Marxist Thought in Latin America

Marxist Thought in Latin America

Sheldon B. Liss

University of California Press

Berkeley / Los Angeles / London

University of California Press
Berkeley and Los Angeles, California

University of California Press, Ltd.
London, England

Library of Congress Cataloging in Publication Data

Liss, Sheldon B.
    Marxist thought in Latin America.

    Bibliography: p.
    Includes index.
    1. Communism—Latin America.   I. Title.
HX110.5.A6L57   1984   335.43′098   83-4838
ISBN 0-520-05021-5
ISBN 0-520-05022-3 (pbk.)

Printed in the United States of America
1 2 3 4 5 6 7 8 9

For Harold Eugene Davis
Historian of Latin American Thought

Contents

ACKNOWLEDGMENTS   ix

1. INTRODUCTION   1

   Political Thought   3
   Social Thought   5
   The Writers' Approaches   6
   The Author's Approach   10

2. MARX AND MARXISM   13

   Marx's Major Interpreters   23
   Historical Backgrounds   30

3. ARGENTINA   39

   Juan Bautista Justo, 42   Alfredo L. Palacios, 46   Aníbal Ponce,
   49   Rodolfo and Américo Ghioldi, 51   Victorio Codovilla, 56
   Silvio Frondizi, 59   Liborio Justo, 63   Jorge Abelardo Ramos,
   67

4. CHILE   72

   Luis Emilio Recabarren, 75   Julio César Jobet, 79   Oscar
   Waiss, 81   Luis Vitale, 84   Volodia Teitelboim, 89   Luis
   Corvalán, 91   Raúl Ampuero Díaz, 93   Clodomiro Almeyda
   Medina, 95   Salvador Allende, 98

5. BRAZIL   103

   Luiz Carlos Prestes, 107   Leôncio Basbaum, 112   Caio Prado
   Júnior, 116   Carlos Marighela, 119   Nelson Werneck Sodré,
   123

6. PERU   127

   José Carlos Mariátegui, 129   Hildebrando Castro Pozo and Ricardo Martínez de la Torre, 138   Hugo Blanco Galdós, 139
   Aníbal Quijano, 143

7. THE BOLIVARIAN NATIONS   149

   Colombia   149
     Diego Montaña Cuéllar, 151 José Consuegra Higgins, 153
     Camilo Torres Restrepo, 155
   Venezuela   160
     Domingo Alberto Rangel, 162 Germán Carrera Damas, 166
     Teodoro Petkoff, 169
   Bolivia   174
     José Antonio Arce, 177 Tristán Marof, 181 Guillermo Lora, 185

8. URUGUAY   190
     Emilio Frugoni, 191 Rodney Arismendi, 195 Francisco R. Pintos, 198 Abraham Guillén, 199

9. MEXICO   205
     Narciso Bassols, 211 Jesús Silva Herzog, 214 Vicente Lombardo Toledano, 219 Alonso Aguilar Monteverde, 226 Pablo González Casanova, 229 Rodolfo Stavenhagen, 233 Adolfo Gilly, 235

10. CUBA   238
     Carlos B. Baliño, 241 Julio Antonio Mella, 243 Juan Marinello, 247 Blas Roca, 251 Carlos Rafael Rodríguez, 253 Ernesto "Che" Guevara, 256 Fidel Castro, 265

11. CONCLUSIONS   271

   GLOSSARY   291

   ABBREVIATIONS   292

   NOTES   293

   BIBLIOGRAPHY   333
   Original Works—Books and Pamphlets   333
   Articles and Unpublished and Miscellaneous Materials   353
   Edited Works   361

   INDEX   365

Acknowledgments

Since I began the preliminary research for this book in 1975, numerous institutions and individuals in Latin America, Europe, and the United States have made my task easier. Those who contributed most significantly to my work are mentioned below.

The staffs of the Hispanic Division of the Library of Congress in Washington, D.C., and the Institute for Gramsci Studies in Rome, Italy, received me warmly and complied rapidly with my often impossible appeals for assistance. The personnel of the Bierce Library of the University of Akron patiently handled my frequent inquiries; in particular, Valerie Johnson of that institution efficiently processed my endless stream of interlibrary loan requests. Garnette Dorsey and Dorothy Richards graciously and patiently waded through page after page of indecipherable handwriting in order to type my manuscripts.

The guidance furnished by fellow academicians strengthened this book considerably. John Womack, Jr., read portions of the chapter on Mexico, which I presented as a paper to the Sixth Conference of Mexican and United States Historians, and his comments helped clarify and broaden my thinking. Donald C. Hodges and Ronald H. Chilcote scrutinized the entire manuscript and offered many sagacious suggestions for its improvement. Their ideas on Marxist theory and praxis in Latin America enabled me to reshape this volume's contours. Most of all, their encouragement provided sustenance. My friend and colleague Barbara Evans Clements also read the manuscript, and her extensive knowledge of Marxist ideology helped me to correct errors, expand positions, and write more precisely. During the final days of his life Joseph R. Starobin spent precious hours with me recounting his personal experiences with some of the movements and thinkers about whom I have written. His insights, derived from a lifetime of analysis, deepened my understanding of socialist political activism and sectarianism.

Finally, a note of appreciation to Estelle Jelinek for expertly editing my manuscript and to Alain Hénon, who believed in my project and skillfully guided it through the editorial processes.

1. Introduction

> More than any other great figure of the past, Marx has suc-
> ceeded to an unusual degree in breaking through the geo-
> graphical, cultural, professional, and even ideological barriers
> which normally confine human reputations. . . . He forms
> part of the living universe both of intellectuals and, through
> the medium of the movement inspired by his ideas, of vast
> sections of the world's population. His reputation is genu-
> inely global.
>
> *London Times Literary Supplement*

More than a century ago Karl Marx articulated a world view that
served as a theory of knowledge, a study in logic, and a general
sociological explanation. His analysis of capitalist society and theory of proletarian revolution became an ideology containing a
program and strategy for changing the existing dominant social
and political order.

Marx's ideas emanated from inherently European thought, combining the Judeo-Christian sense of history with a Renaissance
desire to transform nature. He was not primarily concerned with
Latin America but did envision non-European regions eventually
being involved in world revolution. Subsequently, as explained in
the next chapter, the visionary V. I. Lenin opened the way for the
implantation of Marx's ideas in the Third World where today they
take numerous forms. In this study I attempt to show how Marxist social and political thought came to, and has been used by,
Latin American thinkers and theoreticians.

What constitutes Marxism is a question evoking as much disagreement as concurrence. Raymond Aron points out:

> Marxism may refer to: (1) the ideas of Marx, as reconstructed and
> understood by the historian, in light of man and his times, (2) the ideas
> of Marx as interpreted by various Marxist schools in relation to their
> own times, problems, and objectivity, (3) the social movements and
> parties claiming to be operating according to Marxist ideas.[1]

My nonsectarian socialist perspective often differs from those of
the authors whose works I examine and frequently parallels that

of the late C. Wright Mills, who grouped Marxists into four basic categories: (1) "dead" Marxists, for whom Marxism is a sacred authority with answers to all questions; (2) "vulgar" Marxists, who use specific ideological parts of Marx's political philosophy as the whole; (3) "sophisticated" Marxists, for whom Marxism is a model of society and who mold Marxist ideas to fit new situations, find Marxist answers for everything, and whose rigidity sometimes hinders their analysis and substitutes dogmatism for reflection and inquiry; and (4) "plain" Marxists, on the other hand, who work openly and flexibly, as did Karl Marx, and believe that his ideas are applicable to present situations; they reject forcing realities to conform to hard and fast rules.[2]

No school of thought, except perhaps positivism, has been more pervasive among intellectuals in Latin America than Marxism. The area's social, political, and economic problems have not been solved under capitalism, nor have the techniques of its positivist thinkers yielded a program for thorough reform. Thus, Marxism's utopian promise, its scientific means of comprehending in order to improve societal conditions, holds considerable appeal for many of Latin America's intellectuals who have little faith in the existing system.

Since independence, Latin America has traditionally respected its intellectuals who have often been receptive to foreign political doctrines. Within the region their political and social thought has generally transcended national boundaries, and its form and content have frequently been universal.

U.S. historian Harold Eugene Davis has viewed Latin American thought as basically revolutionary and nationalist whereas his Mexican counterpart, Leopoldo Zea, has contended that it follows a dialectical pattern as it strives to reject the colonial past. Because many thinkers share a revolutionary nationalism and a dialectical approach to social analysis, it is often difficult to distinguish the true Marxists from the more eclectic nationalists or Hegelians.[3] Thus, identification and classification of Marxist thinkers becomes problematical. For example, despite Zea's use of the dialectic, Marxists reject his thinking on the grounds that his basic ideology and methodology consider specific Latin American philosophies from the point of view of self-evolution and the relationship of ideas. This tends to reduce the struggle of groups and classes to simple ideological conflicts.[4]

In this volume I explore the major ideas of a select group of Latin American thinkers who call themselves Marxists, even though they often represent diverse branches of the philosophy. I underscore the importance of the intellectual tradition carried on by these individuals by noting that the Marxist component in Latin America's universities has for a long time been considerably larger than in similar institutions in the United States. Simultaneously, Marxist influence among Latin America's intellectuals has usually been greater than its acceptance by the larger community. We shall see that a number of outstanding Marxist thinkers and theoreticians have been produced south of the Rio Grande.

Latin America's political essayists have always, as did Marx, believed in utilizing ideas to raise consciousness.[5] The quest for a greater comprehension of the region's political, social, and economic reality has traditionally been the province of writers and thinkers whose works, either directly or indirectly, have contributed to an understanding of the historical role of class consciousness in their respective nations. Latin America's intelligentsia, since World War II, has increasingly turned toward the socialist alternative as it became apparent that capitalism was not meeting the needs of most of their people. Marxism enabled its interpreters to compare their respective social, political, and economic ideals with the realities of their defective societies. For those Latin Americans who refused to relinquish hope for a better life, Marxist thought—always on the side of the progressive classes and parties that represent the future in the dialectical struggle between the forces and the system of production—came to symbolize the only alternative to capitalism that had brought an overabundance of despair to the region since the arrival of the first Spaniards over four centuries ago.

Political Thought

By the end of the nineteenth century the belief in the power of ideas over history had diminished in great part because of Marxism. Thought, as Marx conceived of it, had come to be regarded as a key to understanding the history of human actions, but not the basic component of societal transformation. Marxism, as a political philosophy, according to C. Wright Mills, contained ideologies to justify and criticize institutions and attitudes, an ethic or a worked-out body of ideals and beliefs, instruments of change, and a theory of a political movement explaining how people function in society.[6] We might also heed Michael Harrington's explanation that a definite relationship does not have to exist between Marxist theory and political position, and those who agree on methodology can use it to reach contradictory political points of view.[7]

The more we study Marx and the writings of those who call themselves Marxists, the more we realize how far from him, and how divergent from each other, are the views of his followers. Thus, some of the themes provided by Latin American Marxists, although derived from Marx, do not precisely reflect his thinking.

No matter how they differ from Marx and one another, Latin America's Marxist writers all covet radical political change and consider their work to be serious political acts. They point with pride to the impact their ideas have had upon social, political, and economic planning, centralized state control of industrial and agricultural development, and protest movements often led by famous *compañeros* (comrades) from the literary and art worlds, such as Pablo Neruda and Diego Rivera.

In the chapters in this book, at one place or another, I touch on the major postulates of Marxist political thought and view them against the historical background of their intellectual origins. I attempt to illustrate how different writers have joined humanistic traditions to the real problems of politics, show the relationships of Marxism to other philosophies such as *Peronismo* or *Aprismo,* study the role of power in society, comment on the compatibility of individual liberty and central authority, note how the rise of anti-elites has reflected a consciousness of problems requiring new political solutions, and indicate to what degree new Marxist groups have effected political change.

Revolutionary thought designed to effect political and social change has long been an integral part of the Latin American ethos. Traditionalist thinkers such as Simón Bolívar and José Martí subscribed to the almost universal Latin American idea of the validity of humanity moving toward higher goals of social justice through revolution. This belief has made it easier for Latin Americans to accept Marx's theories of revolution, even though they differ from the ideas of Bolívar or Martí. I will illustrate and attempt to define the Marxian revolutionary variants—how they are organ-

ized and their relationship to nationalism and internationalism—
and explain why political revolution is a precondition for social
revolution in the minds of Latin America's Marxists.

Social Thought

Karl Marx, expert on the classics and product of the Enlightenment, invented a type of social criticism that enables us to diagnose social reality and to try to rectify society's ills in a humanistic
way. Although he never believed that there could exist a theoretical system applicable to all times and conditions, or "a key to
open all locks,"[8] he thought it possible to locate the social forces
that create history. To him, ideas did not have their own lives but
were produced by individuals within a historical framework of
social relations.

Marx believed that humanity could be controlled by a conscious
understanding of history and of the ways people have shaped the
world. He felt that humanity could direct history and that its
struggle for consciousness led to the realization that nothing is
preordained. To him, change is history, and all social relationships
must be analyzed historically.[9] Two characteristics set his theory
of society apart from others: first, the insistence on a hierarchy of
social phenomena, and, second, the belief that internal tensions or
contradictions exist in all societies and that they counteract the
system's tendency to remain unchanged.[10]

Marx believed that the existing capitalist order was destined to
change, that humans could restructure and curtail the powers of
its institutions. He predicted the elimination of social classes and
the replacement of competitive life and repression by human fulfillment and liberation. Fundamental to Marx, and of utmost importance to our Latin American social thinkers, is the concept of
liberation or the human right to be free from control by more
powerful interests, from fear, superstition, poverty, hostility, and
enslavement of any type—the right to live unsubjugated in community with others.

Marx did not reduce the structural dynamics of societies to
single factors such as economic determinism or class relationships.
He carefully noted the overlapping nature and complexities of
societies. Most of the writers with whom I deal do not have his
breadth and tend to be less multidimensional. Nevertheless, they

too rely upon historical materialism—a philosophical theory concerned with the specific laws of social development as distinct from universal laws of being[11]—making history more scientific and avoiding some of the oversimplifications of the positivism they seek to supplant. They believe that history proceeds from lower to higher forms of societal organization and that such change is inevitable because the old forms become outmoded and hinder progress. They endeavor to uncover new relationships between various aspects of social development and examine social questions within definite historical and geographical limits. They realize that the transition from capitalism to socialism does not occur automatically but needs, among other factors, a theoretical awareness that evolves only when a historical situation has matured and can be evaluated.

The Writers' Approaches

Historical studies of ideas generally take one of two approaches. The internal approach examines ideas apart from questions of social origin and assumes that ideas have lives of their own that transcend ordinary experience and do not fit a scheme. The external approach traces the relationship of ideas to events rather than to each other. Exponents of external analysis view ideas as catalysts for change and survival. Marxists take exception to the internal approach, for it generally rejects the fact that ideas refer to the material aspects of human experience, and without reference to material conditions ideas are intangibles and do not fit into a scientific scheme of history.

In addition to their external approach to the history of ideas, Latin American Marxist writers believe that they have a special responsibility toward humanity and that they must be free to criticize in order to effect social justice in their class-stratified societies. At the same time they strive to preserve such traditions as cultural plurality and individual liberty. While they encourage a Latin American consciousness, or a sense of hemispheric community of interests, they simultaneously try to protect unique regional or national characteristics.

For Latin America's Marxist thinkers the struggle for survival often takes precedence over the more leisurely pursuit of abstract thought. At times, even some of the most talented of them have felt the need to propagandize rather than to pursue scientific theory that serves fewer people. This book attempts to separate propaganda from theory and concentrates on the latter. I deal primarily with broad works postulating general theories of society, historical analysis of various countries, and interpretations of Marxism as applied to Latin American conditions.

The authors whose works I examine have often suffered from the medieval ideas, still prevalent in Latin America, that writers do not rate remuneration, that they belong in an ivory tower, and that they subject themselves to personal dangers if they write social criticism. They frequently have had to rely upon nonwriting jobs for a livelihood, turning out their articles and books in their spare time, often with little hope of finding a publisher and with the realization that their readership, recompense, and recognition will be small.

Writers who call themselves Marxists have emerged in most Latin American countries, often in diverse societies, but generally, as we shall see, for somewhat similar reasons. That they all do not think alike is evident. Since I do not adhere to an iron-clad definition of Marxism, I will not get involved in sectarian hair-splitting over who represents the "true Marxist." The individuals whose works are analyzed here will sometimes be referred to interchangeably as Marxists and socialists. Such designations are often used loosely for the sake of convenience and with the knowledge that readers can, at times, justifiably quibble with their accuracy. Admittedly, some of the people I deal with might better be described as radicals or progressives who use some Marxist tools of analysis; others could be more precisely categorized as Leninists, Trotskyists, Maoists, followers of Gramsci, or a host of other things. To a great degree I rely upon the writer's self-perception. Thus, when intelligent thinkers like Peru's Víctor Raúl Haya de la Torre and Mexico's Vicente Lombardo Toledano, both influenced by Marx, respectively declare themselves to be and not to be Marxists, I often take them at their word.

In Latin America those most receptive to Marxist thought have not been proletarians but rather students, professors, journalists, professionals, and artists. In particular, Marxism has gained a great deal of respectability in the region by its acceptance by outstanding literary figures such as Jorge Amado, Julio Cortázar, Gabriel García Márquez, and Pablo Neruda.

Although a few of the writers whose works I analyze have produced novels or poetry, most of them are not literary figures or philosophers whose ideas go beyond wordly concerns. They are, generally, *pensadores*—thinkers who try to interpret social reality. Naturally, the level of analysis varies greatly from one *pensador* to another. All examine the facts, most evaluate causal connections, and the best among them propound theories or abstract thought. Basically, they write two types of works: some use a Marxian framework to treat specific subjects, and others deal with Marxist theory per se. The *pensadores* represent diverse versions of the "soft" and "hard" approaches to Marxist analysis. Proponents of the "hard" approach adopt the more rigid view that the process of production determines politics and ideas whereas advocates of the "soft" approach follow Georg Lukács, who argued in *History and Class Consciousness* (1923) that in his later, and less Hegelian, theory Marx saw society as an interacting whole, with material factors, rather than ideas, being basic. In other words, the "soft" approach sees Marx as more of a humanist who realized that ideas can affect the material process of production.

Some of these *pensadores* can be categorized as socialist humanists for whom improving the human condition is the primary objective. In order to give this book greater latitude, I refer to the socialist humanists as Marxists on the grounds that they take off from the works of Marx and use his methods to analyze society.[12]

Most of the writers do not belong to the "aristocratic" school of intellectual history which sees ideas and opinions originating in an intellectual elite and flowing downward. Instead, they come from what has been called the "plebian" school, which considers elitist ideas as well as those originating in other sectors of society.[13] However, they all tend to think of themselves as intellectuals with an obligation to use their critical faculties to challenge authority and established institutions, to delegitimate conventional wisdom, to search for solutions to social problems, and to provide leadership in the realm of thought.

To define the term *intellectual* in the context in which it appears in subsequent chapters, I turn to the Italian Marxist Antonio Gramsci. In his "vertical" view, intellectuals are "all those who exercise a technical or directive" role in society, such as managers, administrators, bureaucrats, politicians, and organizers of culture like artists and scholars. In his "horizontal" view, Gramsci distinguishes between "traditional intellectuals," who think that they have a character of their own and are independent of the dominant social group—those who represent a "historical continuity uninterrupted by even the most radical and complicated changes of social and political systems"[14]—and "organic intellectuals," who are more directly related to the economic structures of their society and more consciously work for their own social class, often to obtain mass consensus for the state they control with the belief that it has a historical right at a given moment. When writing of "traditional intellectuals," Gramsci calls their feelings of independence illusory and sees them inevitably tied to the ruling class of their society. He feels that their true duty should be, as Marx and Engels suggested in the *Communist Manifesto* (1848), to break away and join the revolutionary class. On the other hand, Gramsci feels that the "organic intellectual" group includes "traditional intellectuals" who comprehend the direction in which history is moving and those intellectuals put forth by the revolutionary class as its leaders. To him, history has not been made by intellectual elites but by intellectuals conscious of their organic ties to a popular mass.[15]

Latin America's Marxist writers are "organic intellectuals" who share many common characteristics. They possess a good deal of expertise about capitalism, and their Marxism is to some extent the analysis of capitalism and its contradictions. They have a sense of knowing and perhaps even making history. Their radicalism is idealistic and visionary, not simply the product of rebelliousness. Their interests run to two types of knowledge. First, they seek understanding through interpretative studies of social action, like historians who reconstruct traditional meaning to provide comprehension of societies by connecting them to earlier times. Second, they pursue critical knowledge to free us from false consciousness and the domination of forces beyond our control. They reject the "mainstream" social science belief in the validity of neutral analysis. However, they are, in general, as objective as their capitalist counterparts whom they frequently criticize for failing to realize that all thought emanates from an ideological base.

Although the breadth of Latin American Marxists' thinking goes beyond Marx, like him they are determinists who believe in man's ability to order society, the inevitability of progress, the inherent goodness of human nature, and the dialectical method.

Above all, they hold that these principles are as applicable to the struggles of present-day Latin America as they were to the conditions of Marx's nineteenth-century world. They interpret Marx for their people, using history as a vehicle for the liberation of the working classes. In the words of Thomas Kuhn, they want to effect a "paradigm shift," to use ideas to open new roads for humanity. Like Marx, they want to illustrate to the workers that one does not have to be poor, that poverty is not attributable to one's failure, or the will of God, but that it originates in the political and economic conditions of capitalism and can be eliminated by abolishing that system under which the profit or luxury of one is paid for by the deprivation of another.

The Author's Approach

A brief word about the organization of this book is in order. Assuming that what a generation thinks is far more important in determining the way it treats events than where it obtains its ideas, I use both internal and external analyses with emphasis on the latter. I endeavor to establish each writer's relationship to the means of production, individual ideologies, political and social objectives, relationships to earlier and later doctrines, approaches to Marx, unique theories of society, and views on power and institutions. I examine, where possible, each thinker's style of operation, concept of a "socialist person," ideas on revolution, search for community, relationships to social movements, organizational efforts, role in his nation's intellectual life, how the person's ideas were implemented and whether or not they endured, and the historical significance of his ideas and actions.

This book confronts most of the questions facing Marxists in all parts of Latin America. To avoid repetition, some problems characteristic of the region and analyzed by more than one thinker, are handled in conjunction with a single country and one writer. Although many of these thinkers deal with Latin America as a whole, for the sake of expediency their ideas appear in chapters corresponding to their regions or countries of origin. Their thoughts are compared with those of their countrymen before being examined in a wider context. I try to determine if, because of Marxism, these writers hold universal views and prefer to interpret Latin America in terms of the world rather than the Americas.

Social scientists and humanists in the United States have tended to neglect Latin American thought in general, and Marxist thought in that region in particular. No book of this kind has ever been written and little of what is examined between these covers has been translated and published in the United States where Marx is more talked about and misquoted than read. Among many Latin Americanists in the United States there exists an anti-intellectual tendency to approach Marxism from a negative point of view, as dissent that is not a social philosophy but merely a means of expressing dissatisfaction. I note sadly that at a recent American Historical Association meeting when I stated publicly that the scholar who fails to consider Marxist thinking is as inadequate as the one who believes it to contain the last word, two young academicians complained that my remark was out of order and said that they had gone beyond the Ph.D. without knowledge of Marxism and could and would continue to function without it. This volume is intended primarily for those with a sparse knowledge of Marxist thought in Latin America.

Unlike the few books on Latin American Marxist topics published in the United States, this one is not primarily concerned with socialist or communist political parties or organized labor. Theory and historical interpretation predominate in this exploratory work designed to serve as a springboard to more detailed analyses. It affords the reader a broad, but cursory, look at Marxist thought in most of Latin America and focuses primarily on thinkers who have passed their fiftieth birthdays and whose major studies were published before 1970. To prevent this from becoming the work of a lifetime, whose size would prohibit publication, some writers such as Argentina's Rodolfo Puiggrós have been omitted. Also, a few internationally known multitalented younger Marxists, like Peru's Aníbal Quijano, who bridge the gap between the old and the new guard, are included. But it remains for another volume, perhaps one published ten years hence, to document the contributions of today's outstanding younger Marxist theoreticians, such as Bolivia's Silvia Rivera, Brazil's Vania Bambirra and Theotonio Dos Santos, and Chile's Marta Harnecker.

Subsequent pages deal more with how and where Latin American Marxists agree or disagree with their European counterparts than with how the latter differed or concurred with Marx. For the most part, I refer to a sort of generalized Marx rather than an early or late Marx. While my analysis per se endeavors to avoid the internal arguments of the diverse schools of Marxist thought, I point them out and illustrate how the authors relate to them—a difficult task in that the thinking of these writers, like that of Marx, often changed during various stages of their lives. Their early writings often reflect the entrenched elitist ideas of their respective societies, and sometimes only their later works reveal mature socialist mentalities.

This book does not criticize Marx but rather shows how Latin American thinkers have interpreted him. For example, the conflict between "state" and "free Marxism," which occupies so much space in anti-Marxist tracts, receives no attention here. Marxist-oriented literature and literary criticism, although they might serve as commentary on political and social thought, are not part of this volume; nor is pure economic thought, although, like Marx, Latin America's Marxist authors are involved with political economy. What follows are essays, not a formal history or identically structured analyses of the Marxist thought produced in each geographical area or by each individual thinker. To know the thought of Marx completely, let alone that of all of his Latin American interpreters, is impossible. A lifetime could be spent on each set of ideas or person mentioned in this book. I realize that my omissions are numerous and that my margin for error is great. I also know that ideology is no substitute for critical analysis and that there exists a need for critical analysis of ideology.

I have tried to put as much of what follows into intelligible prose while at the same time following as closely as possible the language and thinking of those whose works I examine. The passages in this book that contain an abnormal amount of esoteric jargon or rhetoric, for the most part, reflect an attempt to portray accurately the style of the works under discussion.[16]

2. Marx and Marxism

> For each individual is the synthesis not only of existing rela-
> tions, but of the history of these relations. Structure ceases to
> be an external force which crushes man, assimilates him to
> itself and makes him passive, and is transformed into a
> means of freedom, an instrument to create a new ethical po-
> litical form and a source of new initiatives.
>
> Antonio Gramsci

One must understand what influenced Marx and how he thought before analyzing the works of his Latin American interpreters. Like him, most of them have considered their primary task to free man to think—to rid his mind of dogma and rigid authority. Unlike him, none of them has ever created an entire movement by sheer force of intellect.

Marx never considered his ideas sacrosanct or unchanging for all times and places. He changed his mind, made errors, and his intellectual endeavors, spread out over a half-century, show inconsistencies and contradictions. At various times he was interested in different aspects of society. Whether one takes the "hard" or "soft" approach to Marxist thought, one can agree with political scientist Bertell Ollman, who has contended that the thinking of the young Marx did not differ greatly from that of the older Marx and that no profound "break" in his thought occurred—rather, an evolution in his thinking took place—and that its tendencies are visibile in his early thought.[1]

Depending upon which of his works you read and when they were written, one can, using non-Marxian categories, call Marx a sociologist, an economist, a historian, or a political scientist. He might also be referred to as a philosopher, humanist-moralist, or propagandist. His thought may be further subclassified as that of democrat or authoritarian, gradual socialist or revolutionary, humanitarian or utilitarian, determinist or voluntarist, and materialist or idealist. Moreover, his writings are so extensive that one can find in, or read into, them almost anything beyond what he intended.

Before I comment on the bare essentials of Marx's thought that are needed to comprehend how his Latin American followers interpret, or even distort, his thinking, his countryman, colleague, and financial benefactor, Friedrich Engels, deserves mention. Perhaps reference to this study as Marxist-Engelist thought in Latin America would be appropriate as Engels contributed frequently to, and helped broaden, the thinking of Marx. For example, Engels formulated the doctrine of dialectical materialism in *Anti-Dühring* (1878). He concluded that the fundamental laws of nature, society, and thought could be understood by viewing everything that exists as matter and through the use of dialectical logic, which sees contradictions as the productive collision of ideas from which higher truths can be discerned.

The ideas of Engels, a brilliant student of Kant, Fichte, and Hegel, will often, in this study, for the sake of convenience, be considered as interchangeable with those of Marx. Preferring to credit Marx for what they produced jointly, as many of us have been prone to do ever since, Engels, in his funeral oration for his friend, noted that as Newton had discovered the law of motion of the planets, Marx had discovered the law of motion of the capitalist method of production for the middle classes which that method had fostered. Engels then equated Darwin's discovery of the laws of evolution in organic nature with Marx's discovery of the laws of evolution in human society.[2]

Marx never believed that he posited a sacred theory, but felt that he applied new scientific tools of analysis to the complexities of situations in order to develop new understandings. He emphasized that action had to be added to theory to bring about change—that analyzing capitalist society and explaining historical change were not enough. He felt that what will occur is not determined by natural laws, independent of man, but by how man perceives situations and what he does about them. He approached society dialectically, not considering it as something immutable but as something developing, and he sought out the qualitatively specific stages of its development—its socioeconomic formation.[3] He was original in that he affirmed that history is simultaneously dialectic and determined by economic change.

Marx and Engels held a determinist theory of social development. But they did not propound an iron-clad system of sociological laws by which one could predict the inevitability of socialism. They attacked philosophical idealism and rarely lost sight of the fact that the initial step in the transition to socialism had to be theoretical. They asserted that harmful existing situations have to be studied and understood before initiating actions to rectify them.

To Marx, history represented a continuous struggle for human freedom and the social, political, and economic conditions to achieve it. He based his theory of history upon four fundamental elements: the mode of production, the principle of social dynamics or the dialectic, the class struggle, and the derivation of ideas.[4] By using these four tools, he felt history could be evaluated scientifically and used to provide a rational guide to building a new order.

Marx subsumed all cultural and intellectual changes under the laws of history. His theory of history was optimistic and not based upon elements of conspiracy. He realized that most people can, and do, only think within their own times, but he stressed the necessity to think about the past as well as the future. Like his Latin American followers, Marx believed that "man makes his own history, but not out of whole cloth," that individuals play a role in society, but that their aggregate or collective roles are paramount.[5]

Before I delve into the major elements of Marxist thought that appear in this book, some remarks on terminology are in order. Marx never concerned himself with the language he used. Unfortunately at times, he used words awkwardly and without precision or clarity. His interpretations tended to explain his ideas through his own frames of reference. For example, when he talks about social relations, he has reference to machines as well as to people. His lack of accuracy and unique means of expression gave his followers almost a free hand to interpret him or fill in the gaps in his thinking with their own ideas. As a result, much of today's Marxist vocabulary would be unrecognizable to him. For instance, he never used the term *dialectical materialism* and always used the words *communism* and *socialism* interchangeably, as I do in this book on occasion.

Engels served as the first interpreter of Marx in an effort to gain recognition for his friend's, and his own, ideas. He identified Marx with scientific, rather than utopian, socialism in *Anti-Dühring,* where he tried to transform Marx's social theory into a proletarian philosophy of life. Engels popularized his colleague's work so that other sophisticated thinkers of the day soon understood that Marx rejected the metaphysical bases of knowledge, that he advocated a coherent scientific synthesis of all social phenomena by extending Hegel's metaphysical dialectic to social relations and materialism, that he analyzed problems by examining connections between social factors in order to find historical relationships, that he sought to understand the material conditions necessary to free the working classes and to nurture a social revolution or to forge a new society.

Marx put forth ideas that had appeal beyond intellectual elites. His system attracted all types of people dissatisfied with bourgeois society and encouraged them to define and articulate their grievances and to work toward action designed to redress them. His devastating indictment of capitalism illustrated how it operated and how it basically changes because the workers involved in production conflict constantly with the way its economy is organized by the owners of the means of production and the state they control. Marx contended that social and political relationships were determined by human needs and the mode of production created to satisfy them and that by understanding the way changes occur and by participating intelligently in societies' actions, people can rationally order the world and fulfill their needs.[6] To Marx:

> Men make their own history, but they do not make it just as they please, they do not make it under circumstances directly encountered, given and transmitted from the past. The tradition of all the dead generations weighs like a nightmare on the brain of the living.[7]

Demonstrating great flexibility, he argued that under certain circumstances a set of social relations is determinate, but at other times and under different conditions people can break them and restructure social reality.[8]

Marx claimed that he could not postulate a methodology for interpreting a society continuously in motion and that his ideas, too, had to be constantly revised. Thus, what he gave to subsequent generations of thinkers was basically a model, one that even non-Marxists could use as a heuristic device.

At this point it might be useful to note a few things that Marx did not believe. We must bear in mind that during his last years he often criticized the dogmatism of some of his followers. He did not conceive of his ideas as a new philosophy but rather as a perspective containing a conception of man and his world. He did not contend that he had created a new political creed. He never wished to see the relinquishment of "personal liberty to the idea of collective man, but rather felt that society should not be an abstraction opposed to the individual."[9]

What primarily concerned Marx was capitalism, a term used repeatedly on subsequent pages and meriting definition. He devoted most of his life to the study of capitalism with its belief in progress, the future of science, technology, and production. He believed that capitalism carried the seeds of its own decay and that socialism could best be understood in terms of its emergence from capitalism. To him, modern capitalism dated from the sixteenth century—the time of the conquest of Latin America. He believed that from that time on the evolution of the international division of labor was a consequence of capitalism. In relating his theory to the Americas, he stated in 1848:

> You believe perhaps, gentlemen, that the production of coffee and sugar is the natural destiny of the West Indies. Two centuries ago, nature, which does not trouble herself about commerce, had planted neither sugarcane nor coffee trees there.[10]

To Marx, capitalism contained three fundamental faults. First, its primary motive was profit, not human development. Second, capital is the collective product of social labor, but industry is controlled by private capitalists who determine the course of social labor; thus products are not apportioned socially, but according to capitalists' wishes. Third, capitalism lacks overall order as each capitalist produces what and as much as he can, then competes with other capitalists for markets without being sensitive to the needs of the community.[11] Marx saw capitalist and worker locked in a symbiotic relationship, creating increased wealth for the former and increased poverty for the latter. He envisioned a dialectical process out of which wealth and poverty eventually produce a classless society devoid of misery and exploitation. He saw the capitalist stage in the development of society characterized by bourgeois domination, which had been ushered in by a democratic revolution. He felt that the proletariat would support the bourgeoisie only until the time was ripe to end capitalism by a socialist, worker-led revolution.

In building his theory of capitalist development, Marx relied upon the ideas of British economists David Ricardo and Adam

Smith, both of whom tried to isolate the economic factor from political and social influences. Unlike them, he showed that economics do not function in a vacuum but within a social structure necessary to support the economic structure. He did not believe that the economic base determined every aspect of the superstructure but asserted that the mode of production, or substructure, was the most essential aspect determining the social superstructure and its changes. To him, economic determinism belonged to capitalism, not socialism, and when his interpreters analyzed him purely in terms of economic determinism he asserted: "Then all I know is that I am not a Marxist."[12]

Just as Marx disclaimed being an economic determinist, he rejected the idea that he first introduced the concepts of class analysis and struggle, which he attributed to capitalist historians and economists. However, he accepted credit for showing that the existence of classes is linked to historical stages in production methods, that class struggle would lead to a dictatorship of the proletariat, and that this dictatorship is only part of the transition from a class to a classless society.[13]

Marx used the term *class* in a collective sense to refer to a group that thinks and functions differently from the way its members might if acting alone. His use of classes to categorize did not mean that he stripped individuals of their unique characteristics. But he thought that class relationships conditioned personalities.[14] His ultimate objective was to build class consciousness, which included a distinct ideology, a world view, and a program of action designed to maintain or change the existing system.

He believed that only by class analysis could one locate and understand power relationships. For example, he believed the state to be an organ of class domination. He further contended that the state, by creating "order," legalizes and perpetuates oppression by moderating the clashes between classes. In a Latin American context, according to Marx's thinking, we might conclude that *caudillismo* (bossism) has historically been a part of the system used by the landed aristocracy to perpetuate their class rule through the state.[15] To Marx, not the welfare of man but the protection of wealth was the aim of the capitalist state.

In *German Ideology*, written in 1846, Marx postulated that those who own the means of production constitute the ruling class, which dominates the economy and establishes the institutions and even the ideology to justify the system it has created. But we must not view Marx's ideas on class in simplistic terms such as: "In a capitalist society the government always does what the capitalist class wants it to do." To him class rule had a far richer and more complex meaning than this shallow notion that reduces the political process to relations between the will of a class and government policy.

Marx studied capitalism and class analysis to develop his thoughts on revolution, which he believed embodied the most lasting values of Western humanism. He intended his writings as a guide to the action necessary to free the proletariat, not as a program for revolution per se. He never indicated precisely how the proletariat would achieve its revolutionary role. While he talked about the inevitability of revolution, he simultaneously stressed that it had to be brought about by those who wanted it.

Marx, who abhorred senseless bloodshed, did not claim that violence was the most significant factor in revolution but rather that the contradictions in the old system were primarily responsible for its destruction. He concerned himself mainly with social revolution, which he saw evolving from the conflicts in the mode of production, which developed into antagonisms, expressed in class conflict, which ultimately overthrew the state. He believed that the seizure of power by one class from another required force, that there exists no historical evidence of a ruling class yielding its control without violence, but that once power has been acquired, new institutions have to be constructed, and they could be based on proletarian democracy. He viewed social revolution not as perfect, but as a compromise between utopia and historical reality.

Laymen commonly associate Marx with revolutionary thought and often erroneously attribute to him some theories on imperialism. While the majority of our Latin American Marxists deal with imperialism, it did not preoccupy Marx. He and Engels expressed an interest in imperialism and pointed out the harmful effects it had upon humanity, especially as it pertained to India and Ireland. But they never constructed a systematic view of it. All of the "Marxist theories of imperialism" have been the work of Marx's interpreters, most of whom took off from Lenin.

At this point we might consider briefly what Marx knew and thought about Latin America. Hegel, in his lectures on the philosophy of history, referred to the Americas as the land of the future. Although Marx and Engels knew Hegel's views, they never had more than an indirect or tangential interest in the region. Engels had a cursory knowledge of the pre-Columbian civilizations and a vague idea of their social organization gained by reading the popular works of Herbert H. Bancroft.[16] Marx read the books of William H. Prescott on the conquests of Mexico and Peru and obtained some insight into the division of labor among Peru's Incas. He saw production in Inca society based upon communitarian principles, not the value of monetary exchange between private individuals.[17] He wrote about the discovery of America in terms of the European impulse to circumnavigate the world enroute to Africa and about the colonization of America in relationship to the world marketplace. He understood the role of the conquest of the Americas in the process of capital accumulation. He knew about the quest for *El Dorado,* the British and French designs on the region, and was aware that precious metals found there had contributed to the international capitalist system—that they were used to accelerate European industrialization.[18] In their brief essays on the discovery and conquest of America, Marx and Engels analyzed its impact upon European society, not upon the Americas. Marx saw the expansion of trade in Latin America as a fundamental element in the transition from the feudal to the capitalist mode of production.

Marx wrote some newspaper articles on Spanish America's independence and Spain's reaction to losing its American colonies and its mid-nineteenth-century desire to regain part of its American empire. His articles in the *New American Encyclopedia* on the Battle of Ayacucho, which sealed Peru's independence, and on Simón Bolívar attracted little attention. He did not profess to know Latin America or Bolívar very well[19] but wrote the articles to earn some money to fend off starvation. His descriptive, rather than analytical, piece on Bolívar, portrayed the Spanish American as an authoritarian leader of a national liberation movement—a possible step toward socialist revolution in colonial areas insofar as Marx was concerned. He concluded that Bolívar, rather than enrich himself from his exploits, expended nearly all of his own fortune in the "people's service." Also, despite his fondness for "pleasure, fame and power—patriotism and love of freedom were his ruling passions."[20] Marx probably understood Bolívar's elitism but paid little attention to his role in the class struggle engaged in by South American Creoles who wanted to gain political and economic control of the region and perpetuate their interests there. For our purposes, the most significant feature of the unreliable article on Bolívar is that it reveals Marx's opposition to enlightened dictatorship, which he felt prepared the people only to oppose it, instead of readying them for democracy.[21]

Argentine historian Jorge Abelardo Ramos hypothesized that at the time Marx wrote about Latin American independence, he was formulating his thoughts on the national question and that he picked up from Dionisio Inca Yupanqui, a Latin American legislator, the idea that "a people that oppresses another is not able to be free."[22]

Marx's writings also show an interest in foreign intervention in Mexico, especially the "guerrilla war" between Mexico and the United States during the 1840s. Engels wrote about the United States' desire for California's mines and access to the Pacific coast. He saw the United States acquiring territory in the war with Mexico in order to create new capital and to protect the Isthmus of Tehuantepec, which it coveted as a possible Atlantic-to-Pacific route. He also contended that the United States envisioned a transcontinental railroad terminating in California as a means to increase commerce. Marx and Engels viewed the United States' annexation of California as opening up trade to Chile and Peru—and subsequently to Asia—thereby making the Isthmus of Panama important strategically. After examining the arguments for all of the potential Atlantic-to-Pacific canal routes, they concluded that the Panama one was best.[23]

During the 1850s Marx expressed interest in the Spanish troops in Cuba and Puerto Rico. At that time, his writings indicate that he understood the United States' fear of Russian expansion and probably saw the Monroe Doctrine as an attempt to thwart such moves. He also understood the expansionist tendencies of the United States. He claimed that James Buchanan had obtained the U.S. presidency by publishing the Ostend Manifesto of 1853, which proclaimed that the United States would take Cuba by payment, or by force, and that obtaining Cuba was a great national objective.

Marx denounced the French, British, and Spanish occupation of Mexico during the early 1860s as a monstrous act and called the intervention a prelude to a grander one against the United States, which he predicted would occur as a result of capitalist competition. In 1861, Marx noted the interest of U.S. land speculators in the Mexican states of Chihuahua, Coahuila, and Sonora. He indicated that the White House directed filibusters in Central America and reasoned that many people in the United States looked upon Latin America as an area with great potential for the spread of slavery.

In *Das Kapital* (1867) Marx wrote:

> The discovery of gold and silver in America, the extirpation, enslavement and entombment in mines of the aboriginal population, the beginning of the conquest and the looting of the East Indians, the turning of Africa into a warrant for the hunting of black-skins, symbolized the rosy dawn of the era of capitalist production.[24]

Marx knew that the African slave trade in Latin America initially provided capital for European manufacturers and the Industrial Revolution. He considered the exploitation of the Indians in Latin America to be another form of slavery. He viewed both types of slavery as worse than proletarian subjugation. He alluded to the existence of slavery in Cuba, Brazil, Jamaica, Mexico, Surinam, and the United States and also referred to the servitude of the Chinese coolie labor in Peru after 1854 when slavery was abolished there.[25] He viewed slavery as a vital step in the development of colonies and as necessary to the construction of capitalism.

Toward the end of the nineteenth century, Engels demonstrated considerable interest in the plans of the French-owned Universal Interoceanic Canal Company of Panama to construct an Atlantic-to-Pacific waterway across Panama. When that organization went bankrupt in the 1880s, numerous individuals lost considerable money, and a scandal ensued. Engels attributed the abortive venture, and the fact that 22,000 Latin American, Chinese, and Indian workers suffered needlessly while trying to build the canal, to the inherent weakness and inhumanity of capitalism. He thought that the publicity surrounding the canal fiasco would build sentiment for socialism and that Panama, being considerably more European than other Latin American areas, would be an ideal base from which to launch a socialist campaign.[26] Engels knew that the destruction of the Paris Commune had caused the dispersal of many of its socialist supporters to Latin America, that the first section of the International had been founded in Argentina in

1872;[27] and he maintained a strong interest in building the movement in Central and South America.

Marx's Major Interpreters

Just as no examination of Marxist thought in Latin America would be complete without some explanation of Marx's ideas, so too would it be negligent not to look at some of the beliefs of his major interpreters from whom Latin American *pensadores* have extrapolated. Foremost is V. I. Lenin, the twentieth-century Russian revolutionary who showed how to implement the thinking of Marx. Lenin spent his life trying to achieve Marxist socialism, which he felt consisted of public ownership of the means of production, distribution, and exchange, as well as popular democracy that enabled each worker to participate in state management.

Lenin never admitted to having revised Marx's thought, but he did so by successfully adapting it to Russian conditions, thereby creating a theoretical model for revolutionary thought and action in backward societies like those of Latin America. In the more than fifty volumes comprising his complete works, Lenin refers to Latin America only eighteen times, but his ideas concerning the subjective conditions for revolution and his belief in preparing socialists for taking power simultaneously by armed insurrection and parliamentary means have had considerable influence in the region.

Lenin devoted his efforts to making Marx's theory of a dictatorship of the proletariat a reality. After the revolution in his homeland, the Russian theoretican-activist included in the category of *proletarian*, the intelligentsia, which generally received pay as a result of the capitalist mode of production. He felt that distinctions between manual workers and brain workers had to be abolished, that each worker must have access to all varieties of culture and the opportunity to develop fully his or her talents, ideas later embraced by Latin American socialists.

To his Latin American constituency, the Comintern meant: (1) victory for the Russian revolution, which could be emulated by others; (2) establishing Communist parties in all capitalist nations; (3) becoming part of an international socialist system; (4) the elimination of colonialism; and (5) the use of revolution to destroy capitalism and imperialism. Lenin emphasized the role of the political party in raising proletarian consciousness and in becoming the vanguard of the revolution. He believed in the efficacy of coalitions or cooperation with bourgeois political parties when necessary, but not in subordination to them. He stressed that political education of the masses is more important than minor parliamentary gains—the latter being inferior to a good uprising at the outset of a social revolution.

Unlike Marx who viewed social revolution as the fundamental act, Lenin thought social and political revolution to be synonymous. He had no tolerance for reform or evolutionary socialism. He believed that the bourgeoisie was incapable of completing its own revolution. He thought that the peasantry was backward but demonstrated its potential for revolution in a nation that had not passed through to its capitalist stage of development. He made Marx's ideas more relevant to Latin America by showing that the decisive factor in revolution is the nature of the political organization rather than the existing stage of social or economic development. He refined Marx by stressing that the proletariat could seize power during, instead of after, a bourgeois-democratic revolution. Following Clausewitz's thinking, he emphasized struggle not as an end in itself but as the continuation of politics by different means. He contended that the military, once instilled with revolutionary fervor, could become a political arm and bearer of revolution, an idea subscribed to, as we shall see, by the makers of the Cuban revolution. He warned of the dangers of state control exercised by elitist bureaucracies after the triumph of the revolution.

Lenin's thinking on imperialism, perhaps, made him most germane to Latin America. His book *Imperialism: The Highest Stage of Capitalism* (1916), based on John A. Hobson's *Imperialism* (1902) and Rudolf Hilferding's *Finance Capitalism* (1910),[28] indicated that the supremacy of capitalism was achieved by 1900. He stated that monopoly capitalists, searching for gains by investing abroad, caused imperialism, which enabled them to sustain themselves temporarily by extracting profits from foreign areas through political and economic control. He predicted that ultimately this situation would lead to war between the major capitalist powers. To him, Germany and the United States epitomized the monopoly capitalism spreading unevenly throughout the world. He made Marx's ideas particularly pertinent to nonindustrialized, underdeveloped areas affected by European and U.S.

investment, as was Latin America, by giving nationalism the revolutionary respectability it lacked by directing it against Western imperialism.

Lenin read A. B. Hart's *The Monroe Doctrine* (1916), which heightened his awareness of the growth of "protectorates" and of the role of the United States in Latin America.[29] He referred to the Latin American republics as "dependent countries; . . . which, officially are politically independent, but which are in fact enmeshed in the net of financial and diplomatic dependence."[30] His thinking formed the foundations upon which were built the dependency themes that became popular among some Marxist and non-Marxist Latin American scholars in the late 1960s and 1970s.

A second interpreter of Marx who has influenced Latin American thinking was Leon Trotsky, whose ideas have been significant there since the 1930s. Numerous groups in the region, representing diverse positions on the socialist spectrum, refer to themselves as Trotskyists. Donald Hodges, a leading U.S. interpreter of Marxism, believes that Latin American Trotskyists are split into a number of sects whose strategies and politics differ.[31] But they generally all reject Stalin's contention that the revolution would first pass through a bourgeois and then through a socialist stage and accept Trotsky's theory of Permanent Revolution, in which he telescoped the two stages and viewed the revolution as a single process. They share Trotsky's desire for world revolution to achieve a dictatorship of the proletariat composed of productive workers who will constitute the ruling class. They also emphasize the Russian revolutionary's belief in the need to combat bureaucracy, which tends to lead from above and thereby usurps the power of the people.

Liborio Justo, an Argentine thinker, also known by the pseudonym Quebracho, saw two clear tendencies in more recent Trotskyist thought. According to Justo, one Trotskyist faction deemphasizes the semicolonial status of Latin America and the influence of imperialism there, depicts the national bourgeoisie as the major enemy of the workers, supports direct socialist struggles, believes that bourgeois-democratic revolution has been completed in some Latin American nations, and denies the relevance of the Chinese revolution to the area. The other faction emphasizes Latin America's semicolonial status, sees imperialism as the area's primary enemy, suggests antiimperialist agrarian revolution as the initial step toward socialism, and believes that the Chinese revolutionary experience is relevant to Latin America.[32]

Although Stalin never gave up on international revolution, he believed that revolution could be victorious in one nation, even when that country was in a backward stage of capitalist development. His countryman Trotsky thought that the revolution had to transcend national boundaries to remain alive. He believed that proletarian support from other countries was essential to revolution and that proletarians must lead the revolution. He also advocated the incorporation of the peasantry into the socialist system rather than permitting it to remain as a potential petty bourgeois opponent.

Just before his assassination in Mexico in 1940, Trotsky wrote a number of articles on Latin America. In them he noted that fascism in the area was an expression of dependence and asserted that it was necessary to struggle against imperialism in order to eliminate fascism. He saw the Monroe Doctrine and U.S. imperialism inherent in the Good Neighbor Policy, which he felt was conceived to unify the hemisphere under Washington's hegemony.[33] He deplored U.S. support of authoritarian leaders like Cuba's Fulgencio Batista and Brazil's Getulio Vargas. He feared the growing tendency in the region to organize the workers, and sometimes the peasantry, under the control of the capitalist state. He believed that the best method of struggle against authoritarianism was agrarian revolution, and he advocated proletarian solidarity, even a United Socialist States of Latin America in the region to maintain the permanent revolution necessary to combat the Good Neighbor idea. Today's Latin American Trotskyists follow his lead by continuously reminding other socialists about the dangers of pursuing a policy of peaceful coexistence with capitalism.

In recent decades Latin American *pensadores* have added the thought of Mao Zedong to that of Marx, Lenin, and Trotsky in their quest for revolutionary models. The great appeal of Mao, especially to students and intellectuals, rested on his humanism, his stress on the importance of people over the Hegelian state, his ability to adapt Marx critically to nonindustrial Chinese society, and his emphasis on innovative rather than imitative revolutionary thinking. Mao accepted Lenin's belief that Marxism must be molded to historical conditions and must adopt a specific national form before it can be put into practice. He shifted the focus of revolution from urban to rural areas by maintaining that world revolution did not have to start in proletarian centers but could begin in colonies or in the agrarian sector. He developed a peasant-based communist party, insisted on a class alliance between peasants and proletarians, and stressed military conflict based on peasant guerrilla warfare. To Mao, the seizure of power by armed force, the settlement of the issue by war, is the central task and highest form of revolution.[34] He believed that Latin America, Asia, and Africa stood at the forefront of world revolution because they were the earth's countryside, and whoever controlled it thwarted world imperialism by closing off raw materials and markets.

From Wang Fu-chih, a seventeenth-century anti-Manchu philosopher from his home province of Hunan, Mao borrowed the idea that political and social systems were changeable, as were human nature and social customs. From the same thinker he adopted the belief that action was more likely to foster change than ideas. These concepts he added to Marx's and Lenin's thoughts on the class struggle. Although he too saw everything in terms of juxtaposition of opposing forces, he took exception to Marx and Lenin by insisting that contradictions exist in socialist societies, albeit in more limited fashion than under capitalism.[35]

From Lenin, Mao took the idea that proletarian consciousness does not manifest spontaneously among the proletariat but must be encouraged by an elite or vanguard. Unlike Lenin, he saw no insurmountable contradiction between being a nationalist and an internationalist. Latin American thinkers, with their deep nationalist heritage, could identify with his bold political and social programs designed to transform radically China's society and with his idea that only national liberation would enable the workers to emancipate themselves. On the vital question of the role of the national bourgeoisie, he theorized that it vacillated between revolution and reaction, that it supported capitalism but opposed imperialism and feudal oppression. He contended that one could rely, to a limited extent, upon the noncomprador bourgeoisie, which has not betrayed the nation by collusion with imperialism.

Mao called imperialism the major instigator of revolution in colonial and semicolonial nations, and he added to Lenin's theory of imperialism the idea that hostile classes in dependent societies are united by a common desire to offset foreign exploitation. He maintained that a politically aware, armed, and dedicated people cannot be defeated, and he contended that human beings, not machines, won wars, that people with a will to victory can defeat strong imperialist powers.

Finally, Mao repudiated the Leninist concept of the party leadership going to the people with a program for revolution. He held that the people have to make the program, that they are the intellectuals who teach, not vice versa. Latin America's Maoists have also revised Trotsky's concept of Permanent Revolution. They feel that capitalist nations, led by the United States, will not permit socialism to spread. Thus, they maintain that only continuous revolution will enable socialism to gain the balance of world power.

The thought of the Italian newspaperman, Communist party leader, and theoretician Antonio Gramsci (1891–1937) has of late surpassed that of Mao Zedong in terms of its popularity among Latin America's Marxists. Gramsci learned from historian Benedetto Croce that the study of history dominated all other intellectual activity by relating the past to the present and the present to the future. Gramsci looked upon the position of historian as a high calling and wrote well—creatively, objectively, and with integrity. His ideas were fresh, the products of penetrating reflection. Even those that appeared to approximate the thinking of others were arrived at through independent critical analysis.

Gramsci believed human will capable of transcending the limitations of historical and personal experience, and he claimed that the first step toward achieving that objective was to develop the popular creative spirit, culture, and understanding of Marxism. He reasoned that one class's ability to rule others was not just the result of economic and physical power but also of its ability to persuade the ruled to accept its system of beliefs, to share its social, cultural, and moral values.[36] To lead the way from capitalism to socialism, he advocated the creation of a new cultural consensus around a "historic bloc" furnished by the working class and its intellectuals. He envisioned this "historic bloc" eventually exercising ideological and political hegemony as a result of its ability to solve a nation's problems. He urged his party to begin influencing culture by winning the allegiance of the intellectuals and teachers by placing its members in the media and publishing houses.

Gramsci challenged the dominant Marxist view that changing the economic base was the first step toward revolution. He saw class struggle as the primary move toward both radical change and altering the economic base. Gramsci emphasized the need to study the historical development of civil, rather than political, society, contending that civil society can attain consensus whereas political society tends toward class dictatorship.[37] To him, the mysteries of consensus contained the answers to how culture and hegemony (class domination) operate. He asked how civil society acquired its structure, what intellectual currents influenced the process and by what channels in relation to which historically determined social forces it operated, and how it could be radically transformed to attain socialism. He felt that socialism could resolve the problems not handled by liberalism and stressed that to do so it must promote the cultural unity of mankind. To improve social conditions, even in a socialist society, he believed that theoretical discussion had to remain open to all new contributions and to be continuously verified in relation to historical circumstances and the experiences of the masses.[38]

Gramsci contended that the party must offer immediate tangible gains and hope for the future, must organize the masses of workers, and then exert hegemony over them and the middle classes in order to establish a state for all members of society. He rejected the idea of waiting for the inevitable revolution; instead he urged the party to develop a revolutionary consciousness among the masses to prepare them for broad political, social, economic, and cultural revolution. These revolutions, he believed, alternated between active and passive phases, thus causing slowdowns in the permanent revolution. He contended that revolutionary movements could endure despite the fact that capitalism had not been destroyed as Marx predicted. He thereby provided renewed hope for socialism in areas like Italy and Latin America.

Taking off from Italian humanism, Gramsci built a bridge for liberal intellectuals to cross to socialism. Latin American Marxists regarded this bridge as vital if they were successfully to appropriate liberal and domestic institutions and turn them toward solving the problems that the bourgeoisie could not work out. Gramsci showed the way to create a new cultural consensus—with intellectuals leading the way by fostering historical awareness and interpreting it for others. His interest in the role of intellectuals in Italian society elicited Latin American intellectuals' interest in him, as will be revealed in subsequent chapters.

Gramsci's intensity, his tight emphatic style, and his intellectual rigor appealed to Latin American Marxists. They shared his view of positivism as the major philosophy that strove to develop only the privileged sectors of society. They approved of his refusal to follow slavishly tactics and strategies used elsewhere and his insistence that the Italian Communist party adopt policies that conformed to Italy's historical conditions, which they deemed more analogous to their own than those which existed in Marx's England or Germany or Lenin's Russia. They agreed with Gramsci's belief that fascism of the variety so prevalent in Latin America "was the illegal aspect of capitalist violence . . . the attempt to resolve the problems of production and exchange with machine guns and revolvers."[39] His belief that fascism was the only way that capitalists could preserve their economic system heightened Latin American Marxists' sense of urgency in their quests to eliminate capitalism.

Gramsci reasoned that at the outset of the Russian revolution, despite Lenin's theory that the urban proletariat served as the vanguard of the movement, the peasants provided the revolution's impetus and gave it mass reinforcement. His idea of a broad base of support for Italy applied equally to a Latin America more rural than urban. In Italy, as in Latin America, the peasantry always looked to middle-class intellectuals or the church for political leadership. Gramsci advocated organizing the countryside to break these traditional holds on the peasants and emphasized the need to counter the efficient propaganda of the organized church.[40] He worked to create a citizen militia through which the peasants could enter political life, and he believed that a worker-peasant alliance was an indispensable element in the struggle for socialism.

Gramsci's six-volume *Quaderni del Carcere* (1948–1951) (Prison Notebooks) serves as an extremely useful tool for understanding the problems of creating a socialist revolution in conservative authoritarian societies. His approaches to the study of the development of Italian society, especially his thoughts on the role of intellectuals and on the battle for hegemony, provided workable models for those interested in effecting change in Latin America.

Historical Backgrounds

The seminal thought of Karl Marx originated in the history of ideas of the Western world, primarily from the humanist tradition of the Renaissance and eighteenth-century rationalism. Scholars have traced the antecedents of Marxism to precursors such as the Greek philosopher Heraclitus (ca. 510 B.C.), who first propounded the idea of dialectical materialism regarding social relations; to Spartacus, who fought for "equality among men"; and to the Spanish *Comuneros* of early sixteenth-century Castile who advocated liberty and opposed the monarch Charles V. One can find numerous examples of class conflict, worker solidarity, national liberation, social revolution, imperialism, and the justification of violence to eliminate tyranny in pre-nineteenth-century history. But this type of detective work falls outside the scope of this book, which examines how the thought of Marx and his interpreters has been accepted, rejected, revised, and adapted to Latin American reality by mature thinkers.

Latin America, colonized by capital-seeking, class-conscious Spaniards and Portuguese under orders to expand the empires of the Iberian mother countries, provides historical conditions well suited to Marxian analysis. Although Marxist thought did not arrive in the Americas until more than two and a half centuries after Columbus, some Iberian traditions established during the colonial period contributed, indirectly, to its subsequent acceptance in some quarters. For example, although the colonial powers did not exhort *pensadores* to question the rationale for the existing system, they encouraged education among the ruling white elites, and Spanish- and Portuguese-born and *Criollo* (a person born in America to European parents) leaders acquired a taste for new European ideas before independence.

After independence Latin America gave birth to a few new ideas in the area of international relations but contributed little in the realm of political thought. Thinkers in the new nations looked to the United States for ideological inspiration and support while trying to construct their respective national philosophies, but they also sampled every new form of political thought that surfaced in Europe. Latin America's intelligentsia established a tradition of seeking ideas from abroad which might be used to solve the social, economic, and political problems that confronted their societies.

It is sometimes easier to attribute society's ills to the prevailing system and to look for foreign alternatives than to find local solutions to the problems. Marxism came to Latin America not as a mature and practical native doctrine but in piecemeal fashion as an ideology absorbed slowly by young workers and intellectuals.

Among the new European social doctrines attracting attention in the 1840s was the utopian socialism of Frenchman Henri de Saint-Simon (1760–1825), an early practitioner of class analysis, student of the role of labor and property in social development, advocate of social reform as the major function of government, and believer in the proletariat as an entity with a special mission. In addition to the ideas of Saint-Simon, French, Italian and German immigrants carried to Latin America the thinking of the French utopian Charles Fourier (1772–1837), well known for his doctrine of the pervasive "power of attraction," which posits that an ever-present power unites people for action and that obstacles in the way of this attraction cause antisocial behavior that will abate in favor of universal harmony when the obstacles are removed. Fourier's theories influenced a few intellectuals such as Argentina's José Esteban Echeverría (1805–1851) and Chile's Francisco Bilbao (1823–1865), who had fought on the barricades of Paris in 1848. But for the most part, at this time, Latin America's thinkers—middle-class people who lacked a proletarian class consciousness—felt more comfortable with positivism and did not respond to socialism.[41]

Well into the twentieth century the positivism of Auguste Comte (1798–1857), who had broken with the followers of Saint-Simon on the issue of public versus private ownership of property, dominated Latin American thought. Comte's philosophy, determinist in nature, with an emphasis on science and reason, promised to bring about the "order and progress" Latin Americans desired.

During the 1860s a handful of Argentine intellectuals became familiar with the ideas of the International Working Men's Association—the First International of Labor—for which Marx wrote the declaration of principles, and they spread his thoughts to Chile, Cuba, and Mexico. Chilean historian Benjamín Vicuña Mackenna wrote in 1870:

> The founding of the International was in itself a revolution, a big advance toward socialism, the harbinger of a revolution that will confront the exploiters with the organized workers who will deliver the knockout blow to the entire system of exploitation.[42]

European immigrants, some with exposure to the Paris Commune, the Italian Risorgimento, and the Spanish struggle to cast off monarchy, brought to Latin America a preference for anarchy and an understanding of trade unionism and socialism. Some of the Paris Communards established a section of the International in Buenos Aires in 1872 and published Argentina's first socialist newspaper *El Trabajador* (The Worker).[43] Their influence spread across the Río de la Plata to Uruguay where a section of the International was established in 1874, a time when most of Latin America was in a handicraft stage and its workers unorganized.

European colonial expansion reached a high point at the time of Marx's death in 1883. Anticapitalism was not in vogue, and even England and France had few Marxist thinkers. *Das Kapital* was first published in Spanish in Latin America in Buenos Aires in 1895, six years after the founding of the Second International in Paris. But Marxist ideas of social justice through the class struggle were not popular among Latin America's political and social thinkers, most of whom belonged to the elites that governed in their respective countries and whose primary interest was economic growth.

Millions of dollars in U.S. and European funds flowed into the region at this time, fostering new industries and creating new, and enlarging old, urban centers. While the area's intellectuals looked to U.S. and European capitalist centers for inspiration to help solve their countries' problems, European immigrants brought over to provide a labor base for the new industries arrived with radical ideas. Dominant among them were anarcho-syndicalists who looked to trade unionism to improve the workers' economic situations and advocated strikes to lead to the abolition of capitalism. In Latin America the anarcho-syndicalists placed great faith in the general strike as an instrument for bringing industry under worker's control. Seeking better living and working conditions than they had experienced in Europe, these socialist-oriented workers organized, ran candidates for office, agitated for welfare programs and social insurance legislation, and laid the foundations for the political and economic struggles of the twentieth century.

During the nineteenth century Latin American thinkers displayed considerable faith in automatic progress and evolutionary reform, but failure to solve the region's problems caused many of them, in the twentieth century, to turn toward radical bourgeois reform or organized socialist revolution. As the twentieth century progressed, the region became increasingly more involved in world affairs, fewer *pensadores* regarded Marxism as exotic, and interests in various types of socialist alternatives grew.

Light industry, small businesses, and commerce, encouraged by the expansion of British capital, grew in Latin America during the early years of the new century. Between 1900 and 1910, European-inspired socialism gained adherents in the region, with particular strength among workers in Brazil, Chile, Colombia, Cuba, Mexico, and Uruguay. Socialist parties emphasized the eight-hour working day, lower costs of living, safer working conditions, the right to strike, inheritance taxes, and free education.[44]

World War I halted, briefly, the flow of utopian, anarcho-syndicalist, and Leninist ideas into Latin America, and the region's social democrats began to form alliances with national bourgeoisies and to reject proletarian internationalism. Nevertheless, all types of socialists in the area saw the war as a result of capitalist competition and often urged their countrymen to take a pacifist line toward the European conflict.

The October 1917 revolution in Russia renewed interest among Latin American thinkers and workers in Marxist ideas. In particular, in the nations where socialist parties existed, thinkers and workers expressed sympathy for the successful Russian revolution. *Pensadores* like José Ingenieros of Argentina and Brazil's Lima Barreto praised the "maximalists," as the Bolsheviks were known. Lenin's writings were translated and circulated in Latin American nations by 1919. Intellectuals and workers read his works on socialism and war, the state and proletarian revolution, and left-wing communism and were especially intrigued by his denunciation of U.S. imperialism in Latin America. After World War I, Latin American thinkers began to interpret Marx and Lenin in light of the problems that surfaced in the area, in particular those caused by expanding productive forces combined with a backward socioeconomic system based on *latifundismo* (large landed estates) and U.S. and British domination of basic economic sectors.[45]

Argentina's 1918 University Reform Movement, initiated to give students greater voice in university governance, spread throughout Latin America. Many of its vociferous supporters, who in subsequent years became the region's democratic political leaders, expressed faith in radical politics and in socialism.

The Third or Communist International (Comintern), formed in Moscow in 1919, took an active role in the cause of world revolution, and by 1922 Communist parties existed in Argentina, Bolivia, Brazil, Chile, Mexico, and Uruguay. Marxist thought in

Latin America was now divided between Marxism-Leninism—generally known as "Communism" and associated with the Russian-oriented Communist parties—and a more utopian philosophy associated with the area's national Socialist parties.

In the wake of continuous U.S. military intervention and gunboat diplomacy in the Caribbean since the turn of the century, most notably in Cuba, the Dominican Republic, Haiti, Mexico, Nicaragua, and Panama, new waves of thought hit Latin America. *Pensadores* began to make the connection between imperialism and steadily deteriorating economic and social conditions, and they criticized the greed of foreign capitalists and the human exploitation that occurred as a result of it. Writers such as Uruguay's José Enrique Rodó, whose famous essay *Ariel* (1900) had set in motion a surge of Yankeephobia by stressing the retrograde influence of a United States determined to make the world in its own image, and Nicaraguan poet Rubén Darío, who condemned the cultural imperialism of the United States, had aroused the consciousness of Latin American thinkers during the early years of the century. In subsequent years their ideas added credence to the antiimperialist pleas of social revolutionaries.

By the 1920s thinkers like Peru's Víctor Raúl Haya de la Torre, influenced by the teachings of Marx but not a Marxist, concurred with the antiimperialism of Rodó and Darío and added to it new ideas on *Indianismo*, solidarity of the oppressed peoples of the world, and nationalization of land and industry. At the same time the Communists followed the Comintern policy of turning Latin America's proletariat against imperialism.

The Comintern, during the late 1920s and early 1930s, broke all alliances with the Socialists in Latin America, castigating them as petty bourgeois and rejecting their contention that Latin America was still semicolonial. This occurred just as left-wing radicalism gained adherents among the petty bourgeoisie as a result of the disillusionment of the Depression. By the Depression, Communist parties, other than those noted above, existed in Colombia, Costa Rica, Cuba, Ecuador, El Salvador, Paraguay, Peru, and Venezuela. Their growth was largely attributable to good organizing and to party platforms stressing economic independence and greater political democracy. Meanwhile, the strength of the social democrats declined in the region primarily because of theoretical weaknesses and the failure of the various Socialist parties to create effective ties between Latin America's small industrial proletariat and its large peasant sector.

With the rise of Hitler in Germany and Mussolini in Italy the Socialists and Communists were the first Latin American groups to organize systematically to fight fascism and to warn against the impending war in Europe. Left-wing sectarianism broke down by 1935, as Communist and various socialist groups exhibited a willingness to work together and even ally with liberal capitalists to defeat fascism. Until the end of World War II, a "Popular Front" or alliance strategy included consultation among left-wing and liberal groups, the formation of electoral coalitions, and a common effort to destroy fascism. Throughout World War II Latin America's Marxists generally curbed their talk of Yankee imperialism and went along with the idea of Pan-American solidarity.

The notion of fighting World War II to preserve democracy provided ready grist for the Marxist mill. The altruism of the Atlantic Charter and the United Nations concept, combined with the defeat of European fascism, gave rise to antidictatorial attitudes in Latin America. The organized Left, strengthened by the Soviet-United States Alliance during the war, pushed for the establishment of constitutional democracy and emphasized the connection between the overwhelming poverty of the region and the inability of its dictators to foster economic development. Thus, the struggle for socialism accompanied the struggle for democracy— economic, political, and social.

By the end of World War II there existed a more homogeneous urban proletariat in Latin America as a result of nearly a half-century of European immigration and increased industrialization fostered by the unavailability of European and U.S. goods during the conflict. Traditionally, socialist leadership in the area had come primarily from intellectuals and secondarily from trade unionists. However, the former had never attained influence in government without the support of the latter. Now *pensadores* began to relate the problems of the area to class consciousness and to look for solutions through Marxist analysis, and for the first time they could appeal to a growing working class that was receptive to socialism. Also, some Latin American Marxist thinkers began to deviate from the orthodox revolutionary theory of the necessity of developing capitalism followed by a long bourgeois-democratic revolution before beginning the socialist revolution.

They talked about achieving a Marxist revolution in the underdeveloped world without passing through the stages outlined by Marx and before attaining full-scale industrialization.

After World War II Latin American scholars began to analyze modernization, and their studies placed more emphasis on growth, change, and development, as Marx had done a century before. This new trend, in conjunction with the dynamic economic progress in the Soviet Union and the revolutionary upheaval in China, brought about new interest in Marxist thought in Latin America where Marx's vision of a fully modernized society operated by its people for their benefit now had greater appeal than ever. *Pensadores* applied their talents to solving problems like nation-building; industrial, agricultural, and commercial expansion; public education; demographic control; as well as U.S. imperialism. Marxists and many non-Marxists agreed that imperialism was at the root of the other problems and had to be eliminated. Intellectuals and workers, if they could somehow be unified, now had sufficient numbers to be an effective force against imperialism.

The Cold War both damaged and aided the development of socialism in Latin America. The area's governing elites and the U.S. government realized the potential revolutionary strength of an allied working class and expended a great deal of effort to curtail social reform and revolutionary movements. Washington sought to buy ideological allies and to pave the way for U.S. investment with military and economic aid; and its "democratization" policy appeared hypocritical in light of its support of tyrants of the ilk of Cuba's Fulgencio Batista, the Dominican Republic's Rafael Trujillo, Haiti's François Duvalier, Paraguay's Alfredo Stroessner, and Venezuela's Marcos Pérez Jiménez. The venality, brutality, and lack of social concern of such despots, at a time when Latin America received enormous amounts of U.S. private sector capital investment, increased the credibility of Marxist anti-imperialism. Deteriorating economic conditions among the region's majority turned many intellectuals and workers to the left. Young academics, and even clergy, began to question the benefits of the capitalist system, and popular demand for social reform and revolution engendered interest in Marxian analysis.

China's successful revolution, followed by the Soviet Union's launching of the first space satellite, increased Latin American interest in the way these two nations dealt with underdevelopment. Rising U.S. support for Latin American dictators, whose repressive tactics helped provide the political stability and security necessary for foreign investment, turned nationalist sentiment against Yankee imperialism and called attention to the ways international capitalism operated to the detriment of the masses living in the nations south of the Rio Grande.

First Mao Zedong, then Fidel Castro, demonstrated that a militant, unorthodox Marxist approach to revolution could succeed in nonindustrial societies. Third World revolution became a reality as, under the tutelage of *pensadores* radicalized in the 1930s and 1940s, a new generation of Marxist thinkers reached maturity in the 1950s and 1960s. At this time the Sino-Soviet split polarized Marxists but also caused more of them to pursue socialism independently, without ties to an ideological leader, and in a form more adaptable to conditions existing in their respective countries.

By the 1960s, more than ever, Latin American intellectuals accepted variations on Marx's thought. The theories of Castro, Guevara, Lenin, Trotsky, Mao, and Gramsci combined with aspects of nationalism, Indianism, existentialism, and even Christian theology to work toward effecting what Ortega y Gasset called "the revolt of the masses"—bringing the common person to political and social power.

3. Argentina

> Given one system, the capitalist system, which promotes in-
> equality, and another system, the socialist, which at least has
> its goal a form of equality, I had to opt for the latter.
>
> Julio Cortázar

The sentiments of internationally known Argentine novelist Julio
Cortázar[1] represent a recent link in Latin America's longest and
widest chain of socialist *pensadores*. Until the 1960s Argentina
had been the home for more socialist thinkers with different sectarian leanings than any other nation in Latin America. Inevitably
those familiar with the Argentine Left will find a favorite *pensador*
or school of thought, which, for lack of space, has been omitted.

Discussion of socialism in Argentina must begin with the pre-
Marxist thinker José Esteban Echeverría (1805–1851), who,
while studying in France between 1825 and 1830, came to admire
the utopian socialist thinking of Saint-Simon and Pierre Leroux.
Subsequently, Echeverría became the intellectual leader of the Argentine Generation of 1837 and the Association of May, which
opposed dictator Juan Manuel de Rosas, who controlled Argentina from 1829 to 1852. Echeverría believed that the major collective task of society was to provide the greatest individual freedom.
Essentially a rationalist, Echeverría did not accept the idea of class
equalization on the grounds that it was not the people but their
reason that was sovereign. To him, collective reason alone was
sovereign, not the collective will. He preferred the rule of reason
to the rule of the masses, which he feared could be irrational.[2]

Echeverría's *Dogma socialista* (Socialist Creed), written in 1839
and first published in 1846, became the revolutionary creed of the
Association of May. This liberal document emphasized freedom,
equality, fraternity, and the idea of progress. Echeverría's beliefs,
at best social-democratic, differed from their European proto-
types. He espoused an individualistic bourgeois socialism based on
the romantic idea of economic equality to eliminate poverty. He
did not pursue a revolutionary objective, nor did he seek to radically restructure society.[3]

39

Echeverría appreciated the attempt of Europe's 1848 socialist movement to alter life and attain a more humane society. By making his country's intelligentsia more aware of social science and social history, he laid foundations for socialists to strive for similar goals in Argentina. He was the first in his nation to publicize a belief in Saint-Simon's principle "from each man according to his capacity, to each man according to his work," and "the people are the origin and create total power." Saint-Simon's belief in the "conciliation of all classes" was too advanced for Echeverría's class-bound contemporaries, who gave him scant support.[4]

Not until after his death was Echeverría's significance felt. His ideas were referred to by socialists who came to Argentina to escape the backlash against the Paris Commune of 1871 and the repression of Bismarck. References to Echeverría began to appear in print more often after 1872 when Frenchman Emile Dumas founded the socialist journal *El Trabajador* in Buenos Aires.[5] Echeverría's *Dogma socialista* was quite well known among intellectuals and workers by 1880 when *El Obrero* (The Worker), a newspaper run by Herman Lahlman, began actively to promote the ideas of Marx in Argentina. Simultaneously, anarchists began to arrive in the country, foremost among them the Italian Enrico Malatesta, who landed in 1885 and remained until 1889 and who urged his Argentine cohorts toward less individual and more collective action. By 1892, thanks to Malatesta and his countryman Pietro Sori, the anarcho-syndicalist periodical *La Protesta* was launched successfully. As in most major South American nations, clashes between anarchists and socialists eventually impeded the growth of Marxism.

Many socialists during the 1890s associated the ideas of Marx with the philosophies of Kant, Comte, or Spencer, and as a result Argentina's first working-class organizations had an eclectic, rather than a specific, revolutionary character. Even the Socialist party, founded in 1895, was reformist and revisionist and did not have a precisely Marxist ideology.[6]

Thousands who immigrated to Argentina by the turn of the century found no *El Dorado* there. They joined an ever-growing mass of wage earners who felt that they were exploited by the capitalists for whom they toiled. Workers directed their collective actions for better conditions to political parties that began to agitate for changes within the legally established systems and stayed away from violent confrontations. Meanwhile, the nation's embryonic trade union movement remained subordinate to the political parties during the pre-World War I years.[7]

Argentina had a contingent in the Second International before World War I. During this period, through the efforts of activist intellectuals, political parties, and trade unions, urban workers attained better working conditions than existed elsewhere in Latin America.[8] In addition to struggling for better working conditions, anarchists as well as socialists generally concurred in their opposition to World War I. Later, the 1917 upheaval in Russia aroused a new revolutionary fervor among Argentine urban workers. By 1918 dissidents from the Socialist party helped found the International Socialist party in the nation, which became the Communist party when it joined the Third International in 1920.[9]

Events in Europe together with socialist and anarcho-syndicalist influence played a major role in the University Reform Movement, which originated in Argentina in 1918. The University Reform Movement and socialism nourished and reenforced each other. Both aroused the national consciousness and gave greater impetus to freer thought. Intellectual interchange grew in Argentina during the 1920s. The nation's writers, teachers, and politicians exhibited considerable receptivity to new ideas, those imported from Europe as well as from elsewhere in the Americas. Argentina's socialists, in particular, spent a great deal of time discussing political theory and their country's potential for revolution with their comrades from Chile, Brazil, and Uruguay. Socialists, Marxist-Leninists, and Trotskyists argued the relative merits of their respective interpretations of Marx in journals and newspapers and for a time enjoyed considerable respectability among the nation's academics and urban workers. They established foundations for subsequent generations of Marxist *pensadores* to build upon.

Vicente Sierra notes in his history of political ideas in Argentina that the country has a liberal historiographical tradition that accepted the idea of progress.[10] If one takes his word, it follows that, at least among the historically oriented, it is easy to make the transition to the Marxian concept of progress. Since the days of the Association of May, the idea of progress has played a prominent role in Argentine thought, and even today's Marxists express a relationship to that nineteenth-century group of humanists.[11]

Luis Pan, whose books constitute an outstanding repository of information on socialist thought and history in Argentina, points out the connections between the thinking of Echeverría and subsequent socialist writers such as Juan B. Justo, the Ghioldi brothers, and Alfredo Palacios and indicates that there exists a Marxist intellectual tradition in Argentina.[12] On the other hand, historian Alberto Pla contended that domination of the Left for so long by the Stalinist Communist party eclipsed and diminished the socialist image of writers like Justo. He maintained that the counterrevolutionary-reformist attitudes of the Communist party helped erode the socialist respectability built up before the 1930s.[13] Pla intimated, and Pan would probably agree, that since World War II the Argentine government has tended to follow the United States' Cold War policy of attaching a negative connotation to anything remotely resembling socialism; thus by the 1970s Marxist historiography, but not Marxist thought, ceased to be created in Argentina.[14]

Regardless of how Argentine Marxist *pensadores* feel about the theories of Pan and Pla, they all, more or less, subscribe to the ideas enunciated in Carlos Lombardi's *Las ideas sociales en la Argentina* (1965) (Social Ideas in Argentina), which analyzed the entire range of Argentine thought as a dialectical process. Lombardi viewed the liberalism of the period since the 1860s as an ideology with ideas but no action.[15] He carefully illustrated how historical materialism permits the social sciences to function as rigorous tools of analysis in the following six areas: (1) political economy—studying the laws of social relations of production and economic relations between people, (2) law—investigating legal codes to see the evolution and development of the state, (3) ethics—confronting moral problems and the formation of human conduct and its values, (4) history—studying the path of the people, humanity, and the creation of life, (5) linguistics—examining the role of language in the phenomenon of human development, and (6) aesthetics—analyzing the social form of art and reality.[16] With these broad areas in mind, we now examine Argentina's individual socialist *pensadores* in order to determine to what extent they have constructed a Marxist historiographical tradition.

Juan Bautista Justo (1865–1928)

Like many Latin Americans desirous of eliminating human suffering, Juan Justo's first calling was medicine. While studying in

Europe, he became acquainted with socialism and began to explore the relationship between the human biological struggle for existence and the fight for political solidarity. Justo soon found that the political component of the struggle interested him more than the biological one. Drawing on the ideas of Marx, the revisionist Eduard Bernstein, the French socialist Jean Jaurès, and above all Herbert Spencer, he began to integrate their thinking into a philosophy relevant to his native Argentina.

After completing his studies, Justo returned to Buenos Aires, began teaching medicine, and plunged into the socialist movement. He joined with Américo Ghioldi, Nicolás Repetto, and Alfredo Palacios in trying to analyze and find solutions to the problems plaguing Argentina in the 1890s. Together they formed a radical component of the *Unión Cívica de la Juventud* (Civic Union of Youth), Argentina's first major organization dedicated to social progress through political change.

In 1894 Justo founded the socialist journal *La Vanguardia* and the following year helped create a Socialist party committed to evolutionary parliamentary ideas, an organization seeking political power to achieve socioeconomic goals. Years later (1912) he would be elected to Argentina's congress as a Socialist deputy. In the midst of his political activities, he managed, in 1895, to translate *Das Kapital* into Spanish, in 1909 issued the first edition of his book on the theory and practice of history,[17] and later put a collection of his essays into *Socialismo* (1920), an excellent scientific analysis of Argentine history and politics.[18]

Justo's writings revealed that he read Marx and understood revolutionary theory as well as anyone of his day, but he was equally impressed by Spencer's thinking on evolution and as a result remained more a reformer than a revolutionary.[19] He expressed his beliefs in simple, elegant prose and conveyed the essence of socialism with unparalleled clarity.

To Justo, work constituted the essential material of history; thus the study and analysis of its patterns and relationships were central, as we can ascertain from his *Teoría y práctica de historia* (1915) (Theory and Practice of History), which treated the diverse social aspects of work and developed a general theory of human activity.[20] Justo maintained that private ownership of technology and control over the means of production by a specific class made it dominant over the physical and biological

tools and other materials of work, thereby hindering the
workers' struggle for existence. Thus, the proletariat, under capitalism, could never attain the freedom necessary to creative individual development. He claimed that social inequality existed as
a result of the monopoly of the means of production, and this he
believed to be an attack on nature that retarded the development
of the human species. To him, the bourgeoisie interfered with the
worker's ability to improve himself; thus health suffered, and the
weak lost out. He contended that all people, not just elites,
needed every opportunity to benefit from technology, to transform their environment.

Justo, to some extent, disagreed with the Hegelian concept of
the ever-present dialectic being the route to progress. He looked to
the past for laws to govern the evolution of societies. He understood class struggle and recognized the importance of the economic factor in history. He was a materialist who did not accept
all of Marx's thinking but liked Marx's grand vision of history,
which he interpreted flexibly. He believed that Marx had become
lost in abstractions and had neglected the practical ways to rectify
existing social inequities. He disagreed with Marx's assumption
that socialism was inevitable and thought that man had to experiment to find out how, scientifically, to alter society. He could not
accept the idea of a dictatorship of the proletariat. He contended
that all of society, not another elite, had to be prepared to man-
age. To him, education was preferable to revolution because, in
the former, habits necessary for social cooperation and the proper
use of technology could be developed, but they might be lacking if
an uneducated proletariat came to power via revolution.[21] Picking
up nineteenth-century Argentine writer and president Domingo
Sarmiento's theme that education could rid the nation of the barbarity that curtailed its progress, Justo put it in the perspective of
the class struggle by stressing that socialist education would enable the masses to cast off the shackles placed on them by the
elites that Sarmiento viewed as the "civilizers."

Although he lived in an era of growing imperialism and was
familiar with the warnings about it set out so eloquently by his
fellow Socialist party member Manuel Ugarte, who believed that
Latin America was in danger of being controlled or absorbed by
the United States,[22] Justo said that foreign capital was necessary to
develop Argentina because the nation's inept national bourgeoisie

could not do it alone. He maintained that foreign investment would accelerate the evolutionary process that laid the foundations for eventual socialization of the means of production.[23] He was never clear about how the latter would occur.

Justo deviated from the Marxist emphasis on the role of the proletariat. In adapting socialism to Latin America and Argentine conditions, he stressed that the rural sector, where 80 percent of the population were tenants subject to the dictates of landowners, needed restructuring. As a matter of practicality he advocated a progressive tax on the land to reduce the power of the landed aristocracy.[24]

Justo's thinking about rural questions, on a more theoretical level, emerged in 1909 when Enrico Ferri, the Italian socialist, in a public forum in Argentina, criticized Justo's comrades as middle-class radicals and said that they had no business being socialists since socialism was a European, not an indigenous, creation and that the proletariat Marx referred to was industrial and Argentina was basically rural. Justo replied that although an industrial proletariat did not exist, a mass basis for socialism existed in the rural towns.[25] He noted that in Argentina all wage earners, rural and urban, lower and middle class, had to be mobilized. Justo said that Ferri did not understand that the ruling landlord class in Argentina had been creating an urban proletariat not by industrializing but by excluding workers from access to the land and forcing them into the cities. He stated that Marx's observation that the supply of exploitable labor made industrial capitalism possible could pertain to the starving rural population of Latin America.[26]

Justo, while searching for solutions to Argentina's most acute problems at a time when his nation was affirming the preeminence of nationalism, pointed out to his countrymen the international dimension of the factors that impeded their nation's economic and social progress. At a crucial point when Argentina endeavored to democratize its political institutions, Justo symbolized the socialist alternative and also flexibility. He condemned the notion that all socialist doctrine was rigid and talked about the existence of socialist or Marxist theories that could be altered. He said that "socialism is more than an historical theory, an economic hypothesis, and a political doctrine, it is a mode of thought."[27] He criticized Marxist theorists who made artificial gestures and whose grand plans often deteriorated in the face of action or proved to be merely pedantry.[28] His appeal for a more realistic blend of theory and action had enormous impact on the embryonic socialist movement in Argentina and surrounding countries, and his ideas were reflected in the writings of their Marxist *pensadores*.

Alfredo L. Palacios (1880–1966)

If we think of Juan Justo as the "elder statesman" among the energetic and talented group of Argentine Socialist party activist-intellectuals who worked together during the early decades of the twentieth century, then Alfredo Palacios might be thought of as the dean of that socialist school which also included in its ranks Adolfo Dickmann, author of a book detailing the divisiveness of nationalism;[29] Enrique Dickmann, a Talmudic-type scholar who wrote on population problems,[30] ideas and ideals,[31] and Marxist theory; Américo Ghioldi, whose work we will subsequently investigate; and Jacinto Oddone, the relatively uncritical chronicler of the Socialist party[32] and trade unionism in Argentina.[33]

Palacios was a great orator, a law professor, a "people's lawyer" who did not charge the poor, rector of the University of Buenos Aires, the first Socialist deputy in Argentina's congress (1904), a senator, a man who fought a duel for his party's honor and was expelled from it for doing so, and the author of over thirty major books on topics such as literary criticism, law, military justice, the university, socialism, sovereignty, imperialism, the working class, women's rights, economic conditions, and international conflicts. Like Justo, Palacios leaned heavily on the thinking of Jean Jaurès, and he criticized the exclusive emphasis placed by some Marxists on the economic factor in history. He and Justo agreed that the lot of the worker was improving.

Palacios tried to make socialist thought compatible with the creative and vibrant aspects of the liberal tradition.[34] In some ways he regarded socialism as a spiritual force. Yet he stated: "I do not consider the social movement as a natural process governed by laws independent of the will of consciousness, and of intention."[35] He was a materialist who also felt that idealism and individualism were important. These beliefs sometimes set him apart from his Socialist party colleagues.

Palacios's major quest was for social justice, which he believed socialism could foster in all aspects of life. He thought that one had to understand the history of the concept of justice in order to comprehend injustice, and he tried to explain both in *La justicia social* (1954) (Social Justice), a treatise on the philosophy of justice that trod the middle ground between the classical Aristotelians and Marx. Like Juarès, Palacios recognized the importance of economic as well as idealistic values. He indicated that justice could be wrought out of human values and ideas, not only out of the regulation of the means of production. To some extent these beliefs modified the materialist view but did not obscure it.[36]

Palacios traced the notion of justice in human relations from the ancient and the classical worlds to the present, describing the social systems Marx used to develop his concept of emancipation of the workers in relation to the modes of production. He located the predecessors of current totalitarianism, slavery, exploitation, and antisocial human behavior, or the components of injustice.[37] He then showed how these facets of injustice developed in Argentina and theorized how Marxist humanism, of a variety espoused by Justo, could eliminate injustice.[38]

He picked up the history of the Argentine threads of injustice in *Masas y élites en Iberoamérica* (1960) (Masses and Elites in Iberoamerica) where he cited the native revolts against the Spanish as examples of the struggle for justice. In addition to the indigenous desires for justice he related the European thoughts on the matter to the idea of sovereignty residing in the community of man, as had the Thomists Francisco Suárez and Francisco de Vitoria, whose thinking was popular in learned circles during the colonial period. Palacios demonstrated how this early form of "people's sovereignty" developed historically in Argentina, along with the concept of the rights of man.[39] To him, the struggle for the rights of man and "people's sovereignty," along with the influence of Echeverría's *Dogma socialista* culminated in the 1853 constitution, which, theoretically, provided social justice. He viewed the constitution as the result of workers' agitation, in conjunction with elite understanding, which forged a new set of governing principles, and concluded that the masses and elites have to work together to produce the revolution.[40] Palacios, perhaps using himself as an example, assumed, like so many Argentine liberals of the day, that mass-oriented elites would work to further the lot of the workers.

Palacios examined how capitalism had historically affected progress in Argentina. For example, he noted how the postindependence *emphyteusis* program of 1824, under which the nation retained dominion over its lands but provided for their rental to individuals and corporations, enabled vast public lands to pass into the hands of a few people, and when the law was repealed in 1869, these elites became the political and economic dictators of the country. He viewed this attempt to increase public revenues as the major cause of *latifundismo* and the concomitant exploitation of the rural workers.[41] Only nationalization of the land under socialism, he thought, could transform the nation into a place that respected human dignity.

Palacios formulated ideas consistent with the development of Argentine society but stressed socialism within an international context. He strove to build in Argentina a socialist international mentality while criticizing national symbols like flag flying and anthem playing.[42] He enjoyed writing and debating on international subjects, and in this realm appeared to be more influenced by the thinking of José Martí and Manuel Ugarte than by Lenin. In 1925 he helped form the Latin American Union, an organization dedicated to continental solidarity and opposed to U.S. expansion in the Americas. His *Nuestra América y el imperialismo* (1961) (Our America and Imperialism), a highly literate but not particularly profound work, displayed the influence of Martí and Ugarte, as well as that of José Ingenieros, José Mariátegui, and Mexican diplomatic historian Isidro Fabela.[43] In this book he wrote that "the flag follows the trade," and he claimed that Yankee advocacy of Pan-Americanism was designed to further U.S. capitalism in Latin America.[44] He advocated using the Pan-American Union as a vehicle for social justice, not for U.S. imperialism. He opposed U.S. control of Panama and of Cuba under the Platt Amendment, defended Augusto Sandino's attempt to eliminate U.S. influence in Nicaragua, and supported Puerto Rico's independence movement. Palacios held that World War II did not alter the basic structure of the capitalist world but that it rearranged the balance of world power, tipping it a bit toward socialism. He disagreed with Soviet Communism but also believed that the United States overreacted to it. In 1960 he traveled to Cuba and found that the Cuban revolution lacked ideology but was inspired by the humanism and love of liberty of Martí. He admired Castro's successful defiance of the United States, and during the last years of his life Palacios defended the Cuban revolution, especially its agrarian reform policy,[45] and delighted in watching Cuba achieve, in a "creative" socialist fashion, some of his lifelong objectives.

Aníbal Ponce (1898–1938)

The strongest link between the thinking of José Esteban Echeverría and Lenin, between Argentina's sometimes positivist-oriented Socialist party *pensadores* and the country's more radical Marxist thinkers was Aníbal Ponce, the man Rodolfo Ghioldi called the greatest intellectual spirit of Argentine Marxism[46] and whose work introduced a new stage in the history of Argentine culture.[47] Perhaps the best essayist of his time to apply historical materialism to his investigations, Ponce distinguished himself in medicine, sociology, education, psychology, and philosophy. Inspired at an early age by the writing of Lenin, Palacios, and Martí, he was later influenced by the Cuban poet Nicolás Guillén, Cuban *pensador* Juan Marinello, and his close friend, Mexican historian Jesús Silva Herzog, who imbued him with the hope of the Mexican Revolution.

While professor of psychology at Argentina's National Institute of Secondary Education, he coedited, with José Ingenieros, the *Revista de Filosofía* (Magazine of Philosophy). He founded in 1930 and presided over the Free College of Advanced Study and in 1936, directed the magazine *Dialéctica* dedicated to rigorous social analysis.

Ponce's initial fascination with scientific reasoning and biology led him to positivism; then, unlike some of his Socialist party comrades, he made the transition to orthodox Marxism. He ultimately concluded that people modify the conditions of their existence by their actions, that historically humans have created and transformed economic relations and social conditions. He believed that once people accepted these ideas, their horizons were opened to philosophy, which would explain the world and also transform it.[48] An advocate of developing the intellect to its fullest, he mastered Marxist thought, British economics, French utopian socialism, and German philosophy.[49] But he emphasized that Marx was the only one who met contemporary problems with "relentless analysis" and rigorous method, "with the integrity of his criticism and with the revolutionary meaning of history."[50]

Ponce believed that close scrutiny of the classics would reveal much about the lot of the proletariat and the class struggle. He considered Shakespeare's works, such as *Richard III, Julius Caesar,* and *Antony and Cleopatra,* model realistic creations through which the class systems could be seen.[51] He talked about "socialist realism" or the factual history of events observed through the classics, which demonstrated how societies acted and interacted and exposed the reality of life to be not its dreams but its forces and how they operate and what they do.[52]

Ponce tried to foster socialist humanism in Argentina where he believed that the machine age, rather than liberating the proletariat, caused dehumanization and exploitation.[53] In his 1935 book *Humanismo burgués y humanismo proletario* (Bourgeois Humanism and Proletarian Humanism), subsequently republished in Cuba where it had considerable impact on Castro's social planners, he stated that humanism characterized by a return to the study of the classics was a prologue to the Renaissance, from which there emerged an intellectual elite whose view of man was too abstract. He said that Erasmus's bourgeois humanism proclaimed the freedom of man, but man was only freed from one master to serve another—those who owned the means of production. He contrasted bourgeois humanism with Marxist humanism, which views people as living beings, not abstractions,[54] and concluded that humanity can flourish only if class distinctions are destroyed.[55] This could be done, he felt, by creating a love for the humanities, literature, art, and music and a classless culture with which all could identify equally. He saw correlations between transmitting the classics to the masses and ridding man of poverty; between opening up universities to all and enabling everyone to understand how exploitation works in order to eliminate it.[56]

Aníbal Ponce, a product of the University Reform Movement, never lost his desire to improve education. He believed that the concern Argentina's bourgeoisie had for education was designed to foster its own class interests, and he advocated a "New University," in which there would be liberty and freedom from the class-bound mentality. In *Educación y lucha de clases* (1936) (Education and the Class Struggle), Ponce showed how the rise of capitalism affected education in the Western world. He saw in primitive education a social responsibility reflecting a collective sense of community.[57] But, from classical times on, he contended, that education had become an arm of the ruling classes and their state, used to maintain slavery and feudalism. The Church, he believed, taught irrationality, passivity, fatalism, and faith in the supernatural. By the eleventh century and the founding of the first universities, the bourgeoisie, which saw education as the path to benefits formerly reserved for the nobility and the clergy, began to dominate intellectual life.[58]

Educación y lucha de clases, reprinted in Castro's Cuba, contributed significantly to that country's new revolutionary educational system. In it Ponce demonstrated how the dominant class had directed the social organization of the state through education, which conveyed selected information but did not teach people to think for fear that they might then question the system that the education was designed to support.[59] He lamented the fact that too often average people do not realize that their children are being prepared to function as subordinates. He also negated the concept of the "neutral" scholar and pointed out the dangers of those who think that they are objective or value-free in their judgments.

This flexible, "plain" Marxist was driven into exile for teaching well, for urging people to question the "truths" that he felt contributed to Argentina's historical myopia and its limited ability to comprehend the need for societal restructuring.

The Ghioldi Brothers—Rodolfo (1897–) and Américo (1899–)

Rodolfo Ghioldi was born to Italian immigrant parents in Buenos Aires where at age sixteen he helped form a socialist youth group. A few years later he joined the antiimperialist, anti-World War I movement that was partially responsible for keeping Argentina out of that conflict.[60] Between 1910 and 1921 he led Argentina's National League of Teachers; and in reaction to the revisionism of Argentina's Socialist party and Juan Justo whom he praised but also criticized as a reformist,[61] he helped found, along with Victorio Codovilla, the International Socialist party, forerunner of the Communist party.[62] He visited the Soviet Union in 1921 and returned a lifelong devotee of Leninism and Argentine interpreter of the Communist party position. The Comintern sent him to Brazil to organize the National Liberation Alliance, an activity that brought him in contact with Luiz Carlos Prestes (to whom he served as an ideological mentor) and landed him in a Brazilian jail in 1935. During World War II, he believed that Argentina was caught in a crossfire between Germany's desire to take over the world and the United States' desire to take over Latin America,[63] but his ties to Russia caused him to support the United States against Germany. After the war the Perón regime forced him into exile. He later returned to Argentina and served as a Communist party delegate to the country's Constituent Assembly. An outspoken critic of Trotsky and Mao and defender of Stalin, Ghioldi devoted his time and energies to trying to clarify the ideas of Marxism-Leninism for his people.

Like Ponce, Rodolfo Ghioldi was influenced by the University Reform Movement, which tried to open Argentina to new ideas. However, he held that the nation ultimately reacted against the University Reform Movement by turning to the right and eventually became an authoritarian corporate state. He believed that a resurgence of positivist thought, the conservatism of the Church, and the military's desire to be the arbiter of politics eliminated most of the gains of the 1918 University Reform Movement. The survival of the fittest, elitist ideas of the "positivist church," he said, were analogous to bringing the Falange or Hitler to Argentina.[64] To him, positivist thinkers like Alejandro Korn, a disciple of Kant and of idealism, erroneously believed that moral order presupposes human freedom and the existence of God. Although Korn recanted and moved toward scientific explanations of society toward the end of his life when he joined the Socialist party (1931), Ghioldi claimed that his early elitist ideas had a profound adverse affect on Argentina.[65]

Ghioldi contended that, in addition to the thinking of Korn and Kant, the ideology of existentialism popularized in Argentina by the works of Spanish philosopher José Ortega y Gasset, was also nonscientific and worked against the antiimperialist and agrarian revolutions needed in Latin America.[66] He criticized Ortega's *Revolt of the Masses* (1932), which depicted the masses as causing chaos and violence, as an extension of Nietzsche who, unlike Marx, believed that elites will always be necessary to lead the masses.[67]

On a more practical level, Rodolfo Ghioldi attacked the generally accepted theory that the nineteenth-century conflict over the benefits of Argentina's import and export tax revenues that came through Buenos Aires, the struggle between Argentina's *porteños* (residents of the port city of Buenos Aires) and the *provincianos* (those who lived in the hinterlands) hindered progress in the country. He stated that the contradiction that severely hurt Argentine society was not between *porteños* and *provincianos* but the alliance of foreign imperialists with the ruling oligarchy against the working class. He claimed that the people of Buenos Aires and those of the interior are natural allies against the common enemy.[68]

To him, imperialism primarily meant the United States, the Monroe Doctrine, and Manifest Destiny.[69] He read the writings of Alfred Thayer Mahan, who believed that the Caribbean was the strategic key to both oceans and Cuba the key to the Caribbean[70] and that they expressed the same point of view as did the work of U.S. historian Samuel "Wave the Flagg" Bemis written decades later. In Washington's Latin American policies, too, he noted little change. As recently as the 1960s, he viewed Raúl Prebisch's essentially diffusionist theory of development upon which the Alliance for Progress rested as an instrument of the capitalist-controlled International Monetary Fund.

Over the years, Rodolfo Ghioldi's tone mellowed, but his fundamental ideas remained the same. He never wavered from the belief that one cannot proceed directly to socialism without going through the preliminary antiimperialist and democratic revolutionary stages. His 1967 book *No puede haber revolución en la revolución* (You Cannot Have a Revolution in the Revolution) viewed the *Fidelistas* as extreme adventurers and called Régis Debray an advocate of pre-Marxist nonclass socialism.[71]

In the final analysis, Rodolfo Ghioldi's thinking has moved over the decades from that of a Stalinist to a standard interpreter of the Communist party and sometimes sophisticated Marxist, who has functioned most effectively as a critic of ahistorical nonscientific bourgeois sociology which emphasizes group concepts, but not group conflict, and masquerades under a false illusion of objectivity while pursuing its mission of social control designed to maintain the capitalist order.[72]

In contrast to Rodolfo Ghioldi stands his brother Américo, a socialist humanist theoretician and practical Socialist party politician. Influenced by Jean Jaurès and Juan Justo with whom he worked closely, Américo Ghioldi agreed philosophically with socialist thinker Henri Lefevre, who called Marxism an expression of an epoch, but not totally the thinking of Karl Marx.[73]

Luis Pan referred to Américo Ghioldi, along with Justo, as the most vigorous interpreters of Marxist ideas in Argentina; an accolade borne out by Ghioldi's theoretical treatise *Marxismo, socialismo, izquierdismo, comunismo, y la realidad argentina de hoy* (1950) (Marxism, Socialism, Leftism, Communism, and Today's Argentine Reality)[74] and his *Juan B. Justo: Sus ideas históricas, socialistas, filosóficas* (1933) (Juan B. Justo. His Historical, Social, and Philosophical Ideas), which clarified the thinking of Justo and demonstrated that Ghioldi shared his belief in the natural democracy of socialism, his notion of what constitutes the Left, and his economic analysis of Argentine history.[75]

Américo Ghioldi wrote books on socialism, Sarmiento, pedagogical theory, and the 1943 and 1966 military takeovers in Argentina. These volumes and many long pamphlets display a deep knowledge of Argentine historiography and an understanding of the contradictions inherent in it. In his writings he integrated the thinking of most major Argentine *pensadores,* Marxist and non-Marxist, in order to explain the social relations of each epoch in his nation's history.

Ghioldi, in his impressive book *Marxismo, socialismo, izquierdismo, comunismo, y la realidad argentina de hoy* (1950) examined the relationship of Marxism to the history of socialism and criticized the "extreme leftists" in Argentina for their simplistic analyses of Marx. He would have placed his brother Rodolfo among the "simplistic" but not the "extreme left." One wonders how Américo's "extreme left" differed from that which Rodolfo took to task. Neither brother resolved these sectarian differences satisfactorily, but their efforts to do so must have engendered many lively dinner discussions.

In *El socialismo en la evolución nacional* (1946) (Socialism in the National Evolution) Américo Ghioldi described the factors that have enabled socialist orientations to gain footholds in Argentina. He showed how the class struggle has united diverse ethnic components of the working class, helped them assimilate, and forced them to acquire the political education necessary to alleviate poor conditions.[76] He contended that most Argentine socialists and nonsocialists share a belief in democracy and a disdain for totalitarianism. He believed that most knowledgeable Argentines respected the democratic goals of socialism and realized that its proponents represented a tradition that proclaims the excellence of a method, of a conduct, of a work—an ongoing process.[77] He claimed that syndicalism, inspired by the ideas of Sorel, began a desire for a tradition of liberty among Argentina's workers, which was subsequently pursued by the *descamisados* (shirtless ones) of the *Peronista* movement. He concluded that Juan Perón propagated the concept of worker liberty primarily to gain proletarian support but that he deceived the workers whose desires he did not fulfill.

For him, World War II clarified the connection of fascism to the capitalist economy and made socialism more synonymous with democracy in Argentina. To counter the socialist threat to *Peronismo,* he noted that the fascist-leaning Perón incorporated socialist expressions of social justice into his program. In other words, Perón endeavored to replace socialism with Peronism by co-opting it as Hitler and Mussolini tried to do with their national socialism.[78]

Ghioldi explained that by the Perón era, Argentina had passed into a new stage of primitive capital accumulation and had experienced some preliminary economic progress. Argentines were psychologically prepared for conditions to continue to improve when Perón offered them further hope. Thus, socialism, which accepted the idea of utopia as an ideal goal or inspiration but still had to contend with reality, could not compete with the unrealistic promises of Peronism.[79] In describing how the cult and power of Perón worked, Ghioldi showed admiration for the ingenuity and disdain for the lack of commitment of the Argentine strongman who incorporated traces of Marx, Lenin, Justo, and Clausewitz into his cleverly conceived propaganda and carelessly constructed policies on war, power, and politics.[80]

Ghioldi did not share the fascination Argentina's working class had for Eva Perón and her women's wing of the Peronista party. His profound interest in the social emancipation of women caused him to campaign against Evita, who he believed promoted female subordination. He considered her elaborate social service foundations part of an insincere dictatorial program by which the Peróns beguiled the Argentine people with false hope while gaining their support for a society based upon corporatist, fascist, clerical, and military principles.

Throughout his extended career Américo Ghioldi distinguished himself as an articulate, forceful, and highly rational spokesman for Argentina's oppressed minorities and majorities. A sagacious, creative, "plain" Marxist analyst of his own society, he ranks with

Juan Justo, Alfredo Palacios, and Aníbal Ponce as one of the most effective of the large group of Socialist party *pensadores* who kept socialism alive through two world wars, the Depression, and the Perón era. Ghioldi and his respected Socialist colleagues, while providing their countrymen with a viable political alternative, constantly challenged Argentina's capitalist ruling political elites through their literature, in the press, and as participants in all branches of government. Although their socialist revolution never came to pass, they figured prominently in most of the progressive reforms that were effected in Argentina, and their tenacious opposition and omnipresence reduced the harmful excesses of Argentina's rulers until the 1960s when the military took over the country.

Victorio Codovilla (1894–1970)

Italian-born Victorio Codovilla arrived in Argentina in 1912 and immediately joined a socialist youth group; later he became a member of the Socialist party. In 1918, he declared his Socialist party comrades, especially Justo and the Dickmanns, "revisionists," and he and Rodolfo Ghioldi founded the International Socialist party, forerunner of the Communist party. Like Ghioldi, Codovilla became virtually synonymous with the Communist party, serving as one of its leading essayists, polemicists, social critics, and as a party historian.[81] He began writing in the 1920s, and from the Depression through the Cold War era into the 1960s he loyally defended the Stalinist line.

Although Codovilla lived most of his life in Argentina, he thought in terms of developing European-style socialism there. For example, he could not accept the idea, as had Prestes in Brazil, of allying with the national bourgeoisie enroute to socialism. He viewed Prestes, and those who sought a "Latin American" road to socialism as deviants from classical European socialism who overemphasized nationalism to the exclusion of internationalism.[82]

In *¿Resisterá la Argentina al imperialismo yanqui?* (1948) (Will Argentina Resist Yankee Imperialism?) Codovilla stressed that communism is not anti-United States or anti-England, but antiimperialism. He pointed out the deceptive nature of the Good Neighbor Policy, which pretended to be antiinterventionist but which merely represented a new, more covert, way to intervene.[83] He concluded that the Good Neighbor Policy opened the eyes of workers to the character of the expansionist-exploitative U.S.

businesses.[84] Despite the invidiousness of the Good Neighbor Policy, Codovilla held that the United States' reaction against fascism during World War II fostered liberalization in Latin America, which subsequently enabled Communists to hold ministerial posts in Chile and Cuba.[85]

Codovilla contended that after World War II President Truman reestablished "dollar diplomacy" along with the development of an inter-American system designed to protect the economic, political, and ideological solvency of the United States. To build Cold War solidarity, the United States forced the Latin American governments to create militaries disproportionate to their financial capabilities.[86] Codovilla noted the contradiction between the avowed aim of the Good Neighbor Policy to increase commercial interchange and lessen dependency in the Americas and the Truman Doctrine, which did the opposite and also prevented the workers and populist masses from developing a political base.[87] He opposed the Organization of American States concept, arguing that in that body the Latin American nations would be under the hegemony of the United States. He also rejected the idea of a separate Latin American bloc dominated by Argentina or Brazil. He took the Stalinist approach that after World War II there existed two world markets—one capitalist with no rhythm or predictability, and the other socialist—the capitalist system building dominant and dependent relations and the socialist working for classless equality. In Latin America, Codovilla felt that you could have either colonialism under one capitalist power or another or equality under an antiimperialist Communist party striving to build socialism.[88]

Although international affairs occupied a great deal of Codovilla's thinking, he also concerned himself with national policy. He viewed the rise of Argentina's Radical party, the country's major civilian political organization since the 1890s, with skepticism, believing that it was progressive and represented the bourgeois-revolutionary stage of political development, but that it left the workers out of the political process and sought no structural changes in the social relations of production in the rural sector. He claimed that the Radical party included many reactionaries who feared the development of a mass movement and preferred rule by an elite, which would lead to strongman rule, as in Germany, to protect the system. In essence, Codovilla predicted the rise of Peronism.[89]

Codovilla was a leading public exponent of women's rights, a difficult idea to propagate in Argentina's *macho* society. He supported equal salaries for equal work and tried to build female unity. In 1947, he urged the Communist party to establish separate men's and woman's cells, to attract women who could, by working together in highly supportive groups, overcome the sense of subordination to men they experienced at mixed meetings. Codovilla's thinking contrasted vividly with that of the Peronista's women's organization, which worked for female gains and rights but, for the most part, accepted the superior status of men.[90]

Codovilla provided an interesting analysis of the Perón era. He said that during the flux period between the world wars, industrial capital began to overshadow that of the *latifundistas* (owners of large landed estates) and the petty bourgeoisie. This permitted Argentina to be subject to the greatest foreign exploitation of its natural wealth in its history. Urban masses formed, and after the Depression the workers could either become an independent entity in conflict with the new capitalists or could become an extension of the capitalists who controlled them while allowing them to organize for their own and the capitalists' benefit.[91] When Juan Perón assumed the position of secretary of labor in the military government in 1943, he began to build a political machine around the labor unions under his control. He was elected president in 1946, again in 1951, and served until 1955. Codovilla granted that urban workers fared somewhat better during the Perón era, but the government was never in their hands as their leader had them believe.[92]

To Codovilla, the anti-Yankee rhetoric of Perón masked further foreign penetration. Despite propaganda about *Peronista* control, Argentine society was under the direction of the foreign and domestic industrial and commercial bourgeoisie.[93] *Peronismo* was also supported by the military and police who controlled the state apparatus, the less politicized workers, the landed oligarchy, the church, university students, and some intellectuals, professionals, and artisans.[94] With such broad-based support, much of it predicated on false hope, Perón almost succeeded in destroying the Left in Argentina and the Communist party in particular.[95] Codovilla claimed that the Communist party raised worker consciousness and Perón capitalized on it, despite the fact that *Peronismo* basically favored imperialism and foreign monopolies.[96]

Peronismo proclaimed itself a movement between capitalism and socialism, but, according to Codovilla, it was not a new synthesis but a form of capitalism where most of the benefits of labor accrued to the dominant classes. He felt that "social justice" was given considerable lip service but could not be nurtured in a society divided by class antagonisms. Nevertheless, Perón did a magnificent job of publicizing and making people believe that he created a social revolution.[97] A primary example of Perón's attractive propaganda was his contradictory and pseudoscientific philosophy of *justicialismo* (justice), which contained something for everyone—idealism, materialism, individualism, and collectivism under an aura of Christianity.

Codovilla found Perón to be a social demagogue[98] whose nationalism militated against the international solidarity of the workers. Perón fostered a Sarmiento-type of nationalism that discredited the existing foreign or immigrant influence and negated cultural pluralism.[99] On the other hand, Codovilla contended that it was healthy to incorporate positive foreign experiences, like socialism, into the national ethos. He believed that an artificial prosperity brought on by World War II, not Perón, caused an unrealistic euphoria in Argentina, a false hope that the lot of the masses was on the upswing. But the relations of production did not change during the Perón era, and the workers developed a bourgeois mentality rather than a proletarian class consciousness.[100]

Silvio Frondizi (1907–1974)

It is difficult to find a greater contrast on the Left than that between Victorio Codovilla and Silvio Frondizi, although both were of Italian extraction, belonged to the same generation, and were initially influenced by Socialist party *pensadores*. However, Argentine-born Frondizi's thought, as we shall see, was more akin to that of those who reached their intellectual prime in the second half of the twentieth century than those who represented the ideas of the first half like Codovilla.

Frondizi, trained as a lawyer but with a solid grounding in classical and Marxist economics, acquired a nationwide reputation as a professor of history and political science at the University of Buenos Aires. His brilliant career included the writing of numerous theoretical books on the modern state, world capitalism, the crisis in democracy, Argentine reality, and dialectical materialism.

Silvio Frondizi, the brother of Arturo Frondizi, the leader of the most liberal wing of the Radical party and president of Argentina between 1958 and 1962, founded the *Movimiento Izquierda Revolucionaria* (MIR) (Movement of the Revolutionary Left), an organization designed to develop revolutionary methods for Latin America. He established MIR in response to the Socialist party, which, he felt, espoused revolutionary theory but was reformist in practice, and to the Communist party, which, he believed, did not pursue revolution because of the stagnation of its Soviet-style-bureaucracy and its popular frontism. Unlike the Communist and Socialist parties, Frondizi's MIR advocated proceeding with socialist revolution before the bourgeois-democratic revolution was completed. Frondizi never completed the work of MIR. After denouncing the military's murder and torture practices in Catamarca Province, in 1974 he was assassinated. Had he lived another decade, this independent, highly creative "plain" Marxist would probably have been recognized internationally as the Argentine counterpart of C. Wright Mills.

Frondizi discussed the German origins of Marxism in *El materialismo dialéctico* (1966)[101] (Dialectical Materialism). Influenced by the economic thought of Harold Laski and that of Gramsci on social and political questions, Frondizi agreed with the latter's contention that the intellectual plays a fundamental role in completing society's superstructure. In this book he presented a critical analysis of the economic, political, and spiritual components of the liberal state, which he characterized as impersonal and uncaring. He questioned intellectuals' tendencies in Europe and America to defend the existing economic system and their failure to reconcile individual liberty with the freedom to act without economic restraints. He felt that to survive, democracy had to safeguard the moral value of the individual, even at the expense of economic liberty. In other words, only state economic controls might be able to protect individual values. He argued that the bourgeois-liberal state provided the minimum political liberty necessary for the pacification of the majority of the people—to keep them from espousing serious change.[102] In the modern liberal state, he said, the lack of economic liberty and equality negates the other liberties and that different degrees of liberty and democracy exist for different classes.[103]

Frondizi, in addition to commenting on political and economic liberty, discussed spiritual liberty. To understand the position of spiritual liberty in the bourgeois-liberal state, he went back to the thinking of Kant and Rousseau. Kant believed that we only know what we perceive and that this governs our actions, that we are ignorant of other value constructs that might be more beneficial or valid for our society. Kant also claimed that ethical good coincides with that which is imposed—an action which Frondizi believed could be injurious. Rousseau, a deist, accepted the liberal idea that the moral norm is the language of the function of feeling of the conscience, not the intelligence. Frondizi pointed out, through the divergent ideas of Kant and Rousseau, how liberal states breed a mentality that limits spiritual liberty.[104]

Frondizi also noted the incompatibility between the theoretical liberties espoused by the Church, especially in Argentina where there is an official (Roman Catholic) religion. He saw a basic incongruity between the reason for the state and that for religion.[105] To him, Latin Americans, with their Catholic heritage, have become accustomed to accepting "revealed truth," which retards their problem-solving processes. The idea that supreme liberty resides in the possibility of the approximation of God—that is to say, the truth—Frondizi asserted, was a concept belonging to the Middle Ages.[106]

He stated that totalitarianism came from the elevation of the state, which tended to annul the values of the individual and to raise politics to the supreme category of life. He tied in the elevation of the state to the elevation of the Church and analyzed the relationship between the two entities, which militate against liberty. He indicated that only the abolition of the bourgeois-liberal state, with its official Church in Argentina, could liberate the individual. He also examined the battle between the Church and Marxism, based on the old "atheistic-godless communist" idea. He saw emerging a new group of young antibourgeois, people-oriented priests and laymen who understood the possibility of accepting social Christianity and foresaw the potential for Christians for Marxism bringing about social change, the possibility of turning the traditional Church-Marxism adversary relationship into collaboration. More than most Marxist *pensadores* of the Old Left, of which he was critical, he saw closer agreement between humanistic dialectical materialism and social Christianity.[107]

In *Teorías políticas contemporáneas* (1965) (Contemporary Political Theories) Frondizi discussed the "neoliberalism" of the in-
terwar years, such as existed in the United States during the New
Deal, which he felt was a middle ground between totalitarianism
and socialism and differed from bourgeois liberalism because it
understood the necessity of state intervention in social relations.
By the 1960s, he noted that neoliberalism was being replaced by
existentialism, neo-Catholicism, and neo-Marxism.[108] Existentialism, which grew in popularity after World War II, particularly
interested Frondizi because it militated against Marxism or any
kind of system per se. He pointed out the negative qualities of
existentialism, which is predicated upon despair, and contrasted it
to Marxism's optimism. Like Jean-Paul Sartre, he maintained that
Marxism and existentialism could find some harmony since both
assume an antibourgeois attitude toward ethics, social life, and
liberty.[109]

On a more practical level, Frondizi attempted to explain Latin
America's proclivity toward Bonapartist regimes, which he, following Marx and Engels' lead, defined as the imposition of conciliation of the classes from outside by force. He believed that Latin
America's bourgeoisie does not have the stuff to rule directly, and
when its oligarchy is not strong enough, or too disunited, to take
over the management of state and society in the interests of the
bourgeoisie, Bonapartist semidictatorships, like that of Perón, assume control.[110]

Frondizi tried to explain Argentine society in a monumental two-
volume work *La realidad argentina* (1956) (Argentine Reality).[111]
He contended that Argentine politics were a manifestation of world
capitalism, which had enabled bourgeois democracy to develop in
the country at the beginning of the twentieth century. But he saw
little revolutionary potential in the national bourgeoisie, which, due
to industrialization, had become economically linked to and dependent on foreign capital. To him, the interests of the national bourgeoisie were not those of the Argentine masses, but those of their
foreign partners who controlled industrialization.[112]

Like other Latin American Marxist *pensadores* Silvio Frondizi's
lifelong dreams of socialism in the Americas came true in the
Cuban revolution. In *La revolución cubana: Su significación
histórica* (1961) (The Cuban Revolution: Its Historical Significance) he asserted that the Cuban revolution, more than any single

twentieth-century event in Latin America, awakened people to the dangers of dependency and to the feasibility of successful action to change the dominion-dependence relationship. He saw the Cuban revolution as the beginning of the destruction of imperialism in Latin America, which would lead to the replacement of capitalism by socialism and thus to progress. Unlike some other socialist thinkers, Frondizi was not hoisted on the petard of sectarianism. He viewed Cuba as "a" model not "the" model for revolution. He realized that some of the theory and strategy followed by Fidel Castro would not work everywhere in Latin America, that conditions on the relatively small nonindustrial Caribbean island differed greatly from those in a large developing country like Argentina. He believed that it was counterproductive and counterrevolutionary to condemn the Cuban road to socialism and that all people interested in the welfare of humanity could appreciate and be encouraged by Cuba's revolution.[113]

Liborio Justo (Quebracho) (1902–)

One of the most fascinating and energetic Marxists in Latin America is Liborio Justo, best known in literary circles as Quebracho but also identified by the pseudonym Lobodón Garra. The son of General Agustín P. Justo, president of Argentina from 1932 to 1938, Liborio gained a reputation as a writer of short stories and novels and achieved notoriety as a political gadfly, pamphleteer, and author of works on Trotskyism, the Bolivian and Chilean revolutions, the history of Argentina, and imperialism.

Justo was deeply influenced by the University Reform Movement, which he saw as a struggle against the static society represented by the class of his famous father and as a rejection of U.S. values in Latin America. After reading the work of antiimperialist Waldo Frank, he decided that the powerful neighbor to the north had a Babbitt value system and that Latin America had to be liberated from capitalism and cultural, economic, and political imperialism.

Justo's vehement opposition to U.S. expansion was well known in Argentina. He invariably turned up at political meetings to denounce the Colossus of the North. For instance, on December 1, 1936, when Franklin D. Roosevelt rose to address a meeting of the Pan-American Union in Buenos Aires, presided over by President Agustín Justo, a loud cry of "Down with Yankee Imperialism" echoed from the back of the room. A scuffle ensued followed by a few thuds, and then silence was restored as Roosevelt began to speak. After the meeting, as the notables left the platform, President Justo whispered to a policeman: "Was that my son Liborio?" *"Sí, Señor Presidente,"* replied the officer.[114]

Liborio Justo devoted his life to searching for "the truth of my epoch"—hoping for the day there would be a "Union of Socialist Republics of the World."[115] Originally a Trotskyist purist, he subsequently renounced Trotsky, who he felt betrayed Marxism-Leninism by allying, during his last years in Mexico, with U.S. interests. After breaking with the Fourth International, Justo became the principal director of the relatively uninfluential Revolutionary Workers' League and, without much success, advocated changing the name Latin America, which he felt symbolized imperialism, to "Andesia," which he believed signified unity and liberation of the nations he hoped could operate under a Fifth International.[116]

Justo spent a great deal of time explaining Trotskyism. In *León Trotsky y el fracaso mundial del trotskyismo* (1975) (Leon Trotsky and the Failure of World Trotskyism), he provided an excellent history of the Fourth International and its internal problems that led him to seek a Fifth International dedicated to overcoming the superimperialism of the United States, to uniting proletarians and *campesinos* (rural workers), to unifying all races, and to establishing world socialism.[117] Justo believed that Trotsky and the Fourth International were ignorant of Latin American politics. He categorized Trotsky's approach to the region as petty bourgeois and opportunistic, too inclined to think of liberal reformers like Mexico's Lázaro Cárdenas and Peru's Haya de la Torre as revolutionaries. He believed that while Trotsky was in Mexico, Cárdenas used him to help promote an essentially nonrevolutionary government.[118] Justo believed that Trotsky let his feud with Stalin supersede the fight against capitalism and that Trotsky accepted Yankee imperialism because it actively supported the struggle against Stalinism.[119] Haya de la Torre, Justo said, was a pseudorevolutionary who acquiesced to the Good Neighbor myth and Dollar Diplomacy during World War II when he liked the idea of working closely with the United States for hemisphere defense. Haya de la Torre, too, denounced the USSR but accepted its belief in coexistence, which Justo called an abandonment of socialism because it disregarded the inherent contradictions between capitalism and socialism.[120]

Justo, in addition to being a severe critic of Trotsky, was a keen analyst of Argentine society. His *Pampas y lanzas: Fundamentos histórico-económico-sociales de nacionalidad y de la conciencia nacional argentina* (1962) (Pampas and Lances: Historical, Economic, and Social Fundamentals of Nationality and the National Conscience of Argentina) demonstrated familiarity with the sweep of Argentine historical literature. He analyzed the works of various historians and constructed his own revisionist history of the nation.

Justo explored the mystique of the pampas and displayed great concern for the frontier tradition. He rejected the commonly accepted theme of the gaucho as the nineteenth-century symbol of national unity and freedom and emphasized the suppression of the Indian and the gaucho by the ruling oligarchy. Also, to him the gaucho represented a symbol of white supremacy over the Indians, and he pointed out the racism in the bourgeois attitudes of Sarmiento who wanted to see "civilized" white class behavior adopted by the more "barbaric" classes. Justo related the sad tale of Argentina's Indians who, like the indigenous folk in the United States, were pushed farther and farther west or exterminated. He viewed nineteenth-century *caudillo* (strongman) Juan Manuel de Rosas as the leader of the *porteño* ranchers who in their struggle for land and cattle strove to pacify the Indians. Ironically, as the Indian lands were acquired by the *latifundistas,* a new Argentine nationality formed, and an economic order led by a native oligarchy and foreign forces converted the gaucho into a peon who relinquished his freedom to become an exploited wage earner.[121] Liborio Justo retained his optimism and, like Juan Justo, talked about the unbreakable spirit of the small contingent of Argentina's *montoneras* (country folk) for whom liberty has always been paramount and who resisted the power of the commercial bourgeoisie, just as they earlier opposed the colonial system.[122]

Justo studied Latin American history and observed political and social change in the region as part of his search for successful precedents, or an opening wedge, for socialism. Thus, he was intrigued by the Bolivian revolution of 1952, which he wrote about in *Bolivia: La revolución derrotada* (1971) (Bolivia: The

Revolution Destroyed). His clear analysis of class and economics in Bolivia, from the communal era of the Incas of Tahuantinsuyu to the 1960s, reflects the thinking of José Mariátegui and Bolivian scholar José Antonio Arce. Justo claimed that Tahuantinsuyu had an economic system akin to Marx's "Asiatic Mode of Production"—a class-stratified system in which the dominant state exploited the communities by exacting from them either tribute or labor or both.[123] He might refer to Inca society as communalism but not socialism.

Justo argued that after independence, Bolivia's basic system remained the same, with the landed gentry (including the mine owners), the military, and the commercial bourgeoisie in control. By the War of the Pacific (1879–1883) international companies began to take great interest in Bolivia and by the 1920s controlled its natural riches as well as its politics.[124]

After the Depression, the Chaco War (1932–1935), World War II, and the start of Cold War rivalries, antiimperialism grew in Bolivia. Justo believed that the bourgeois-directed *Movimiento Nacionalista Revolucionario* (MNR) (National Revolutionary Movement) attempted to bring about a bourgeois-democratic revolution in alliance with the proletariat and that Bolivia's relatively powerful Trotskyists and the Communists agreed to the alliance in order to pass through the bourgeois-democratic stage enroute to socialism.[125] He pointed out that this egregious error forced Bolivia closer to the capitalist powers that were at the root of its problems. He maintained that despite the antiimperialist thrust of the revolution, Bolivia capitulated to the mineral policies of the United States, succumbed to U.S. manipulations through the United Nations, and accepted military assistance from the United States under the anticommunist Mutual Security Acts of 1951 and 1952,[126] the grave consequences of which are discussed in my chapter on Bolivia.

Justo agreed that Bolivia's Agrarian law of 1952 attempted to create small properties and to smash *gamonalismo* (rural bossism) and that the revolution changed some political and social conditions.[127] He called the Bolivian experience the first partial proletarian revolution in Latin America. He said it did not triumph because no Marxist-Leninist party wrested power from the middle class, which controlled the revolution and the government. Remaining true to the sentiments of Lenin and the early teachings of Trotsky, Justo asserted that one cannot reconcile control or the sharing of it by two classes, that the mechanics of political revolution consist of passing power from one class to another.[128] He claimed that the Bolivian revolution showed that the Trotskyists did not know how to take advantage of their influence in the powerful Tin Miner's Union. He criticized the Trotskyist *Partido Obrero Regional* (Regional Workers' Party) for limiting itself to Bolivia, for not solidifying the continental and international ties necessary to support a revolution. To him, Latin America represented a fragmented nation that required unity to foster revolution.[129] Justo also believed that proletarian-peasant solidarity, which he saw as essential to revolutionary success, did not exist in the Bolivian situation. He conceded that the Cuban experience proved the possibility of success without proletarian strength, but like a true independent Trotskyist, he maintained that structural and institutional change could be effected in Bolivia and surrounding countries only if the region's urban and rural workers joined forces in an international Andean revolution.[130]

Jorge Abelardo Ramos (1921–)

Liborio Justo was succeeded as the leader of Argentina's independent Trotskyists by Jorge Abelardo Ramos, professor of history at the University of Buenos Aires and head of Argentina's Popular Left Front. A prolific author and critical analyst of the Left in Argentina, Ramos also gained reknown as a literary critic. An ardent opponent of Stalin and the idea of revolution in a single country, he combined the thinking of Ugarte, Lenin, and Trotsky. Like Marx, Ramos contended that, theoretically, workers have no country,[131] that their problems, and the solutions to them, are universal.

As the ideological mentor of the Popular Left Front, he developed its program: (1) political sovereignty, (2) economic independence, (3) social justice, (4) a popular worker's government, and (5) a United Socialist State of Latin America working for the end of imperialism, agrarian revolution, and the incorporation of the Indian into the working class.[132]

Ramos became known as the initiator of the *izquierda cipaya* (Sepoy left) criticism of Marx in Argentina. He postulated (after 1939) a revolutionary socialism that expressed itself in terms of the nation's political and social realities. He was part of the generation responsible for popularizing the theories of the National Left, which culminated in the establishment of the small Revolutionary Socialist Workers' party in the early 1940s, which, after the fall of Perón in 1955, integrated with the Socialist Party of the National Revolution.[133]

Ramos asserted that the struggle for socialism shifted, in the middle of the twentieth century, away from the large developed centers toward less developed regions like Latin America. He believed that Latin America had to emancipate itself from the Marxism of European tutelage, that European bourgeois-capitalist development could not be reproduced in the area. He refuted the idea that the expansion of capitalism in Latin America in the twentieth century was progressive, as might be claimed for that of the nineteenth century.[134]

Ramos contended that the struggle for socialism had been immobilized by ultraleftists whose contributions had been purely verbal. He criticized the glorification of Sorel by Marxists whom he called neo-Sorelian advocates of violence in the abstract.[135] He claimed that Latins had to study and realistically redefine Marxist ideology in terms of Latin America's character. He echoed Trotsky who saw the struggle against imperialism in Latin America as progressive in two ways. First, it prepared favorable conditions for development; second, it laid foundations for *golpes* (blows) against foreign imperialists and their native allies.[136]

Ramos viewed the twenty Latin American states as artificial and believed that their boundaries impeded development and enabled foreign entrepreneurs to provide goods and services that could be produced at home under a united Latin America. He said that the only development imperialism permits the Latins is that of literature about it—which provides words but little action.[137]

Ramos thought that since 1945 relations between the dependent world and the metropolis changed, as did relations between the proletariat and the bourgeoisie. Socialist beliefs grew in opposition to the ideas of the church. The destiny of Latin America, its people began to realize, was in their hands, not those of the oligarchs, the military, or God.[138] Frequent Yankee incursions into Latin American life increased solidarity against the United States. This unity, he believed, worked to overcome nationalism and regionalism and rekindled an interest in Bolívar's idea of a Latin American confederation and in terminating the Balkanization of Latin America, which began after independence from Spain and Portugal.

In his book *América Latina: Un país* (1949) (Latin America:

One Country) Ramos demonstrated the inability of Latin America's national bourgeoisie to achieve a democratic revolution, the region's incapacity to develop heavy industry and its necessary internal market, and the area's inability to effect agrarian reforms. He argued that to achieve these changes, the twenty Latin states had to unify to rid themselves of dependence on the United States. During the 1940s, he supported working with the *Peronistas,* who had a plan for Latin American unity based upon antiimperialism and labor reforms. Perón's successful mobilization of Argentina's urban workers against the United States, Ramos believed, provided a good example for the rest of Latin America.[139]

Shortly after the fall of Perón came the Cuban revolution, which provided the impetus, in Ramos's estimation, for hemispherewide rebellion. To him, Castro proved that popular forces can win a war against the army, that an insurrectional center or *foco* can create revolutionary conditions, and that in underdeveloped Latin America, the major area for struggle is the countryside. Ramos did not maintain that all of Cuba's experiences were repeatable in countries like Argentina or Venezuela, but he believed that they indicated that the Communist party idea of waiting for propitious conditions was not correct. To him, the road to socialism lay somewhere between the Cuban experience and what the Communist party espoused.[140] Ramos felt that the Cuban revolution pursued the idea of Bolívar and Marx—that national barriers can be broken down. He advocated "*Marxismo-Bolivarismo,*" a combination of the two forms of struggle incorporating parliamentary political activity and action, unionization, guerrilla war, and propaganda—as phases of the movement toward a United Socialist States of America.[141]

Although he advocated socialism on a Latin American basis, Ramos studied Argentina's problems, which he considered to be a microcosm of hemispheric conditions. His five-volume *Revolución y contrarevolución en la Argentina* (1974–1977) (Revolution and Counterrevolution in Argentina) spanned the period from 1810 to 1973, providing an overall appraisal of his country's constant struggles for survival. When read in conjunction with his history of the Communist party in Argentina,[142] one derives the impression that a revolutionary workers' party can never flourish under a world center (Moscow) and that Argentina's workers belong to a Latin American group that is more likely to work and to transform the gaucho into a modern proletarian.[143]

Ramos thought that to liberate a semicolonial nation like Argentina, one must reevaluate its past and distinguish the degree to which foreign influences have distorted its life. At the same time one has to understand its traditions, such as oligarchical control, which existed in Argentina from the rule of Juan Manuel de Rosas through that of Perón.[144] He pointed out that the European idea of liberation by a pure class (proletariat) was inapplicable to Argentina even by the early years of the twentieth century when the "internationalization" concept of Juan Justo began to gather adherents among the nation's intelligentsia and urban workers and when Socialist Alfredo Palacios had a large enough constituency to be elected to the Chamber of Deputies. Ramos believed that during the heyday of the Socialist party the proletariat was too small and precapitalist to seize control of the nation. To do so, it needed to ally with the discontented and exploited urban petty bourgeoisie and the *campesinos*.[145]

Like most Argentine Marxist *pensadores*, Ramos credited the University Reform Movement with raising political consciousness and assisting the rise of socialism. He also recognized that the movement's major contributions were to liberalism and reformism. He believed that in 1930 when the military took over the government, the liberal state withered along with socialism.

Not until 1943, with the emergence of Perón and the *descamisados* did Argentina's proletariat regenerate and display some potential for political action. Ramos stated that by 1943 power in Argentina rested in the national bourgeoisie and the army but that the old oligarchy had lost its grip.[146] At this time Argentina began to be transformed from a semicolony of Great Britain to a dependency of the United States as a result of World War II and the curtailment of Argentine access to Europe. After the war Argentina's first predominantly native-born proletariat had a chance to progress, but unfortunately under *Peronismo* the worker's parties were hindered by their petty bourgeois base.[147] Simultaneously, splits between the intelligentsia and the masses and between the proletariat and the young petty bourgeois elements enabled foreign imperialists to reestablish their hegemony.[148]

To Ramos, *Peronismo* displayed the classical confluence of classes in a semicolonial country. Socialist thunder was stolen by Perón's national antiimperialist front containing sectors of the army, the industrial bourgeoisie, the urban and rural workers, and the Church. These factions elevated Perón to a position of limitless power, which he proved unable to wield to the advantage of most Argentines.[149] Ultimately *Peronista* rule brought Argentina economic and social instability, from which it never recovered.

It is fitting that we close this chapter on Argentina with Jorge Abelardo Ramos, whose scholarly works take into consideration the thinking of all of the Argentine Marxist *pensadores* mentioned here. He had the advantage of more historical hindsight than most of them, was able to analyze critically the ups and downs of the various socialist movements in Argentina, and demonstrated how for many years they contributed to progessive social and political measures effected by the nation's liberals.

Ramos's thinking enhances our understanding of why liberal reformism eventually fell victim to the conservative policies of the military, which has dominated Argentine politics since 1930 and which, by the time of this writing, had all but eradicated socialist humanism in the country that had the greatest tradition of it and potential for its development in Latin America. Since its 1976 takeover from the Justicialist Front (*Peronistas*), which in an effort to unify the country it permitted to return to power through elections in 1973, the military has worked to eliminate socialist thought through censorship and radical political activity through the use of "death squads."

4. Chile

From the nitrate deserts, from the submarine coal mines, from the terrible heights where the copper lies buried and is extracted with inhuman labor by the hands of our people, a freedom movement of magnificent proportions sprang up. That movement raised a man named Allende to the presidency of Chile to carry out reforms and measures of justice that could not be postponed, and to rescue our national wealth from the claws of foreigners. . . .

Here in Chile a truly just society was being erected, based on our sovereignty, our national pride. . . . On our side, on the side of the Chilean revolution were the constitution and the law, democracy and hope.

Pablo Neruda

José Victoriano (1817–1888), an outstanding nineteenth-century Chilean intellectual, advocate of independent American scholarship, and critic of Spanish colonialism, organized a literary society in Santiago in 1841. The society's activities stimulated the quest of its member Francisco Bilbao (1823–1865) for a new political, philosophical, and historical synthesis. His search led to the publication of *Sociabilidad chilena* (1844) (Chilean Sociability), which referred to historical determinism and discussed the "old synthesis" of Catholicism and feudalism and a "new synthesis" of beliefs that developed after the Middle Ages and that brought about what he termed the "equality of liberty." His ideas caused him to be fined for blasphemy and sent into exile in Europe where he befriended the Liberal Christian Félicité de Laminnais, historian Jules Michelet, and poet Edgar Quinet, from whom he learned about the revolutionary ideas of 1848.[1]

While Bilbao was in Europe, a society of artisans with social objectives but devoid of class consciousness formed in Santiago. Upon Bilbao's return to Chile in 1850, he and Santiago Arcos established the Sociedad de la Igualdad (Equality Society) inspired by the French utopians and based upon the principles of sovereignty of reason as the foundation of all political life and upon universal love and fraternity as the moral rule.[2] The society met secretly to discuss citizens' rights, labor, and industrial and banking laws. It was suppressed in 1851, accused of participating in an armed revolt against the government, but its ideas resurfaced in 1859 in the periodical *La Igualidad*.

Chile's Democratic party, Latin America's first avowedly socialist political organization, formed in 1887 and elected a member to the Chamber of Deputies in 1894. The party moved increasingly to the right, and in 1912 a militant faction broke off and formed the Socialist Labor party.[3] The Socialist Labor party opposed participation in World War I, agitated against clerical influence in politics, and tried to build a trade union movement. By 1919 it altered its program to conform to that of the Comintern, became the Communist party in 1921, and dominated Chile's leftist politics until the 1930s when the Socialist party, partially inspired by Peru's José Mariátegui, was born.

Chile experienced both constitutional democracy and military dictatorship during the 1920s. Strongman Carlos Ibáñez fell from power in 1931 and was succeeded by a conservative government. Left-wing elements in the country feared the return to power of the aristocracy, which had long blocked progress in the country. Then, on June 4, 1932, Colonel Marmaduke Grove led a junta, which proclaimed a "Socialist Republic" standing for progressive taxation, government monopoly of vital industries such as coal, copper and nitrates, public control of foodstuffs, the break-up of large estates, and government management of credit facilities. This reformist movement, whose leader felt that Marx glorified physical work excessively and who never spoke of worker domination, was devoid of long-range ideological plans. It managed to establish a national bank during Grove's twelve days in power. Carlos Davila controlled the movement for the next one hundred days and brought some economic relief to thousands who had lost jobs during the Depression. Davila's administration then fell victim to a military coup.

Chilean Socialists, Communists, radicals, radical socialists, and democrats formed a "Popular Front" and won some electoral victories during the late 1930s, but the coalition eventually broke up over doctrinal differences. For the next three decades Chile's disparate socialist factions tended to reject Lenin's doctrines of the inevitability of war and violent revolution, preferring to pursue electoral politics. The country's Old Left, inspired by the Russian revolution, met serious challenges in the late 1950s and 1960s by a new generation of socialists excited by the possibilities opened by the Chinese and Cuban revolutions. The aristocratic oligarchy, which traditionally controlled Chile's Senate and blocked progressive legislation, lost some power in the mid-1960s, providing an opening wedge for economic and social reforms that presaged the people's democratic movement that brought Marxist Salvador Allende to the presidency in 1970.

Before analyzing Chile's Marxist *pensadores* who contributed to the ultimate election of Allende, a brief word about the country's various schools of socialist thought is in order. Since Chile's socialist factions predate the Russian revolution, they have given an indigenous cast to Chilean socialism. Their strength has generally been more in their ability to mobilize than to postulate doctrine. The Socialist party, in particular, has had a unique character, which historian Paul Drake attributed to its founders, for whom "Marxist theory represented more of a protest symbol than a precise ideological commitment."[4] The Socialists claimed allegiance to Marxist doctrines but declared their independence from specific world revolutionary movements. Political scientist Ernst Halperin noted that Chilean Socialists were susceptible to "intellectual fashions" and open to new ideas from Popular Frontism, to Peronism, Titoism, Castroism, and even aspects of Maoism. Over the years the Socialists have been highly nationalistic, opposed to parliamentarianism, and oriented to the proletariat despite the fact that their leaders have generally been intellectuals born to the middle class.[5] As the Cuban revolution progressed, Chile's Socialists became more radical.

The main differences between Chile's Socialists and Communists have been their attitudes on foreign policy and middle-class parties. The Socialists have rejected alliance with middle-class parties, even radical ones, and until the 1960s preferred the more neutral "Tito-type" foreign policy. Although Chile's Communist party members have been less typically Stalinist then their Argentine comrades, they have basically adhered to Soviet foreign policy. The Communists have perceived two revolutionary stages. The first, or "democratic stage," opposed feudalism, imperialism, and monopoly and advocated state domination of the economy in order to raise living standards. In the "second stage" the working class would become the leading force on the way to socialism.[6] But the Communists have no revolutionary record whereas the

Socialist party, which grew out of dissatisfaction with the Communist party, has a more radical tradition extending from the 1932 uprising.[7] The Socialists have generally been led by intellectuals or professionals, particularly members of the legal and medical fields, and the Communists by labor leaders.

More than any other single event after the Russian revolution, the Spanish Civil War opened the way for Chile's intellectuals to move to the left. For example, world famous poet Pablo Neruda joined the Communist party in 1939 after witnessing, first hand, the struggle in Spain. Neruda cogently characterized Marxist thinking in Chile when he said that "out and out originality is a modern invention," a fetish that he did not believe in,[8] and spoke for a broad segment of the Chilean Left when he asserted that aside from his dislike of capitalism and faith in socialism, he understood humanity's persistent contradictions less and less.[9]

Luis Emilio Recabarren (1876–1924)

Luis Emilio Recabarren, who excelled at turning theory into practice, had as much impact on Latin America's workers' movement as José Mariátegui had on the region's Marxist political theorists. A typographer by trade, he thought that socialist literature was a necessary and effective tool and contributed to it as a militant journalist, pamphleteer, poet, and playwright.

Don Reca, as his associates respectfully called him, was initially influenced by the thinking of his countryman Francisco Bilbao, as well as by the utopian socialists Charles Fourier, Robert Owen, and Etienne Cabet, and anarchists Pierre-Joseph Proudhon and Mikhail Bakunin. Between 1906 and 1908 he traveled to Argentina, France, and Belgium and met Alfredo Palacios, Juan Justo, the Spaniard Pablo Iglesia, and the Frenchman Jean Jaurès, all of whom helped radicalize him.[10]

Volumes have been devoted to this self-proclaimed "socialist revolutionary," who served as a conscience to Chile's workers whose causes he championed. Known affectionately as *El abuelo* (the grandfather) to Chile's poor, Recabarren organized them into unions, educated them politically, and urged them toward nonviolent revolution. He continuously exhorted Chile's proletarians to follow the lead of the French and Russian workers, who had won considerable gains for themselves.

Recabarren began editing the newspaper *El Trabajador* (The

Worker) in 1903, then performed similar duties for other workers' periodicals such as *El Proletario, La Vanguardia,* and *El Grito Popular*.[11] In 1906 he was elected to Congress, representing the mining district of Antofagasta. When he refused to take the oath of office, which included swearing allegiance to God, he was singled out as a dangerous revolutionary by his fellow deputies, who refused to seat him in Congress.

He then created the first significant Marxist labor movement in Latin America in Chile's northern nitrate mining regions, and in 1912 he founded his country's Socialist Labor party, hoping to unite the working classes. The party advocated transferring private property into common property, promoting the freedom of association and the press, increasing voter registration, abolishing the standing army, confiscating church wealth, and making education mandatory and free.[12] The party, led by Recabarren, felt that World War I should be followed by revolution in which the proletariat took over from the collapsing bourgeois civilization, that socialists should carry out disarmament and establish world peace.[13]

In an effort to eliminate the class differences, which he thought had increased in Chile since independence, Recabarren unsuccessfully sought the presidency in 1920. He was elected to Congress in 1921 where he served the Socialist Labor party and then the Communist party, which he helped form. The following year he represented Chile at an International Communist Congress in Moscow. He was impressed by the way the Russians had eliminated capitalism[14] and concluded that the Russian people possessed the qualities necessary to construct a communist society but that the conditions for it were more propitious in Russia than in Chile. While in Russia, he also became more familiar with the works of Trotsky and Lenin, which led him to believe that Chile's proletariat lacked the discipline and the political organization to build socialism.[15] He was fascinated by Russian attempts to emancipate women, felt that they had participated equally in the revolutionary struggle and were attaining equality.[16] The Russian successes caused him to study the problems of working women in Chile, and he called the Soviet experience a laboratory of social experience from which Chileans could learn.[17]

He struggled for almost four years in the Chamber of Deputies to expose the tragic working and living conditions confronting the

Chilean miners, simultaneously endeavoring to build workers' class consciousness. He tried to transform the proletariat into a powerful disciplined organization by encouraging and organizing strikes, which he believed were the most effective weapons workers could use to emancipate themselves.[18] Upset by the impotence of his Communist party in the struggle against the military dictatorship, Recabarren committed sucide in 1924.

Recabarren's ideas, especially those on worker control, remained alive in the Chilean labor movement for years to come. He, like the anarchists, espoused a system of unions with major roles at all levels for workers in the governance of Chile. Under his ideal constitution three basic governmental divisions would exist. First, industrial assemblies composed of workers from each geographical region would represent all agricultural, industrial, and service sectors. Second, municipalities run by delegates named by each industrial assembly and governed by commissions would assume responsibility for the well-being of their inhabitants. Third, a national assembly, with delegates from each municipal territory with over 10,000 inhabitants and run by committees, would legislate for the entire republic.[19] Under the system, all citizens over eighteen years of age could participate somewhere in the government.[20]

Recabarren thought that workers were primarily responsible for all facets of societal growth. He believed in the labor theory of value and claimed that a salary was insufficient recompense for worker's contributions. To him, a salary was not participation in the wealth produced, which he thought workers were entitled to share and thereby participate in the amenities of life.[21]

In *El socialismo* (1912), a primer explaining what socialism had been and how its followers should function, he inveighed against individualism and the ego-building that it encouraged, which he believed had proved destructive to Chilean society.[22] He pointed out to the urban workers that economic factors determined social and moral conditions. He argued that socialism meant more than the transformation of poor to rich; it included altering mentalities to understand that redistribution of wealth did not get at the root of the basic economic problem—private property. He maintained that the redistribution as well as the abolition of private property would lead to progress toward individual and moral perfection and justice.[23]

To Recabarren, class struggle was paramount, and he categorized class collaboration as reformism. He impugned religion, contending that the capitalist class used it as a political force to defend its privileges and its system.[24] He urged that religious ideas be replaced by scientific ones.[25] To him, religion's offer of a better life in the hereafter resigned people to suffering on earth,[26] was barbaric, insufficient consolation for human exploitation, and a perversion of the teachings of Christ, who died protesting corruption and tyranny.[27] In many ways his views presaged those of the Christians for Socialism movement discussed later in this book.

He postulated a time and space theory, which, to some extent, served as a foundation for the ideas of Peru's Víctor Raúl Haya de la Torre. Recabarren refuted the concept of a supreme creator, stating that the material, or the universe, always existed in infinite space and time eternal. To him, the material, which can be visualized, was the only truth. He was confident that humans could eventually unlock the mysteries within themselves. He noted the differences between dialectical materialism and Christian metaphysics and questioned how the existence of a supreme creator could account for cultural, racial, moral, and religious diversity in different parts of the world. To him, the only valid explanations were evolutionary and environmental.[28]

Julio César Jobet, whose work is discussed later, credited Don Reca, "the creator of the worker's press," with making the workers' struggle synonymous with political action in Chile. Recabarren's pamphlet *El socialismo* became the theoretical platform of the Socialist Worker's party.[29] Subsequent generations of Chilean socialists of all sectarian leanings have accepted his theories that "life is an equal circumstance for all" and that equality of opportunity, which does not mean biological equality, should accompany all of life and transcend all human relations.[30] His sometimes creative moralistic views on social, political, and artistic interaction, derived from his analysis of life's totality, were pervasive—even extending into Argentina and Uruguay. His was a cohesive and scientific, but easily understood, plan for building a socialist system in which women and men could reach their full potential. Paralleling Lenin, who said "with illiterates you are not able to build socialism," and Antonio Gramsci, who believed that the Communist party had to be an intellectual collective,[31] Recabarren maintained that the first step toward socialism in Chile was to educate the working masses.

Julio César Jobet (1912–1980)

Julio César Jobet belonged to Chile's Generation of 1930, composed mostly of university students who saw an emerging crisis in capitalism (the Depression) and tried to understand how Chile's economic problems of the 1920s led to the Ibáñez dictatorship (1925–1931). They felt a strong social responsibility and conceived of themselves as a vanguard of a new political and social movement.

While a student at the University of Chile during the early 1930s, Jobet joined the newly formed Socialist party, and in subsequent years he became one of its ideological mentors and an outstanding economic historian[32] who believed that the leading histories of Chile were written by erudite upper-class elites who overemphasized political chronology and neglected social interaction. During the 1930s Jobet's ideas approximated those of the European social democrats as he represented the right wing of the Socialist party, which often approached historical materialism without stressing economic determinism. In subsequent decades, he moved to the left, became more doctrinaire, and denounced the Socialist politics of the 1930s as liberal and reformist.

Jobet was a disciple and biographer of Recabarren, whom he called a *caudillo popular* (popular boss), and considered him Chile's leading builder of working-class consciousness and the spirit of struggle.[33]

Jobet viewed Chile as subservient to the United States' monopolies, which attained their position by subtle diplomacy rather than violent gunboat action. He noted that his nation's economy depended almost exclusively on copper and saltpeter exports and assailed the landed aristocracy for allowing these basic industries to fall into the hands of foreign interests. He said that such denationalization brought a change in human feelings, that corruption and opportunism grew and morality declined. He concluded that as a result of Chile's economic dependency, its workers had more in common with proletarians elsewhere then they did with Chileans from other classes.[34]

Jobet examined Chile's class consciousness and relations in *Ensayo crítico del desarrollo económico-social de Chile* (1955) (Critical Essay on the Socioeconomic Development of Chile), a strong antidote to uncritical histories written by scholars like Luis

Galdames, whose work was quite popular among academics in and out of Chile. Although at times he engaged in polemics, Jobet also clearly described how Chilean labor's consciousness arose from conflicting social forces in the nation. Unlike the mainstream of Chilean historians of his time, he categorized the country as semifeudal, semicolonial, and extraordinarily dependent. He diverged from the "cozy" picture of Chile as a bastion of constitutional democracy painted by liberal and conservative academics,[35] who he believed deluded themselves into thinking that their scholarship was objective and free of ideology, a claim he did not make for his own works.[36] Jobet pleaded for socialist interpretations of Chilean history and assumed that socialism was not merely a possibility or an abstraction, but practical and real.

Santiago Arcos Artegui's noted *Carta a Francisco Bilbao,* which appeared in 1852,[37] inspired by the French utopian socialists, constituted the foundation upon which Jobet tried to build a solid Marxist historiographical tradition in Chile. His efforts began to bear fruit in the 1950s with the publication of a series of profound Marxist works that moved away from chronology and narrative and toward analyses of the causes and effects of Chile's social development and other class-oriented history. This occurred before such treatments became popular elsewhere in the Americas.[38] Jobet and his followers produced historiographical studies that examined society from the bottom up, eschewed the glorification of Chile, and told about its people's incredible pain, misery, and poverty.[39]

In addition to his histories, Jobet produced some theoretical works. For example, his *Los fundamentos del marxismo* (The Fundamentals of Marxism) drew distinctions between socialism and communism. Under socialism, Jobet said, the means of production are socialized, leaving the fruits of production for private consumption, while communism also allocates the fruits of production. Under socialism, he maintained, the fruits of labor are distributed according to the quantity and quality of work, but in communism they are distributed according to need. He noted that "totalitarian communism" perverted Marxist doctrine by deifying the state, by allowing a privileged buraucratic class to dominate,[40] by stripping citizens of their human rights, and by diminishing democracy.[41]

Jobet viewed Latin America as an organic entity, which through continental unity was capable of replacing capitalism and imperialism with its own brand of socialism.[42] He contended that each Latin American nation should pursue independent economic development, but with an eye to eventually integrating the countries economically and politically. He argued that this was the only feasible way to eliminate the imperialist control over the area's primary resources perpetuated by Creole oligarchs who promoted nationalism.[43]

In the wake of the Cuban revolution, Jobet, along with Oscar Waiss, emerged during the 1960s as the chief socialist advocates of attaining political control through nonelectoral means. "Revolutionary violence is inevitable and legitimate. Pacific or legal means of struggle alone do not lead to power," he stated, arguing that power could be attained only by circumventing the established political process and engaging in "armed struggle."[44] The members of Salvador Allende's Popular Unity government, whose ideas prevailed, disagreed with these thoughts of Jobet, but in light of what befell that administration, one is hard pressed to reject his stance. At the same time, like Recabarren and the Popular Unity government, Jobet stressed education as the primary means to build humanistic values, which would enable Chileans to understand the importance of revolutionary periods in human development as eras of creativity and that only pluralistic socialism, free of dissension and sectarianism (which he likened to class warfare), could stabilize and free their nation.[45]

Oscar Waiss

Santiago lawyer Oscar Waiss served as the Chilean Socialist party's secretary for international relations and as one of its leading theoreticians until ousted from the organization in 1961. He then affiliated with the Trotskyist Popular Socialist party,[46] for whom he toiled as a disseminator of ideas. His vituperative style caused one scholar to refer to him as "the Thersites of the Chilean Left."[47]

During the "Popular Front" days of the late 1930s Waiss emerged as a Marxist ideologist of national stature. Although the Communists, Socialists, and non-Marxist radicals joined forces behind Radical Pedro Aguirre Cerda, who captured the presidency (1938–1942), Chile's Socialists resented the ties, despite their benefits, to capitalists. Waiss felt that it was impossible to move toward socialism by decree, that in the Latin American context you must pass through the bourgeois democratic revolution, but he repeatedly pointed out the differences between the objectives of Chile's bourgeois-democratic parties, including the Radicals, and the workers.[48] He claimed that the "Popular Front" was designed to achieve goals desired by all participants, in particular, to combat the imperialism of U.S. "Manifest Destiny," which caused it to dominate Chile's copper market and credit. He lamented the fact that outsiders construed the alliance as an ideological accord.

Waiss was impressed by Mariátegui, whom he felt correctly viewed Latin America's independence not as a social movement but as a class struggle between *Criollos* and the *peninsulares,* from whom they wanted to wrest power.[49] He regarded Recabarren as the other outstanding Latin American Marxist writer and had a great deal of respect for his workers' programs.[50] Among Waiss's Latin American Marxist *pensador* friends were Uruguay's Rodney Arismendi and Argentina's Silvio Frondizi.

He spoke of the need to create a revolutionary system—one organizing Latin America's masses on collective principles to overcome the power traditionally held by false leaders or opportunists. He talked about the road to socialism in Chile but was not so naive as to believe it could be passed over peacefully. He admitted that the *vía pacífica* was the more democratic way and, as the Allende tragedy ultimately proved, doubted that power could be transferred from the oppressors to the oppressed without bloodshed.[51] He also contended that "democracy," as it existed under capitalism, was a political form that uses the state to regulate relations between social classes—enabling the democratic bourgeoisie to control. To him, genuine democracy, of a socialist variety, was not synonymous with subordination by the majority to a minority but vice versa.[52]

A brilliant and creative "plain" Marxist with a solid understanding of Third World politics, especially as they related to western and eastern Europe, Waiss constantly searched for a viable way to build socialism in Chile. Historical evidence led him to believe that the major obstacle to that goal was sectarianism.[53] In *Los problemas del socialismo contemporáneo* (1961) (The Contemporary Problems of Socialism) he broke down socialist thought into four major categories. He equated Soviet orthodoxy with strong rigid bureaucratic control and the idea of using peaceful coexistence and alliances with the petty bourgeoisie to attain power. Chinese socialism connoted inevitable clashes, permanent revolution, decentralization rejecting bureaucratic control, and emphasis on rural workers. Yugoslavian socialism meant a revolution that does not devour its young, an autonomous system stressing decentralization, active and neutral coexistence, and the right of people to choose their path to socialism and not to be subject to inflexible ideology. Finally, he spoke rather vaguely about "revolutionary socialism," which attacks coexistence and by-passes the stage of bureaucratic terror.[54]

His *Los problemas del socialismo contemporáneo* (1961) reenforced Marxism, not just as political economic theory, but as a way of life. For example, it contains an outstanding chapter on the socialist principles of freedom and creativity. Like Lenin, he asserted that each artist has the right to create with full freedom. Artists, in his opinion, should not be restricted to reflecting only the class struggle, and socialist governments must not dictate to artists, thereby stripping them of creativity. He contended that socialist artists, using the great Russian filmmaker Serge Eisenstein as an example, are part of their society, and their works naturally reflect it and its class struggles.[55]

Besides analyzing the components of socialism, Waiss liked to interpret revolutionary processes in Latin America, which he believed operated on three general theories. First was the "Petty Bourgeois Theory," whereby political parties such as Peru's *Apristas,* Paraguay's *Febreristas,* and Venezuela's *Acción Democrática* (AD) work for individual liberties and raise living standards but repudiate the class struggle and do not stress structural changes in the means of production.[56] Included in this category would be nationalist movements such as those in Mexico (1910), Boliva (1952), and Guatemala (1944), which installed popular governments and worked to procure democratic rights but rather than building socialism advanced capitalism while trying to liquidate the feudal relations of production.[57] Second was the "Dogmatic Theory," the strict application of vigorous class struggle leading to proletarian dictatorship. This theory included the belief that the landed and the bourgeoisie are identical in Latin America and that one cannot rely on the bourgeoisie at all, even to fight against imperialism. He called this scheme dogmatic because it reduced the complexities of Latin America's social and political structure to a pat formula wherein only the urban proletariat and the rural *campesinos* can be capable of aiding the revolution. It precludes middle-class help for socialism and implies that for revolutions to occur, interchangeable people must follow the identical proce-dures (stages) under the same conditions.[58] Third, he advocated the "Dynamic and Properly Marxist Theory," the forging of revo-lution by changing the fundamental relations of property and work, but allowing for and anticipating different contingencies as the revolution progresses. The objective here is not only the eman-cipation of the workers but also national and continental indepen-dence from imperialism. Like Lenin, Waiss agreed that the revolu-tion did not have to be repeated identically in each nation and that its development had to be adjusted to the differences in structures and superstructures. Above all, he wanted to replace simple and rigid formulas with clear thinking.[59]

Luis Vitale (1927–)

Argentine-born Luis Vitale became a citizen of Chile where he gained a reputation as a professor of history and geography and as an analyst of contemporary social problems. A prolific author, his work included books on Marxist personalities, Zionism, Cuba, and a six-volume study of Chilean history. His special interests were imperialism, the labor movement, agrarian reform, and in-dustrial development in Chile.[60]

His teacher, Argentina's José Luis Romero, developed Vitale's interest in the history of political ideas. Vitale subsequently ap-plied his disciplined mind to the study of Marx and adopted his belief in the stages of development. He incorporated the thinking of Mexico's Silvio Zavala on the colonial era and the political analyses of Peru's José Mariátegui into his own Trotskyist views.

Vitale argued that the modes of production of the pre-Colum-bian civilizations were in an advanced stage of the Metal Age (copper and bronze) when the Spanish arrived. He saw the Span-ish Conquest as a result of the Muslim invasion of Spain, the desire to fortify the monarchy, a quest for external markets, and the rise of a new commercial bourgeoisie. He refuted the demo-cratic left idea that Spain was a feudal nation and felt that "liber-als" confused economic backwardness with feudalism.[61] He be-lieved that during the Conquest Spain was making the transition from feudalism to capitalism while simultaneously developing a voracious clericalism and savage militarism. The colonial economy was organized with great amounts of capital, and workers were, however slight, salaried.[62] The Spanish continued the historical process of creating a world capitalist market by replacing the pre-Columbian agrarian society.[63] Spain's *encomienda* system, which granted Indians, and in effect their lands, to Spanish soldiers, was not feudal in nature but part of a hybrid capitalism.[64] Vitale noted that the "Black Legend," popularized by British writers did not reveal clearly the situation in Latin America, which approximated that which existed in all overseas areas where European nations sought profits. On the other hand, he deplored the "Pink Legend," which tried to justify the *encomienda* system and defended the Church.[65]

The desire on the part of the Creole bourgeoisie to develop internal markets generated a movement to take political and economic power away from Spain and the peninsular monopoly and caused the 1810 rebellion. Independence increased political autonomy but did not stop imperialism; nor did it alter the political and economic system or foster agrarian reform or industrialization. Vitale contended that the course of Latin American history has been one of a frustrated bourgeois-democratic revolution that has continued through the twentieth century.[66] Thus, Chile's national bourgeoisie emanated directly from the colonial era without passing through the European cycle. It was not an industrial bourgeoisie, but rather a commercial one, with small internal markets.

After independence, power passed into the hands of an exporting bourgeoisie, which sent primary materials abroad. Thus, the tragedy of Chile, Vitale thought, was not that it was the product of feudalism but of a bourgeoisie that blocked the major possibilities of development in a semicolonial continent that could not break its ties to imperialism because of its dependence upon foreign finance capital. No independent national bourgeoisie developed, and imperialism was built into the Chilean system.[67]

By the end of the nineteenth century, Chile's bourgeoisie worked with the land holders and foreign investors, and the idea of a progressive bourgeoisie was remote.[68] Chile did not replicate nineteenth-century Europe where the middle class overthrew feudalism and began the cycle of democratic bourgeois revolution. Instead, it went directly from primitive indigenous communities to incipient capitalism.[69] Vitale also contended that beginning with the first Pan-American Conference in 1889, the United States began a dual method of direct military and economic intervention and indirect diplomatic intervention in Latin America, which solidified ties between oligarchies in both areas.[70]

Vitale maintained that during the era of Recabarren activity in the class struggle did not become a permanent part of daily life in Chile but that Don Reca strengthened the nation's proletarian tradition, and his suicide symbolized the political independence of the workers' movement in his nation.[71]

Vitale pointed out that the cooperation between the bourgeoisie and the working class during the 1920–1932 period established a tradition leading to the 1938 "Popular Front," a precurser of Allende's *Frente de Acción Popular* (FRAP) (Popular Action Front) in the 1960s and 1970s.[72] He saw a partial development of a bourgeois-democratic revolution during the Allessandri years (1920–1925), but without the expulsion of imperialism that Trotsky said should occur during this stage of the Permanent Revolution. He also noted that the Ibáñez regime (1925–1931) replaced the upper-class oligarchs with the bourgeoisie while labor began to organize and Marxist ideas gained respect. However, Ibáñez thwarted labor by placing it under government control instead of the other way around as Marx wanted. What started out under Ibáñez as a Bonapartist revolution turned out to be more like Mussolini's corporate state. Although both labor and the bourgeoisie were antioligarchy, their brief alliance led to bourgeois supremacy.[73]

The "Socialist Republic of 1932," Vitale described as a clear expression the the numerous contradictions existing in Chile as a result of economic chaos: political and social instability and crisis in the parliament, the army, and the political parties. Colonel Marmaduke Grove, leader of the "Socialist Republic," did not take power because of the workers but as a result of a *golpe* (coup d'état) by some military units. His movement was antiimperialist, antioligarchy, and petty bourgeois in orientation. It did not last because the petty bourgeoisie leaders were afraid to arm the workers, did not institute an antiimperialist program, and failed to disarm their enemies.[74]

In Vitale's estimation, during the 1932–1938 period, Chile's Left began to unite but was prevented from taking power by sectarianism. To him, the collaboration of the classes during the

Popular Front era made economic sovereignty, especially over raw materials, impossible for Chile. Following his reasoning, one can see that from the "Popular Front" era until the Allende days, class collaboration enabled foreign entrepreneurs to retain considerable control over Chile's economy.[75]

Vitale analyzed the basic concepts of social Christianity and labeled it pseudorevolutionary. Under the guise of social good it changed Chile's laws to better the lot of the capitalist class, both foreign and native. To him, the ideology of Aquinas and Augustine, in conjunction with Christian democracy, sustained the idea of political and social compromise that in Chile proved sterile and retrograde.[76]

Vitale depicted how the revolutionary process unfolded in Chilean politics and labor as the nation went through the stages of capitalist development. He inveighed against simplistic dogmatic solutions to complex problems and emphasized the need for socialist solidarity. In *Los discursos de Clotario Blest y la revolución chilena* (1961) (The Lectures of Clotario Blest and the Chilean Revolution), in which Vitale edited Blest's works and added his own essays, Cuba is considered the most vital psychological prod to Allende's movement in Chile.[77] The Cuban revolution confirmed Vitale's belief that every revolution liberates new forces, speeds the contradictions between rank and file and the bureaucratic leadership, and gives rise to processes of differentiation, centripetal and centrifugal tendencies, violent ruptures, and the birth of new organizations.[78]

Vitale believed, as did Marx, Engels, Lenin, and Trotsky, that the communist revolution had to be international because only within the framework of the global market could world production be reappropriated by humanity and only in this way could people be liberated from the local and national limitations that impede their universal development.[79]

Thinkers such as C. Wright Mills believed that the Marxian sequence from feudalism to capitalism to socialism would not necessarily happen because nowhere had socialism sprung out of capitalism, but rather out of feudalism. Vitale disputed Mills's belief and contended that even when in a colonial or semicolonial nation there is no advanced industry, but there exists a system of capitalist production in mining, ranching, agriculture and light industry, a social class—the national bourgeoisie, allied with imperialism—is governed not by the laws of feudalism but by the laws of surplus value, profit rates, and capitalism in general. He cited Cuba as a capitalist nation not in a feudal stage but in a stage of capitalist development when Castro took over. He did not deny the possibility of an historic leap but emphasized the existence of transitional societies.[80]

Repeatedly, Vitale made the point that the workers' states in the world are transitional to socialism and did not arise from feudal nations but from states with a retarded capitalist development of uneven and combined characteristics.[81] He constantly reiterated Trotsky's view that the peasantry could be a valuable driving force in revolutions in such backward nations but regarded it as the weakest link in the revolutionary chain. To him, peasants' individualism made it difficult for them to adapt to collectivist society,[82] a contention which one could refute by recalling the communal aspects of some pre-Columbian societies.

Vitale questioned whether revolutionaries fought from countryside bases in the post-World War II era because landless peasants provided impetus for the revolutionary process or because the countryside was the only place where the modern bourgeois and imperialist armies could be defeated, or both. To him, whether the first stage of revolution was rural or urban depended on the historical circumstances in each country.[83]

Luis Vitale expressed great concern for deepening the theoretical study of workers' states in transition. He believed that special conditions caused history to detour and make the backward countries the place to put the ideas of Marxism into action.[84] To him, the world steadily advanced toward socialism; over one-third of humanity had entered some phase of it in confirmation of Marx's prediction that it would supplant capitalism. This, he reasoned, caused the capitalist nations to postpone their demise by keeping humanity on the brink of a nuclear holocaust.[85] Nevertheless, he did not lose his faith in the idea of progress, especially in Chile. Although he warned during the 1960s that Chile's workers were, by and large, more militant thant the political parties represented in Allende's FRAP, he was delighted by the electoral victory of *Unidad Popular* in 1970. After Allende's election, Vitale called for a theoretical rearmament of the Left to defend the socialist government and advocated an organization of workers ready to use violence to protect their government.[86] His sagacity went un-

Luis Corvalán (1916–)

In contrast to his more creative Communist party comrade Volodia Teitelboim, the ebullient politician Luis (Lucho) Corvalán excelled at implementing the ideas of others and at explaining briefly and precisely the essence of complex issues. He too was influenced significantly by Recabarren and like Teitelboim felt that communism in Chile was the highest expression of humanism. He served the Communist party as an idealogue, a newspaper editor, pamphleteer, senator, and as its secretary general. He worked closely with the Popular Action Front (FRAP), an electoral coalition of the Communist and Socialist parties, which later expanded, by incorporating other political parties, to form the Popular Unity government that came to power under Salvador Allende. After the military takeover in Chile in 1973, Corvalán was imprisoned until 1976 when he went to the Soviet Union in exchange for Russian dissident Vladimir Bukovsky.

Corvalán believed that each country had its own fundamental problems, such as the land tenure system and the Catholic Church, which produced and perpetuated extreme conservatism and impeded social progress in Chile, and that revolutionaries in every nation must understand their own national problems and determine the direction of their movements accordingly.

As a result of the Cuban revolution, Corvalán saw in Chile a revolutionary structure arising from a petty bourgeois foundation, one that tended to underestimate the proletariat, one that was nationalistic, and one that inclined toward the use of terrorism. He contended that unlike Cuba, in Chile violence could not erupt in the countryside, only in the cities.[96] Nevertheless, he averred that the revolutionary ideas emanating from Cuba should be reconciled with the thinking of the more established revolutionary groups such as the Communist party. Although he heeded Lenin's warnings against the dangers of adventurism, as he categorized Fidel Castro's early actions, he simultaneously advocated left-wing coalitions, a situation that briefly achieved political power for Chile's socialists. For his own country, he believed in fostering revolution without armed struggle and supported multiparty government, yet never explained how such a regime could be sustained once in office.[97]

In a series of articles compiled in *Nuestra vía revolucionaria*

(1964) (Our Road to Revolution), Corvalán took up the question of the possibility of a peaceful transition from capitalism to socialism, a concept long advocated by Chile's Communist party, which believed it could come to power through the electoral process. He stressed the fact that although achieving political victory through democratic means is the objective, even if it fails, the movement is strengthened, and that in itself is an accomplishment.[98]

He maintained that "the proletariat and its party have never been supporters of violence for the sake of violence," a belief that no sane person could contest. He noted that "if the ruling classes resort to violence, it is possible that the people's movement will be forced to follow another path, the armed struggle." For him, violence seemed to exist only when those in power used it on a daily basis. Corvalán's left-wing opponents said that as long as a façade of bourgeois democracy existed in Chile, he viewed the situation as normal and nonviolent. He construed violence in terms of bloodshed, not premature death, malnutrition, poor health, lack of sanitation, unemployment, and human exploitation.[99]

Corvalán knew that many Marxists argued that a democratic or a national liberation revolution could not come about peacefully and realized that Lenin rejected this possibility, but he insisted that historical situations differ and that Lenin also thought that all roads to socialism did not have to be identical. Paradoxically, Corvalán was also cognizant of Lenin's prediction that entrenched powers would never voluntarily give up and that if you defeated them in an election, you could expect a counterrevolution. Ironically, the Chilean experience bore out the Russian revolutionary's prophecy.[100]

Corvalán noted that his party agreed that each nation should select its own path to socialism and that the Soviet Union did not give political and ideological commands, only direction. On the other hand, Chile's Socialists construed "direction" as subordination. For example, they objected to the Warsaw Pact as drawing the world into a military struggle, which Socialist leader Raúl Ampuero Díaz (discussed later) said divided the globe into two camps—a situation leading to the subordination of the worker's struggle to national security.[101]

Corvalán also rejected the Chinese theory that each party should simultaneously prepare for peaceful transition and armed struggle.[102] Despite the Cuban experience, he continuously expressed his preference for the peaceful road to socialism in Chile, to the chagrin of his political opponents on the left who pointed out that his approach denigrated class struggle.[103] Whether one attributes Corvalán's views to vulgar Marxism, dogmatic adherence to the Soviet line, personal idealism, or utopian naiveté it is noteworthy that even during the tumultuous days of the Allende government, he never wavered from the contention that a general strike could defeat a right-wing armed insurrection.[104]

Raul Ampuero Díaz (1917–)

One might call Raúl Ampuero Díaz the Socialist party's counterpart of the Communist party's Luis Corvalán. A lawyer, master politician, ideologue, distinguished senator and party organizer, like Corvalán he excelled at interpreting and implementing Marxist theory. During the 1950s he took control of the Socialist party and shaped it into a disciplined and autonomous organization. He strove to eliminate personalism in politics and moved the party away from populism toward traditional Marxist socialism. When necessary, he allied with other parties, never compromising the Socialists' goals, while steering an independent course during the Cold War.[105]

Although he was not a particularly original theoretician, Ampuero had a solid knowledge of Marxist ideology. He especially understood the thinking of Mao Zedong and, like him, was not bound to strict stages of Marxist development. In fact, he noted that had Fidel Castro followed orthodox Marxist methods, Fulgencio Batista would still be in power in Cuba. Like Corvalán, he claimed that each country had to adapt tactics and strategies to fit its own conditions.[106] Within the Socialist party, Ampuero was recognized as the expert on economic and social matters, the man who adapted Marx to the Chilean reality more than did Salvador Allende.[107]

Ampuero rejected the Communists' claim to a socialist ideological monopoly in Chile, as well as their "Peaceful Road to Socialism" theory.[108] To him the Communists and the social democrats, who advocated working through the established order to bring about revolution through the parliamentary process, were unrealistic. He believed that the world was not divided into two political (party) camps but into the forces of the bourgeoisie and the proletariat. To him, party differences and sectarianism in Chile damaged the socialist cause. He viewed socialism as a reality that socialists could achieve but which remained an abstraction until they reached accord.[109] He worked to fill the gaps between the socialist sects and eventually aligned the Socialist party with the FRAP, whose program opposed imperialism, the oligarchy, and feudalism; respected workers' rights; and advocated democratic collectivism and the elimination of agrarian exploitation.[110] Nevertheless, he always maintained that the road to socialist unity in Chile was harder to travel than not; for the differences between Chile's socialists, to use Hegel's thoughts, were born in the mind and translated into life.[111] Personal and ideological discord caused him, late in 1967, to withdraw from the Socialist party, which he accused of engaging in populism and, paradoxically, allying too closely with the Communists. He then founded the Popular Socialist Union (USP), which did not support Salvador Allende in 1970.[112]

Ampuero believed that the Cuban revolution served as a catalyst for other revolutionary movements in Latin America but that it also placed Latin America under a United States-directed state of siege—one resurrecting the Monroe Doctrine to prevent ideological colonization.[113] He thought that the United States had moved quickly to institutionalize Latin American dependency after the Cuban revolution, and he pointed to the Alliance for Progress and extensive aid to Latin America's right-wing militaries as examples of this policy.[114]

Chile had to contend with an assertive United States and simultaneously resolve internal problems, many of which were inextricably bound to foreign imperialism. For example, Ampuero believed a major obstacle existed in Chile's inability to resolve the disequilibrium between agriculture and the other facets of its economy. He noted that foreign investment and monopoly were difficult to combat and that it was hard to sustain a high level of gain with low productivity, especially with a workers' movement that lacked political awareness.[115] Ampuero realized that the old landed oligarchy controlled finances and politics and collaborated with foreign capital to the detriment of the development of native capital and that the agrarian sector was paralyzed by a precapitalist form of land use and exploitation. He felt that all the aforementioned problems could not be overcome until worker control became a reality.[116] As a model, he pointed to the Yugoslavian system of worker management, which he said prevented the evils of Stalinism and demonstrated that multiparty systems are not necessary for democracy as long as the workers are directly represented in the economy and the government.[117]

On another level, Ampuero believed that coexistence between socialism and imperialism was preferable to nuclear war but that the struggle between capitalism and socialism had to go on. Class struggle had to be waged in capitalist states—wars of national liberation were essential—but world wars could be avoided.[118]

In the pamphlet *El socialismo ante el mundo de hoy* (1964) (Socialism Before Today's World), Ampuero indicated that the Chinese had a clearer understanding of the Third World than the Russians but that the international struggle must be better coordinated. He deplored disruptive situations like the Sino-Soviet split. His plea was for fraternal cooperation and pluralistic paths to socialism.[119]

Ampuero discussed whether or not Chile had to pass through a bourgeois-democratic stage enroute to socialism. He concluded that Peru's Haya de la Torre was correct when he said that imperialism is the last stage of capitalism in developed regions, but in the underdeveloped areas like Chile it is the first phase of capitalism.[120] Ampuero urged his countrymen to be critical, pragmatic, and flexible and to experiment with diverse facets of Marxist theory that might enable Chile to attain the socialist independence he so admired in Yugoslavian society.[121]

Clodomiro Almeyda Medina (1923–)

The youngest, and in some ways the most articulate Marxist *pensador* of the Allende era with whom we deal is Clodomiro Almeyda Medina, a former lawyer and professor of social science at the University of Chile. During the 1950s he supported Carlos Ibáñez, who he hoped would provide the authority Chile lacked, and he was the general's minister of labor and later minister of mining.[122]

Recognized for his incisive mind, Almeyda subsequently became a fixture in the *Unidad Popular* movement. He served the Allende administration as minister of foreign affairs and as chancellor of Chile. After the military takeover in 1973, he became the executive secretary of *Unidad Popular* (in exile), a position he has used effectively to coordinate worldwide condemnation of and resistance to the Pinochet dictatorship.

Almeyda established himself as a thinker of substance with the publication of the thesis *Hacia un teoría marxista del estado* (1948) (Toward a Marxist Theory of the State) that he had submitted for the *licenciado* (law) degree at the University of Chile. In the thesis he identified the university as the place to initiate revolutionary thinking, as in essence he did by presenting this solid Marxist analysis of the historical antecendents of the state and politics.[123]

Basically a Leninist, Almeyda also incorporated into his thinking the utopian concept of a state where political authorities do not exist and where administrative and techical officials exist only to serve the public and satisfy social necessities. Almeyda opposed the parliamentary process as it functioned in Chile, believing that it operated for class interest and feeling that it did not provide sufficient authority to resolve social problems such as that of the *latifundios*.[124] He also subscribed to Harold Laski's belief in the limitations of democracy in a capitalist state. In dealing with the relations of the capitalist state to politics, law, economics, government, authority, the nation, and class dictatorship, he differentiated between the state and the nation. He emphasized that human (nationality) groups make up the nation whereas the state contains a theoretical political component by which the groups are governed. He concluded that the state ought to elaborate an ideological synthesis that satisfies the diverse constituencies found there and guarantee freedom for all. To him, classes are the product of historical devlopment, and the state is an instrument of the dominant classes that try to stabilize the existing structure. Thus, the state is the agency that oppresses the dominated classes—in essence a minority class dictatorship exists.[125]

He advocated a dictatorship of the proletariat consonant with a "workers' democracy" leading to a state of communism, or a classless society which created liberty in diverse forms. Although he believed that the U.S.S.R. had the first workers' state, he noted that it had degenerated into a society dominated by bureaucracy and the military and had deprived people of some rights and liberties.[126]

Almeyda was also one of the first Latin American Marxist *pensadores* to attempt to clarify the differences between corporativism and state intervention, both of which became more prevalent in the area during the 1960s. To him, corporativism was increasingly replacing the liberal state in Latin America. It is scientific, on a high plane, while intervention is a practical, often immediate act, not conceptually thought out and the results of which are not calculated in advance. Corporativism represents a planned society where all political power resides in the professional groups and social entities that constitute the corporation. Theoretically, in corporativism, decisions are made by the groups representing the people whereas in state intervention the old dominant class elites make them. He views corporativism as a preferable way of conducting a capitalist state because in theory it is more representative than free enterprise liberal-bourgeois democracy.[127]

In addition to his analysis of the state, Almeyda's essay on the concept of man perhaps best displays his breadth as a Marxist thinker. He cites three basic concepts of man: (1) the traditional concept wherein man is seen as governed by natural, inevitable laws and biological orders, where agriculture and economic activity form the basis for power and prestige, and where belief in God plays a major role and helps maintain a social (and feudal) order wherein the promise of another life should suffice for the present; (2) the modern (seventeenth-to-nineteenth century) concept where Renaissance thinking predominates, where there exists a vision of man at the center of human existence, and where there is confidence in the power of reason in a bourgeois world; and (3) his Marxist concept, following the thinking of Henri Lefebvre, that socialism does not resolve all human problems but inaugurates an epoch in which people are able to understand them and thus can work toward their resolution.[128]

Almeyda constructed a political philosophy based on his perception of Latin American reality. He felt that the major problem affecting Chile was imperialism, which caused disequal development of capitalism and domination and dependence.[129] In *Reflexiones políticas* (1958) (Political Reflections) he contended that U.S. political, economic, social, and ideological penetration compromised Chile's sovereignty, culture, and ability to build a more equitable society. He noted that for a few decades after independence Chile enjoyed a greater degree of sovereignty but that subsequently the ruling aristocracy began to import considerable European culture, which led to a takeover by foreign lifestyles and ideas.[130]

He believed that the socialist movement could also be overly influenced by foreign ideas. He pointed to Argentina's socialists, for whom he thought the French revolution was a model and who he contended were intellectual elitists insufficiently concerned about the common man.[131] He believed that Chile's Marxists had also relied too heavily on European ideals and nineteenth-century values, including parliamentary democracy, the party system, liberty, and abstract democracy, all of which he averred were not in tune with Chilean reality.[132] He inveighed against adopting foreign values and pointed out that in Europe democratic liberalism permitted the development of people's movements in advanced capitalist states, but in dependent nations like those of Latin America, it caused political confusion and strengthened the rule of reactionary minorities under the guise of public liberties that do not reach the masses.[133]

Almeyda's belief that Latin America's dependent people need to break their subordination drew him to the Chinese strategy of employing national liberation movements. Like the Chinese he believed that the danger of war could only be eliminated by the destruction of imperialism, that the struggle for peace is related to the struggle against imperialism. He realized that the Chinese did not deny the possibility of avoiding a world war and certainly did not advocate such conflict.[134] Almeyda, a long-time opponent of socialist sectarianism, thought that a flexible Organization for Latin American Solidarity might be the best way to begin to unite the Left for the revolutionary struggle. To him, *Unidad Popular,* a coalition of eight political groups, was a major step on the national level in that direction.

While serving as Chile's foreign minister under the Popular United government, Almeyda, in contradiction to some of his ideas stated above, functioned as a social democrat much as he had done while serving the Ibáñez government in the 1950s. Under Allende he backed a three-pronged program. He supported ideological pluralism in Latin America and in the Organization of American States, worked to create the external conditions necessary to build toward domestic socialism, and strove to strengthen groups struggling internationally to transform world capitalism into world socialism.[135]

Salvador Allende (1908–1973)

Salvador Allende, more a practical politician than a political or social theorist, had the knack of putting the ideas of others into simple language, which the masses understood and often construed as reformist rather than revolutionary. He appears in this volume primarily because his 1970 election to Chile's presidency was the culmination of the efforts of many of the *pensadores* we have discussed. A brief look at how he interpreted the socialist cause in Chile will help clarify how a Marxist-oriented regime first came to power through electoral politics in a Latin American nation.

The son of a lawyer, Allende attended medical school in Santiago where he became active in politics. He helped found the Socialist party in 1933, by 1937 was elected to the Chamber of Deputies, became minister of health under the Popular Front government of Pedro Aguirre Cerda in 1939, and secretary general of the Socialist party in 1943. He served in the Senate from 1945 to 1970 and as its president for five years. He also ran unsuccessfully for the presidency of Chile in 1952, 1958, and 1964.

Allende identified with the mainstream of Socialist party thinkers from the 1930s until the 1950s when he broke with them briefly over their support of the presidency of General Carlos Ibáñez. However, during the 1940s he thought that Socialist support of the Popular Front government merely postponed the conversion to socialism.

He saw World War II as a catalyst for socialism in his country. To him, a major contradiction existed in that conflict wherein fascism was represented by the Axis but also by bourgeois Chilean interests, which had traditionally displayed right-wing tendencies. Thus, the war pitted fascists against those with a similar orientation. At the same time, some fought the war for democracy. He reasoned that the war signified a change in social and economic relations and was basically a breakdown of capitalism.[136]

Building upon the democratic currents produced by the victory of the Allies, during the postwar period Allende stressed collective social change rather than industrialization, hoping to reduce the privileged position of foreign and domestic elites and to improve the lot of the masses. In the 1950s he pursued a "Workers' Front Thesis" entailing no deals with the aristocracy, the middle class, the conservatives, or the reformist-centrist political parties. He sought alliances only with working-class parties,[137] assuming that history had not demonstrated that a single party was necessary in the process of transition to socialism.[138]

El pensamiento de Salvador Allende (1974) (The Thinking of Salvador Allende), a collection of his writings, reveals that Allende was an activist who sought socialist unity rather than personal power, a man who believed in the value of Marxism as a method of historical interpretation.[139] He sometimes expressed himself in writing quite eloquently, but his works contain no major contributions to Marxist thought. He had a firm grasp of Marx and Engels and followed the thinking of Almeyda that the Chilean state had been a vehicle of oppression used by the dominant class. Allende emerged as a democrat who wanted economic development, social well-being, and national independence for his country.[140]

He rejected the role of a Marxist theoretician,[141] but he tried to understand the works and the roles of *pensadores*. He said that Lenin's "State and Revolution" contained key ideas but that they should not be used as a "catechism."[142] He often alluded to Lenin's *Left-Wing Communism: An Infantile Disorder* (1920) with whose theme he concurred. Engels's "Our doctrine is not a dogma, but a guide to action" essentially summarized the philosophy of Chile's Socialist party, which Allende saw as a synthesis embodying the reality of an underdeveloped American country, a dependent economy, the aspirations of a people, and the concept of Latin American solidarity.[143] He shared Engels's dream that "it is possible to conceive of peaceful evolution from the old society to the new in countries where representatives of the people have concentrated in their hands all the power, where in accordance with the constitution anything may be done that is desired, from the moment when the majority of the people are behind one."[144]

When first organized, the Chilean Socialist party pursued a radical antiliberal program. Labeling itself "Marxist," it developed an indigenous orientation, concentrating on the masses and opposing the middle class, which it felt had lost the capacity to innovate and had accepted upper-class values.[145] Diverging from orthodox Marxism, the Socialists molded their own revolutionary theory. According to Allende, in some nations the road to socialism traversed a transitional zone marked by a dictatorship of the proletariat with two major functions, one political, the other social. Dictatorship serves primarily a political role whereas the proletariat pursues social change. In Chile, he said, the idea of the dictatorship had been supplanted by a different (electoral or constitutional) device, but the social or proletarian aspect remained.[146]

Allende was proud of the "Chilean Road to Socialism" and stressed that it constituted a Marxist interpretation of history, free of international ties but supportive of the right of China, Cuba, Yugoslavia, or Romania to choose their own course to socialism.[147]

Additional Allende insights can be found in *Citas de compañero presidente* (1973) (Quotations of Comrade President), his version of Mao's *Little Red Book*,[148] which applied historical materialism to a wide range of areas of social concern—from diet, to agriculture, to alcoholism, to feminism. It demonstrated his commitment to improving the human condition through technological and administrative means.[149]

Allende realized that the world was increasingly interdependent and that Chile had a need to equalize or lessen dependency. To him, the existence of two sectors or blocs in the world endangered global peace. But this potentially dangerous situation could be neutralized by balancing or equalizing dependency, especially between the developed nations and Asian, African, and Latin American countries. He also thought that the latter had to coordinate their own revolutionary efforts.[150] On an international scale he advocated Latin American efforts through the United Nations to build solidarity with the dependent Asian and African peoples, Latin American economic and political integration and cultural interchange, and universal arms limitations.[151]

Pursuing a "Chilean Road to Socialism" while functioning within a democratic system with the theoretical acquiescence of some capitalist political parties brought Allende to the presidency of Chile in 1970.[152] By that time he was regarded in many leftist circles as a social democrat who stood at the right wing of the Socialist party. He believed that he could operate through the reformist institutions of an extraordinarily dependent capitalist state to bring about a unique brand of socialism. He gambled that democracy, legality, and Chile's long tradition of constitutionalism would survive while he endeavored to alter the country's political and social systems—a difficult task when his administration did not have the power to dominate the state and when there existed severe external and internal opposition at the practical and theoretical levels.

Allende has been criticized for not arming Chile's workers and peasants and for not producing sufficient class solidarity to unify them against the nation's United States-supported armed forces.

He ignored Lenin's lesson that those who govern are the middle-range technocrats, bureaucrats, and militarists in the government ministries and private corporations—those who cannot be replaced by elections but only by revolution.[153] Ultimately, Allende's idealism—his unwillingness to turn Chilean against Chilean—cost him his life and crushed his dreams of building a socialist state, as the country's military, led by General Augusto Pinochet, destroyed the Popular Unity government on September 11, 1973, and established a brutal dictatorship that eliminated all vestiges of democracy in the nation.

In Marxist-Leninist terms, Allende and the Chilean experiment were doomed from the outset. He tried to build socialism from above, beginning without a revolutionary situation or a vanguard capable of dealing with the reactionary forces. *Unidad Popular* had no ideological unity beyond the belief that it could gradually transfer power from the bourgeoisie to the workers by using the machinery of the state to alter the nation's infrastructure, thereby weakening the upper- and middle-class hold on it.

To some extent Allende's movement adhered not to Marxist principles but to communitarian socialism, based on the idea that the land and productive goods belong to the workers. This superseded the basic idea of capitalism, in which the conflict between the owning class and the propertyless masses who serve them for wages creates obstacles to economic and social development and justice. Under communitarian socialism, capital and labor are united against individual or class exploitation. It differs from state socialism in that the role of the state is subsidiary to the self-management of the workers. The state does only what the workers cannot yet do. Communitarian socialism works on the premise that eventually all functions will be taken over by people's organizations, which will prevent the state from becoming an all-powerful unresponsive organ.[154]

5. Brazil

Capitalism is not a regime instituted by Divine Providence
for eternity, but only an episode in the social development of
humanity.

Leôncio Basbaum

From 1822, when Emperor Pedro I severed ties to Portugal, until
the overthrow of Brazil's monarchy in 1889, nationalism enhanced the mystique of the crown and played a dominant role in
the politics of South America's largest nation. The nationalists,
who governed there, were establishment and reform-minded elitists, who, by the end of the nineteenth century, followed the lead
of philosopher Benjamin Constant, who instilled in them respect
for Comptian positivism with its promise of "order and progress."
Brazil's intelligentsia shared this set of beliefs and did not identify
with the masses or have the capacity to create ferment within their
ranks.[1] From independence to the present, nationalism and positivism have stood as monumental barriers to Marxism in Brazil.

Socialist thought, however, managed to enter Brazil during the
nineteenth century. The nation's leading intellectual journal, *O
Progresso,* edited by Antônio Pedro Figueiredo (1814–1859), was
the first publication in the country to support some pre-Marxist
European socialist ideas. Socialist thought gained the attention of
a few intellectuals when the short-lived *Socialist Review* started
publishing in Rio de Janeiro in 1845.[2] Between the 1840s and the
turn of the century, Euclides da Cunha (1866–1909), author of
the classic *Os sertões* (1902) (The Backlands), was the most famous Brazilian writer to correlate Marxism with his nation's
ethos. In 1901 Cunha founded the International Club—Sons of
Work, in order to reveal the works of Marxism, which he somehow misnamed "rationalism."[3]

During the last quarter of the nineteenth century European immigrants brought socialist and anarchist ideas to Brazil. Anarcho-syndicalism influenced Brazilian physician Silverio Fontes (1858–
1928), who published the journal *A Questão Social* (The Social
Question) dedicated to propagating the social ideas of Marx.[4]

Another respected publicist for socialism in Brazil during this period, Tobías Barreto, a professor at Recife Law School and a pseudo-Marxist whose ideas lacked proletarian consciousness, promoted the concept of scientific analysis. His extensive writings described Brazil's reality in terms of the class struggle, and he drew parallels between monarchial Europe and his country under the reign of Pedro II (1841–1889).[5] He and a few colleagues at the Recife Law School attempted in the 1870s to analyze non-European influences on Brazilian institutions and during the next decade tried to popularize the ideas of Marx. An admirer of Kant, as well as Marx, Tobías Barreto strove to free Brazilian philosophy, literature, and jurisprudence from its heavily French influence and to redirect it to German thinking. The German-language newspaper he published rested on two fundamental principles, a belief in the conditioning of people by the economic process and the historical nature and changeability of humanity.

Brazil's first socialist congress convened in Rio in 1892, attended by socialists and by anarchists who followed Kropotkin's belief that humanity's fundamental goodness would reveal itself in a society without authority or property—one permitting the fullest development of individual autonomy.[6] Although a Brazilian Socialist party was founded in 1895, anarchism, with its preference for federalism over centralism and libertarian ideas on party constraints, remained the dominant philosophy among Brazil's trade unionists.

Both Brazilian Socialists and anarchists campaigned actively against World War I but gained little public acceptance for their political beliefs. The intense rivalry between them endured until the 1920s and seriously impeded the growth of organized labor movements in the country.

The Russian revolution rekindled the interest in socialism in Brazil and in May 1917, Nestor Peixoto Oliveira, influenced by French thinker Jean Jaurès, resurrected Brazil's Socialist party.[7] At this time the anarchists rejected the idea of the dictatorship of the proletariat and maintained that the Bolsheviks had replaced the Czar with a president—a nonrevolutionary, reformist-parliamentarian move.[8] The anarchists attacked the Brazilian Socialists for thinking along similar lines as the Bolsheviks. Although most Brazilian Socialists could not accept Lenin's views on revolution in 1917, by 1922 many had changed their minds. A number of them split with the Socialist party and helped found Brazil's Communist party. Anarchists too, by now familiar with the thinking of Lenin as well as that of Argentina's José Ingenieros on "Maximalism" (as he called Bolshevism), joined the Communist party, which modeled itself after the one in Argentina.

A prominent Brazilian Communist party leader, Otávio Brandão, who in 1924 had translated the *Communist Manifesto* into Portuguese, after reading Lenin's *Imperialism: The Highest Stage of Capitalism,* wrote, in 1926, a major Marxist study of Brazil. *Agrarismo e industrialismo: Ensaio marxista-leninista sôbre a revolta de São Paulo e a guerra de classe no Brasil* (Agrarianism and Industrialization: An Essay on the Revolt of São Paulo and the Class War in Brazil) referred to Brazil's Communists as successors to Tiradentes, Euclides da Cunha, and other past revolutionaries who tried to free their country from political and cultural domination. The author made a strong plea for a revolution to be guided by theory. He presumed that Brazil was economically, socially, and politically at the mercy of a feudal agrarian system that left the nation with an unstable economy based on a nonessential product—coffee; thus the country had constant need for foreign loans. He also analyzed the United States-British rivalry for economic supremacy in Brazil.[9]

Not until the 1930s, after the ravages of the Depression, did many Brazilian writers begin to seriously study their country's sociopolitical problems. By then they had come to appreciate more fully the accomplishments of the Russian revolution and the intentions of the Mexican Revolution. Artistic creativity and intellectual ferment flourished in the wake of the Depression. Brazilian theater, cinema, architecture, and folk and serious music underwent a revival. Progressive thought assumed a major place in the nation's intellectual life, and many artists and writers joined the Communist party. Subsequently, the populism that grew during the Getulio Vargas dictatorship (1930–1945) enabled many members of the intelligentsia to see that working-class participation in government was essential to progress, and they produced articles, books, and pamphlets designed to awaken Brazil's laboring class to the origins of their country's problems.

World War II brought Brazil into the United States-Soviet Alliance, forced import substitution and industrialization upon the country, and raised working-class awareness to new heights.

Brazil's economy was oriented away from Europe and toward the United States. After the war the United States endeavored to secure its hegemony in the South American nation by including Brazil in its plans for maintaining capitalist supremacy in the Americas. In an effort to strengthen its foothold in Brazil, Washington courted Brazil's military, which it considered to be a more stable force than the numerous weak political parties. The United States provided training, equipment, and large doses of anticommunist indoctrination.

State Department-inspired anticommunism took hold among Brazil's military, industrial, and political elites. For example, by the 1950s, Governor Carlos Lacerda of Guanabara State led a successful drive to exclude Marxists from the Brazilian Writers Association. The association collapsed, and many Brazilian Marxists went underground or into exile.[10]

Jorge Amado, a Communist party member and probably Brazil's most famous post-World War II novelist, in his stories that interpret the class struggle in Brazil's underdeveloped Northeast, comments upon the recent impact of socialist thinkers in Brazil by depicting them as rather weak and ineffective in terms of their understanding of, and contributions to, Marxist theory. On the other hand, Jacob Gorender, a leading Communist party theoretician, contends that the great post-World War II development in the country intensified the existing structural discrepancies and caused new ones, thus contributing to revolutionary thinking by heightening contradictions, such as the one between U.S. imperialism and the well-being of Brazil's people.[11]

Brazil's left-wing political parties were crushed within a few years after the military seized control of the country in 1964. Nevertheless, a few Marxists in Brazil continued to turn out theoretically oriented books, which had little or no audience in a nation where the military leaders, most of the remaining intellectuals, and the more literate laymen still believed in positivism. In 1979, when I was surprised to find stacks of volumes by socialists in a Rio book shop, the proprietor explained that the government was not threatened by works that very few could comprehend and that it primarily feared Marxist views reaching the masses. Thus, the censors focused primarily on radio, television, public rallies, and popular journals.

Before proceeding to examine Marxist thought in Brazil, note that within the ranks of the country's organized Left, intellectuals have often been distrusted. Some say that the mystique of the revolutionary proletariat prevails—the belief that manual workers possess a natural revolutionary proclivity that makes them superior to mental laborers.[12] Nowhere is this more evident than in the attitudes of Luiz Carlos Prestes, Brazil's most famous Communist party leader.

Luiz Carlos Prestes (1898–)

No Brazilian Marxist has attracted more international attention than Luiz Carlos Prestes, whose mother taught French and was influenced by the novels of Emile Zola and whose father was a professional soldier and accepted positivism. Prestes graduated first in his class from the Realengo Military Academy in 1919 and received a commission as a lieutenant in the engineer corps, whereupon the affable and tenacious young officer embarked upon what his superiors predicted would be a brilliant military career.

In 1922 a group of idealistic young *tenentes* (lieutenants) of lower-middle-class origin rebelled against the Brazilian government of Artur da Silva Bernardes, assailing its lack of social concern and justice. The revolt was put down rapidly, but *tenentismo* lived on, and in 1924 Prestes recruited a force, including approximately 1,500 of the rebels, for a march designed to dramatize their desire for social progress in the country. From this point on, the life of Prestes became a chapter in the social history of Brazil.

The Prestes Column's two-year march took it over 25,000 kilometers, from the pampas of southern Brazil through the interior to the Paraná Valley, back and forth across the northeast and central Brazil, through Mato Grosso, to the Bolivian border. When the march ended in defeat at the hands of federal troops, assisted by the elements, Prestes sought sanctuary in exile.

Prestes came to view the march as a repudiation of the system that represented the governing class and some bourgeois elements rather than the people. During the march he made the transformation from petty bourgeois reformer to revolutionary and began to see Brazil's strife as a manifestation of the world wide crisis of capitalism in the 1920s and understood that Brazil without an advanced industrial base, but with monocultural dependence on imperialism, could not improve.[13] He had intended the march to awaken the population of the interior, to shake them out of the apathy into which they had sunk, to kill their indifference to our country's fate. . . . Mine was above all a political and social task.[14]

Originally, he had not conceived of the column as the vanguard of the proletariat or the conscience of a class but, as he noted in a 1978 interview, as a means of disrupting the government and building public sympathy and unity. He admitted that the march opened his eyes, turned him toward political and social alternatives, and led him to read Marx and Lenin, from whom he acquired a "new world perspective."[15]

After the march, while in Bolivia in 1927, the "Cavalier of Hope," as Prestes was then known, at the urging of Brazil's Communist party, began to study Marxist theory. In late 1928 he went to Argentina where he encountered the Ghioldi brothers, Rodolfo and Américo, who became his ideological mentors.

Prestes issued a well-publicized manifesto in May 1930 calling for an agrarian and antiimperialist revolution to establish a government run by councils of urban laborers, peasants, and soldiers. Under his plan the government would seize land, distribute it to the peasants, repudiate foreign debts, and nationalize banks, mines, public services, and communications networks. The manifesto did not call for a dictatorship of the proletariat. Prestes felt that the revolution would be hindered by the hegemony of the Communist party and that more Brazilians should be involved in the process. His position elicited considerable criticism from the Communist party.[16] Prestes looked to the Soviet Union for guidance to unite the international proletariat against capitalism and, in the case of Brazil, to help attain independence from British and U.S. capital. He viewed the populist-oriented promises of Getulio Vargas's regime as empty and opposed its collaboration with capitalism and its fascist tendencies.[17] He believed that the Communist party, allied with other popular forces, could mobilize Brazil's masses to save the nation from fascism.

By 1931 Prestes had denounced some aspects of *Prestismo,* called a few of his former *tenente* cohorts agents of imperialism, and declared himself a Communist.[18] At this time, as both a leader of the proletariat and a hero to the middle classes, his humanism transcended class lines, causing some Communist party members to reject him as "petty bourgeois." Nevertheless, he maintained that joining the Communist party was the best way he could help combat Vargas, whose program, despite its rhetoric, was not revolutionary and who represented the classes that held power in Brazil.[19]

After his extensive stay in the Soviet Union, Brazil's Communist party formally accepted Prestes in 1934. The following year he became prominent in a National Liberation Alliance, a "Popular Front" organization that opposed fascism, imperialism, and oligarchy; agitated for the liquidation of *latifundia;* proposed cancellation of the foreign debt; and advocated nationalization of foreign-owned enterprises.[20] Although Vargas suppressed the National Liberation Alliance, Prestes continued to push for its programs and for nationalization of public works, social security benefits, the eight-hour working day, minimum wages, guaranteed individual liberties, and the abrogation of harmful international treaties.[21] The government captured Prestes in 1935 and the following year sentenced him to forty-six years in prison.

While in jail Prestes became deeply committed to the Soviet Union and Joseph Stalin.[22] Upon his release from prison in 1945, he met the celebrated Chilean Marxist poet Pablo Neruda, who noted: "These long confinements are nothing exceptional in the 'free world.' "[23]

During the immediate post-World War II period the international Communist movement considered Luiz Carlos Prestes its most influential Latin American member and looked to him to explain conditions in the area.[24] In his estimation, U.S. imperialism had replaced fascism as the chief reactionary force in the world. He worked to divert Brazil's economy from the United States and toward Russia. He contended that Brazil had a greater opportunity to extend its markets within the huge populations of the socialist bloc, that commerce could develop with the socialist nations without a Soviet monopoly, and that Brazil's sovereignty could increase only by expanding its economy. At the same time, he counseled his followers not to try to bring about revolution immediately but to work through parliamentary procedures until proper conditions—in the pure Marxist scheme of revolutionary development—existed. By the time Fidel Castro successfuly employed guerrilla tactics in Cuba, Prestes still condemned radical revolutionary and terrorist activities in Brazil and advised Marxists there to proceed with caution, explaining that conditions differed from those in Cuba.[25]

Prestes viewed the military takeover in Brazil in 1964 as total abandonment of independent economic policy in favor of dependence upon the United States.[26] In an effort to topple the military regime some Brazilian leftists, including dissatisfied former members of the Communist party, turned to urban terrorist tactics. Prestes criticized the "desperate adventures of ultra leftists" and emphasized their lack of working-class support.[27] He blamed rightest and leftist opportunists in the socialist camp for many failures. To him, "opportunists" such as Carlos Marighela, who pursued urban guerrilla warfare, made grave political errors, worked at a low ideological level, and suffered from impatience. He noted that Marx and Engels warned against impatience and counseled the need to retreat when the revolution waned. He inferred that if people like Marighela understood history, they would know that the time was not right for armed struggle, which would now only cause a senseless waste of life. Prestes drew an analogy between the "left" of Marighela in the 1960s and that in Russia between 1907–1910, which Lenin successfully balanced off against the right-wing socialists. Prestes noted that Lenin in his early works opposed the idea that terror propels the spirit of the revolutionary masses; instead he believed that it impedes the revolution of rising consciousness that is most needed.[28]

During the 1970s, Prestes found himself *persona non grata* in Brazil and departed for Moscow, from where he continued to castigate the "errors" of the revolutionary Left while writing about Brazil and hoping to maintain the resistance there. By the 1980s he favored armed revolution, a stance for which Brazil's Communist party expelled him.

Prestes's name has traditionally been one of the first mentioned in conjunction with Marxist thought in Latin America. Examination of his life and his pamphlets and speeches, where most of his ideas have been set out, confirm his place as a distinguished Marxist organizer and polemicist but not as a profound *pensador*. Abguar Bastos, one of Prestes's biographers, says that the *Prestismo* of the 1930s can best be seen as a sort of hero worship combined with a grand design for the proletariat to whom Prestes symbolized hope. *Prestismo* was a nonscientific, nonintellectual movement rising out of the post-World War I era when the Russian revolution served as a model to a Brazil struggling to industrialize while finding itself increasingly under Western positivist domination.[29] Ronald Chilcote, an authority on the Brazilian Communist party, says that "Brazilian Communist literature is sparse in theoretical writings other than official party documents and the writings of Prestes."[30] Chilcote carefully omits attributing original Marxist ideas to Prestes, whom he claims had an arrogant pride or self-confidence in his ability to find solutions to national problems[31] and whose ambition to control Brazil's revolution led to an extensive advocacy of nationalism.[32]

Joseph Starobin, foreign editor of the *Daily Worker* until 1951, spent considerable time with Prestes between 1946 and 1948 and concluded that he deviated from standard Marxist-Leninist views—that he sought the cooperation of Brazil's national bourgeoisie because he feared that all-out class warfare in Brazil or a move too far to the revolutionary left would cause a right-wing military coup that would seriously impede the Left's ability to progress. The 1964 takeover of the military in Brazil, when the prolabor reformist government of João Goulart was accused of moving too far to the left, corroborated Prestes's fears.[33] Starobin also observed that Prestes lost some of his revolutionary ardor after being imprisoned in the 1930s, that he was consumed by the quest for, and hurt by his inability to find, peaceful solutions to Brazil's problems.[34] Starobin felt that the failure of Prestes's early independent Marxist efforts in conjunction with his inability to attain status in the international Marxist movement on his own led him to turn to Moscow for support in order to be able to effectively confront the Cold War.[35]

The difficulties of assessing the work of Prestes are compounded by the fact that his life has spanned over seven decades, during which he, like political and social conditions, underwent numerous changes. Furthermore, his distrust of intellectuals and the fact that he has never proved to be a methodologically sound theoretician make it difficult and possibly unwise to try to categorize his thinking. In some ways, he sought flexibility within his ideology. His early independent Marxist postures have been noted above, and as recently as the 1960s he asserted: "Marxism-Leninism does not unconditionally reject any form of struggle." He followed that statement by saying that "violent actions have nothing to do with the process of revolution unless they contribute toward raising the level of consciousness and organization of the masses." Thus, he evaded the question of whether it is possible in Brazil to organize the masses by means other than armed struggle against the dictatorship.[36] Prestes's tendency to lapse into such uncritical rhetoric when clear analysis of genuine problems is called for, along with his often dogmatic defense of Stalin and the Soviet Union, lead to the conclusion that he is an extraordinary person, one whose major place in Brazilian history is as a folk hero. Perhaps when Jorge Amado characterized Communist party leaders in his novels as earnest activists but weak and ineffective theorists, he had his close friend and associate Luiz Carlos Prestes in mind.[37]

Leôncio Basbaum (1907–1969)

In contrast to the practical Luiz Carlos Prestes stands the more scholarly Leôncio Basbaum (sometimes known by the pseudonym Augusto Machado), who trained for medicine, became a political activist, joined and broke with the Communist party which he served as an official, held a professorship in economic history, and wrote thirteen volumes on topics such as the sociology of materialism, the Brazilian road to development, and the worker and peasant path to revolution. As a youth he most appreciated the writing of Machado de Assis, the nineteenth-century Brazilian novelist, and the films of Charlie Chaplin; and was especially fond of Don Quixote.[38] In adulthood, Argentine Marxists Victorio Codovilla and Rodolfo and Américo Ghioldi had considerable influence on him, but he reserved his greatest admiration for the works of Italian thinker Antonio Gramsci. Like Gramsci he was a social critic who allowed for human weaknesses, rejected dogmatism, and whose Marxism considered many factors such as race, geography, economics, and population.[39] Following Gramsci, he stressed the importance of culture in the evolution of humanity and that only cultural, not biological, differences exist.[40]

Basbaum strayed from classical Marxism by propounding a humanistic historical theory with existential characteristics like that of Jean-Paul Sartre. He took pride in his scientific approach to history, especially his four-volume study of Brazil, which he felt was unique.[41] He viewed history as a dialectical process whereby freedom under capitalism leads man to become a slave to the products he creates, which in turn leads him to seek the ultimate freedom—socialism. In order to attain socialism, he realized that alienation had to be overcome. Unlike Marx who saw alienation as the conflict between reality and the ideal, but like Herbert Marcuse, he viewed alienation as a reaction against human servitude, machines or work, property, religion, the capitalist market, and the state.[42] He contended that man must elude the slavery of production which produces alienation and begin a new type of consciousness geared to manipulate production to enhance the social value of its ends (products).[43] He believed that alienation could be overcome by humanism, not aimed directly at the proletariat but at all humanity, and that the alienation of work and education, if superseded by humanism, would give people dignity.[44]

Basbaum's memoirs show how his Marxist views evolved as he observed Brazil's political history over the last forty years of his life, beginning with the rise of *Prestismo*.[45] He wrote about himself as a young intellectual, who studied Marx, Lenin, and Tolstoy, and as a teenager intrigued by the exploits of Prestes's Column.[46] His curiosity compelled him to analyze *Prestismo*, Prestes's relationship to Brazil's Communist party, and the internal politics of the Brazilian Left. He concluded that anarchist ideas were important to the followers of the Prestes Column,[47] which he called the most significant military-political act in Brazilian history insofar as consciousness-raising was concerned.[48]

The world crisis of the late 1920s had enormous repercussions in Brazil where the workers sustained severe damage. He viewed the Depression as a rupture in the retrograde system of relations of production, an explosion of an archaic semifeudal system.[49] He linked *Prestismo* and the Depression to the so-called Populist Revolution of 1930 that brought Getulio Vargas to power and which he saw as a transfer of some power to the petty bourgeoisie and the middle class from the landed aristocracy, which was replaced by a monied aristocracy (industrialists) or foreign interests.[50] He noted how the British pound sterling became diminished in relation to the dollar as U.S. corporations with enormous investment in Brazil and their new ally, the national bourgeoisie, supplanted the landed aristocracy and its British supporters.[51] To him, Vargas as chief of the "revolution" was a political boss—not representing finance capital but the leader of the national bourgeoisie or the representative of a small minority desirous of representing the popular masses.[52]

During the late 1930s and early 1940s Basbaum became concerned about fascism, which he found to be a new and bloodier manifestation of capitalism, the ultimate consequence of the inability to achieve the necessary marketplaces under bourgeois democracy. After the defeat of the Axis in World War II he envisioned an international desire to end colonialism and build toward self-determination.[53] At the same time, he found an intensification, in academic and political circles, of the struggle between what he called the "ideology of permanence" (maintaining the status quo) and the Marxist concept of progress and change, or "dialectical transformation of society."[54] He thought that the war opened the road to socialism by showing the inevitability of conflict under capitalism.[55]

Basbaum attributed the military takeover in Brazil in 1964 to the United States. He stated that political instability under the Goulart administration, which U.S. Ambassador Lincoln Gordon and the CIA believed was Communist-connected—in conjunction with the desire of foreign interests to protect their huge investments in Brazil and fear of popular support for another Castro-type movement—led to the antireformist, antirevolutionary conspiracy that put the military in control.[56] He saw the dictatorship as the logical consequence of the country's new class of managers, directors, and public relations people, who wanted to defend their holdings and those of their financial allies.[57]

Basbaum, in one book or another, endeavored to put most of Brazil's political, economic, and social problems into historical perspective. In *Caminhos brasileiros do desenvolvimento* (1960) (Brazilian Roads to Development), written before dependency theories became popular, Basbaum showed contemporary Brazil as a formally sovereign but extraordinarily dependent state, where feudal relations existed in a capitalist framework, with industrial capital in the cities and vestiges of feudalism in the countryside. He believed that the contradiction of this dual society, with a rich and prosperous sector and a poor and degenerating one, accounted for the great problems of social and political dislocation and economic inflation of the post-World War II era.[58] As economist André Gunder Frank did some years later, he saw Brazil as a major example of the development of underdevelopment.[59]

While following Lenin's views on imperialism and showing that industrialization transformed Brazil into a colony, and impoverished the rural masses, he explored two immediate roads to social betterment. First, he advocated destroying feudal relations by breaking up the *latifundias* and liberating the peasants;[60] second, he suggested the possibility of state capitalism, which could remove the foreign presence from Brazil and serve as an intermediate stage in the transformation to socialism. The latter theory lost credibility when the military took over in 1964 and increased government control, and nationalization of some industry made Brazil more secure for foreign investments.

Perhaps Basbaum's greatest talents existed on a more philosophical level. For example, his *Sociología de materialismo* (1964) (Sociology of Materialism)—a comprehensive historical treatise, studying materialism from its Greek and Roman origins, contrasting it with idealism, and explaining the differences between vulgar and dialectical materialism—established him among the most erudite of Brazilian *pensadores*.[61]

His penetrating studies delved into a multitude of philosophical areas. Among his best work is an elaboration on the Marxist concept of "reciprocal action," which he applied to political parties as part of the class struggle.[62] Another excellent piece is his chapter on the psychology of Marxist thought, which explained how it developed, how a national psychology differs from individual psychology, and how difficult it is to overcome national ideas in order to create an international psychology.[63]

His original *O processo evólutivo da história* (1963) (The Evolutionary Historical Process), the finest study in Portuguese of the sociology and methodology of history, breaks down history into eight laws: (1) material factors impel history, (2) these factors are interdependent, (3) they interact reciprocally, (4) history is not reversible but spirals, (5) all factors are transformed dialectically, (6) interaction always exists between the forces of production and the social relations of production, (7) "abrupt leaps" in the dialectic process's transformations are not smooth, and (8) new variables always affect the historical process.[64] He advocated flexible interpretation of these laws and emphasized that Marxists must liberate Marxism from dogmatists. He allowed that Marx would have wanted permanent criticism of the Left and continuous revision of Marxism and that "part of Marxist truthfulness is precisely to negate Marxism."[65] He criticized the rigidity of Brazil's Communist party and at one point singled out Caio Prado Júnior for his "dogmatic servility" to the Communist party line.[66]

The works of this creative "plain" Marxist are not inspirational in an evangelical sense, but they impart a perpetual optimism, an eternal hope for the future. He made a plea for a new kind of history, unlike the old histories of Brazil, which had been written from the standpoint of the dominant class[67] by its own members like Oliveira Viana, Pedro Calmon, and Gilberto Freyre, who presented a false reality and justified privilege and injustice.[68] He rejected the type of history that simply narrates or states facts in order to record "our glorious past." He was also skeptical of those who interpreted Brazil's history on a solely racial or political evolution basis. He emphasized that history should examine all of society's ramifications and historians should search for the fundamental characteristics that determine the historical process and the origins, relationships, and consequences of facts.[69]

Despite his optimism, Basbaum's sense of history forced him to be realistic. For instance, in analyzing the accomplishments of socialism, he pointed to the Soviet Union as an example of over-bureaucratization and agreed with Yugoslav political theorist Milovan Djilas that the bureaucracy in Russia had become a "new class,"[70] which assumed political rule and which, in Trotsky's view, constituted betrayal of the revolution. On the other hand, he was willing to deviate from the classical road to socialism and noted that Cuba could attain it without a dictatorship of the proletariat and that an individual like Castro could act as the conductor of the masses by interpreting their aspirations and helping them to change their historical path.[71]

Caio Prado Júnior (1907–)

The Brazilian Marxist historian best known in all of the Americas is Caio Prado Júnior, some of whose works have been translated into Spanish and English. His studies provide foundations for previously unexplained aspects of areas such as race, rural and urban conflict, external pressures on Brazil, and the social history of the nation, particularly during the colonial era. His scholarly work, noted for its economic analyses and subtle development of dependency themes, written in lucid prose rather than in mathematical terms or sociological jargon, is characterized by the clear-cut methodology of the "plain" Marxist humanist who believes that given a chance, socialism will prevail in the minds of men and women. There exists another, less-known (beyond Brazil) side to Prado—his life as a journalist, head of the publishing house Brasiliense, editor of the significant Marxist social science journal *Revista Brasiliense,* "sophisticated" Marxist, and sometimes supporter of the Soviet Union, who, during the 1960s, disagreed with Djilas and Basbaum's "new class" theory.

Despite long-time membership in Brazil's Communist party, Prado never followed the party line exclusively. For instance, he always differed with the Communist position on feudalism in Brazil. He maintained that it never existed, that production in the country was always market-oriented, and that the socioeconomic structure of the plantation system differed from feudalism.[72] Using Marx's frames of reference, he contended that when slavery was abolished in 1888, Brazil moved from a precapitalist to a more exploitative system he has termed the "peasant economy."[73]

Prado has predicated his analyses on the belief that to understand the present, we must comprehend the past. To him, the colonial past still exists, in modified fashion, in Brazil's economic and social order. He has shown that Brazilian life during the colonial era was organized around commercial interests and that contemporary economic, racial, and political problems stem from settlement patterns based upon colonial commerce.[74] He has demonstrated how the colonial economy, run by a few entrepreneurs and administrators, with the masses providing the labor base necessary to supply international trade with vital natural resources, became institutionalized and later blended into the positivist creed of material progress through order and discipline. Prado designated the Second Empire (1841–1889) as the transition phase between colonial and contemporary Brazil, when some slave labor was transferred to free labor. Brazil's infrastructure expanded, coffee became important, but the nation continued to be a producer of primary materials, and life improved for the upper and middle classes while the gap between them and the lower class widened.[75]

In the book *A revolução brasileira* (1966) (The Brazilian Revolution), Prado tried to formulate a revolutionary theory based on the history of Brazil. He began with, and sustained, the premise that "the class structure of a society and the maturity and hierarchy of its classes and social categories always reflect the economic organization that serves as its base."[76] He categorized Brazil during the 1960s under the military as a nation run by bureaucratic (state) capitalism. In order to forge a socialist revolution, he stated that the urban proletariat must ally with rural workers. However, no tradition exists for this type of merger in Brazil where even under the "populism" of the Vargas era, the peasantry was largely ignored. Prado noted an absence of revolutionary force in Brazil, even on the part of the Communist party. He maintained that there has never existed, more than indirectly, a scientific Marxist theory of revolution in Brazil.[77]

In the prologue to the Spanish edition of *A revolução brasileira* Rodolfo Puiggrós pointed out that the Left made little progress in Brazil because of sectarianism and lack of opportunity to capture the moment with revolutionary action. He said that Prado realized that the workers and the youth in Brazil have understood the valor required of revolutionaries but that the sectarians do not act, that they have preferred to read about revolution and increase their sophistication and alleged authority in their respective groups.[78] Nevertheless, Prado after personally viewing socialist nations, has not lost faith in socialism as the solution to the historical problems and contradictions of capitalism. He has pointed out the futility of comparing the objectives and mechanics of the socialist states with those of capitalist ones. The latter exist for the interests of private property owners and their class whereas the former function for the interests of the workers who constitute the majority and for the collective components of society struggling to achieve human harmony.[79]

He argued that socialism replaces the idea of individual incentive with the concept of collective interest, that under socialism providing necessities for all is more important than maximizing production. Socialism places the social relations of production into sensible proportions; by so doing, it equalizes justice and prevents competitive conflict and discrimination.[80]

He has defended the single party slates that exist in some socialist nations where elected officials are an administrative organ serving the interests of all and noted that in bourgeois states with multiparty systems, elected officials legislate for the interests of private property and a social class. He has warned Brazilians not to compare noncommensurate items by viewing socialist governments through a capitalist lens.[81] He concluded that hostility to socialism based on the defense of capitalism is not valid or constructive. In essence, their competitive mentalities preclude capitalists from analyzing socialism objectively. Indirectly, he has raised the issue of how one gets those imbued with capitalist values to expand their minds to think in terms of humanity as a whole, not just their part of it—to permit themselves to have true freedom of thought.[82]

Carlos Marighela (1911–1969)

Carlos Marighela, known as Preto to his friends, came under the tutelage of Luiz Carlos Prestes during the 1940s. Later he served as a leader of Brazil's Communist party in São Paulo and as editor of the party's journal *Problemas*. After the military takeover of Brazil in 1964, he became disenchanted with Prestes's conservatism, the bureaucratization of the Communist party, and its failure to foster revolution.[83] Inspired by China's Cultural Revolution and the Maoist belief that "it is right to rebel"; Castro, Che Guevara, and the Cuban revolution; and Régis Debray's message in *Revolution in the Revolution* (1967) that the domination of the old tired orthodox communist parties had to be eliminated, Marighela broke in 1967 with Brazil's Communist party. At that time no elected legislature existed in Brazil, and the United States was increasing its presence there by dispatching two-thirds of all its Latin American foreign aid to the generals who controlled the country. Marighela felt that the Communist party had searched too long for peaceful forms of transition to the proletarian revolution while working with national bourgeois elements to achieve that goal. He concluded that "orthodoxy belongs to religion, the old religion," that the new religion is the socialist revolution to be pursued pragmatically. To limit the revolution to the party, he said, would limit it to endless discussions and little progress.[84]

Proclaiming the guerrillas to be the vanguard of the revolution, early in 1968 Marighela and his colleague Mario Alves established the pro-Castro Revolutionary Communist party of Brazil and called for armed struggle. By 1969 they were joined by the Armed Revolutionary Vanguard and launched a political and military campaign.[85]

Marighela declared that revolution through propaganda and ideology had failed in Brazil, that proselytizing yielded few results. Thus, he began violent new departures in Marxist revolutionary thought and action, ones contradicting the views of Prestes. When Prestes subsequently criticized the "ultra leftism" of Marighela as "putschism and adventurism," resting on the disbelief in the revolutionary potential of the working classes and united action,[86] Marighela countered with the statement that he too had always criticized deviation from Marxist thought. He agreed that "Marxism-Leninism is totally opposed to the idea that the only thing that counts in the popular struggle is to advance," but he claimed that Prestes's Communist party suffered from a lack of ideological grounding and was in no position to question his interpretations of Marx.[87]

Marighela maintained that Brazil had reached an early stage of capitalist development when the world entered the imperialist epoch and was divided up between socialism and (capitalist) imperialism. Brazil never caught up with developed countries and could not follow the same course as states that reached the capitalist stage through the Industrial Revolution. He asserted that Brazil's bourgeoisie never had the strength or funds to establish basic industries via private enterprise; thus the state had to establish industry, and state capitalism developed.[88]

Marighela claimed:

> the most the bourgeoisie managed to give the country was a certain economic development. Although dependent on imperialism, this development signified a move forward, a real progress. But the laws of capitalist accumulation immediately applied, and it involved sacrifice, poverty, and exploitation, especially on the part of the rural masses.[89]

In effect, Marighela depicted a classic case of neocolonialism wherein Brazil no longer suffered from a lack of capital but from capitalism. Revolution was necessary to remedy the situation, but he thought that it would never come about under a Communist party that continued to work for unity with the bourgeoisie that maintained the two classes in Brazil in a state of alliance and confrontation. He believed that Brazil needed new cohesion, strength, and politicization at the base, or proletarian and peasant level, not just at the vanguard level.[90]

Marighela, more a strategist than a *pensador,* had the ability to innovate, to blend the thinking of the Old Left with that of the New Left, to fuse the ideas of different theoreticians into a cohesive package. His programs, strategies, and theories for building socialism are summed up in *For the Liberation of Brazil* (1971), which includes his *Minimanual* or *Handbook of Urban Guerrilla Warfare* containing a number of ideas borrowed from Uruguayan theoretician Abraham Guillén, whose work is analyzed in my chapter on Uruguay.

Marighela stressed that revolutionaries need to understand the military before trying to overthrow it. Nelson Werneck Sodré's *História militar do Brasil* (1965) (Military History of Brazil) helped persuade him that Brazil's military had traditionally existed to protect the system by responding to class conflicts to insure that political power is not transferred to a popular base. This had been accomplished by taking actions, ostensibly to protect the constitution, but which thwarted man's desire for progress. Marighela deplored the common conception that Brazil's military, which overthrew the monarchy in the nineteenth century in favor of republicanism, has had a democratic orientation and showed that the military has always sided with the ruling class and even the overthrow only changed the form of Brazil's government, not its rulers.[91]

Marighela advocated forming an armed group to confront the military and convert Brazil's political crisis into a conflict situation forcing the military to admit that a struggle existed. The initial confrontation, he believed, should come in urban areas where the guerrillas could attack and then disappear quickly, unlike in rural areas where they would return to more permanent and vulnerable bases. He rejected the insurrectional *foco* theory (see Chapter X on Cuba) on the grounds that establishing an armed group at a specific point and then waiting for *focos* to form elsewhere was too spontaneous and would fail. He felt the need for a more exact tactical program, one that included the use of rural guerrilla warfare.

Marighela reasoned that once a permanent political crisis was unleashed, discontent would spread throughout the country and the military would be blamed for economic, social, and political failures. When the masses realized that revolutionary action was directed against their enemies, they would recognize the urban guerrillas as allies and come to their aid. At the same time, the alliance with the United States would be discredited, and when the military fell from power, the Yankees would be expelled from the country.[92]

Marighela stressed that the proletariat had to adopt a position toward the military and cited Engels's *The Role of Violence in History*, claiming that two decisive forces existed, organized state force (the military) and disorganized force in the fundamental strength of the popular masses. He believed that the proletariat must see the military as an instrument of the state and understand that the state will never permit the organization of countervailing force that could oppose or hinder the military and thereby upset the class supremacy it protects. He pointed out that the military has had a repressive and conservative class function throughout Brazil's history, that it does not understand the contradictions in Brazilian society, and that its position of class and political leadership precluded it from changing its political course in response to societal needs.[93] He asserted:

> The basic point is that the leading role of the Brazilian bourgeoisie in the revolution is not historically inevitable. . . . The proletariat can exercise its hegemony in the revolution right from the start and can struggle determinedly for this hegemony. . . . This possibility does not modify the antifeudal and antiimperialist national and democratic character of the revolution to be carried through.[94]

Once the revolution took hold, Marighela's Action for National Liberation group planned to call for the abolition of privilege and censorship; liberty of artistic expression and religion; the elimination of political police, CIA agents, and the U.S.-AID Police Mission that conducted witch hunts in Brazil; the expulsion of U.S. business people and the confiscation of their banks, lands, mineral resources, atomic materials, and ill-gotten fortunes; state control of the money market, foreign trade, public services, minerals, and communications; the break-up of land monopolies; guaranteed property rights for peasants; eradication of governmental corruption; educational reform without a U.S. orientation; and guaranteed work under the theory from each according to his capacity, to each according to his work.[95]

Putting theory into practice, Marighela's group, on September 3, 1969, kidnapped U.S. Ambassador Charles Burke Elbrick in an effort to secure the release of fifteen captured comrades. Although the captives were released and flown to freedom in Mexico, the ensuing backlash led to the reintroduction of the death penalty abolished seventy-five years earlier in Brazil and a police crackdown, in which Marighela was killed on November 4, 1969.[96]

After the death of this leading Latin American architect of urban guerrilla warfare, the militant Left in Brazil was virtually extinguished. The forces of reaction, as they did in neighboring Uruguay a few years later, retaliated against the urban guerrillas by brutally repressing all types of revolutionary and social reform action. At this writing, fourteen years after the death of Marighela, the military, operating on the same philosophy and buttressed by the same allies, still controls Brazil.

Nelson Werneck Sodré (1911–)

The most prolific and one of the most consistently profound Marxist writers and thinkers in Brazil is Nelson Werneck Sodré. A graduate of his nation's military academy who rose to the rank of general, like fellow officer Luiz Carlos Prestes he turned to the revolutionary left. Unlike Prestes, Sodré the historian writes penetrating theoretical, rhetoric-free works. He has skillfully composed over thirty books that use Marxism as a heuristic device and take cognizance of the role of class struggle and imperialism in Brazil's history. His *Evolucão política do Brasil: Ensaio de interpretação materialista da história brasileira* (1933) (Political Evolution of Brazil: A Materialist Interpretation) applied principles of historical materialism to Brazil[97] and stood for years as a model of scholarship for Brazilian Marxists.

Sodré has written on diverse topics such as fundamentals of Marxist aesthetics, the Prestes Column, racism, and the ideology of colonialism, modernization, and military history. His *Formação histórica do Brasil*(1962) (Historical Formation of Brazil)[98] traces the development of Brazilian society from its Portuguese roots and shows how it paralleled the formation of capital in the country. In his very significant book *História da burguesia brasileira* (1967) (History of the Brazilian Bourgeoisie) he showed the transformation of Brazil from the "feudal order" through the commercial revolution and noted that as a bourgeois revolution took place in Portugal, feudal relations were destroyed in Brazil too.[99] He depicted how the Brazilian bourgeoisie developed, for the most part, after the transfer of the Portuguese monarchy to the country in 1808 but remained retarded by the prevailing slave, land tenure, and seigneurial systems. After the middle of the nineteenth century the nation's economic emphasis shifted from the northeast and sugar to the south and coffee, and as the country's mercantile class grew, more power transferred to it from the landed aristocracy. At the same time, British investment in Brazil increased. Also, when slavery ended, the class structure changed again as more salaried workers appeared.

Sodré contended that the growth of foreign finance capital in Brazil led to more native finance capital, that the nation's bourgeoisie grew in size and power,[100] and that as the export economy grew, internal colonialism developed.[101] He made a strong case for the bourgeoisie's having built and maintained power by the end of the monarchy in 1889 and for their having solidified it after 1930 when more power of the *latifundistas* was broken. Sodré claimed that the peasantry, with its natural ally, the proletariat, was a potential force for social and political change but that lack of confidence in each other has precluded a mutual effort to break the power of the bourgeoisie.[102]

Years after he wrote the *História da burguesia brasileira* (1967) (History of the Brazilian Bourgeoisie), Sodré filled in some gaps in that book by writing *A coluna Prestes* (1978) (The Prestes Column), which showed Prestes's march as a natural outgrowth of the post-World War I era when many people wanted to eliminate human suffering caused by the world capitalist crisis and Brazil's extraordinary dependence and as a protest against *latifundismo*. To Sodré the march signified the initial step in the agrarian revolution, which led to the diminution of the political power of the landed aristocracy.[103] He saw *tenentismo* as petty bourgeois and reformist, an anarchistic act by some military men who defied the government that they felt did not respect the constitution or its guarantees. Sodré maintained that ultimately the movement helped transform the Communist party into a party of the masses and helped organize the Brazilian proletariat.[104] *Prestismo,* he also said, instead of leading to a proletarian revolution, led to the Vargas era, during which Brazil went through some of the changes characteristic of a bourgeois revolution but without proletarian participation. For example, Vargas's *novo estado* (new state) imposed social legislation on the working class that the latter did not advocate.[105]

Sodré's own studies often offer the best examples of what he believes Marxist *pensadores* should do. His works prove that a solid Marxist approach compels writers to analyze cause and effect, to deal with social relations with respect to material production, and by so doing clarify the relationships between classes and dominant institutions, thereby constructing a clear historical picture of societal formation. How the process works is clarified in his *Ofício de escritor: Dialéctica da literatura* (1965) (The Writer's Profession: The Dialectic of Literature), in which he delved into the interrelationships of art and society. To Sodré, like Gramsci, writers search for social reality, truths, and beauty and also re-create them through interpretations. Writers show societies' perpetual conflicts and dialogue, which are often class struggles. Sodré lent dignity to the art he discusses in a fashion reminiscent of the works of the the Russian Maxim Gorky.[106] Like Gorky, he distinguished between the technicians who transmit facts or "know-how" and intellectuals who stimulate ideas that reshape society.[107] To him, art dominated by technology becomes obedient and loses purity, autonomy, and value as art.[108]

He points out the contradictions between wage labor and intellectual labor, that under capitalism the wage laborer finds himself at the mercy of the owner of the means of production and the intellectual laborer usually does too. However, the former may well be lower class whereas the latter is generally middle class or recruited by the upper class to help preserve its traditions. He indicates that elites can afford, and usually have, monopolies on modes of expression.[109] His *História da literatura brasileira* (1976) (History of Brazilian literature) also reiterated the important role of economics in written works of art.[110]

Sodré believes that the artist should destroy the fantasies of false hope and express the realities that the future holds. To him hope is visible through revolution, not dreaming. The artist can be a missionary for almost anything, but foremost he or she must portray reality. The militant must also convey hope for humanity through creativity. Sodré shows the inherent liberty in communication, its propaganda value, and its authoritarian potential but insists that art forms remain one of the most vital ways of searching for truth.[111] He notes that socialist artists retain individuality and creativity while producing for mass viewing or reading, that social consciousness can be retained in the course of doing an individual piece. Art, he maintains, should be built on the liberation of the mind, dedicated to reflecting social conditions, as well as to encouraging and bringing about change, to foster independence, not to deepen dependency. Written art, in particular, he views as a form of consciousness; thus writing can contribute to liberty of the mind and then to deeds.[112]

Sodré expresses deep concern for maintaining artistic style, form, and content; with the socialist role of the artist and his or her place in the market; and with sustaining high literary and artistic standards within a socialist perspective. He understands the contradiction between the artist who works alone, but produces for mass consumption or the community, and resolves it by asking whether the artist injects individual or collective value into his or her work.[113] He realizes that culture generally has been controlled by bourgeois power but feels that it can be otherwise, a fact borne out by his own life and work.

His profound insights into the origins and effects of Marxist art and literature and the overall quality of his many creative "plain" Marxist analyses of his nation's history mark Sodré as the consummate Brazilian socialist *pensador*. Although his work is generally broader in scope than that of most of his fellow Marxist thinkers, it also evaluates and incorporates the fruits of their respective labors. From *Prestismo* and the exploits of Luiz Carlos Prestes, Sodré derived inspiration and proof that dedicated effort can alter the thinking of a people. Prado's meticulous scientific analyses of colonial Brazil served as a model for Sodré's studies of other historical epochs as did Basbaum's multidimensional applications of Marxist thought.

Sodré, to a great extent, shares a common view of Brazilian history with the Marxists featured in this chapter. They all basically accept the dual society concept, agree on how class structures evolved and on the timing and the mechanics of the transfer of power from one class to another, and on the political and social consequences of *Prestismo* and Vargas's *novo estado*. Despite the fact that, at times, they have advocated different strategies for revolution, these Brazilian thinkers have embraced a common faith in socialism as the more humane road to "progress" and have rejected positivism, which has accentuated the competitiveness of the class struggle and has too often brutally enforced "order" in Brazil.

6. Peru

Marxism is a method that anchors itself fully in reality, in actual events. It is not, as some erroneously suppose, a body of rigid predictions, applicable in the same fashion to all historical climates and social latitudes. Marx took his method from the very entrails of history.

José Carlos Mariátegui

Scholasticism runs deep in Peru, which has produced some of Latin America's outstanding political and social thinkers. Positivism, too, has long roots planted there in the nineteenth century. But in the twentieth century, Marxists have made as significant contributions as any group to the climate of intellectual growth and liberty in the country.

As early as 1884, European-oriented anarcho-syndicalists formed the Artisans Union in Peru. But their ideas, as well as the subsequent thinking of the Russian revolution, were soon eclipsed by those of Peruvian *pensadores,* who emphasized native themes. By the 1920s *indigenismo,* a movement to assimilate the Indians into civilization while preserving their culture, became the major concern of a larger segment of Peru's intellectual community whose ideas quickly spread throughout Latin America. Peruvian thinkers were, and still are, at the forefront of the region's anti-imperialist, anti-Yankee movement, which gained momentum from the 1920s to the 1960s. Peruvian intellectuals were among the first in Latin America during the post-World War II era to combine European Marxist doctrines with new theories pertaining to economically underdeveloped countries and the Third World.

By the 1960s a social-progressive school of thought existed in Peru, based upon the principles of Marxist humanism, historicism, a bit of existentialism, and a little speculation. This mélange of theorists and thinkers produced some of the region's most profound dependency paradigms, which continue to provoke thought and controversy in scholarly circles.

No analysis of Marxist thought in Peru would be complete without mention of Manuel González Prada (1848–1918), who, although primarily a positivist, displayed anarchist tendencies and who some call the father of radicalism in his country.

González Prada rejected historical materialism and socialism but was aware of the class base in Peruvian society and politics. A well-educated aristocrat, he attributed Peru's problems primarily to a socioeconomic structure that kept the masses from participating in national governance while the aristocracy perpetuated its position at the expense of the native workers.[1] He believed revolution could solve most problems, and that it could begin to be forged in urban areas by an alliance between intellectuals and physical laborers. He envisioned it spreading to rural regions as Indian consciousness was eventually raised to revolutionary pitch.[2]

After Peru lost valuable territory to Chile in the War of the Pacific (1879–1883), González Prada became disenchanted with his country's institutions. To him, Peru represented *caudillismo* (bossism) grafted on to a U.S.-style constitutionalism, a system that increased social and racial inequities. He inveighed against Spanish values, the Catholic church, and the military elites, hoping to destroy them by educating the masses. He exhorted the workers to rebel, urging them to adopt the ideas of Bakunin, Kropotkin, and Proudhon. He assailed Peru's laissez-faire economics and pseudodemocratic systems.

González Prada served as a consciousness-raiser who affected all subsequent generations of Peruvian political and social scientists, for whom his collected works, *Anarquía* (1936), were standard fare. He began a new intellectual and literary tradition emphasizing recognition of the social value of the Indian culture and an independent Peru. From his works we see a linear progression in Peruvian political and social thought, one followed by José Carlos Mariátegui, Víctor Raúl Haya de la Torre, and Luis Alberto Sánchez, even extending beyond Peru to the Mexican (1910) and Bolivian (1952) revolutions. For example, he pointed out the antithesis between colonialism and *indigenismo,* just as Mariátegui later noted the antithesis between capitalism and anticapitalism. Although González Prada neglected the idea of the dictatorship of the proletariat, his thinking significantly influenced Mariátegui and the whole Generation of 1919, which believed in political revolution.[3]

José Carlos Mariátegui (1894–1930)

No Latin American Marxist receives more acknowledgments of intellectual indebtedness from fellow thinkers than José Carlos Mariátequi. Born to poverty, afflicted by poor health, and largely self-educated, he became enamored of the printed word while a teenager working as a typesetter. Intellectually, he grew from a devotee of the Spanish mystics to a critical Marxist *pensador* capable of adapting sophisticated principles of European socialism to a Latin American context.

Mariátequi first learned about socialism from his friend and fellow writer Abraham Valdelomar, who had spent time in Europe and was particularly excited by the anarcho-syndicalist ideas of Georges Sorel. Between 1919 and 1923 Mariátegui, while in exile from the dictatorship of Augusto Leguía, traveled in Europe, was impressed by Italy's Communists, and inspired by French socialist Henri Barbusse, who imbued him with a sense of political direction. In Europe his vision of Latin America clarified, and he began to see hope in the struggle between capitalism and socialism.[4] He made the transition from a utopian socialist to a scientific socialist, moving from a sentimental "feeling stage" to one of more profound belief and conviction and deeper analysis of society.[5]

Upon returning to Peru in 1923, he took over the editorship of the periodical *Claridad* (Clarity) from Haya de la Torre, whom he subsequently viewed as a liberal reformer devoid of an international revolutionary ideology. Doctrinal and personal differences caused him to openly split with Haya in 1928, and he then helped form the Peruvian Socialist party and Peru's General Confederation of Workers.

The writings of Matiátegui, who founded the socialist magazine *Amauta*, fill eight volumes and cover a variety of topics, including political theory, international relations, economics, land tenure, regionalism, the Church, Indian problems, and literary criticism. He also wrote under the name Juan Croniqueur for the theater.[6] Historian Augusto Salazar Bondy called Mariátegui's greatest achievement the application of Marxist methodology to a comprehension of Peruvian history and society.[7] He viewed Marátegui as an exponent of "open Marxism," the idea that Marxist thought should be revisable, undogmatic, and adaptable to new situations.[8] Mariátegui knew that Latin America faced different problems from Europe, to which Marx's thinking was tuned.[9]

Primarily an essayist who wrote in a penetrating and vivid style, Mariátegui was not a trained political theorist, and his work often appeared unsystematic. He was, and is, a major force in Peruvianism. He interpreted the spirit of revolutionary Marxism in an effective literary fashion, and his famous *Siete ensayos de interpretación de la realidad peruana* (1928) (Seven Interpretative Essays on Peruvian Reality) served as a rudimentary revolutionary program for his country.

Mariátegui understood the conflict between nativism and Europeanism and advocated Peru for the Peruvians, a premise still paid considerable lip service in the country. According to Jesús Chavarría, his biographer, Mariátegui felt that myth, hope, and faith were essential elements of humanity and would foster a revolutionary consciousness. Myth implied that social revolution embodied an eternal verity, and Mariátegui believed that it could become true and lead to the final struggle. Mariátegui emerged as a voluntarist, who emphasized individual choice in decision making, rather than as a determinist.[10] He believed that deterministic factors in Marxism could stifle creativity and that the revolutionary myth must not be eliminated, or with it would be lost the humanistic qualities of Marxism.[11]

Mariátegui's first priority was to solve social problems. He thought that all intellectuals were obligated to work for social justice. He realized that intellectuals, often with a great appreciation for tradition, frequently were conservative and averse to change[12] and that they all, himself included, operated from a bias. He asserted: "I am no impartial and objective critic. My judgments are nourished from my ideals, my sentiments, my passions. I have a strong and declared aim to contribute to the creation of a Peruvian socialism."[13]

The 1918 University Reform Movement, more than any other factor, he believed, aroused the consciousness of Latin American intellectuals. Although they were not converted to socialism by the movement, some of them were proletarianized by it. Students from aristocratic backgrounds displayed a class consciousness, and some of them, after sorting out class differences, found themselves spiritually aligned with the proletariat. Mariátegui maintained that "new" and "old" socialists would coalesce to form an intellectual elite that would lead the revolution.

This book cannot do justice to one of Mariátegui's stature in intellectual circles in Latin America.[14] Chapters could be devoted to those who influenced him. But for our purposes a few paragraphs will have to suffice. His work reflects the thinking on Indian and land tenure problems of his contemporary Hildebrando Castro Pozo, whose thinking Mariátegui also affected. From González Prada, he gleaned ideas on national integration based upon Indianism and on land reform. He shred González Prada's disdain for European cultural imperialism and his dislike of the Church's intrusions in temporal affairs. He learned from his countryman the value of militancy, of indoctrinating workers and students, and of the need for an intellectual-proletarian alliance for revolution.

The writings of Argentine man-of-letters and statesman Domingo F. Sarmiento enabled Mariátegui to see that European and Western science and thought could be the basis of Latin America's salvation if applied in a flexible fashion compatible with the region's culture and tradition. However, he did not share Sarmiento's racist idea of breeding the barbarity out of the indigenous race.[15] Mariátegui referred to the antiimperialism of Manuel Ugarte[16] and to José Ingenieros as a thought-provoking teacher whose ideas could help transform culture.[17]

Like Spanish philosopher José Ortega y Gasset, some of whose work he read, Mariátegui rejected the capitalist notion of mass man devoid of individual creativity. From Oswald Spengler he acquired the belief that Western Europe and the United States were in a state of decline, leading him to conclude that a new civilization, one built on native ideals, could emerge in Latin America.[18] Marx's writings convinced him that man had the moral obligation to share the material benefits of society instead of surviving by exploiting fellow human beings.[19] He admired the tenacity, not the inhumanity, of Friedrich Nietzsche.

Mariátegui's later ideas on race and class were derived from Nikolai Bukharin's *Historical Materialism: A System of Sociology* (1921), which stressed that the status of a people is derived from its connection to the relations of production.[20] Max Eastman's *Marx and Lenin: The Science of Revolution* (1927) made

Mariátegui aware that both Freudian analysis and Marxian analysis basically reveal self-interest, a major bourgeois characteristic.[21]

Mariátegui's *Defensa del marxismo* (1934) (Defense of Marxism) championed Henri de Man's ethical socialism based on humanitarian principles that elevated the proletariat,[22] yet the book contained a Leninist tone. The Peruvian *pensador* followed Lenin's thinking on imperialism and considered that Russian the ideal revolutionary leader. The thinking of Frenchman Georges Sorel strengthened Mariátegui's view of Marx's "original dynamic revolutionary conception of spontaneous violent class struggle."[23]

Despite the aforementioned contacts, Mariátegui's greatest debts extended to Italy where he formed his socialist sympathies. Through the ideas of Italian writer Piero Gobetti, who emphasized moral regeneration and man's ability to control his consciousness[24] and demonstrated the value of proletarian discipline in the revolutionary struggle, Mariátegui became acquainted with the thinking of Antonio Gramsci.

Gobetti and Gramsci, who collaborated on the publication of the journal *L'Ordine Nuovo,* were both influenced by Benedetto Croce, the neo-Hegelian philosopher whose work convinced them of the validity of Sorel. They both believed in the role of intellectuals in controlling the revolution.[25] Mariátegui, like Gramsci, felt that for him politics included both philosophy and religion. They also agreed that successful socialist revolution occurs only when Marxist theory is attuned to national conditions,[26] that one deals with regional or national problems, often through popular culture, enroute to internationalism. Both Gramsci and Mariátegui advocated flexible, non-deterministic, and dynamic Marxism.[27]

Not until after World War II did Latin American *pensadores* become aware of the extent of Mariátegui's debt to Gramsci. Then the writings of the Italian Communist became popular in the area. It is interesting that although Mariátegui met Gramsci once briefly in 1921, Hugo Pesce, one of Mariátegui's closest intellectual *compañeros*, stated that his friend never referred to Gramsci or his ideas.[28] While at the Institute for Gramsci Studies in Rome in 1979 I uncovered no personal links between the two thinkers, either through printed works or correspondence. Nevertheless, anyone who reads Mariátegui cannot overlook the great influence upon him by the *Ordine Nuovo* group in Turin, Italy, which included Gobetti, the famous communist Palmiro Togliatti, and especially Gramsci.

Mariátegui's Italian experiences helped him adapt socialism to the Latin American and Peruvian ethos. Rejecting the positivist ideas prevalent among his country's intellectuals in favor of the dialectical process in which socialism was the historical stage following capitalism, he theorized that nations learned more about themselves if they analyzed closely what occurred as they moved from stage to stage. Applying this theory to Peru, he concluded that the political and economic structures of Peru had not changed after independence—a movement that he felt was primarily economically motivated. He noted that even the British banking houses wanted the independence movement to succeed to protect their investments in Latin America and to help them place more capital abroad.[29] He reasoned that after independence the European economic system never attained equilibrium in Peru. Monopoly and privilege remained even during nitrate and guano booms when a new wealthy class formed and allied politically with the vestiges of the landed gentry.

Mariátegui spoke repeatedly and fondly of the 1917 revolution, which gave him hope for a new Latin American society where aspects of the Russian experiment could be repeated. He also saw Russian communism as too materialistic and unfit to build upon in a primarily Indian country like Peru.[30] He stated: "socialism is certainly not an Indo-American doctrine. But no doctrine nor contemporary system is. And socialism, although born in Europe from capitalism, is not specifically European. It is a world movement."[31]

Mariátegui realized that Marx did not create socialism; rather he interpreted the historical process that would give rise to it. He tried to perform a similar service for Latin America. He adhered to Lenin's interpretation of Marx, believing that the class struggle first has to be fought on a national level, that before Peru could ally with the oppressed peoples of the world, it had to cultivate national unity and identity. He insisted that he was not a nationalist or an indigenist, simply a socialist.[32] He referred to his theories as "socialist," did not hesitate to declare himself a Marxist, but refused to be subservient to the Comintern.

Mariátegui rejected the idea of achieving socialism through an alliance with the national bourgeoisie and founded the Peruvian Socialist party, which he envisioned being composed of the proletariat, the peasants, and some petty bourgeois elements. Initially, he accentuated a blending of socialist revolution and Indian nationalism but admitted that internationalism was a higher stage of development that would subsequently supplant nationalism.[33] He advocated left-wing unity in Peru, in contrast to the sectarianism he had seen in Europe. Mariátegui, like Gramsci, believed that a spontaneous revolution could occur and pointed out that industry and an industrial proletariat could not be expected for a long time in Peru, and thus the revolution had to come from other quarters.

In some ways he presaged Mao Zedong as he valued ancient indigenous collectivism as an inspiration to revolution—one fostered by the rural masses before the middle classes finished building capitalism. He viewed parts of twentieth-century Peru as still in colonial or feudal stages and concurred with Gramsci's belief that capitalism could be created by socialists on their way to socialism. Simultaneously, he rejected social democracy on the grounds that its followers who wanted to build socialism through the existing parliamentary institutions were too idealistic and doomed to fail.

Mariátegui, like Gramsci, believed that one should not reduce problems solely to economic causes. For him, the class struggle was paramount, and economics were the weapons, or manifestations, of class antagonisms[34] that transcended national boundaries. He saw the creation of socialism as hindered by economic ties to Western capitalist markets. To him, Peru's landowners, or capitalist bourgeoisie, were satisfied to function as intermediaries for foreign capital, which controlled the nation's commerce, transportation, and mines. He attributed such situations, which fostered economic and political dependency, to intellectual dependence—the belief that Latin American thought existed only as an approximation of Western European ideas—and believed that the latter would have to be supplanted by indigenous ideas to lessen dependency.

In *Defensa del marxismo* he explained Peru's dependency by asserting that when production began to exceed consumption in the United States, the nation searched for external markets. Borrowing from Trotsky's thinking, he depicted the surplus of gold flowing into the United States as a detriment since the nation's industrial sector could no longer absorb its profits. Gold reserves built up, and it became necessary to expand overseas to place excess capital, thus extending foreign dependency. Imperialism, he said, went wild, entering the final stage of capitalism on a grand scale. He noted the spread of capitalist monopoly at the expense of free competition—monopoly expressed in terms of imperialism. In a classical Leninist sense, Mariátegui saw the United States accomplishing its historic mission, with imperialism being the final stage of capitalism, which he interpreted as the road to destruction. To him World War I was a major watershed in the deterioration of capitalism. The League of Nations formed in an attempt to restore order to the system. The league epitomized international capitalism, as it was designed to benefit the bourgeois and upper classes, and proved detrimental to the proletariat whose post-World War I needs it ignored.[35] Mariátegui's thinking was, perhaps, borne out by World War II, which erupted as a result of the German people's needs not being met, economic frustration, competition for markets within the capitalist system, and the actions of Adolf Hitler.

Mariátegui attempted to analyze Peru's revolutionary potential by understanding its indigenous past from a materialist perspective. His *Seven Interpretive Essays* combined Marxist analysis of the material base of Peruvian society with his voluntarist ideas on its superstructure.[36] He concluded that given conditions in Peru, it was best to omit the classical Marxist bourgeois-democratic revolution and proceed directly to an indigenous socialist national liberation movement.[37]

Mariátegui had no faith in *mestizo* America or in José Vasconcelos's "cosmic race" (a Latin American melting pot)[38] to lead the revolution. He did not believe that the fundamental problem of Peru was racial in nature but felt it was basically social and economic,[39] an agrarian problem, not an ethnic one, in which the Indians suffered most as their lands fell into the hands of corporations cooperating with Peru's bourgeoisie. He believed that the Indians could effect change in Peru because of their habit of assimilating progress and their spirit and discipline to overcome adversity.[40] He did not expect Peru's fundamentally conservative rural Indians to spontaneously awaken and lead a revolution. He believed that militant urban intellectuals, who comprehended the indigenous spirit, had to work to re-create collectivist attitudes among the peasantry.

By combining socialism and Indianism, Mariátegui hoped to restore the old Inca communal land patterns, which would alleviate land tenure problems and put power in the hands of the people—

actions that would spread beyond Peru's boundaries. He advocated building a mass peasant organization to defeat *gamonalismo* (rural bossism) or the hegemony of the semifeudal landed estate owners over the policy-making mechanisms of the government.[41] To him, *gamonalismo* constituted the greatest impediment to Peruvian development. He asserted that rural labor suffered as capitalism bloomed in the cities. He categorized capitalism as basically an urban phenomenon producing internal colonialism.

Mariátegui extolled the virtues of pre-Columbian life and values as a psychological prod to revolution but did not reject the West entirely. He believed that Indians had to utilize Western political and social theory in order to build a socialist revolution. He was simultaneously a passionate popularizer of Indian culture and art and an outspoken advocate of using Marx's scientific method to solve Latin America's problems. He saw in the Inca past a characteristic that coalesced with his socialist projections for the future— a state that assumes total material and moral responsibility for its citizens, wherein no one went without life's basic necessities. He did not want to use the Inca system as a model per se, with its theocracy, absolutism, and rigidity; he merely wanted to borrow its sense of community.[42]

Mariátegui delved into a myriad of topics. Among the more significant ones was religion. The son of an ultrareligious Roman Catholic mother, he went beyond the basic faith he was taught as a youth and acquired an understanding of religion and its role in society. He concluded that religious sentiment could not be resolved by philosophy as the nineteenth-century rationalists tried to do, that "present revolutionary and social myths can fill the deep consciousness of men with the same fullness as the ancient religious myths."[43] For him Marxism was a truer religion than Christianity. Like the latter-day Cuban revolutionary Fidel Castro, he believed that struggle for economic and social change would produce religious changes, that it was not necessary to wage an antiholy war on religion. He equated Protestantism with the acceleration of the historical process and the rise of capitalism but never condemned Catholicism per se, only the church of Rome.[44] He believed that the Church, Peru's largest landowner, had to be reduced to its proper place in terms of economic and political influence.

Mariátegui understood why González Prada called Peruvian women "slaves of the Church" and hoped that women could attain more independence as they were doing in Europe. Under Mariátegui's direction the journal *Amauta* carried numerous articles to enunciate a political role for women. The journal popularized the works of artist Julia Codesio, sculptress Carmen Saco, and writer María Wiesse and provided other women a vehicle to express themselves both in politics and art.[45]

Mariátegui, like González Prada, thought that all art forms had a social function and helped prepare the way for socialism. He pointed out the vital role played by practitioners of the fine arts, as well as writers, in the creation of anticapitalist revolutionary thought.[46] He claimed that revolutionary artists should emphasize social and political questions and not engage in diversionary forms such as futurism and arielism.[47]

Mariátegui added numerous dimensions to Marxist thought in Latin America. His ideas helped launch both radical reform and revolutionary movements. More than any other Latin American political thinker, except perhaps his countryman Haya de la Torre, he promoted *Indianismo,* which became a vital part of the Bolivian, Guatemalan, and Mexican revolutions, as well as an integral part of Peru's national ethos. He learned from and contributed to the Mexican Revolution, which he considered an important non-Marxian movement dedicated to the overthrow of feudalism and oriented toward land reform and the return of Indian properties.[48] Mariátegui influenced the socialist thinkers and groups that emerged in Peru after his death. Also, in many ways the reformist *Aprista* ideology was derived from Mariátegui, as was the thinking of the highly nationalist state-capitalist military that controlled Peru from 1968 to 1980.

He professed a desire, unique among Marxist *pensadores,* to bring about an inner revolution in man or to add an element of personal radicalism to Latin America's leftist movement.[49] His ideas elicited a great deal of support, but also spawned an anti-Marxist school of thought in Peru during the 1930s led by Víctor Andrés Belaúnde, who created a Catholic replica of the *Seven Interpretive Essays.* However, this Church-supported movement, later joined by advocates of the social doctrine of fascism, never succeeded in diminishing the spirit of the thinking of Mariátegui, godfather of contemporary Latin American Marxism and precursor of Franz Fanon, who postulated the concept of Third World revolution.

Hildebrando Castro Pozo (1890–1945)
and Ricardo Martínez de la Torre

Among Peru's liberal and radical twentieth-century *pensadores* the role of the indigenous folk and their relationship to the land rank along with politics and the state as one of the most dissected themes. An early thinker who confronted systematically the problems of *indianismo* and land tenure was Socialist party leader, lawyer, and political theorist Hildebrando Castro Pozo, whose career overlapped that of his *compañero* Mariátegui.

Castro Pozo, author of *Nuestra comunidad indígena* (1924) (Our Indigenous Community)[50] and *Del ayllu al cooperativismo socialista* (1936) (The Ayllu and Cooperative Socialism),[51] claimed that, despite the disastrous affects of the hacienda system, the Indians had retained their cultural heritage and social values. He believed that capitalism and its colonial component had destroyed their land-holding system and that what existed in the twentieth century had to be replaced by agrarian collectivism if social justice were to be obtained by the peasantry.

Castro Pozo depicted the continuous destruction of the pre-Columbian communal system in Peru and the domination of life by the urban bourgeoisie armed with foreign capital. He advocated adding the spirit of Marx, in the context of Peruvian reality, to the pre-Columbian communal tradition. He viewed the revival of the *ayllu*, the cooperative agricultural community, as a step toward a more socialistic society, which would simultaneously help solve Peru's food shortage problem and break dependence upon foreign capital. By applying historical materialism to Peru, he envisioned recapturing some aspects of a more moral civilization, one with fewer racial, social, and class prejudices and one sufficiently glorious to inspire twentieth-century revolutions.[52]

Castro Pozo did not, by himself, prove a worthy successor to Jose Mariátegui, but with his contemporary Ricardo Martínez de la Torre, he helped bridge the gap in Peruvian Marxist thought left by the premature death of their more well-known colleague. Martínez de la Torre continued Mariátegui's work when he founded, in 1931, the magazine *Frente* (The Front) based on the principles of historical materialism.

The author of the four-volume collection of materials on the evolution of Peruvian socialism, *Apuntes para una interpretación marxista de historia social del Perú* (1935–1949) (Points for the Marxist Interpretation of the Social History of Peru),[53] Martínez de la Torre analyzed the Peru of his day, emphasizing the role of labor in the country's daily life and its politics.[54] Taking off from Mariátegui, he described the social justice aims of the University Reform Movement, which he believed signaled the end of the aristocratic scholastic tradition in education and of the plutocratic system of government that had endured from colonial days. He projected socialism as the logical extension of the University Reform Movement.

Martínez de la Torre touched upon anticlerical and antiimperialist themes and, to a lesser degree, the class struggle in Peru, which, during the time that he wrote, he saw existing primarily in terms of the petty bourgeoisie versus the aristocratic plutocracy. He categorized the Depression as a watershed in Peruvian and Latin American history, a period that exacerbated and clarified the class struggle, especially in the monocultural nations that suffered the most during this period of economic collapse.[55] On a positive note, he realized that the Depression heightened awareness of the defects of the capitalist system, particularly in dependent Peru where the nation suffered under the oppression of foreign imperialism.

In many ways the works of Castro Pozo and Martínez de la Torre did not match the breadth or style of that of Mariátegui, but they provided continuity in Peru's chain of Marxist thought from the master to a new generation of socialist *pensadores,* which began to make itself known during the 1960s.

Hugo Blanco Galdós (1933–)

After the death of Mariátegui in 1930, Marxism was somewhat eclipsed in Peru by Víctor Raúl Haya de la Torre's reformist *Aprista* movement, which stressed antiimperialism, Latin American unity, nationalization of land and industry, internationalization of the Panama Canal, and solidarity with the oppressed people and classes of the world. A whole generation of Peru's outstanding thinkers was attracted to *Aprismo,* which advocated a democratic state run by a populist coalition of workers, peasants, and the petty bourgeoisie, with the backing of private sector industry. Haya de la Torre sought social change, not based on class struggle, but under the direction of a national, multiclass revolution. He offered many of the social and economic changes proposed by Marx without the inevitable grand conflict. He accepted the Marxist notion of history as a series of conflicts, but not universal ones, and he refuted determinism.

Haya de la Torre, like Mariátegui, sought historical reality for Latin America and Peru on the basis of Indo-America apart from Europe. Unlike Mariátegui, he viewed economic imperialism as progressive in that it stimulated the development of a modern proletariat and provided capital for growth.[56] Haya de la Torre believed in the possibility of social and economic change without extreme violence, which appealed to outstanding Peruvian intellectuals like Luis Alberto Sánchez, who rejected Marxism in favor of *Aprismo*.

The *Apristas* and Haya de la Torre dominated left-of-center politics in Peru until the 1960s when it became evident that the nation's military would not permit the election of Haya de la Torre to the presidency. After forty years of struggle and political prominence, *Aprismo* lost influence in Peru. Young intellectuals, sensing the failure of the reformists like Haya de la Torre, who by now were willing to ally with the conservatives in order to capture political office, sought more radical, revolutionary roads to social, economic, and political change. Most successful and prominent among the new generation of Marxist thinker-activists was Hugo Blanco Galdós.

A man of middle-class origins, Blanco as a youth was caught up in the atmosphere of *Indianismo*, which prevailed in the predominantly Quechua area in and around Cuzco. Early in his life he became familiar with the thinking of Mariátegui and Haya de la Torre and gained a healthy repsect for the approach to Indianism taken by Haya de la Torre's *Alianza Popular Revolucionaria Americana* (APRA) (Popular American Revolutionary Alliance).

While studying under Hugo Bressaro at the University of La Plata in Argentina, Blanco became a devotee of the thinking of Leon Trotsky. From Bressaro, he got the ideas of bringing the peasants to action through unions on both the regional and national levels and of eliminating the power of the landowners by organizing workers and seizing the land where its owners did not share their benefits with the *campesinos*.

Blanco returned to Peru, joined the young Trotskyist movement, which had been in existence there since 1944, organized peasant unions in Convención and Lares provinces between 1958 and 1963, and in turn had the unions establish schools and health clinics and educate and heighten the consciousness of the peasants.[57] Blanco worked for the time when his unions would also control rural education, public works projects, and the administration of justice. Blanco's position on the peasants approximated that of Mao Zedong, except that the Peruvian believed that the *campesinos'* revolutionary fervor diminished when they received land and became bourgeois. He contended that the real hope for maintaining the revolution was in the proletariat.

Blanco followed the thinking of the Fourth International, repeatedly repudiated the Communists as reformists, and defended the Marxist-Leninist postulate that there is no possibility of the exploiters relinquishing power without a struggle—that a peaceful transition to socialism is not possible.[58] He maintained that armed struggle is a necessary phase of revolution—part of a process through which the masses raise their consciousness, organize, and are guided by a revolutionary vanguard.

Blanco's book *Land or Death* (1972) explains how, via transitional stages, a revolutionary program can be converted into mass actions, an important contribution to the theory of revolution in Latin America. It is the antithesis of the *foco* theory, as it demonstrates how armed struggle can be derived from mass movements.[59] Blanco criticizes the *foco* theory of Régis Debray and Che Guevara for lacking the party concept and not following scientific Marxism. He warned that one must not confuse simple guerrilla warfare with revolution, that the Cuban revolution underestimated the significance of mass movements and tended to glorify isolated heroic acts.[60] Blanco states that guerrilla warfare should not be used artifically but that it is fine when it evolves naturally out of a given situation, such as the political development of the peasants in Peru. For him, and other sophisticated standard interpretors of Trotsky, guerrilla warfare is a tactic possible in a specific country under particular conditions, but it is not a strategy that has to be used.[61]

Like Mariátegui, Blanco depicted *gamonalismo* as the main obstacle to social and economic progress in Peru.[62] He strove to break the peasants' subservience and to expand their horizons, not to reinforce their isolation. To him, Indian Peru connoted both the communal ideal of Mariátegui and Castro Pozo and a lumpenproletariat dominated by a false consciousness instilled by the Church and the *gamonales* (bosses).[63]

Blanco envisioned two powers confronting each other in Peru, the exploiters representing a shameful past, and the exploited proclaiming the future. He thought of the latter as a union militia leading the armed struggle,[64] eventually taking the oligarchy's power and creating a system wherein power resides in the masses.[65]

Blanco's 1962 letter to his comrades in the Convención Valley summarized his Marxist overview. In it he claimed that the Soviet Union had not attained socialism, nor will it until the revolution is victorious internationally—thus reaffirming Trotsky's theory of Permanent Revolution. He stated that the Peruvian revolutionary process marked the end of the Stalinist theory of "revolution by stages," which incorrectly asserted "that our revolution can only be bourgeois-democratic and that the local capitalists whom they call progressive bourgeois will join us in our fight against land-lordism and imperialism."[66]

Blanco for a time successfully promoted noncooperation, the refusal of the *campesinos* to perform work on *estancias* (estates). Meanwhile, he urged them to cultivate plots of land designated for their own use. His activities on behalf of the peasantry abated when he received a twenty-five-year prison sentence in 1963.

Blanco would say that he failed to build a lasting and viable movement in Peru for two reasons. First, the leftist organizations in the cities did not join the struggle and permit the proletariat to take over from the peasants as he had projected. Second, there never existed a Leninist combat party in Peru on a national scale.

Despite repeated setbacks, Blanco tried to sustain his revolutionary efforts. However, much of the fervor of his movement was lost to the reform-minded state-capitalist military government, which took over Peru in 1968. Using leftist rhetoric, the nationalist military implemented some of the ideas of Mariátegui and Blanco. For example, it promoted *Peruanidad* (Peruvianism or Peru for the Peruvians), land reform, and nationalized foreign industries and conducted a forceful campaign against Yankee imperialism.

Sensing that Blanco had lost the political clout that he had during the early 1960s, the government released him from prison in 1970 whereupon he resumed, briefly, his revolutionary activities and then went into exile in Mexico. He returned to Peru in 1975 only to face exile again. In 1978 he was elected to Peru's Constitutional Assembly, which prepared for the restoration of civilian political control in the nation. Functioning as a member of a student-worker association, he antagonized the government, which feared that a Blanco-led Marxist coalition would capture the presidency in the 1980 elections. Thus, in 1979 he was imprisoned, as the military readied the nation for the subsequent election to the presidency of non-Marxist civilian Fernando Belaúnde-Terry.

Aníbal Quijano

Numerous young Marxist intellectuals appeared in Peru's institutions of higher learning during the 1960s and 1970s. We do not have sufficient space to devote to most of them here. The inclusion of one outstanding creative "plain" Marxist scholar, sociologist Aníbal Quijano, director of the journal *Sociedad y Política* (Society and Politics), will have to suffice for our purposes.

Carrying on the tradition of Mariátegui, Castro Pozo, and González Prada, Quijano developed a great deal of interest in and expertise about peasant movements, which he viewed as the logical extension of *Peruanidad* and *indigenismo*. His work combines scientific Marxist analyses, especially the teachings of Lenin and Mao, with the latest principles of political sociology. Joining theory and praxis neatly, he elaborates formulas tailored to Latin America's reality.

Quijano is critical of Blanco and the Trotskyists, whom he believes uphold the idea of a new state apparatus rising above the masses. He questions that the apparatus represents the people or serves as an adequate model of a revolutionary power structure. Quijano condemns the Trostskyists for failing to build a system based on the direct power of the workers.[67]

He provides an excellent theoretical explanation of why socialism has not taken hold in Latin America in *Crisis imperialista y clase obrera en América Latina* (1974)[68] (The Imperialist Crisis and the Working Class in Latin America). He indicates that Latin America still searches for the proper socialist model and that the Left in the area is divided among those who follow the Bolshevik model, Maosim, the *foco* or Cuban revolutionary theory, the syndicate or trade union lead, or the urban or rural guerrilla paths to revolution. He feels that it is exceedingly difficult to organize these factions and points to the situation in Chile during the early 1970s as an example of the inability to devise a program to function evenly at all levels of proletarian development. This he believes is compounded by the difficulty of constructing political ties between the Latin American nations, not to mention the problems of building internal left-wing alliances.[69]

Quijano notes that the *Aprista* movement retarded the growth of the radical Left in Peru as it provided a viable, less potentially violent, antioligarchic and antiimperialist alternative. In addition to being somewhat co-opted by APRA, he contends that three basic problems have prevented the rise of socialism in Peru and Latin America. (1) There exists no effective Latin American-oriented theory upon which to initiate revolutionary movements. (2) The region's numerically dominant classes have not been organized and mobilized. (3) The masses have not developed the capacity for violent revolution. In other words, Quijano sees that the organized movements lack cohesive theories of revolution, that the connections between groups are tenuous, and that the capacities for organized mass revolution are undeveloped and weak.[70] He cites the failure to revolutionize the workers as the major reason for lack of socialist success or growth. He also notes that mechanization and automation have replaced workers and diminished their revolutionary potential.[71]

Quijano refutes the beliefs that Peru derived from a feudal structure established by the Spanish and that two societies coexist in the nation—each with its own historical characteristics and structural laws but integrated by a common political apparatus, with the capitalist sector directly dependent upon foreign capital and the feudal one only peripherally dependent on the capitalist sector.[72] He indicates how, historically, the middle class has grown in the country as capital intensive industrialization increased, economic growth continued, and unemployment and poverty have increased.[73]

Quijano depicts the historical shifts in Peru's dependent capitalism from Spain to Great Britain to the United States to the latest (post-1968) shift from the United States to dependence upon internationally owned funds in association with native urban capitalists. Under the old dependency arrangements, he notes that foreign capital dominated primarily in sectors like agriculture, cattle raising, and mining, but under the new system it also penetrates urban manufacturing and business.[74] He clarifies the relationship between the bourgeois state, monopoly capital, and international monopolies, between the dependent bourgeoisie and their foreign controllers.[75]

Quijano avers that in the majority of Latin American countries the central model of capital accumulation is semicolonial and the basic mode of relations of production are precapitalist. Most funds come from external sources, and the possibilities of expanding internal markets are blocked by external sources and the inability of the native bourgeoisie to capture total political power. He also indicates that a conflict exists between the imperialists and the native bourgeoisie, as the former exercise a disproportionate amount of power over the latter.[76]

Quijano believes that imperialism is the final stage of capitalism, but only in advanced industrial nations, and that for economically backward countries that receive capitalism, imperialism is the initial stage. In this sense, he concurs with the thinking of Haya de la Torre.[77] He points out how the international division of production changed after World War II, and with it came a revitalization of the class struggle at all levels. He envisions socialism coming to the fore soon because capitalism entered its final crisis after World War II.[78] He believes that in the two decades following the war, the United States proved incapable of leading the capitalist states toward the reestablishment of the legitimacy and respectability of the bourgeois social system. The dependent bourgeoisies and the dependent nation states they controlled, like Peru, began to realize that they had more freedom to maneuver and started to push for new advantages and economic and political ties.[79]

He shows that the aforementioned factors, together with the advancement of international monopoly capital and the failure of the national bourgeoisie to develop a viable economy, led Peru to shift to state capitalism, which he defines as an attempt to absorb and control the contradictions between the degree of internal development and the forces of production that derive from the expansion of new forms of international accumulation and monopoly capital. To him, state capitalism is a means whereby dependency, which will not be totally eradicated, can be modified with the state as the principal negotiator in the process.[80] He calls state capitalism, as it has evolved to some degree in Bolivia, Brazil, Chile, Mexico, and Peru, a Latin American phenomenon.[81] He says that state capitalism has developed to control the conflicts

between capital and labor, that it is dominated politically by a
bureaucratic and technological class that moves it toward a capitalist corporate state, which is nationalistic and antioligarchic.[82]

Quijano distinguishes between the operations of multinational
companies and those of imperialist states. He looks at Latin America from an international perspective and sees the transnational
corporations as today's major instruments of domination. He
shows the changes in the social and political relations of production
on an international level and indicates that contemporary society
proves the Marxian theory of the inevitability of concentration of
capital at the highest or imperialist stage of development.[83] He
demonstrates that since the Depression, as the relations of production changed in Peru, the lot of its peasantry increasingly worsened.

Quijano divides the social struggles of the peasantry into two
main periods. During the first or prepolitical period the peasant
struggles were based on "feudal religion models"—founded on a
view of social reality involving man and God and a natural order
that could not be altered substantially. Peasant movements of this
period broke down into four categories: (1) messianic movements
designed to change the relationship between man and God, (2)
social banditry to protest specific abuses and injustices, (3) racial
movements to protest domination by groups of other ethnic origins, and (4) agrarian movements demanding social reform but
lacking understanding of the fundamental problems of society.[84]
Quijano calls this feudal-religious model a "form of false consciousness, of social psychological alienation." He indicates that
for centuries the dominant classes reenforced this interpretation of
social reality. But then it began to break down as peasants endeavored to identify a community of interests against an opposing class
and thus repress ethnic, regional, and cultural differences in order
to unite for a common goal. In Marxist terms, the peasantry,
according to Quijano, began the process of changing from a class
in itself to a class for itself.[85]

He felt that Peru initiated this second period, or "nationalist-
antioligarchic revolution," during the 1930s, partially as a result
of the revolutionary Left guided by Mariátegui's thinking and the
reform-minded *Apristas*. He contends that instead of the national-
ist-antioligarchic revolution culminating in the institutionalization
of socialism, it ended in the takeover of the country by a reformist
military in 1968.[86]

Quijano claims that ever since the 1930s Peru's peasants have been more politicized and that three basic types of politicization have taken place among them: (1) "reformist agrarianism"—such as that espoused by APRA, dedicated to changing the social order and altering the land tenure system, but not questioning the power structure; (2) "revolutionary agrarianism"—committed to changing the social order and the land tenure system, as well as altering the power structure, and often employing illegal tactics such as those used by Hugo Blanco; and (3) "political banditry"—of a guerrilla type, used to dissolve the old bonds of political repression or dependence.[87]

Quijano discusses three phases of peasant group development. The first originates with agitation by urban-based organizations upon whom the peasants are often dependent. In other words, he says that the class consciousness of the urban proletariat is transmitted in phase one to the rural *campesinos,* often through political parties. During phase two, the peasantry becomes more independent of the cities, attains more rural autonomy and leadership, but still requires urban support. In phase three, peasant organizations, guerrillas, and militias work together to operate ideologically and politically on a national scale. Marx doubted the feasibility of attaining phase three because of peasants' local loyalties, their social and cultural isolation, and their lack of intragroup communication—factors preventing them from becoming a class. Quijano cites examples from Bolivia, Colombia, and Peru as evidence of the peasants reaching phase three and becoming a class. He claims that the greatest agrarian reform in Latin America has come where peasant agitation has been the most intensive and that as the peasantry develops as a class, class conflicts will increase and the peasants can become, as they did in Cuba, a vital ally of total revolution.[88]

As the peasant movement gained importance in Peru through unionization and illegal occupaion of the land, especially in the Cuzco region under the direction of Blanco, Quijano observed that Peru's *cholos* (Indians or people of mixed blood) found themselves moderating between the polarized positions of the increasingly militant Indians (peasants) and the nation's white aristocracy. In *Nationalism and Capitalism in Peru: A Study in Neo-Imperialism* (1971) he asserted that eventually Peru's military sought to preclude conflict and to stabilize the country by taking over the reins of government (in 1968) and effecting a reconciliation of class and ideology under the aegis of nationalism and capitalism, possibly even humanism and communitarianism, but not socialism.

Peru's ruling generals deported Quijano in 1973 for writing inflammatory articles that argued that the military lacked the ability to reconcile the contradictions between the class nature of their economic reforms and political democratization. Quijano maintained that those in power in Peru believed, erroneously, that political change could be effected outside of class struggle by governmental acts, which, he contended, led to repressive policies.

7. The Bolivarian Nations

> The revolution for independence separated us from Spain but did not do away with the local oligarchy. For this reason the work of Bolívar is not finished because we came away from dependence on Spain to fall into dependence on the United States, with the further aggravation that the ruling class benefits from this dependency and defends it against the interests of the majority.
>
> Camilo Torres

Colombia

Within a year after the 1848 revolutions in Europe a tiny socialist club existed in Colombia as a result of the country's position as a trade center. Contacts with European ideologies were made through Colombia's port cities on the Caribbean and on the Magdalena River. A few Colombians were receptive to Marxist ideas, but the nation lacked a politically conscious immigrant proletariat like the ones led by anarcho-syndicalists in Argentina and Brazil during the late nineteenth century, and a viable socialist movement did not begin in Colombia until after the Russian revolution.

During the early 1920s Silvestre Savitski, an energetic supporter of the 1917 revolution, and Luis Tejada, a socialist whose writings appeared in *El Espectador* (The Spectator), started Colombia's first genuine Marxist study group.[1] In 1922 Colombia's Liberal party convention produced a platform dealing with social problems and promoted the idea of the defense of the working classes, themes elaborated upon by the Marxist study group. By 1925 the thinking of Peruvian José Carlos Mariátegui, who tried to work out a new Marxist position for Latin America, was embraced by Colombian students and intellectuals caught up in the University Reform Movement. Mariátegui's *indianismo* stance turned the Colombians toward the study of their own pre-Columbian societies as a way of understanding contemporary Indian and land tenure problems. Marxist analyses became more popular among Colombia's intelligentsia, and anti-Catholicism and antiimperialism grew in academic circles along with a desire to raise the material level of the protelariat and to defend the national domain. Particular sentiment existed to nationalize and conserve petroleum.[2] Nationalism grew in the country, as did the anti-United States attitudes that had begun when Panama, with U.S. aid, broke away from Colombia in 1903. These factors contributed to the rise of a liberal bourgeois-democratic revolutionary movement for social and political change that culminated in violent political conflict in the 1940s.

No study of Colombia's struggle during the 1940s for bourgeois-democratic reform, as a link to the development of socialist thought in the country, would be complete without mention of the nation's most famous liberal exponent of social change, Jorge Elíecer Gaitán. The son of poor parents, Gaitán attended school on an academic scholarship, studied law in Italy, and eventually returned to Colombia's National University as a law professor. While in Europe he was inspired by Lenin, who he felt understood better than anyone what kind of social revolution a country like Colombia needed.[3] In some ways, Gaitán patterned himself after Lenin, whom he respected as an intellectual, a political activist, an advocate of social and political change, a teacher, and an internationally admired man of wisdom.

In 1924 Gaitán wrote a doctoral thesis "Las ideas socialistas en Colombia" (Socialist Ideas in Colombia),[4] a sophisticated work for its day and for a twenty-six-year old. In it he demonstrated a sound knowledge of the history of socialism, of Marx, and also of how the German thinker's ideas could be adapted to nonindustrialized Colombia.[5]

In his thesis Gaitán viewed life as a continuous historical process, leading to, through a dialectical process, the eventual triumph of equality.[6] He saw all fundamental aspects of Colombian life—religion, art, and philosophy—derived from economic origins or part of a common ideology, by which he meant the ability to explain all of these aspects in relation to one another—that they all evolved from, and were part of, common problems.[7] He discussed the functions of capital within a Colombian context and saw the country at the stage where capital was produced—not as the direct result of personal labor but as the result of exploited labor.[8] At this juncture his Marxist analyses ended. He used some of Marx's ideas as heuristic devices to analyze and comprehend Colombia's problems and viewed class discrimination as a major obstacle to progress. He urged the urban proletariat to recast society but never posited a socialist political program or blueprint for restructuring society.

Basically, Gaitán employed an antiimperialist, anticapitalist-oligarchy line based on Lenin, Mariátegui, the early doctrines of Peruvian *Aprismo,* and José Ortega y Gasset's *Revolt of the Masses* (1930), but he did not subscribe to the hierarchical philosophy of Ortega. The charismatic Gaitán chose to work for social change through the left wing of Colombia's Liberal party, which he was representing as a presidential candidate when he was assassinated on April 9, 1948.

Had Gaitán attained the presidency, how would he have worked for social change? This question has long been open to speculation. The most satisfactory answer came from the late Joseph Starobin, a political scientist, authority on communism in the Americas, and shrewd judge of political character, who knew Gaitán and considered him a radical reformer who respected the world Marxist view[9] and who, once in power, might have turned out to be a socialist revolutionary like Fidel Castro. Starobin noted that Gaitán feared U.S. imperialism as an attempt to extend Protestant hegemony over a Catholic nation. Evidently, Gaitán was contemptuous of U.S. insinuations that its development proved the superiority of the Protestant work ethic.

Gaitán became a martyr in the eyes of the Colombian masses, a symbol of the struggle for political and social reform. His death plunged Colombia into *la violencia,* a protracted period of internal political conflict from which it has yet to recover, and radicalized liberals and countless apolitical poor people who realized that little hope existed for change in their country where a social reformer like Gaitán was considered extremely dangerous by those who exercised political and social control.

Diego Montaña Cuéllar (1910–)

Diego Montaña Cuéllar, professor of sociology and one-time rector of the Free University of Bogota, thought of Jorge Gaitán as a romantic whose policies were not coherent or scientific but who sought the elimination of privileges and the acquisition of political power for the popular classes. Like many other Marxists, Montaña Cuéllar uses the term *filisteo* (Philistine) to refer to liberals of Gaitán's ilk who struggle for ideals that most socialists believe cannot be attained under capitalism.

His book *Colombia: País formal y país real* (1963) (Colombia: A Formal and Grand Country) translated the history of his country into Marxist terms. In it he stressed Lenin's ideas on development as he analyzed Colombia's agricultural imbalances brought about primarily by monocultural dependence on coffee, energy deficiencies attributable to the inability to properly develop a native petroleum industry, and foreign penetration of business, which accounts for an enormous loss of vital investment capital. He drew analogies between Marx's observations on the English domination in India and the recent history of Colombia where major economic problems have caused rampant violence, which he viewed as chiefly a manifestation of an internal class struggle and external imperialism.[10] This book, like his earlier *Los partidos políticos y la realidad nacional* (1950) (Political Parties and National Reality), neatly connected the concepts of political and economic liberty.[11]

In *Sociología americana* (1950) (American Sociology), Montaña Cuéllar studied the historical development of Anglo, Spanish, and Portuguese America from pre-Columbian societies to the middle of the twentieth century in order to develop a more thorough understanding of their relationships to one another and their contemporary problems.[12] Although not an exciting book, it deserves mention because it was an early example of social history of the type that barely existed in Colombia or the United States when it was published in 1950. The author used Latin America as a large laboratory and felt that the societies he studied constituted a collectivity. For example, he considered work a collective action since it affects society as a whole and demonstrates the social relations of production.[13] He produced a horizontal portrait of society rather than the top-down vertical type preferred by most social scientists. He stressed the fact that this was a sociological study, an examination of the causal factors that motivate society, as opposed to simply a study of time and space, which he considered to be the function of history.[14] One might construe these thoughts as his way of criticizing Colombia's historians, who, for the most part, thirty years ago, wrote nonanalytical political and military narratives.

Montaña Cuéllar also tied Colombia's political and social ills to racial and geographic determinism, a tradition begun in Latin America by Alexander von Humboldt, who traveled and wrote about the area during the last years of the nineteenth century and concerned himself with theories of causality and evolution. Montaña Cuéllar placed Humboldt in the same category, as a precursor of modern sociology, as Argentine thinker José Esteban Echeverría (1805–1851) author of the famous *Dogma socialista* (1846) (Socialist Creed) explained elsewhere in this book.[15]

For many years Montaña Cuéllar belonged to Colombia's Communist party, but his writings do not reflect the "party Line." Unlike a number of his "sophisticated Marxist" comrades in Latin America, his thinking was generally "critical" and "plain," more influenced by Lenin than by Stalin. The Cuban revolution jolted him out of what he regarded as political complacency and helped mold his more recent thought. After Castro's takeover and early successes in making the transition to socialism, Montaña Cuéllar grew impatient with the coexistence policies of the Communist party, which he felt placed too much emphasis on parliamentary politics and not enough on guerrilla warfare, which had proved so effective in Cuba. He broke with the party over this issue in 1967.[16]

He felt that the Cuban revolution had two major influences on Colombia. It illuminated the need for social revolution in the South American nation, and it emphasized the benefits of eliminating imperialism there, particularly U.S. influence. He realized that Colombia's national bourgeoisie could not begin to expel the Yankees for fear that such a move would lead to a social revolution that would cost it its power.[17] Thus, he began to question the efficacy of passing through the bourgeois democratic phase on the road to socialism.

Montaña Cuéllar interpreted Colombian society for his people and served as an intellectual and ideological mentor for hundreds of them for whom the liberalism of Jorge Gaitán and his associates has proved meaningless.

José Consuegra Higgins

Unlike Jorge Elíecer Gaitán or even Diego Montaña Cuéllar, the younger generation of Colombian Marxist thinkers like José Consuegra Higgins has easier access to a larger corpus of socialist literature, finds the study of Marx more academically, socially, and ideologically acceptable, and has a larger group of like-minded *pensadores* with whom to exchange ideas and argue the relative merits of diverse theories. Consuegra's works, which more closely resemble those of his contemporaries in Venezuela and Mexico than his Colombian predecessors, exhibit an awareness of the thinking of an earlier generation of Marxists like Uruguay's Rodney Arismendi, Cuba's Carlos Rafael Rodríguez, Chile's Luis Emilio Recabarren, and Peru's José Mariátegui.

José Consuegra is best known for refuting the neo-Malthusian pessimism found in capitalist developmentalism. He feels that the former diverts attention from problems such as economic imperialism and the structural dependency it causes.[18] He rejected the idea, which formed part of the Alliance for Progress mentality, that the population explosion in Latin America is the primary obstacle to development, and he demonstrated that the neo-Malthusian thought used by capitalist economists derives from Spencer, Darwin, and Comte, relates to the survival of the fittest, tends to be based on speculative and unscientific data, and responds to the interests of the economically powerful.[19] He showed that, paradoxically, Malthus's ideas impede development in Indo-American states where those in control have used them to spread the myth that no hope for social and economic progress exists, when in fact the main existing problem is not overpopulation but the poor distribution of wealth.[20] Like Marx, Consuegra views Malthusian thought as antirevolutionary and as an apology for the misery of the working classes. To him, neo-Malthusian thought—more precisely the birth control movement—treats a symptom not a cause (the economic system). He sees birth control as a device to maintain the existing system that perpetuates underdevelopment, which causes hunger rather than overpopulation.[21]

Consuegra finds that attributing Latin America's problems and underdevelopment to excessive population diminishes the real cause—imperialism.[22] In his book *Lenin y la América Latina* (1972) (Lenin and Latin America), he related Lenin's thoughts on imperialism to current Latin American problems, concluded that capitalist underdevelopment results from capitalist development, and then showed how current Latin American dependency fits the Leninist concept of imperialism.[23] Consuegra imparts the feeling that most Latin American economists, whether they realize it or not, owe a debt to Lenin whose ideas they use to interpret events in their own countries and to clarify the fundamental laws and traits of development.

He believes that Lenin and the 1917 Russian revolution served as the models, both psychologically and functionally, that made possible subsequent movements, like that led by Castro in Cuba.[24] To him, Lenin was a composite José Martí and Fidel Castro. These men all exerted the same kind of influence, understood imperialism, and tried to overthrow it by practical actions. For them the revolution organized and defined the strategy and the practice by which the people use their natural capacities to transform sociopolitical conditions. To the "plain" Marxist, José Consuegra, Fidel Castro is to Latin America what Lenin was to the world.[25] Above all, the respective revolutions of Castro and Lenin represent successful examples of creative adaptations of Marx, whose ideas Consuegra believes can be modified to help foster socialism in Colombia.

Camilo Torres Restrepo (1928–1966)

The son of a free-thinking Bogota pediatrician and an outspoken feminist mother from an aristocratic family, Camilo Torres left an indelible imprint on Latin America as a sociologist, priest, and revolutionary. An energetic and rebellious young man, his desire to be socially useful led him into a Roman Catholic seminary in Bogota, then to the Catholic University in Louvain, Belgium, where he became familiar with the neo-Thomist French philosopher Jacques Maritain's "purification of structures" theory, which encouraged Christian democracy to go beyond both capitalism and Marxism. Maritain also advocated Catholics' entering secular politics, aroused their social consciousness, and opened them to new humanistic ideas. In addition to the thinking of Maritain, Torres acquired an appreciation of neo-Marxism, which the great disparity between the classes in Colombia later caused him to try to reconcile with Christian theology.

Padre Camilo returned to Colombia's National University in Bogota in 1959 where he tried to organize a progressive faculty of sociology in a country known for its conservative university curriculum.

Following the Latin American tradition established by priests Manuel Hidalgo and José María Morelos, who led Mexico's flight for independence from Spain, Torres adopted the attitude that theology was best expressed in action. As a sociologist he advocated social pluralism; as a priest he supported religious ecumenism.[26]

Colombia's Liberals and Conservatives had agreed in 1957 to establish a National Front through which the parties alternated in the country's presidency. This accord officially ended *la violencia,* but repression continued as the nation's oligarchy still exploited the poor in order to maintain control. By the early 1960s Camilo's work with peasants led him to advocate the breakup of large landed estates, to agitate for political power for Colombia's disenfranchised majorities, and to speak out for female equality, including birth control and the right to divorce. He began to think that only violent revolution could achieve social justice in Colombia. He reasoned that Marxist revolutionaries need not be atheists; that socialism, based upon the history and needs of Colombians, could be in keeping with the tenets of Christianity; and that Christians and Marxists should collaborate to foster structural change.[27]

Camilo Torres viewed U.S. imperialism, abetted by Colombia's national oligarchy, as the main impediment to progress for his countrymen. He quesioned the existing social and political conditions and structures and concluded that radical departures were in order. He did not directly invoke Marx's name in public speeches or in his writings for fear of alienating potential allies. But he laced his language with such phrases as "the people's mission" and the word *bourgeois,* and his preachings, writings, and actions suggested a spiritual Marxism directed toward uniting Colombians in the struggle against foreign and native exploiters.

In Colombia, the most conservative—in a religious sense— nation in Latin America, Camilo's Roman collar opened doors closed to lay revolutionaries. He never rejected God, whom he referred to as *El Patrón.* Even after formally leaving the Church to pursue full-time guerrilla activities, he maintained considerable prestige among the faithful who respected his great honesty. He apparently never reconciled the fact that nothing metaphysical can exist in Marxism and that historical materialism, the cornerstone of Marx's theory of history, explained religion as a manifestation of material and economic conditions of life, a concept incompatible with Roman Catholic theology. Nevertheless, before taking leave of the Church he contended: "I am a revolutionary as a Colombian, as a sociologist, as a Christian, and as a priest."[28]

When his sense of mission and the futility of the liberal existence caused him to give up the cloth and take to the mountains in October 1965, he asserted: "I took off my cassock to be more truly a priest. The Catholic who is not a revolutionary is living in mortal sin."[29]

Fighting for the Army of National Liberation, in February 1966 he was killed in a battle with a Colombian army patrol. The man who believed that "when one is ordained one remains a priest forever,"[30] provided a model for fellow Catholic clergy and laymen alike, who believed that Christ's objective was to liberate all souls, not to save individual ones.[31] Throughout Latin America, his death radicalized Christians, united the Left, and inspired others to continue the struggle for social justice.

Camilo Torres embodied the spirit of the worker-priest movement, perhaps best exemplified by French philosopher Emmanuel Mournier, who accepted Marx's theory of alienation and advocated working toward the kingdom of God by total commitment to humanity, especially the poor, homeless, and hungry. Mournier's ideas were accepted after World War II by Latin America's "people's priests," who lived with the deprived and the alienated, shared their quest for social justice, and accentuated Christ's brotherhood by inveighing against human oppressors, especially United States-based transnational companies. Camilo followed this line of reasoning and joined it to Pope John XXIII's *Pacem in Terris,* which recognized the good in Marxism and emphasized the relationship between peace and development.

Padre Camilo and his clerical associates searched for the meaning of life, thought it to be the quest for basic necessities, for respect, dignity, and collective fulfillment. They viewed the existence of hunger, exploitation, racism, poverty, and alienation in Latin America as manifestations of greed for wealth and power, which was sanctioned neither by Christ or Marx. Torres agreed with his countryman Diego Montaña Cuéllar who found it difficult to understand why all scholars who used Latin America as a sociological laboratory did not see the same evils in capitalism as had Marx. To Camilo every Christian, as well as every Marxist, had an obligation to free man from oppression. Both Christianity and Marxism stressed the need for personal sacrifice, and both condoned the use of violence to secure freedom.

Torres thought that most bourgeois sociologists, who used scientific methodology in their studies, believed their analyses to be objective but that they failed to comprehend the degree to which their ideas were colored by cultural imperialism. On the other hand, he viewed the work of Marx and Engels as proof of the scientific ability to escape ethnocentrism and to be objective. He did not mean that Marx's and Engels's studies were value-free but that they had avoided the contradictions of their class background.

Torres never developed a totally Marxist analysis of Colombian society. For example, he hoped that *la violencia* would force the ruling class to undertake a development program, an unlikely occurrence since *la violencia* served a useful purpose for Colombia's rulers who needed an opponent to justify their repressive actions while consolidating their power. Torres believed that *la violencia* stimulated a class consciousness in the peasants and gave them a feeling of group solidarity. But also in non-Marxist fashion, he viewed *la violencia* as opening up the peasants' possibilities for social ascent.[32] His 1962 study of *la violencia* demonstrated familiarity with Che Guevara's *foco* theory, indicated that Torres believed that violence could foster change in Colombia, and showed that he thought that guerrilla efforts to topple the government were breaking down Colombia's old order.[33] At this juncture, it is too early to see whether his assessment was correct. Evidence both to support and refute his theory exists.

Torres attained political maturity in the shadow of the Cuban revolution, which he saw as the first movement in Latin America to institutionalize change. In contrast to Cuba's revolutionaries, he held that Colombia's liberals like Jorge Gaitán effected transitory and often illusory reforms and that their altruism and sentiment were no match for the scientific socialist methods being used in Cuba under Castro. Torres contended that the long-standing Liberal-Conservative conflict in Colombia helped the ruling classes, as the basic two-party system divided Colombian society vertically and grouped the popular class into opposing factions in electoral struggles and impeded the formation of class solidarity.[34] He advocated the formation of a party of the popular class and suggested—until it attained sufficient strength to take power— that the masses refrain from participating in elections for the traditional party candidates.

By 1965, Camilo's liberation ethics gave way to revolutionary values. He publicly condemned Colombia's ruling class, "the local oligarchy," which benefited, to the detriment of the masses, from the nation's ideological and economic dependence on the United States.[35]

He issued a "Platform for a United Popular Movement," which included agrarian reform, the building of agricultural cooperatives; urban reforms, including the collective use of space; the abolition of free enterprise; worker ownership and participation in management; nationalization of industry; a government-run public health system; and pluralist socialism.[36] He launched the *Frente Unido de Pueblo* (People's United Front) in an unsuccessful effort to unify nonaligned progressive groups in Colombia. But his increased radicalism, fear of Marxism on the part of some liberals, and sectarianism caused the alliance to disband.[37] Although he thought that the Soviet system was incompatible with Christianity, he believed that the Church should not be anticommunist, and he accepted the support of Colombia's Communist party for the Army of National Liberation, which he helped lead after the breakup of the United Front.

Camilo's willingness to serve as a link between radical Christianity and varieties of Marxism and his advocacy of violent social revolution helped to split the Church in Latin America. Going on the premise that the Church accepted dialogue and that socialism looks for it, on August 5, 1965, he wrote:

> If the efficacy of love of neighbor can not be obtained except through a revolution, love of neighbor must consider the revolution as one of its objectives, and if in revolution they coincide in action and in practice with some Marxist-Leninist methods and objectives, it is not that the Marxists are becoming Christians or the Christians Marxists, but that they are united for the technical solution of the problems of the majority of Colombians and that this solution must not only be permitted for Catholics but obligatory for the priest.[38]

Camilo Torres, often referred to as "Che in a cassock," propagated the idea that the guerrilla had a social conscience, as opposed to the bandit, a view accepted by the clergy, who constituted the "Latin American Camilo Torres Association," which gained strength, after his death, in Bolivia, Brazil, Chile, the Dominican Republic, Mexico, and Colombia, and who insisted that it was the duty of every Christian to be a revolutionary. This idea came under attack by opponents of socialism, especially Colombian ecclesiastical leaders allied with the nation's political and economic powers, who went to great lengths to defame Torres's authenticity by trying to turn him into a myth. In explaining this type of historical phenomenon, Lenin wrote:

> In the life of great revolutionaries the oppressor classes subject them to constant persecution, hear their doctrine with the most furious hatred, with the most immoral campaign of lies and calumnies. After their death, they try to convert them into inoffensive canonized icons, surrounding their names with a certain aura of glory in order to 'console' and trick the oppressed classes, castrating the content of their revolutionary doctrine, dulling the revolutionary edge of this doctrine, degrading it.[39]

The ideas of Camilo Torres did not die with him in the mountains of Colombia but lived on with the guerrillas who still endeavor to overthrow the increasingly repressive government of Colombia and in the minds of those who formed the backbone of the 1968 Medellin Conference of Latin American Bishops, which called for reform and revolution and denounced institutional violence, international capital, and imperialism. Camilo's thoughts and actions led other priests and theologians to the use of social science techniques and scientific Marxist methodology. Liberation theologians emerged all over Latin America, stressing that trying to keep the gospel in a sanctuary and out of politics is in itself a political move legitimizing the existing political situation or submission to the status quo.[40] This thinking formed a direct link with that of the Christians for Socialism movement, for which the best system is one based on social ownership of the means of production and where the organized majority participates effectively in the conduct of the historic process.[41]

Venezuela

Revolutionary idealism initially appeared publicly in Venezuela in 1928 when workers, students, and intellectuals banded together and agitated for social change. Known as the *generación del veintiocho* (Generation of '28), these energetic opponents of dictator Juan Vicente Gómez, who had ruled since 1908, sought political participation for leftist groups such as the Committee of Democratic Defense, the Workers Front, and the Workers National

Front.[42] Inspired by the Mexican Revolution of 1910 and the Russian experiment of 1917, idealistic Generation of '28 members hoped to oust Gómez and install a democratic regime in Venezuela.

The Generation of '28, searching for new paths to political and social change, opened Venezuela for the first time in the twentieth century to alternative philosophies. Some members became life-long devotees of Marxism, others had a passing affiliation with it, and some were attracted to less radical political programs like Peruvian *Aprismo*. For instance, Rómulo Betancourt, a student leader who became an anticommunist president of the republic some thirty years later, after being imprisoned by Gómez spoke of a Bolshevik revolution in Venezuela and joined the Third International. He and approximately eleven associates, while in exile in Colombia, formulated the "Barranquilla Plan," an attempt to develop a theoretical base to analyze and solve such problems as how to liberate the nations of the Caribbean from what they called feudalism.

Some Generation of '28 members helped establish Venezuela's Communist party in 1931. By 1935, when the tyrant Gómez died, some members of the group had renounced Marxism. Rómulo Betancourt, for example, helped found *Acción Democrática* (AD) (Democratic Action), a left-of-center reform-oriented political party. But the study of Marxist thought had gained respectability in Venezuela, and other Generation of '28 members pursued it on the academic level; some even tried to build a socialist movement in the country. As the government's antileft campaign subsided during the late 1930s and the 1940s, new Marxist currents took hold, particularly in the universities.

From the ranks of the student activists of 1928 came Marxist political thinkers whose writings began to appear in Venezuela in the late 1930s. For instance, Carlos Irazabal's *Hacia la democracia* (Toward Democracy), published in 1937, accepted the teachings of Engels and stressed the people's struggle. Two years later Manuel Matos Romero in *Vene„uela y México ante el imperialismo* (Venezuela and Mexico Before Imperialism), analyzed the role of imperialism in the petroleum industry and explained how it deepened dependency,[43] a concept, until then, primarily associated with Lenin's thinking on imperialism as the final stage of capitalism.

By the 1950s as the gap between the poor and the wealthy widened in the oil-rich nation, Marxism was more widely debated there, and by the 1960s, after Castro's successful revolution in Cuba, Marxist thought became an accepted part of Venezuelan academic life. A new generation of educated Venezuelans were aware of Marx's interest in their national hero Simón Bolívar and regarded the Peruvian José Carlos Mariátegui as the father of Marxist thought in Latin America.

Despite the fact that Marxism had become a legitimate subject for study and Marxists had some freedom to function in the academy, the Venezuelan government, after the takeover by Castro in Cuba, pursued a successful, and sometimes brutal, anti-Marxist policy, which often caused scholars to confine their Marxist analyses to bygone eras rather than the twentieth century. Marxist historians, in particular, produced a great deal of fine class-oriented critiques of the colonial and independence eras.

Regardless of government interference and, often, not too subtle pressures, Marxist thought over the past quarter of a century has added methodology, direction, new form, diverse perspectives, coherence, and more penetrating analyses to Venezuelan scholarship. It also helped to inspire a futile guerrilla war against the government, strongly supported by U.S. military aid during the 1960s, a bloody conflict which did not enhance agreement on tactics among the nation's diverse socialist groups.

Domingo Alberto Rangel (1923–)

When the reformist Democratic Action party failed to meet his expectations for social and political change in Venezuela, Domingo Alberto Rangel left it and liberalism and became a leading inspiration behind the *Movimiento Izquierda Revolucionaria* (MIR) (Movement of the Revolutionary Left), a political party formed in the late 1950s that espoused Castro-type social revolution. Influenced by the Black revolution exponent Franz Fanon (1925–1961), who called upon the peasants of Asia, Africa, and Latin America, rather than the industrial proletariat, to lead the "true" revolution, Rangel came to believe that only revolutionary violence frees the native from his or her inferority complex, despair, and inaction and restores self-respect.

Rangel, a disciple of the Generation of '28, congressman, respected university teacher, journalist, and political economist, became the ideological mentor of MIR and Venezuela's most prolific and prominent Marxist writer. His *Los andinos en el poder*

(1964) (The Andeans in Power),[44] a political history of Venezuela from 1899 to 1945, showed how the middle class at the end of the nineteenth century—before the appearance of an oppressed proletariat—was the most progressive element in Venezuela. To him, before 1899 a dualist society existed wherein mercantile capitalism functioned in the state of Táchira while the rest of Venezuela, more or less, existed in a feudal stage. When Cipriano Castro, Táchira's first *caudillo* of note, took control of the country in 1899, the Andean region began to take national power.[45] Rangel believes that Castro initiated an antiimperialist movement that did not culminate in internal political reforms; nor did it give rise to the political and social consciousness necessary to bring about social justice.[46]

Rangel credits the Generation of '28 with bringing ideological awareness to Venezuela and with beginning the quest for social and political change that started to take hold after the death of dictator Gómez when political parties became viable instruments in Venezuela. Rangel noted that at this point when Venezuela's potential for class struggle and worker supremacy reached a peak, it diminished in the wake of the populist promises of the middle-class reformers who gained political control of the nation.[47]

In *La revolución de las fantasías* (1958) (The Revolution of the Fantasies),[48] Rangel spoke about the political fantasies that had been a part of Venezuela from 1811 to 1958—the romantic notion that democratic tendencies always existed in the nation, despite its succession of authoritarian rulers. He also related what it was like to be part of the resistance to Venezuela's last despot, Marcos Pérez Jiménez, who was overthrown in 1958. He claimed that during the 1948-to-1958 period of dictatorial rule and foreign economic, military, and ideological penetration, many Venezuelan liberals turned to the Left.

He demonstrated that, despite the transfer of Venezuela's political power from dictatorship to the middle class, the country's masses continued to be exploited, and he stressed that the implantation of democracy is not consonant with social revolution, that the abstraction of electoral liberty does not equal opportunity for all classes. To him, Venezuela does not have representative democracy but instead a government acting for the middle class and led, not by an intellectual elite, but by mediocre uncreative politicians.[49] Politics in Venezuela, he said, is the parties controlled by the middle class, which assumed prominence as a result of the petroleum boom.

Rangel categorized *Acción Democrática,* which has held the presidency in Venezuela for three of the last five-year terms since 1959, as a hybrid of bourgeois democracy operating on a formula of centralization inspired by Lenin.[50] He showed how the government—when it did not meet popular demands—resorted to repression but also credited the system with a capacity to absorb the antagonisms of society and acknowledged the existence of reforms. He pointed to the Central University as a microcosm of Venezuelan society where leftists meld with the authorities and integration is the result of co-optation or manipulation. He predicted that the contradictions among the political, economic, and military elements that govern Venezuela might cause a future breakdown leading to either right-wing tyranny or a socialist revolution.[51]

Rangel saw party politics replacing the old vanguard but thought that a new vanguard was emerging independent of the party system. Thus, he criticized the Venezuelan Communist party and *Movimiento al Socialismo* (MAS) (Movement to Socialism), a Leninist party, for playing into the hands of the establishment by engaging in conventional electoral politics.[52]

In his two-volume work *Capital y desarrollo* (1971) (Capital and Development) Rangel examined the history of the relations of production in Venezuela and explained how the petroleum industry transformed the nation from a self-sufficient to a dependent importer of foodstuffs. Putting Venezuela's economic development, or lack of it, into historical perspective, he agreed with Brazilian economist Celso Furtado, who viewed underdevelopment as a specific condition emanating from the colonial system, not just a passing phase, and as an integral part of the dependency that accompanies imperialism.

Rangel indicated how the discovery of vast petroleum reserves in the 1920s was a watershed in Venezuela's history and how foreign penetration occurred as oil replaced coffee as the nation's major export and capital-producing commodity. He pointed out that Venezuela ran true to Trotsky's belief that capitalism causes the rural sectors to become subordinate to the cities—in this case agriculture was supplanted by "black gold," and the political power in the country shifted from the landed aristocracy to urban elites. Petroleum also helped develop among the workers Venezuela's first genuine organized working-class consciousness but exacerbated class antagonisms by increasing discrimination against them by greedy oil producers.[53] Petroleum moved the nation toward industrialization, urbanized it, and strengthened capitalism. Capitalism based on oil needed national unity and centralized institutions, and to attain and maintain them, Rangel feels, Venezuela developed a more professional military, which became a dominant political force in the nation and a primary pillar of support for the middle-class *criollos,* who, by 1944, endeavored to put the petroleum economy under their own control rather than that of foreign capital.

He cited *Acción Democrática,* one of the two major parties (the other being the Christian Democratic Party [Comité de Organización Política Electoral Independiente, or COPEI]), representing the new middle-class rulers, as having moved toward state capitalism rather than socialism as its rhetoric would have one believe. He criticized the gradualist politices of *Acción Democrática,* specifically for not pursuing a vigorous agrarian reform program and for not counteracting U.S. imperialism.

Rangel explained that after World War II, Latin America replaced Europe and Asia as the major supplier of raw materials for the United States. He asserted that the United States needs Latin America in order to exist and that this need led to Yankee military and ideological control in the region by a tactic defined by former Guatemalan President Juan José Arévalo as "anti-Kommunism," or the use of negative feelings about communism as an excuse to curtail any activity one deems objectionable by labeling it "communist-inspired."[54] Although U.S. ideological hegemony grew in Venezuela, the nation moved toward taking control of its own natural resources, culminating in the nationalization of oil in 1976, but then became more dependent upon international finance capital and technology.[55] Drawing inspiration for his dependency analysis from Marx's thoughts on India,[56] Rangel imparted the feeling that petroleum provides Venezuela with the potential to break dependency but that under either imported or native Creole capitalism, it will never happen.

Rangel is a contemporary example of the traditional Venezuelan intellectual, political-activist writer. His thoughts on the political economy of Venezuela are representative of those of most of today's well-educated "critical plain" Marxist *pensadores.* Naturally, some would differ with his tactics, especially his nonparliamentary approach to social revolution. His fundamental ideas on Venezuelan dependency are subscribed to by both Marxist and non-Marxist dependency theorists. Rangel best serves his cause by maintaining the respect of thinkers and practitioners of all ideologies and by functioning as a social critic whose analyses and suggestions for improving the quality of political, social, and economic life in Venezuela occasionally prod the nation's power elites into effecting reforms.

Germán Carrera Damas (1930–)

Central University history professor Germán Carrera Damas, more than his colleague Domingo Alberto Rangel, melds with mainstream Venezuelan academics. He does so without being co-opted or manipulated.

While studying in Mexico, he realized that the Mexican Revolution lacked the ideology and scientific rigor necessary to solve political and social problems, and he began to learn how to devise and apply methodology to historical problems. Carrera Damas returned to his native Venezuela and gained enormous respect among academics as an essayist and editor who uses new and innovative approaches to the study of Venezuela's past. He has been a leading Latin American proponent of emphasizing ideas in the study of history rather than the traditional narrative-chronological approach favored by most Venezuelan historians.

He is best known for applying Marxist techniques of analysis to the colonial and nineteenth-century history of his country. In his "Estudio preliminar" (1971) (Preliminary Study) to *Materiales para el estudio de la ideología realista de la independencia* (Materials for the Study of Ideology Resulting from Independence), he noted the complexities and contradictions in colonial Venezuelan society—that initially diverse constituencies wanted independence from Spain for different reasons. He advocated new structural analyses of the independence movements to correct the deficiencies in most histories of that period, which he found simplistic. Somewhat as Charles Beard did for U.S. history, he commented on the relationship between the development of Venezuela's bourgeoisie and the independence movements. He noted that the forms of struggle adopted corresponded to the degree of ideological development and the maturity and level of consciousness of the social classes involved in independence.[57]

He felt that independence was a class struggle, pitting slaves against Creoles, Creoles against *peninsulares,* and *pardos* (a racial mixture of black and white) against Creoles, a theory subject to debate if one considers Creoles and *peninsulares* part of the same class and their differences as hierarchical.[58] He stated that one cannot speak strictly of an ideology of emancipation, that the various participants in independence had different ideologies, and that one must see the period in terms of pluralistic dynamics for change. In his examination of the *pardos,* a group generally ignored by scholars, he referred to them as a fundamental group in Venezuela's economic process. The *pardos,* whose struggle for independence he depicted, included Venezuela's dominant producers of export goods, the majority of its artisans, and a small part of its commercial and professional liberals, many of whom had a higher cultural level than their Creole counterparts.[59]

He asserted that emancipation was not an end in itself and that it did not attain all of the goals of its diverse participants.[60] To him, the new "liberal 1811 republic" that emerged expressed a Creole character that was arbitrary, intolerant, discriminatory, and proslavery and that bred inequality. The new Creole rulers made few social changes and maintained the old military and political orders.[61]

Carrera Damas viewed abolition as a result of slave hostility, a class struggle to be free, not a benevolent middle-class action on the part of the Creoles, who had their own battle for equality with the *peninsulares.*[62] He also pointed out the contradictions between the struggles for equality and political power and top positions by Creoles, who were often more sophisticated, better educated, more financially secure, and had greater regional control than the *peninsulares* they sought to replace.[63]

Besides dispelling some myths about independence, Carrera Damas tried to eliminate the cult of Bolívar that has pervaded Venezuelan history. In explaining Venezuela's emancipation from Spain, he reduced *Bolivarismo* to a single factor. He questioned Bolívar's negative view of the masses and maintained that "The Liberator" has been made a hero by writers who possess an extreme individualist concept of history—that they have created a cult that has become an "opiate for the people," one whose functions have been to dissemble a failure and delay a disillusion.[64] To him *Bolivarismo* is a hoax, which deludes people into thinking that independence brought liberty, equality, and fraternity to the masses when it primarily served the commercial bourgeoisie. Bolivarism, he contended, is based upon supernatural ideas and predestination, which tend to raise expectations beyond reality.[65]

Carrera Damas writes precise critical history. His "plain" Marxist approach to the study of the independence era serves as a model for other historians of Latin America. Particularly innovative is his breakdown into phases of the period from the late eighteenth century to 1830 and his analysis of the diverse segments of Venezeulan society during that time.[66]

However, his research and writing go beyond the eighteenth and nineteenth centuries. *La dimensión histórica en el presente de América Latina y Venezuela* (1972) (The Historical Dimension in Today's Latin America and Venezuela)[67] demonstrated familiarity with the sweep of Venezuelan economic history. In it he characterized Venezuela as a dependent society, of an implanted rather than indigenous nature, controlled by foreign traditions beginning with colonial subordination to Spain followed by postindependent dependence upon England and then the United States. He subdivided postindependence dependency into: (1) commercial dependency: 1821–1970s, (2) absolute commercial dependency: 1821–1960s, (3) imperialist dependency: 1870–1970s, (4) modernizing imperialist dependency: 1870–1930; (5) monopolistic imperialist dependency or dependence on minerals: 1930–1970, and (6) the current era of thermonuclear revolution, which introduced changes in the relations of dependency.[68]

He spoke about the imposition of the culture of the metropolis (Spain) on an indigenous and African people[69] and about *imperialismo anglonorteamericano*. He viewed Venezuela's fate as inescapably bound to capitalism and the United States, as it is today, or to socialism and a socialist superpower and cited Cuba's dependence upon the Soviet Union as an example of the latter. Carrera Damas distinguished between the two varieties of dependency by noting that Cuba is not exploited by Russia as the capitalist dependencies have been and are by the Western superpowers.[70] Like Rangel, he believed that Latin America's common problems of modernization are retarded by its lack of independence within the international order.[71]

Although he would like to think that Latin American regional unity is possible, he noted that cultural idiosyncracies and national differences make the concept of Latin America artificial and that such differences can overcome implanted cultural imperialism in the area of literature and the creative arts, but not in the realm of technology.[72]

In assessing Venezuela's potential for revolution Carrera Damas considered the role historians have played in his nation's history and concluded that they have generally subjected their countrymen to ideological manipulation. He relegated most contemporary Venezuelan historians to an "intermediate ideological zone," a euphemistic way of chiding them for their reluctance to venture into what the elitist academic establishment considers unacceptable modes of historical analysis[73] and for their refusal to admit that all history is value-laden and that objectivity only exists within ideological perspectives.

Teodoro Petkoff (1931–)

Teodoro Petkoff represents a new breed of Venezuelan Marxist. The son of radical parents from a middle-class, immigrant background, Petkoff rose to prominence through the *Juventud Comunista* (Communist Youth Group) at Caracas' Central University. From student militant fighting against dictator Marcos Pérez Jiménez who controlled Venezuela between 1948 and 1958, he moved into national politics, won a seat in Congress, became a guerrilla leader dedicated to toppling the Venezuelan government and forging a socialist revolution, and finally rejected extreme vanguardism, in which the revolution is envisioned as an act of will. He realized that Venezuela's peasants had never joined the revolution, accepted the premise that one cannot make a revolution out of nothing, and went on to found in 1970 the parliamentary-oriented *Movimiento al Socialismo* (MAS) (Movement to Socialism) political party.

MAS now calls for a nonviolent transition to socialism that rejects popular frontism but respects socialist democratic pluralism and approximates the tenets of Eurocommunism. The party advocates a neutral foreign policy, including friendly relations with the United States, to which it looks as a market for Venezuelan oil and purveyor of needed technology. MAS seeks to strengthen Venezuela's military in order to preserve the nation's neutrality. Its theoreticians, such as Petkoff, believe that by construing institutions like the military and countries such as the United States as perpetual enemies, the Left has in the past become feared and isolated, factors that have hindered its progress. By 1980, MAS's political strategies attracted a following sufficient to enable the party to hold eleven seats in Venezuela's lower congressional chamber and two Senate seats and to permit Petkoff to become a respected congressman.

Petkoff has always believed that Venezuela constitutes a special case in Latin America, and because of its potentially great wealth it needs different means to develop. To him, the nation's plentiful supply of petroleum has caused native capital to become tied to foreign, particularly United States, business. He has pleaded for economic diversification as a step toward breaking Venezuela's economic and concomitant military and ideological dependence on the United States[74] and as a step toward building socialism.

Petkoff has maintained that given the structure of contemporary Venezuelan society, small groups cannot do much for the revolution but that the masses must, and can, be turned to socialism. In his book *¿Socialismo para Venezuela?* (1970) (Socialism for Venezuela?), he criticized the divided Venezuelan Left and searched for a way to unify it without creating a monolithic Left as he believed existed in the Soviet Union.[75]

He concurred with Lenin that revolution will come in stages, the democratic-bourgeois, followed by the socialist. His analyses of Venezuela have led him to a conclusion similar to the one that Herbert Marcuse made about the United States, that most workers belong in the petty bourgeoisie category;[76] thus, as we shall see, they will be part of the democratic-bourgeois revolution.

Like Gramsci, Petkoff has wanted a "concrete utopia" where the quality of life is paramount, people are freely socialized, no official culture is created, and dissent exists. He has predicated his theories upon the goodness of man and a profound belief in the possibilities of a planned society. In order to effect change, he has contended that one has to comprehend the nature of the society for which one plans, and he wrote *Razón y pasión del socialismo* (1973) (The Reason and Passion of Socialism)[77] to help provide that fundamental understanding.

He wrote about Venezuela not as a classic capitalist society but as a developing capitalist society in a dependent position, where the proletariat plays a marginal role in politics and where the middle class controls and blocks political and social transformation. With the knowledge that violent and nonviolent vanguardism has failed in the recent past in Venezuela, he contended that societal transformation cannot be effected by dogmatic socialists, but only by flexible ones whose ranks include students, factory workers, and peasants who are willing to involve themselves in an immense national debate in order to make a case for their ideology.[78]

He noted two types of capitalism to be combatted in Venezuela—a "large" type tied to foreign interests, and a "small" type, often national and not necessarily associated directly with imperialism but limited by it, for example, by its credit and banking facilities.[79] He then illustrated the relationship between dependent capitalism and political power, basically showing how U.S. corporations, generally supported by their government, built business alliances with Venezuela's ruling class. He claimed that this relationship was strengthened by close World War II ties that helped Venezuela's bourgeoisie grow, especially through the Democratic Action party (AD) from 1945 on. Like Domingo Alberto Rangel, he saw an enormous growth of neocolonialism in the postwar era, led by the proimperialist petty bourgeois AD.

Before Venezuela can move toward socialism, he said that the means of production have to be put into the hands of "small" capitalists. He maintained that the national bourgeoisie has the potential to break Venezuelan dependency and to stimulate the development of independent capitalism. Once dependent capitalism is eliminated, he favors the creation of a force to take power away from the native capitalists,[80] which is possible because more and more Venezuela's petty bourgeoisie turns away from leaders like AD's Rómulo Betancourt and toward advocates of state capitalism like the generals who ruled in Peru between 1968 and 1980 or socialists like Cuba's Fidel Castro or Colombia's Camilo Torres.[81]

Petkoff's strength lies in his ability to criticize socialism as well as capitalism. He has rejected the Soviet model with its top-heavy bureaucracy as unsuitable for other countries; he also knows that Cuban *foquismo* (the use of insurrectionary centers) cannot work in Venezuela where, instead of combatting a military dictatorship, socialists have to contend with a form of representative democracy.[82] He has said that the right wing correctly accuses the left wing of pursuing a revolution with foreign (Russian, Chinese, or Cuban) characteristics. By so doing, the Right defends nationalism and casts blame on foreigners for political and social upheaval. Then the Left acts as though these criticisms were valid by defending internationalism and identifying with foreign socialist brothers and sisters. Thus, the Left confuses solidarity with the parties that rule in socialist states. By using these foreign models, the Left exhibits somewhat of a colonial mentality, which it constantly has to defend. In arguing for a nondogmatic leftist approach, not just the status quo of the models,[83] Petkoff has accused the Left of using syllogistic logic. For example, he cited the frequently stated belief that the state is the machinery by which one class oppresses another, that Venezuela is dominated by the United States and executes its orders; therefore the Venezuelan state only exists to execute U.S. orders. If this situation prevails, then when the Venezuelan state accomplishes some good for its people, the Left is at a loss for an explanation; and because of its rigidity, rather than search for genuine social, political, and economic explanations for what occurred, it says: "This good is a plot to deceive the people."[84]

Petkoff, the Communist youth leader and guerrilla figher, always exhibited finely honed critical facilities and tended to follow the "hard" and "sophisticated" approaches to Marxist thought. Although his fervor for social revolution never diminished, his thinking changed along with his strategies and tactics. Today, an older Petkoff supports the parliamentary process and takes a "soft" more flexible "plain" Marxist approach, which can perhaps best be seen in his ideas on religion.

Once a vociferous opponent of religion, Petkoff now, like Germán Carrera Damas, has accepted the existence of basic Roman Catholic values in Venezuela and believes in the usefulness of the dialogue between Marxist revolution and progressive Christianity. He contends that the inhumanity and irrationality of capitalism, with its moral and ethical failures, have stimulated a return to the original ideas of Christianity to "liquidate private property and disequality among people."[85] Petkoff wants to get away from the Marxist idea that religion is the opiate of the masses and the Christian tendency to view Marxism as Satan incarnate. However, he has found the belief that religion brings order to society morally and politically unacceptable.

Marxist thinkers with the depth and perspicacity of Teodoro Petkoff, Germán Carrera Damas, and Domingo Alberto Rangel surfaced late in Venezuela compared with their counterparts in the Southern Cone of South America. But these descendants of the Generation of '28 have established a tradition of Marxist thought and scholarship. Young Marxist theoreticians and activists increasingly take off from Petkoff, Carrera Damas, and Rangel and contribute to the corpus of knowledge about Venezuelan society and the nation's political debates.

Two outstanding young "critical" and "plain" Marxist thinkers, Héctor Malavé Mata and José Silva Michelena, deserve mention here. Malavé Mata's *Formación histórica de antidesarrollo de Venezuela* (1974) (Historic Formation of Antidevelopment in Venezuela), an economic history from precolonial times to the present, showed how emphasis on petroleum production and the accompanying neglect of other sectors of society have deepened Venezuela's neocolonial dependency.[86]

Social scientist José Silva Michelena endeavored to tie empiricism to Marxism. In Platonic fashion, he also built a Marxist-dependency model through which to diagnose Venezuela's past and present in order to predict its future. His study of the violent acceleration of structural changes in the country since the 1930s led him to the conclusion that the forty years of upheaval created cultural contradictions and conflicts that have affected the creation and implementation of viable development policies. He demonstrated that democracy is an illusion in Venezuela where there exists a direct correlation between socioeconomic status and political capacity, and both rest in the hands of United States–dominated elites. In the economic realm, he applied the vested interest theory to Venezuela and concluded that while all social groups have undergone substantial change, more people are hurt by Venezuelan development than benefit by it, thus concurring with economist André Gunder Frank's ideas on the "development of underdevelopment." He added a social-psychological dimension to his analysis of Venezuela; and using Marx's basic thoughts on class consciousness and alienation, he explained why organized discontent might appear. His application of the dialectic to Venezuela yielded a new view of the nation as a dependent political entity,[87] one in which popular dissatisfaction with the government is growing, and he predicted that a revolutionary situation could arise by the mid-1980s if touched off by a powerful catalyst such as the depletion of the nation's petroleum reserves—a definite possibility.

All of our Venezuelan Marxists realize that no modern nation can be totally independent. But they also stress that for more than four and a half centuries Venezuela has been in either a colonial or neocolonial position, and its ability to make autonomous economic, political, and social decisions has been severely limited by extraordinary dependence upon dominant foreign nations and businesses that have not been primarily concerned with its national interest. In addition, these Marxists have all been severe critics of Venezuela's liberals—AD and COPEI, which have controlled the nation's government since 1959 and which they condemn for increasing dependence on the United States and for failing to effect adequate social and political changes. Ironically, the outstanding contribution of Venezuela's Marxist *pensadores* has been to sustain the national debates on the dependency and social change issues, which in turn has pressured the ruling middle-class elites to pursue some social, economic, and political reforms.

Paradoxically, in Venezuela where socialist alternatives are spoken about frequently by manual workers, students, and intellectuals, primary barriers to social and socialist revolution have been the moderate reforms enacted by the capitalist Democractic Action and Christian Democratic parties, which use leftist rhetoric, stress democratic nationalism, and emphasize reducing Venezuela's dependence upon other capitalist nations while building independence within their system.

Bolivia

Bolivian *pensador* Guillermo Francovich holds that Marxism evolved in his country in two stages: the speculative and the political. During the first stage, Marxism existed as a sociological doctrine, with historical materialism confined to academic discussions. In the second stage, Marxism became a politicized social force.[88] Enrique Anderson-Imbert, the noted Latin American literature specialist, corroborates the views of Francovich by dividing Bolivia's Marxists into two groups: those who advocate economic, political, and social communism, and psychic communists.[89] Both schools of thought dichotomize between Marxism as theory and as theory blended with practice.

It is difficult to pinpoint when Bolivian Marxists began to combine theory with activism. We know that a Workers' Social Center in La Paz operated on socialist principles as early as 1906. By 1921 an anarchist group began to form in the country. Interest in Marxist ideas burgeoned in the period between the world wars. Simultaneously, José Ingenieros's *Sociología argentina* (1918) gained a readership in the nation and gave Bolivians another set of insights into the scientific analysis of human behavior by providing an historically oriented economic view of the region from the Spanish conquest, through the independence era, to the disorderly republican period.[90]

Marxist literature gained popularity in Bolivia's universities by the 1920s, especially in reaction to liberalism and positivism. Socialists like José Antonio Arce and Arturo Urquidi Morales began to formulate scientific critiques of Bolivia and searched for a way to substitute socialism for the liberalism that many intellectuals in their country, particularly those influenced by the Peruvian Haya de la Torre, thought to be its salvation. Marxist ideas, primarily those of Peru's José Mariátegui, also became popular among Bolivia's thinkers. Mariátegui's *Seven Interpretative Essays on Peruvian Reality* were published in Bolivia in 1928, and his themes pertaining to economic evolution, industrialization, religion, and racial questions were adapted to Bolivian conditions.

Despite the popularity of the ideas of Ingenieros and Mariátegui and the establishment of anarchist Workers' Literary Centers in La Paz and Cochabamba and a Women Workers' Federation in La Paz,[91] left-wing radicalism did not develop early in Bolivia in contrast to other Latin American nations. By the late 1920s, no totally Marxist political group existed in the country. At that time Peruvian *Aprismo* exerted the greatest influence in the country's academic circles, especially after Manuel A. Seoane, a well-known *Aprista,* wrote *Con el ojo izquierdo mirando a Bolivia* (1926) (Looking at Bolivia from the Left), which focused on the indigenous situation and the privileges of the mine-owning class[92] and advocated social and political changes that could be effected without building a classless society.

Once the Depression began, Bolivians searched for new solutions to old problems and read more translations of European works, especially those of Lenin, Plekhanov, and Bukharin.[93] The Chaco War (1932–1935), a bloody territorial conflict between Bolivia and Paraguay over the potentially mineral-rich Chaco Boreal, in which Standard Oil of New Jersey sided with Bolivia and Royal Dutch Shell backed Paraguay, caused Bolivians to examine domestic and international colonialism more closely and raised questions about the ownership of Bolivia's mines and *latifundios.*

Francovich indicated that, to some extent, the Chaco War set the stage for Bolivia's entry into the second or politically active Marxist stage. He noted that consternation about the causes and effects of the war moved Bolivia's embryonic Marxists out of the phase of intellectual speculation. They began to establish contacts with international Marxist groups in order to build a viable movement against the exploitation of the masses. The Chaco War heightened awareness of the degree of Bolivia's subordination to foreign capital, primarily that from the United States, but also from England, Germany, Italy, and Japan.[94]

The effects of international exploitation caused most Bolivian *pensadores* to follow either a strong reformist or a Marxist path toward social and political change after the Chaco War. Even nonsocialists realized the value of Marxism as an analytical tool. Víctor Paz Estensorro, a one-time economics professor who subsequently served as president of Bolivia (1952–1956 and 1960–1964), expressed an attitude that prevailed among Bolivia's intelligentsia in the early 1940s when he said that he believed that Marxism was the best instrument for interpreting national realities and that he thought capitalism would eventually disappear.[95]

After World War II, Marxist influence grew in Bolivia's labor movement, particularly among tin miners, where the thinking of Trotsky gained a strong foothold. Nationalism, seeking progress as an objective and the nation-state as the vehicle of progress, made enormous gains at the same time among mine and urban workers.

It is frequently difficult to separate nationalist from Marxist thought as both movements shared some goals and employed similar rhetoric. Marxist and nationalist thinking affected the Bolivian National Revolution, which began in 1952 and brought about, temporarily, the break-up of large landed estates, the distribution of land to peasants, the nationalization of the mines and diminution of the power of the mine owners, increased government ownership or control of commerce and industry, a greater voice in government for workers and peasants, and antiimperialist sentiment.[96]

Unfortunately, from a Marxist point of view, the revolution (1952–1964), led by a nationalist group called the *Movimiento Nacionalista Revolucionario* (MNR) (National Revolutionary Movement), which appealed to some extent to most socialist elements in the nation, effected petty bourgeois agrarian reforms and did not provide for capital development, thus leaving the country's small national bourgeoisie economically and ideologically dependent on imperialism.[97] During this period orthodox Marxists considered what the MNR did as part of the bourgeois-democratic revolution and necessary to modernize and industrialize the nation before it could make the transition to socialism. Meanwhile, Bolivia's Trotskyists, led by Juan Lechín and the mine workers who represented the left wing of the MNR, disagreed and felt that the socialist revolution could proceed without the transitional bourgeois-democratic phase.[98]

Despite Marxist representation in the MNR, the reformist thinking of the majority in the organization, in alliance with the *Central Obrera Boliviana* (COB) (Bolivian Labor Central), during the 1952–1964 period, destroyed revolutionary fervor in the country's proletariat. The Bolivian National Revolution also curtailed the growth of solidarity among socialist groups in the nation, a factor that has continued to prevent them from gaining political influence. This is best exemplified by the case of Ernesto Che Guevara, whose efforts to replicate the Cuban experience in Bolivia in the mid-1960s were thwarted by conflicts among leftist groups in the country and by Bolivian nationalism, factors subsequently causing him to lose his life in the struggle to build socialism.

José Antonio Arce (1881–1968)

José Antonio Arce stands as one of the outstanding Marxist *pensadores* in Bolivian history. An outspoken man with a reputation for impeccable honesty, enormous enthusiasm, and strong convictions, his public life began as a student leader of the University Reform Movement and founder in 1928 of the Bolivian University Federation, which stood for university autonomy, a revolutionary stand on Indian problems, and termination of the Monroe Doctrine of Pan-Americanism controlled by the United States.[99]

A sociologist by profession, Arce in 1939 founded the *Frente de la Izquierda Boliviana* (FIB) (Bolivian Leftist Front), which merged in 1940 into the *Partido de la Izquierda Revolucionaria* (PIR) (Party of the Revolutionary Left), a Marxist organization advocating building a revolutionary movement gradually from below but led by a radical intellectual elite. The PIR gave primacy to industrial development and rejected the idea of a permanent revolution on the grounds that before socialism could be attained, Bolivia would have to go through a period of capitalist development.

Despite clashing with the followers of Marxist writer Tristán Marof, whose desire to build socialism from above helped split the Left in the nation, the PIR contributed significantly to the radicalization of the labor-artisan movement in Bolivia by continuously exposing the nation's "false reformist" national counterelites. Arce, while teaching at universities in La Paz and in Sucre, founded the Institute of Bolivian Sociology, acted as his party's leading spokesman, and ran for the presidency of Bolivia in 1940 and 1951 and in the interim served in the national Senate.

Arce's historical approach to sociology and his fascination with the pre-Columbian societies led him to translate into Spanish a volume by Georges Rouma that depicted Inca civilization as a continuation of autocracy and Louis Baudin's well-known *L'empire socialiste des Inka* (1928) (The Socialist Empire of the Incas),[100] which Arce believed illustrated the communal aspects of Inca society but did not prove it to be socialist as its economics were rudimentary and it condoned slavery.

Arce's analysis of Bolivia's history led him to break it down into three stages: (1) precommunism existing among the pre-Columbian peoples, (2) feudalism during the colonial period, and (3) independence and the emergence of capitalism.[101] He believed pre-Columbian society offered more to its citizens compared with how they fared after the arrival of the Spanish. Those facts, in conjunction with what he saw as the results of the Chaco War, helped create his hostility to all foreign incursions in Bolivia. Borrowing from the ideologies of Mariátegui and Marof, he espoused alliances between Bolivians and Indianist parties in all of Latin America to ward off political, economic, social, and cultural imperialism. He saw in the revolution of the international proletariat a way for semicolonial peoples to oppose dominant foreign capital through world struggle.

Arce believed that only materialism provided a scientific conception of the universe and a practical method for eliminating capitalism and the class system, thereby emancipating the earth's people.
He thought that economic planning and technology could provide
abundance for all. Through his writing and as an activist he championed equality for women and promoted accessible lay-supervised
coeducation from primary grades through the university. He also
stressed the need for a universal language transcending national
boundaries in order to curtail nationalist rivalries and conflicts.[102]

Arce advocated incorporating the Indian into the mainstream of
Bolivian life. In order to accomplish this, he sought the emancipation of the Indian by breaking up the *latifundios* as the Mexican
Revolution had begun to do. He claimed that democracy was
incompatible with Bolivian capitalism and called for socialization
of private wealth, more specifically the nationalization of the
mines and petroleum.[103]

On a more abstract level, Arce considered the relation of science, art, and philosophy to one another. He felt that positive
sciences studied the universe to discover past and present realities;
philosophy existed to find out what possibilities exist in reality
and what ought to be; and art, used in a broad sense to mean the
practical or applied sciences, aimed to transform reality into what
it ought to become. First, he viewed sociology as a positive science
in that it investigates family relations, economics, politics, religion,
law, and morality. Second, from a philosophical standpoint, he
felt that sociology studies various hypotheses and goals of social
evolution. Third, he considered applied sociology to be concerned
with practical matters like eugenics, legislation, and political
action.[104] In "plain" Marxist fashion, Arce adapted this method to
Bolivian society.

The thoughts and actions of José Antonio Arce influenced significantly two other PIR members, Arturo Urquidi Morales
(1905–) and Ricardo Añaya, who attained considerable stature
as Marxist thinkers. Urquidi, one-time rector of the University of
Cochabamba, also studied the sociological antecedents of the Bolivian *campesino*. In his *La comunidad indígena: Precedentes
sociológicos, vicisitudes históricos* (1941) (The Indigenous Community: Sociological Precedents, Historical Vicissitudes), he concluded that Bolivia's Indian problems could be rectified by nationalization of land, progressive socialist modes of production,

technical education for Indians, and reversion to economic-administrative bases conforming to ancient indigenous regional characteristics. In other words, he proposed preserving traditions while modernizing—bringing technology to existing communal situations.[105] Urquidi held that Bolivia was semimodern and semifeudal. Thus, he took a determinist view of the country's agrarian problems, agreeing with Arce that socialism cannot be achieved without passing through a well-developed capitalist stage. He envisioned the peasant as the generator and protector of the revolution and felt that to go through the bourgeois-democratic stage of development, one initially has to bring capitalist forms of production to the countryside, then give land to peasants and organize them into militias and unions, which would form part of the revolutionary party. He favored destruction of the *latifundios* and distribution of their land to the Indians but advocated leaving the medium-sized landholdings intact. The MNR subsequently adopted many of Urquidi's ideas and incorporated them into the 1953 Agrarian Reform Law.[106] Also, his ideas that students should be a force for the transformation of society and should carry on the struggle against class privilege and imperialism and that the universities should be political organisms became the norm in Bolivia during periods of civilian governmental control.[107]

Ricardo Añaya, another influential Bolivian Marxist, professor of public law at the University of Cochabamba, outstanding parliamentarian, and author of the program of the *Partido de la Izquierda Revolucionaria* (PIR), wrote a number of noteworthy books, including *La nacionalización de las minas* (1952) (The Nationalization of the Mines). In that volume he concurred with Arce that Bolivia's mines had to be nationalized in order to rid the nation of imperialism. He propounded ideas on how to nationalize, administer, and establish a popular democratic polity. A key to modernization in his estimation is government use of revenues from the nationalized mines for land reform, electrification programs, industrialization, education, and health reforms. This process will enable the nation to curtail its dependence upon foreign capital and to recoup its sovereignty and dignity. He realized that increased independence would not mean the end of all dependency, for in the modern world Bolivia would have to retain interdependent ties. Añaya saw two choices for interdependency, either with the U.S. bloc or that of the Soviet Union and other socialist nations. Since Bolivia already knew the consequences of affiliation with the former, while he never supported ties to the Third International, he opted for links with the latter, which he believed would be more mutually beneficial and less exploitative.[108]

Tristán Marof (1898–)

Gustavo Adolfo Navarro, better known by his Russian-oriented pseudonym Tristán Marof, has become a legendary figure in Bolivia where his popularity has rivaled that of the Russian novelists Tolstoy, Chekhov, and Dostoevski, from whose writings about life under the tsars Bolivians have drawn analogies to their own social conditions.

Born in Sucre to humble parents, Marof displayed a great deal of intellectual curiosity and maturity at an early age. By the time he reached his twenties, he had acquired a solid reputation for his articles, novels, and political tracts. During the 1920s he served as Bolivian consul in Paris where he became fascinated by France's post-World War I revolutionary political movements, which he wrote about extensively. He particularly admired the social activists in the French Clarté Circle, especially Henri Barbusse, author of the powerful antiwar novel *Le feu* (1917) (The Fire).[109]

Upon returning to Bolivia in 1925, Marof organized the Socialist party. His radical political activities landed him in jail in 1927. He subsequently escaped to Argentina. While in exile in 1934 he and fellow Bolivians founded the *Partido Obrero Revolucionario* (POR) (Revolutionary Workers party). Two years later he returned to Bolivia with a great deal of international stature as a writer. His *La justicia del Inca* (1926) (Inca Justice) became a Marxist primer for university students,[110] and the slogan he coined, *Minas al estado, tierra al indio* (Mines to the state and land to the Indian), became a battlecry of the Bolivian Left, which adopted his belief that foreign capital could only be beneficial to advanced industrial states and that in Bolivia, where minerals dominated the economy, the mines should be used for the national benefit, not for the benefit of private investors.[111]

In 1938 he organized the *Partido Socialista Obrero Boliviano* (PSOB) (Bolivian Socialist Workers' party), in his estimation the first disciplined socialist party to follow the *indigenista* ideas of

Mariátegui. Marof then served his party in Bolivia's Chamber of Deputies, where he functioned primarily as a spokesman for Marxism.

The work of Marof, the politician, essayist, literary critic, novelist, playwright, and biographer, has always rested upon historical materialism. Marof the critic could be devastating, as he illustrated in his analyses of the histories of Alcides Arguedas, whom he took to task for not understanding the role of materialism and for worshipping *mestizo* thinking representative of a corrupt class that believes in middle-sector superiority.[112] Marof never thought of his literature, plays or literary criticism primarily in terms of expressing creativity but rather as vehicles for his political ideas, to encourage skepticism, to reject everything Spanish, and to foster a belief in social legislation.[113] He is, perhaps, best known for his play *El jefe* (The Chief), an exceptionally humorous political comedy that pokes fun at the system and deplores the corruption in Bolivia's government.[114]

Marof's nonfiction pieces generally assume an antiimperialist stance based on the ideas of Rubén Darío and José Enrique Rodó, whose works he read. He acknowledged an intellectual debt to Peru's José Mariátegui, whom he knew personally; to Mexico's Andrés Molina Enríquez, whose book *Los grandes problemas nacionales* (1909) (The Great National Problems) he felt clearly depicted conditions in most Latin American nations; and to Aníbal Ponce of Argentina, whose writings he read and whose socialist interpretations he favored.[115] Marof's writings also reflect the thinking of the French philosopher Jean-Jacques Rousseau and the American novelist Jack London, both of whose concepts of liberty he respected. From the man known best as the tutor of Simón Bolívar, Simón Rodríguez, in whom Marof saw elements of utopian socialism,[116] he obtained ideas about the United States, especially its potential danger to Latin America.[117]

According to his countryman Guillermo Lora, Marof's greatest talent was not as an historian or theoretician, nor as an organizer or politician, but as a novelist, who wrote excellent critical political works such as *Los cívicos* (The Civics),[118] and as a salesman for socialism. Lora points out that Marof's analysis of Bolivia is somewhat European, devoid of a Bolivian theory of revolution or a clear picture of what type of government could best serve the workers' struggle.[119]

Some observers have labeled Marof a Trotskyist, but close examination of his life and works leads to the conclusion that he represented no sectarian Marxist viewpoint. He was an independent "plain" Marxist, who vehemently opposed imperialism and oligarchical government. He did so by appreciating, but without utilizing, disciplined Marxist methodology.

Marof defined revolution as a social movement—a transposition of classes. He pointed out that what has been called revolution in Bolivia has been only the replacement of one government by a similar one. What Bolivians have called "revolutions" have transferred nothing. This he blamed on a lack of orderly planning and forethought. He rejected the idea that the masses, despite engaging in considerable subversion, have been the instrument of revolution, on the grounds that they have been too hungry, ill-informed, and unorganized to plan successful structural changes. He agonized over the fact that the masses have not had the education necessary to read Thomas More, Bakunin, or Marx.[120] To him, what has passed for revolution in Bolivia has been brought about by bourgeois democrats who care only temporarily about the people.[121]

On the other hand, Marof advocated violent revolution to effect social change. He linked revolution to the return to indigenous political and social traditions and to the return of land to the Indians. His *indigenismo* contained a mystical quality, related to man's attachment to the land—the belief that humans can conquer nature if they can handle or cultivate the land successfully. In conjunction with these beliefs, he urged the nationalization of the mines and the expulsion of foreigners who encroached upon and took over the land.[122]

He agreed with Mariátegui that the Indians need their own land, signifying their freedom, before the destruction of Bolivia's feudal system can begin. Marof's 1934 book *La tragedia del altiplano* (The Tragedy of the Highlands) examined the plight of Indian society in Bolivia[123] and cited the absence of initiative on the part of intellectuals and the government to improve social conditions. He praised the greatness of the pre-Columbian civilizations, condemned the Spanish for degrading them, noted that the Incas understood and could cope with the problems of their times, and stated that if Bolivians analyzed contemporary conditions by socialist methods they could make social improvements.[124] Marof categorized the Incas as a communal society, not as a scientific socialist or a classless state. He realized that their government was autocratic but appreciated their social solidarity and liked the idea that their natural wealth was at the disposal of the state.[125]

Since the Indians lost their independence to the Spanish, Bolivia has never been free, thought Marof. After the expulsion of the Spanish, the country came under the control of the British, Chile, and, subsequently, the United States.[126] He contended that those who have suffered the most under foreign domination have been workers and peasants who deserved a better life. He found in the twentieth century proletarian characteristics similar to those of the pre-Columbian peoples—a mystique of desire, a feeling of fraternity, and a need for abundance and liberty.[127]

Marof believed that foreigners brought racism, a manifestation of class antagonisms, to Bolivia. Whites desirous of economic gain created the myths of the hapless Indian and the untrustworthy *mestizo*.[128] He buttressed his theories on racism by pointing to the Chaco War as an example of white foreign elites endeavoring to manipulate the economic future of Bolivia. He also noted that the extensive nationalism of the conflict weakened the feudal system by spreading the notion that something better existed.[129] He saw the Chaco War as an attempt to obtain a port for Standard Oil tankers and to preserve that corporation's interests; and he thought, at the time, that the conflict would awaken Bolivian workers, soldiers, and students, who could ally and turn their energies against the oligarchy and toward social revolution.

Marof belonged to the Tupac Amaru Revolutionary Group, dedicated to converting the Chaco War to a social movement opposing imperialism. The group held the unique idea that the war would enable the military to understand that it fought for the wrong reasons. After the conflict over the Chaco, which cost Bolivia most of the disputed territory and approximately 60,000 lives, a secret society of former soldiers *Razón de Patria* (RADEPA) (Reason of the Fatherland), formed to further nationalist, statist, and social revolutionary goals. Although the group's program was vague and overly romantic, its existence supported Marof's contention that the war educated some who were forced to serve in it.

He hoped that the nationalism of the war would foster a movement for nationalization of the mines and that funds available to the country from such a move could be used for social betterment. He explained in *La verdad socialista en Bolivia* (1938) (The Socialist Truth in Bolivia) how Creole reactionaries had liquidated Bolivian nationality and that it could only be reclaimed by socialism.[130] He maintained this belief throughout subsequent decades, including the period of the Bolivian National Revolution, which he assessed as a reform era during which society was not sufficiently restructured to bring about lasting political and social change.

Guillermo Lora (1922–)

Known by Marxists throughout Latin America for his vigorous style and biting critical analyses, Guillermo Lora has been one of the area's most articulate exponents of Trotskyism. Over forty years ago he founded Bolivia's (Trotskyist) Revolutionary Workers' party (POR), which he subsequently served as secretary general. Despite being harassed by Bolivian authorities for decades, Lora has continued his scholarly studies and writing. But his active efforts to build a general Trotskyist movement in Latin America have diminished.

Lora's three-volume *Historia del movimiento obrero boliviano* (1967–1970) (History of the Bolivian Workers Movement), winner of critical acclaim in Latin America, Great Britain, and the United States,[131] is a tribute to his high academic standards and tenacity, especially in light of what he terms the handicap of working with the poor bibliographic, library, and record-keeping resources in Bolivia, to which he attributes the low overall quality of history done there. More than any other piece of scholarship, this monumental social history depicts the evolution of Bolivia's working class, analyzes the nation's class structure, assesses the country's role in South America's economy, and tries to understand how Bolivia's intellectuals think. Lora provides evidence for some of Tristán Marof's generalizations by studying some of the same problems but by using a more scientific methodological approach than did his countryman.

He shows how, during the colonial and early republican eras, the indigenous masses were virtually enslaved[132] and how, as a result of the War of the Pacific (1879–1883), the United States became prominent in Bolivia's economy.[133] He clarifies how, during the second half of the nineteenth century, Bolivian liberals began to replace, or vie with, the conservative oligarchy for political power.[134] He notes the entry of monopoly capital into the country on a large scale between 1870 and 1880 and how, during this major era of imperialism, finance capital began to leave the country.

According to Lora, one of the first socialists to have a significant impact on Bolivia was Gerardo F. Ramírez, an admirer of the European anarchists, who published in 1921 a pamphlet *La Sociedad Futura* (The Future Society), outlining a plan for a federal socialist state.[135] Lora noted that later in the 1920s, Ricardo Jaime Freyre (1868–1933) an Argentine militant, poet, historian, and diplomat who studied Marx, Tolstoy, Ingenieros, and Palacios, spread his ideas in Bolivia.[136] Lora also credited the works of Argentine socialist Alfredo Palacios and Chilean Marxist Luis Recabarren with influencing the workers' movement in Bolivia.[137] He mentioned that the first Bolivian syndicates were based on the principles of classical Marxism[138] and that the student federation of the 1920s, an outgrowth of the 1918 University Reform Movement, relied heavily on Marx.[139]

An intellectual rather than a manual worker, Lora identified with and has been active in Bolivia's labor movement. He believes that whoever controls Bolivia's mines controls the country. He has long advocated a special role for the mine workers as a revolutionary vanguard to replace the military, which has traditionally held political power.

In 1946 Bolivia's Miner's Federation adopted Lora's Thesis of Pulacayo, the first time that a Latin American trade union formally accepted Trotsky's ideas on permanent revolution.[140] The Thesis—based on the idea of the proletariat as the new class in Bolivia and the mine workers as the most advanced revolutionary sector in that class—stated that the struggle against international capitalism was paramount to the struggle for socialism, that the mine workers should lead the fight, that all workers should be armed, that a worker's government should be armed, and that a worker's government should be the dictatorship of the proletariat. It rejected compromising alliances with the national bourgeoisie but stressed ties with the peasants and artisans who would fulfill the traditional democratic-bourgeois role in the transition to socialism.[141] Lora's Thesis was predicated on Trotsky's theory that in backward nations the bourgeois-democratic revolution against feudalism and the socialist revolution against capitalism would follow each other in a continuous process.[142]

Adherence to the Thesis of Pulacayo marked the high point in the history of Bolivia's working class as it contradicted the MNR, which called for a movement based on multiclass nationalism led by a middle-class elite, a position which Lora attributed to the exceptional backwardness of Bolivian capitalism, which was incapable of effecting a democratic revolution.[143]

In his *Balance de la huelga minera* (1963) (Liberation by the Miner's Strike), Lora presented a critique of the years the MNR controlled Bolivia, when the trade union movement was run by the government bureaucracy and Stalinists and Trotskyists engaged in reformism.[144] He portrayed the unions of that era as anachronisms, playing into the hands of imperialists through the *Corporación Minera de Bolivia* (COMIBOL), the state-capitalist government- (not worker-) controlled mining corporation founded after nationalization of the mines in 1952.

In *La revolución boliviana* (1963) (The Bolivian Revolution), Lora depicted the Bolivian trade union movement as following a U.S. model during the McCarthy era. Despite their antiimperialist rhetoric, Bolivia's unions were controlled by the bourgeoisie and not representative of an independent working class.[145] His analysis of the MNR and the Bolivian National Revolution approximates the views of Cuban Julio Antonio Mella and Peru's José Mariátegui on *Aprismo*. They all see the respective struggles of the MNR and APRA as counterrevolutionary—directed against imperialism not to abolish private property but to protect native private property from foreign imperialism.[146]

In addition to studies of workers' movements and the Bolivian National Revolution, the indefatigable Guillermo Lora wrote a brief history of guerrilla warfare.[147] This book leaned heavily on the works of China's Mao Zedong, Vietnam's General Vo Nguyen Giap, and Cuba's Che Guevara. Lora explained that Guevara erred when he stated that a guerrilla war could not succeed when the incumbent government has popular support and the appearance of constitutional legality. Lora contended that a guerrilla movement can still get underway when a legitimately elected government exists if the military is subordinate to an imperialist power and if other conditions for revolution are favorable, such as an organized party to lead the insurrection.[148]

He maintained that a worker-peasant militia constituted a good counterweight to the old military and noted that one factor in the failure of the Bolivian National Revolution was that it reorganized the army as an arm of (Yankee) imperialism and that the government disarmed the people. He argued that guerrillas need to be coordinated by a political party and must undergo a continuous revolutionary education process as did Fidel Castro's army.[149] He agreed with Marx and Clausewitz that "war is no more than the continuation of politics by other means" and said that a spontaneous military action can be useful but that the political party, operating as the vanguard of the proletariat, can raise the level of the guerrilla struggle and permit the guerrillas to become a more regular force.[150] He stated that waiting for the proper conditions for a guerrilla war is for the social democrats or orthodox Communist parties; and he also contended that situations and political development (consciousness) are unequal in all Latin American states and that one cannot simply apply Cuba to Bolivia and hope to succeed.[151] Lora thought that Guevara should not have expected a *foco* to create a revolutionary party in Bolivia and that he failed there in 1967 because he deviated too far from Lenin by not adhering to the need for a cohesive and developed party to guide the guerrilla insurrection.

Postures such as those described above, generally articulated in well-researched, soundly reasoned, scholarly books, helped solidify Lora's position as one of Latin America's foremost creative "plain" Marxists who preferred Trotskyist ideas, but always worked openly and flexibly. Lora, like his fellow Bolivian Marxist thinkers, envisioned his country relinquishing its inferior position in the capitalist system and assuming a productive and noncompetitive role among the developed and developing socialist nations of the world. He and his *compañeros* held no false illusions about "instant success" either in making the transition to socialism or in developing a healthy, diversified socialist economy. They realized that economic development in Bolivia had historically been limited by concentration on the mining industry and that the prospects for a successful socialist revolution were not optimal in a nation that has not attained a minimum standard of development and which for the major portion of its history has languished under the control of a military subordinate to the native land- and mine-owning class and its foreign partners.

From 1964 until 1982 various military-led or -controlled governments increasingly forced Bolivia's radicals underground or into exile. Today, the impact of the thinking of Tristán Marof, Guillermo Lora, José Antonio Arce, Arturo Urquidi Morales, and Ricardo Añaya can occasionally be gleaned in the rumblings of restive peasants and disenchanted students. But for the most part, Bolivia's active intellectual Left has literally been eliminated by the old aristocracy supported by a new business elite grown powerful through U.S. military and economic aid.

8. Uruguay

> Socialism is more than Marxism, because it is not just a
> point of view or a historical, sociological, philosophical, and
> economic criterion. It is also a movement which answers
> needs that are far removed from any theory, a current of
> anxiety, of hopes, of desires for social and human justice.
> For these things, Marxism is a channel, and as such it acts as
> a guide, but certainly a channel is not the whole river.
>
> Emilio Frugoni

No analysis of modern Uruguay would be complete without mention of José Batlle y Ordóñez (1856–1929), whose ideas dominated his nation's social and political thought until the 1960s.
Founder of the prestigious newspaper *El Día*, critic of Church
policies, advocate of separation of church and state, and president
of the nation (1903–1907 and 1911–1915), he epitomized the
staunch liberal democratic constitutionalist. Philosophically, *Batllismo* rested primarily upon nationalism, Comte's positivism, and,
to a lesser extent, the idealistic social consciousness found in the
spiritist thinking of Krausism.

Batlle, who has been erroneously called a Marxist, understood
the labor theory of value, and his thinking reflected an appreciation of the plight of workers. But his ideas were decidedly non-
Marxist. He rejected the dialectic and believed inequality not to be
deliberate but merely the result of difficulty in achieving a just
distribution.[1] He felt that class struggle furthered inequality. To
foster equality, he advocated state intervention and regulation of
distribution. He held utopian views about man's ability to control
conflicts but dismissed the notion of conflict's having an economic
base. In his book *La ideología de Batlle* (1967) (The Ideology of
Batlle), Antonio Grompone analyzed him from an historical-mate-
rialist perspective and concluded that he was purely a product of
bourgeois thought—an early advocate of the theory that most of a
society's ills will be eliminated by the ascendence to political
power of a socially conscious middle sector. Alberto Zum Felde,
author of *Proceso intelectual del Uruguay* (1941) (The Intellectual

Process of Uruguay) and that country's most frequently read *pensador,* also finds Batlle's thinking to be middle class.

Why begin our examination of Marxist thought in Uruguay with Batlle, a nonsocialist social reformer? We know that during the late nineteenth century and early twentieth century Uruguay had a sizable school of materialist thought; however surprisingly few of its members were Marxists. But in this period the freethinking, open-minded Batlle encouraged open debate about new ideas, both foreign and domestic, helped make Uruguay a Latin American center for the development of international and inter-American law and diplomacy, and created the intellectual climate that permitted Marxist thought to take root and subsequently flourish there. He believed that in a democracy ideas of all types should be introduced, scrutinized for potential value to society, and understood. During his first term as president, Uruguay's Socialist party was organized (1910), and a new generation of Marxists was spawned. Under Batlle's aegis Uruguay adopted protective labor legislation, a progressive social security system, and numerous public welfare services, thereby establishing a tradition upon which the country's Socialists and Communists endeavored to build a working-class movement.

Emilio Frugoni (1880–1969)

Nurtured by the intellectually stimulating climate of Montevideo, Emilio Frugoni gained reknown as a diplomat, lawyer, professor, journalist, orator, defender of women's rights, poet, writer, social critic, and founder of the Karl Marx Study Center in 1904 and of Uruguay's Socialist party, which he served as its first elected representative to parliament in 1911 and unsuccessful presidential candidate in 1938.

A prolabor social democrat who adhered to the tenets of the Second International,[2] Frugoni claimed that he was inspired by Cuba's writer-freedom-fighter José Martí.[3] He combined historical materialism with an almost primitive idealism in order to gain his primary objective—getting his socialist ideas across to the Uruguayan people. To do so, he strove to combat the thinking of Batlle whom he viewed as a reformer who broke the power of the *caudillos,* brought about state capitalism, and began to make the bureaucracy into a new ruling class in Uruguay. His *Socialismo, nacionalismo, y batllismo* (Socialism, Nationalism, and Batllism) demonstrates the uphill battle he fought against Batlle's successful reforms, which he felt expanded capitalism at the expense of the people. He claimed that Batlle-inspired democracy would flourish for a time in Uruguay but warned against a takeover of the nation by the right wing.[4]

Frugoni led Uruguay's and the Socialist party's struggle against World War I, which he called an "imperialist war." When the Socialist party affiliated with the Communist International in 1922, he led a minority that withdrew from that body and established an independent Socialist party that remained rather orthodox for the next three and a half decades.

Adhering to the Marxist idea of theory and praxis, he continued to work actively in politics while writing continuously. In 1935 he published *La revolución del machete: Panorama político del Uruguay* (The Revolution of the Machete: Panorama of Uruguayan Politics), a condemnation of his nation's shift toward dictatorship after Batlle's death.[5] He viewed his Socialist party as the main force resisting fascism during the 1930s and warned that eventually Uruguay's reformers would fall victim to hard times, that the country's economy would falter, and that fascist types would seize political control in the name of the capitalist power elites. He denounced the false illusion of democracy in a country where the electoral processes were controlled by those who held the means of production and where the workers had little political power.

By the late 1950s Frugoni's predictions of the 1930s proved true. Uruguay's welfare state economy began to run huge deficits. When Uruguay appeared in danger of collapse, the Socialist party moved to the left and adopted a Marxist-Leninist line. When the economy deteriorated further in the 1960s, the Socialist party became a spawning ground for the Tupamaro guerrillas, who unsuccessfully led the battle against the military, which seized control of the country and ended its democratic tradition.

Turning from the practical to the theoretical level, we see that Frugoni brought to Uruguay the teachings of Argentine socialist Juan Justo. He believed that Justo, more than anyone else, explained world socialist thinking in a Latin American context. Frugoni pointed out that conditions differed considerably between the more developed Argentina and Uruguay, especially in the predominance of early democratic sentiment in the latter, which he attributed to the pastoral environment, the thinking of independence leader José Artigas, and the diversity of thought brought there by postindependence European immigrants.

In his significant book *Ensayos sobre marxismo* (1936) (Essays on Marxism), Frugoni went beyond the lessons of Justo and displayed an incredible breadth of knowledge about the history of political thought in the Western world. His chapter "The Determinism of Hunger" argues brilliantly that all thought emanates from the process used to satisfy hunger or the basic search for food. Using ideas to my knowledge never before expressed by a Latin American socialist, Frugoni constructed an interpretation of history based upon human need for money in order to purchase food.[6] Taking off on the thinking of the Spanish philosopher Miguel Unamuno and the Spanish biologist R. Turró, Frugoni contended that a person's first social act is to satisfy hunger, that hunger motivates human intelligence, and he ties these facts to Marx's beliefs that one's social existence determines one's consciousness and that the mode of production determines social evolution.[7] In order of priority, he saw three basic hungers to be satisfied: (1) the hunger to feed the body or the need to produce food, (2) the hunger to feed the spirit or the need to produce the elements of commerce and civilization, and (3) the hunger for social life or the need to produce articles of beauty and fruits of knowledge. In other words, first you produce food, then more luxurious items, then beautiful ones. Frugoni concluded that hunger is the matrix of violent revolution.[8]

Frugoni also concerned himself with the function of the spirit in relation to the process of social evolution. His *Ensayos sobre marxismo* conveys the conviction that materialism dominates the spirit, that social materialism directs man rather than his spirit. He believed that in order to progress, Latin America had to understand its material drives and to place less emphasis on the spiritual.[9] He also postulated the belief that class thought dominates, that what man construes as "ideal" is derived from his class orientation. To him, social systems are material in origin, and as such class-related. He explained that man's ideas according to the laws of dialectical materialism, not his spirit, determine his destiny. He stressed that Latin Americans have to believe that intellect can control social forces.[10]

Frugoni's large two-volume work *Génesis, esencia, y fundamentos del socialismo* (1947) (Genesis, Essence, and Fundamentals of Socialism), demonstrated, impressively, a comprehensive understanding of the philosophical and intellectual bases of socialism.[11] Aside from his comments on European Marxist thought, his most cogent insights in this work pertain to the Mexican Revolution and Peruvian *Aprismo*. He viewed the Mexican Revolution as a romantic-democratic movement using the rhetoric of socialism but advocating state capitalism. He drew an analogy between the Mexican Revolution and the French revolution where the rights of man are declared but implemented in a class-oriented fashion and where economic and social privilege prevail.[12] *Aprismo,* he stated, was originally based on Marx but was more anti-United States and antiimperialist than anticapitalist. He said that for Peru the last stage of foreign capitalism (imperialism) is also the first in a semifeudal area where the proletariat is very small, where emphasis is on agriculture and mining, thus where, in a Leninist sense, a proletarian party has little potential and must ally with the peasantry to succeed. He saw APRA, despite its propaganda about being a party of manual and intellectual laborers, not involved in the class struggle, but as an alliance of classes, and he thought the organization was more in tune with the antiimperialist thinking of Rubén Darío than with the ideas of Marx.[13]

Frugoni believed that one cannot comprehend the present without a solid grasp of the past, and he, as well as many of his socialist colleagues, understood the course of world history and was thoroughly acquainted with all of the zigs and zags of the diverse leftist movements operating in and out of Latin America. This creative, "plain," and "critical" Marxist thought it a grave error to interpret Marx narrowly. To him, Marxism was not merely economic determinism but a broad sociological science based upon dialectical materialism. He thought that nondogmatic theory and practice provided the maximum liberty—a unique situation that can only be brought about under the leadership of the working class, which has no privileges.[14]

Perhaps the greatest accomplishments of Frugoni were his viable intellectual opposition to *Batllismo* at the height of its success and his ability to sustain socialist thoughts, which increasingly gained greater credence after *Batllismo* failed to live up to expectations.

Rodney Arismendi (1913–)

In contrast to the "plain" Marxism of Emilio Frugoni, Rodney Arismendi exemplifies the "sophisticated" Marxist. For many years he labored to build a continental corpus of thought around which to unify Latin America's Communist parties in theory and action. He has served as first secretary of Uruguay's Communist party since 1955 and simultaneously as its unofficial historian until he was sent into exile to Moscow in 1974. A follower of Lenin, he wrote clearly, had a good head for politics, and, despite a tendency to propagandize, possessed sufficient creativity to be categorized as an activist-theoretician rather than strictly a rhetorician.

Like Frugoni, he opposed the Zum Felde-Batlle school of thought. He objected to Zum Felde's contention that Marxism interpreted history solely from an economic standpoint. He felt that Zum Felde misunderstood the unity of the historical process, tended to see it as a series of isolated events, which led him to view Marxism as dogmatic.[15] He agreed with Zum Felde that Batlle was progressive, but reproached the latter for not handling *latifundismo* effectively and for permitting British and United States monopoly capital into Uruguay. To Arismendi, Batlle represented national bourgeois interests; although he tried to democratize Uruguay, in the long run, he failed to do so. Following Lenin's thinking Arismendi stated that it is sometimes necessary to censure aspects of the old regime, but only the proletariat can bring true democracy and that Batlle did not subscribe to that belief.[16]

Among Latin American intellectuals Rodney Arismendi is best known for his 1946 work *La filosofía del marxismo y el Señor Haya de la Torre* (1946) (The Philosophy of Marxism and Mr. Haya de la Torre), a definitive study from a socialist perspective on the political thought of the Peruvian Haya de la Torre. Arismendi concluded that Haya de la Torre's philosophy represents a variety of idealistic relativism or a skewed dialectic, in which the thesis of the Russian revolution and the antithesis of fascism synthesizes to bourgeois democracy. He disputed Haya de la Torre's contention that capitalism existed in Peru in the 1920s and claimed that for the American "space and time," imperialism is the first stage of capitalism. He stated that Haya de la Torre negated the historic function of the proletariat in America in favor of the idea of populists bringing about the revolution. To him, Haya de la Torre, like Batlle, was a progressive whose main force for change was the national bourgeoisie and who also did nothing to change essentially his country's economic system.[17] He noted that Haya de la Torre, along with other Latin American leaders such as Venezuela's President Rómulo Betancourt (1959–1964) and Costa Rica's Chief Executive José Figueres (1953–1958), represented the "big bourgeoisie" allied with imperialism, not the antiimperialist "national bourgeoisie" of President Juan José Arévalo of Guatemala (1945–1950). To him, men like Haya de la Torre, Betancourt, and Figueres are guilty of conciliation with imperialism in that their phraseology often confuses some people who mistakenly see them as leftists striving to liberate their nations from foreign domination.[18]

Rodney Arismendi successfully articulated Latin America's problems in Marxist terms. His thinking approximated that of Peru's José Carlos Mariátegui with whom he agreed that after independence Latin American politics were susceptible to bourgeois economic and political theories, which reflected the rise of capitalism in the region as a result of contact with the world market. Both Arismendi and Mariátegui did not refer to the bourgeoisie in the conventional sense, for they believed that Latin America had no industrial base.[19]

Arismendi spoke of Latin America in terms of the Third World and drew analogies between Asia, Africa, and Latin America. For example, he depicted the Catholic Church as a prime instrument of colonialism in both Africa and Latin America. His writing arouses the class consciousness of the Third World, making it aware of its history in order to forge a revolution leading to socialism.[20] He viewed World War II, especially the Soviet victory over fascism, as opening the way to further socialist gains in the Third World between 1945 and 1975, an era when colonial empires began to disintegrate, the antiimperialist movement gained momentum, and socialism won major victories.

A proponent of armed struggle, Arismendi, like Lenin, at times preferred mass action to isolated acts of terrorism. In his study *Lenin: La revolución y América Latina* (1970) (Lenin: The Revolution and Latin America), he demonstrated a sound understanding of the Russian leader's thinking and then applied it to Latin America.[21] He saw all Latin American nations at some stage of the permanent revolution and believed that in most countries a socialist revolution needs a revolutionary party to lead it to victory but that there could be exceptions. He concurred with Lenin about the difference between a revolution in an imperialist country and one in a nation dependent upon imperialism. In the latter the agrarian problem enables the national bourgeoisie to participate in the democratic front of national liberation as it did in China. He viewed Latin America's national bourgeoisie not simply as an instrument of imperialist rule and noted that the antagonisms between the national bourgeoisie and imperialism are constant. He saw the national bourgeoisie as a potential participant in a national liberation movement, one that can be subsequently converted into a socialist ally or eliminated. To him, temporary collaboration was sometimes necessary to further the revolution, but class alliance was less desirable.[22]

He cited numerous examples of successful cooperation between socialists and antiimperialist national bourgeoisies. From Brazil during the heyday of Luiz Carlos Prestes in the 1930s, to Bolivia and Guatemala during the 1950s, to Cuba under Fidel Castro and Colombia's Camilo Torres in the 1960s,[23] he noted the rise of revolutionary democrats or social reformers inspired by socialist ideas, who led movements for change and eventually embraced Marxism-Leninism and allied with the country's established working classes.[24]

He warned against Pan-Americanism, which manifests itself in projects like the Alliance for Progress, an antisocialist attempt to unify Latin America's bourgeoisie under the economic and ideological hegemony of the United States. He demonstrated that while Washington gave lip service to a "democratic front" in Latin America, the Alliance for Progress for the most part weakened democracy and deepened dependency in the region.[25]

Underlying all of Arismendi's thoughts on imperialism, revolution, his analyses of other thinkers like Haya de la Torre, and his political and social theory are Marx's stages of development to socialism. The Uruguayan thinker never wavered from the belief that the bourgeoisie must complete its historic function—the destruction of feudalism, capitalist development of agriculture, industrial expansion, and the creation of political democracy before society can make the transition to socialism.[26]

Francisco R. Pintos (1880–1968)

Less famous and less flexible than his Communist party comrade and countryman Rodney Arismendi is historian Francisco Pintos. In his *Historia del Uruguay (1851–1938): Ensayo de interpretación materialista* (1946) (History of Uruguay [1851–1938]: Essay on the Materialist Interpretation), he successfully pleaded for and showed that the application of scientific Marxist analysis to historical problems can yield potential solutions. In a basically pastoral nation like Uruguay, he maintained that agrarian reform was the vital first step toward achieving social justice for most of its citizens. He demonstrated that class antagonisms have constantly engendered economic disparities between Uruguay's elites and its masses, which, in conjunction with pressures from its powerful neighbors Argentina and Brazil, have prevented the nation from maintaining social and political equilibrium. For example, he showed that when Argentina's bourgeoisie centralized its government in the 1850s, many Uruguayans suffered from the repercussions of alliances between the bourgeoisie of both nations.[27] He pointed out how Uruguay, perhaps proportionately more than any other Latin American state, has been subjected to capitalist cross-currents and foreign ideas.

Pintos viewed the 1903 election of José Batlle as a triumph for the progressive bourgeoisie, the petty bourgeoisie, and the workers. Like Frugoni and Arismendi, he saw the Batlle era as one of national reform not revolution. He detailed in his book *Batlle y el proceso histórico* (1960) (Batlle and the Historical Process), how, during the 1876 to 1933 period, U.S. investment began to replace that of Great Britain in his country[28] and how international capitalism gained strength there. Uruguay, like most client states, suffered more than dominant nations during the Depression. Pintos showed that the Depression forced introspection upon the Uruguayans, made all classes aware of the need to industrialize to reduce trade deficits, emphasized the importance of agrarian reform to political democracy, and strengthened the country's socialist movement.

Pintos's work exhibited a strong concern for the disenfranchized, especially the working classes. In *Ubicación de Artigas*

(1965) (The Position of Artigas), he viewed the struggles for Uruguay's independence as a precursor of labor's future battles.[29] He drew causal connections between aspects of the early liberation movements and twentieth-century Uruguayan socialism in his *Historia del movimiento obrero del Uruguay* (1960) (History of the Worker's Movement in Uruguay).[30]

Better than any other Uruguayan writer, Pintos illuminated the history of his country's working class. His "sophisticated" Marxist analyses of Uruguayan society from the bottom up furnished valuable insights into its political economy and a framework around which broader Marxist studies have been, and can be, based. He provided historical guidelines enabling socialists and nonsocialists to gain a deeper understanding of Uruguayan society.

Abraham Guillén (1913–)

The most prominent "plain" and "critical" Marxist in Uruguay in recent years has been Abraham Guillén, a brilliant Spanish exile who fits Gramsci's definition of an "organic intellectual." A veteran of the Spanish Civil War, Guillén, who sometimes used the pseudonym Arapez, first established a reputation by writing about Spanish political problems. From Franco's Spain he fled to France; after World War II he went to Argentina and eventually settled in Uruguay.

Guillén's observations of the Communists and Socialists in Spain led him to conclude that at times they were opportunists rather than believers in the class struggle,[31] a conviction he carried to Latin America where he gained respect as an economic analyst. In 1957 he published his two-volume work *La agonía del imperialismo* (1957) (The Agony of Imperialism), which led the Argentine government to dismiss him from his position in its Ministry of Economic Affairs and subsequently to accuse him of working with the *uturuncos* (tigermen) guerrillas, a suspected *Fidelista* group. Imprisoned briefly in 1961, he sought political asylum in Montevideo in 1962 when Uruguay still prided itself on being a haven for exiled intellectuals and receptive to new modes of thought.

Once ensconced in Uruguay, Guillén went to work for the newspaper *Acción* and began to put into book form philosophies that within a few years guided urban guerrilla movements in Argentina, Brazil, and Uruguay. His clarity of thought, ability to apply Marxist principles to contemporary problems, eloquence of writ-

ten expression, and willingness to devise strategies for and participate actively in Latin America's struggle for socialism under
workers' control caused many Uruguayan leftists to look to him as
an ideological mentor. Perhaps the greatest tribute to Guillén's
sagacity and the influence of his pen is the fact that his works
were suppressed. Almost no one in the United States, outside of
the Defense Department and the Central Intelligence Agency, ever
came in contact with his more than twenty published volumes.

Guillén's *La agonía del imperialismo* and his *El imperialismo
del dólar* (1962) (Imperialism of the Dollar) established him as a
"dangerous" intellectual who called for a second war of independence for Latin America. He envisioned eventual conflict between
the United States and Latin America as the latter's dependency
upon the former grew. Guillén praised Cuba as the initiator of the
process of breaking U.S. domination and predicted that national
liberation movements would emerge in all Latin American countries and unite in a hemisphere war against the United States and
its oligarchic allies in Latin America. Once deprived of its Latin
American dependencies, he predicted that in the United States
living standards would fall, poverty and unemployment would
increase, and labor would be aroused and begin to push for a
social revolution.[32] Peace in the Americas, he claimed, would only
come about when there is socialism in the United States, which he
believed had to be triggered by revolution in Latin America.[33]

By 1965 and the publication of *Teoría de la violencia* (1965)
(The Theory of Violence), Guillén had gained reknown in South
America as a flexible Marxist theoretician and guerrilla strategist.[34] He, like Mao, rejected the idea of coexistence between
socialism and capitalism and urged Latin American socialists to
oppose the ideas of Argentine economist Raúl Prebisch, whose
diffusionist plans for the region he saw, in the long run, primarily
benefiting foreign corporations.

In lieu of Prebisch's liberal-reformist approach to Latin American development, Guillén posited a plan for socialist development
but warned that it could only be accomplished if the Left stopped
its internecine warfare and united. He called for hemispheric solidarity, perhaps even a Federal Republic of Latin America, which
could successfully control foreign economic interests in the area,
unrealistic recommendations in light of the petty national jealous-
ies in the region and its lack of political stability. On a more

practical note, he warned of the perils of the struggle ahead and, without mentioning Chile specifically, noted what would happen in terms of U.S. response if an Allende-type situation arose.[35]

Guillenismo combined the historical and economic method of Marx with Bakunin's belief in direct action, nineteenth-century French socialist Auguste Blanqui's faith in a group of professional revolutionaries seizing power directly, and Che Guevara's strategy of establishing an insurrectional *foco*. Guillén disagreed with the Cuban contention that the struggle for national liberation brought on socialist revolution. He believed that all classes must work together to foster social revolution, but in Latin America he saw three classes—the peasants, the exploited proletariat, and the middle classes—constantly battling the landowners and the exploiting sector of the middle classes supported by the United States. Thus, he concluded that revolution for national liberation is not necessarily socialist in nature.[36]

On the other hand, Guillén saw rivalries and conflicts in the capitalist world between the Americas and Europe and Japan as irreconcilable and helpful to the socialist movement. At the same time he noted that divisions in the socialist world weakened it in relation to capitalist society.[37] In particular he cited intersocialist antagonisms originating in Soviet imperialism, the economic gap between developed and underdeveloped socialist states, and the tendency of technocrats in socialist nations to keep workers from managing their own industries.

He urged socialists to engage continually in both self- and world analysis. To him, Marxist thought anticipated change by searching for revolutionary potential and by examining the agents of social change. Guillén felt that Marxist philosophy should prepare for action, not merely discover the laws of thought.[38]

His analysis of Uruguay's potential for revolution led him to conclude that urban guerrilla warfare could succeed there. Going on the premise that neither technological superiority nor firepower but the ability to endure the longest wins guerrilla confrontations, he argued that the cities where most who serve capital live are the best places to launch and protract the conflict.[39] When Uruguay's *Fidelistas* talked about emulating Cuba by forming revolutionary *focos* in the mountains, Guillén, ever mindful that Uruguay has no mountains, counseled them to concentrate their efforts on the cities, not the countryside. However, he stressed the guerrillas' need to have allies in the hinterlands to disrupt the flow of supplies to the cities and thereby increase their vulnerability. He concurred with Che Guevara that *focos,* in this case both urban and rural, serve the armed struggle well and that a vanguard party could emerge from the *focos.*[40]

To Guillén, urban guerrilla warfare constituted a link in the revolutionary process, not terrorism. It was designed to destroy the state by constantly striking its weak points and destroying the myth of its invincibility. He saw urban guerrilla victories as political and moral, not military. He advocated attracting the oppressor to an area where the populace supports the revolution and then defeating the oppressor in a protracted demoralizing war. Repeatedly illustrating that the inhumanity of the regime in control is central to winning popular support for the revolution, Guillén, contradicting the belief that it is easier to start a revolution under a moderate government than under a repressive one, contended that revolutionary struggles should begin in Latin America in nations controlled by military dictatorships, not in representative democracies.

Guillén's *Estrategia de la guerrilla urbana* (1966) (Strategy of the Urban Guerrilla), as we shall see, became the model for Uruguay's revolutionary uprising, as well as the inspiration for his Brazilian friend Carlos Marighela's *Minimanual of the Urban Guerrilla.*[41] In Chapter VI of *Estrategia* Guillén demonstrated how the dialectics of politics explains the social structure based on a class system and illustrates the fundamental antagonisms in society. It showed that by stressing economics the masses can be made to understand the revolutionary aspects of urban guerrilla warfare—that by the guerrillas pointing out the corrupt and manipulative manner of the system and a viable alternative to it, the people can fathom the possibility of escape from underdevelopment.[42] Once popular support for the revolution is gained, Guillén warned the guerrillas against revolutionary elitism, counseled them not to place too much faith in electoral politics, and noted the traditional Latin American Marxist tendency to overstress social reform instead of social revolution.[43]

Uruguayans remember Guillén as a theoretician-strategist, some of whose ideas were adopted by the Tupamaros (*Movimiento de Liberación Nacional*) (MLN) (National Liberation Movement), which attained its pinnacle of notability between 1968 and 1972.

Led by Raúl Sendic Antonaccio, a socialist, the Tupamaros also drew support from anarchists, Maoists, and Trotskyists. Advocating nonsectarian armed struggle and deriving inspiration from the Cuban revolution, the Tupamaros endeavored to publicize their movement, often using "Robin Hood" tactics while exposing the dependence of the Uruguayan government on a military that employed death and torture squads.

In 1968 the Chilean journal *Pinto Final* published "Thirty Questions to a Tupamaro," explaining the goals and functions of the movement that borrowed many of Guillén's ideas.[44] The urban *foquismo* of the group bore the stamp of Guillén but also reflected the thinking of Che Guevara, who believed that the taking up of arms and preparing for and engaging in actions against the bastions of bourgeois law create a revolutionary consciousness, organization, and conditions. The Tupamaros also followed Lenin's teachings by adhering to the role of the revolutionary in the revolution and the belief that spontaneity is escapism and can be costly in terms of lives.[45] The Tupamaros wanted to build an independent national socialist community after defeating the capitalists in an armed revolution. They saw workers and students as the nucleus to carry out the revolution that would rectify Uruguay's economic problems by nationalizing banks and export businesses and by expropriating large and underused land holdings.

For a few years the Tupamaro movement grew as it successfully raised the consciousness of Uruguay's young idealists, its steadily growing impoverished sector, and its intelligentsia. It briefly overcame socialist sectarianism by rallying most elements of the Left around revolutionary nationalism. Following Guillén's thought, the Tupamaros operated without a revolutionary party, which they considered a nonmandatory political apparatus. They avoided internal splits by never formally adopting the *foco* theory, which they referred to as a method of struggle. They maintained that Marxist parties and *focos* were compatible, not mutually exclusive,[46] that they could be combined, but were not always necessary.

The Tupamaros attracted worldwide attention in July 1970 when they kidnapped the U.S. AID and CIA official Dan Mitrione, who was teaching Uruguay's military and police how to conduct and combat terrorism. The subsequent killing of Mitrione, himself responsible for the deaths of hundreds of social reformers and revolutionaries in Latin America, led to a stepped-up anti-Tupamaro campaign, in which the revolutionaries proved no match for the Uruguayan armed forces, which soon assumed total control of the nation. Many Uruguayan socialists died in the bloodbath that followed the death of Mitrione.

Guillén criticized the way the Tupamaros handled the Mitrione situation. He felt that had they sentenced Mitrione to death and then released him after telling the story of his crimes to the international press, they would have won support for their movement,[47] that by killing him they lost credibility. Commenting on Tupamaro errors, Guillén stated: "In a revolution, every guerrilla action that has to be explained to the people is wrong: actions should be evident and convincing in themselves."[48] He felt that the Tupamaros failed to educate the masses sufficiently, and perhaps the world, in order to gain acceptance. Furthermore, Guillén contended that the MLN too closely approximated a counter state but offered no counter institutions to the masses other than negative ones like political executions and people's prison. Before the Tupamaros could build a strong mass line, they were demolished.[49]

Guillén's thinking helped foster a movement whose actions triggered a right-wing reaction, which ended Uruguay's long traditions of democracy and freedom of thought and eliminated some hope for immediate socialist revolution in that country. Although his books and those of fellow Marxist thinkers like Frugoni, Arismendi, and Pintos are among the progressive works that have been removed from Uruguay's libraries and burned, their ideas survive clandestinely in the minds of radicals who believe that out of the ruins of Uruguay's once highly successful liberal state, socialism will ultimately arise.

9. Mexico

The new humanism embraces for the first time in history all men
on earth, the yellow and the white, the black and the red. There is
no East nor West nor North nor South in the eagerness to live
with the same ideal and with the same hope.
  Now the beings of all nations are truly brothers and in the
tongue characteristic of each all sing in imposing chorus the
same hymn of liberty.
                                    Vicente Lombardo Toledano

The 1848 revolution in France caused Mexico's well-known nineteenth-century writer and thinker José María Luis Mora to draw
analogies between the lot of the French and the Mexican worker
and, indirectly, to make his countrymen aware of aspects of socialist thought. At that time Karl Marx had as little interest in
conditions in Mexico as its thinkers had in his ideas. But by 1861,
writing for the *New York Daily Tribune* and the German newspaper *Die Presse*, Marx expressed outrage at the French, Spanish,
and English intervention in Mexico. He ascribed most of the
blame for the intervention on England, which he characterized as
an industrialized nation bent upon including Mexico in its empire.
For the next decade his articles referred to Mexico as a colonial
pawn in international politics,[1] and Mexican *pensadores* paid a
little more attention to him.

  By the 1850s the ideas of French anarchist Pierre Proudhon
(1809–1865) were translated into Spanish and circulated in Mexico. Some Mexican liberals borrowed freely from Proudhon's
maxims, especially his belief that God was bad and that private
property encouraged theft. Greek-born Plotino Rhodakanaty arrived in Mexico in 1861 and soon founded an anarchist movement[2] whose followers produced a Fourierist journal, *Falansterio*.
Under Rhodakanaty's direction the anarchists contended that government kills the concept of equality, that to develop democratic
institutions government authoritarianism had to be eliminated.
Rhodakanaty's book *Cartilla socialista* (1861) (Socialist Note),
based on Fourier, argued that the reduction of government would
lessen tyranny.

Rhodakanaty's disciples established the *Gran Círculo de Obreros de México* in 1872—a workers' federation utilizing the ideas
of Proudhon and of utopian socialist Louis Blanc (1813–1882),
who maintained that the workers, not the privileged classes, had
to bring about social transformation. Blanc advocated state-run
social workshops to replace private enterprise, coined the formula
"from each according to his ability, to each according to his
needs," and served as a link between the older utopians and the
Marxists. Building upon foundations laid by the two French
thinkers, the *Gran Círculo* defended political guarantees, advocated free elections, promoted artisan expositions, and publicized
the ideas of trade unionism and workers congresses.[3] It paid close
attention to new trends in European socialism, brought the idea of
combating problems common to international labor to Mexico,
and made some workers aware of the perpetual antagonisms between themselves and the owning and ruling class and realize that
their only weapon against the capitalist state was the general
strike. These messages appeared in articles in *El Socialista* (The
Socialist) and *El Hijo del Trabajo* (The Son of Work) as well as in
other socialist journals and newspapers, which reached 12,000
members of the *Gran Círculo* in various parts of Mexico.[4]

Word of the Paris Commune spread in Mexico in 1871, and
names such as Guiseppe Garibaldi and Auguste Blanqui were
printed there for the first time as were new theories of socialsm.
That year the periodical *El Socialista* awakened some workers as
it dedicated its efforts to defending the rights of the working class.
Three years later the journal *La Comuna* appeared and added the
dimension of agitating for the elimination of the military from
politics.[5] Mexico's first labor congress was held in 1876. Within
two years the workers' movement and embryonic socialists added
to their intellectual baggage a contemporary variant of spiritual-
ism. Thus, there developed, among Mexican left-wing *pensadores,*
the theory that hand-in-hand with social betterment went a humanistic spirit dedicated to social justice. A moral position that
socialism represented the uppermost stage of humanity became the
major theme of Santiago Sierra, who wrote for *El Hijo del
Trabajo.*[6] Anarchist José María González, one of the influential
thinkers of the *Porfiriato* (era of Porfirio Díaz's control, 1876–
1911), wrote in the same journal about the slavery of the workers,
on liberty, equality, and fraternity as elements of French socialism,

and maintained that, despite the fall of the Paris Commune, socialism was the perfection of society—that working conditions in Mexico were particularly harsh and that the workers needed liberation from the enslavement of U.S. capital.[7]

Despite the existence of the anarchists and socialist-oriented periodicals in Mexico, a Spanish translation of Marx did not appear in the country until 1883. Then, as today, there could be found "Marxists" in the nation who had never read the works of or had a reasonable understanding of Marx. In fact, prior to the 1910 revolution the anarchist version of Marxism represented the major ideological expression of the Mexican working classes.

Prominent among Mexico's anarchists was Ricardo Flores Magón, who had read Engels and Marx but took his lead from the thinking of Michael Bakunin and Peter Kropotkin. From the latter he got the idea of removing all government officials and capitalists in order to build a communal society. He contended that the working class should organize to rebel against the state, which it could destroy, and then it should expropriate capitalist means of production and reorganize society on convenient and federalist lines without parliamentary action. Flores Magón realized that such objectives were very difficult to achieve because of close ties between U.S. capital and the Mexican government. He accused the White House of practicing the politics of absorption and asserted that Mexican society could not be restructured without curtailing U.S. imperialism.[8] Flores Magón propagated his ideas through the organ *Regeneración,* especially directing his antigovernment and anticapitalist diatribes toward the indigenous communities, which he viewed as potential catalysts for socialism. To him, the Indian communities had been bound together for centuries by a penchant for liberty, and *indianismo* would be the foundation upon which a Mexican revolution would be built.

Subsequent pages discuss numerous theories about the Mexican revolution, which began in 1910. One should not be deceived by the sometimes radical rhetoric of that movement into thinking that it was Marxist in nature. Marxist intellectuals often feel that there cannot be a revolution without a revolutionary plan or theory, and bourgeois thinkers have tried to construct one for the Mexican Revolution. As we shall see, little agreement exists among Marxists, who have been hard pressed to fit their ideas to established revolutionary models. Political observer Víctor Alba stated that perhaps no one in Mexico had read Lenin in 1910. If they had, they would have realized that the following conditions basic to every revolution were missing. The ruling class was not in a state of decay and did not believe the existing situation to be deteriorating; the oppressed classes were not always conscious of a need for change, and some folks who were did not consider it feasible; and there existed no theory by which to orient the revolution and no organization capable of directing the pressure for change.[9]

Most Mexican Marxists have not accepted the Revolution as a complete or thorough movement that restructured society. At times scholars have referred to the Revolution as part socialist and part capitalist, a concept unacceptable to Marxist analysts who believe in the fundamental incompatibility of the two systems and prefer to think of the Mexican experience as some variety of state capitalism.

During the constitution-making years of the Revolution, few significant socialist *pensadores* were found in government circles in Mexico. An exception was Rafael Nieto (1883–1926), who served the Carranza administration as undersecretary of treasury and public credit. An able economist, sociologist, and statesman, who also at one time or another was governor of San Luis Potosí and minister to Italy and Switzerland, Nieto had read Henry George and Marx. A radical whom Jesús Silva Herzog called "an advanced thinker," "an indecisive Marxist," and "a revolutionary *hacendista*,"[10] Nieto understood some of the major themes of Marx but not scientific socialism.

Nieto tried to prepare Mexico's Left, especially its rural labor sector, which he wrote about and whose interests he tried to protect, to participate in the ideological debates and political life in the years following the implementation of the 1917 constitution.[11] A dedicated internationalist, too, his book *El imperio de los Estados Unidos y otros ensayos* (1927) (The Empire of the United States and other Essays) noted that in an increasingly economically interdependent world the businessmen and industrialists controlled Mexican internal and external politics and economics. He believed that imperialism exploited Mexico's scarce natural wealth and weakened the spirit of its people.[12]

Nieto searched for a social science counterpart of Einstein's theory of relativity in order to explain the arrangement of human conduct, moral doctrine, and political systems.[13] Although he was dedicated to a materialist view and an economic interpretation of history, paradoxically, he contended that civilization could be salvaged by a vigorous reform of the capitalist economic and social system. At the same time he thought that government should exist for the people and believed that Mexico's governments had historically been general agents of political aggression and instruments of economic privilege.[14]

Nieto contended that class struggle was not a socialist creation, nor a simple economic classification, nor a tactic of a proletarian movement; rather it represented an essential truth emanating from the capitalist system. He saw Mexico's class struggle compounded by external imperialism and internal *latifundismo* of a feudal type. He believed that the Mexican Revolution could not be legislated when so few at the top had everything and the majority at the bottom had so little. To him, political equality provided for by the 1917 consitituton was a farce.[15]

When Mexico's Constituent Assembly met to draw up the 1917 constitution, only Luis Monzón, among its members, was a declared Marxist. A few of the other framers of the constitution had read some Marx and knew that he believed that the quest for private property fostered violence generally aimed at the workers. Thus, they inserted some collectivist principles and protective devices for the workers into the document but did not eliminate private industry or property. For example, Article 3 of the constitution stipulated: "Education will be socialistic . . . it will combat fanaticism and prejudice, creating in the young a rational and accurate conception of the universe and of society." Octavio Paz, Mexico's best-known poet and essayist, called the "socialistic" aspect of the constitution absurd, as the document glorified private property in a nation where the proletariat had no say in governing, and he wondered how communal land ownership (the *ejido* system) could become part of a society involved in a capitalist stage of development and the conflicts of world imperialism.[16]

Expressing another point of view on a different level, N. M. Roy, the leader of Mexico's Communists, claimed in 1920 that revolutionary movements could succeed in the West only after Europe no longer had colonies from which to draw profits. Lenin contended that capitalism could not be overthrown in colonial areas until after a socialist revolution succeeded in Europe. Although Roy conceded that revolutions could proceed simultaneously in Europe and America, he and Lenin agreed that the timing was not right for a socialist revolution in Mexico during the first decades of the twentieth century.[17]

Although Mexico was not in the throes of a socialist revolution when the Russian Revolution occurred, Marxist-Leninist ideas were discussed in the country's intellectual circles, and the study of Marxism was not frowned upon by the government during the 1917–1925 period when the United States and some European states tried to prevent the proliferation of Marxist thought or political activity.

Marxism was not studied formally in classrooms in Mexico until the 1930s when university professors, led by Vicente Lombardo Toledano, encouraged the scientific socialist analysis of society. By this time the influence of Marxism-Leninism had reached the top echelons of Mexico's government. President Lázaro Cárdenas (1934–1940), by no means a socialist, had high regard for the thinking of Lenin, especially his ideas about imperialism, the relationship of the people to the land, and the contradiction between capital and labor.[18] Some of Cárdenas's cohorts held Marxist views. His secretary of education, Gonzalo Vásquez Vela, asserted that "dialectical materialism was the philosophic groundwork of Mexican education." Inexpensive pamphlets, distributed by his ministry, contained writings by Marx, Lenin, and Stalin. Books such as *Detalles de la educación socialista implantables en México* (1936) (Feasible Details of Socialist Education in Mexico) by Luis Monzón, a Communist Senator and member of the Ministry of Education, emphasized the class struggle produced by capitalism and the duty of the schools to terminate corruption by creating a socialist state.[19]

During the Cárdenas era Leon Trotsky, who took asylum in Mexico where he was subsequently assassinated by Stalin's agents, became a defender of the Mexican Revolution, especially after Cárdenas expropriated the foreign-controlled oil industry in 1938. Trotsky categorized Mexico as a semicolonial nation waging a war for independence. However, he noted that Mexican labor was not preponderantly Marxist in orientation and that its participation in national bourgeois government should not be construed as socialism.[20]

By the 1940s most Marxist scholars tended to view the Mexican

Revolution as a democratic bourgeois movement while a few "elastic" or optimistic Marxists such as Jesús Silva Herzog, whose works we shall subsequently examine, preferred to believe that the Revolution produced a new synthesis and thus was part of the dialectic of historical materialism.[21]

By the late 1960s Marxist interpretations of history appeared to be gathering acceptance among Mexican academics, but the number of Mexican intellectuals who championed liberalism declined. Although Mexico has a long tradition of left-wing pamphleteers and polemicists, during the last two decades a greater proportion of Marxist theorists has emerged among the ranks of the nation's intellectuals, who are basically dissatisfied with the course of the Mexican Revolution. To understand their thinking, we now examine a few of the ideas of some of their more influential precursors and contemporaries.

Narciso Bassols (1897–1959)

Narciso Bassols influenced some of Mexico's most important social legislation. A professor of law, Bassols studied formally with the noted *pensador* Antonio Caso. He also learned a great deal from his friends philosopher Samuel Ramos and historian Jesús Silva Herzog. His desire to serve his country led him into numerous governmental posts, including secretary of public education, secretary of interior, secretary of treasury and public credit, and minister to Great Britain, France, and Russia.

A brilliant analyst who wrote on the philosophy of law, government organization, education, sociology, and economics, he won a great deal of respect for his book and many articles.[22] His writings show a steady movement to the left. For example, in 1925 he rejected historical materialism as well as Rousseau's idea that man was naturally good and only needed liberty to prove it. But constant analysis of the inequalities of Mexico's class system, wherein 75 percent of the population was isolated from the upper 25 percent,[23] led him, by 1932, to a socialist orientation, but one far from scientific Marxism. Bassols used Marxist phraseology in his speech and writings but ignored the dialectical method in his work as minister of education. After leaving that post, he studied Marx's thoughts in depth and became consumed by them.[24]

By 1937 when he wrote the prologue to the Spanish edition of John Strachey's *Theory and Practice of Socialism,* Bassols displayed a remarkable grasp of Marxist theory, called what existed in capitalist society "false democracy," and saw liberty as an illusion for 95 percent of the population of capitalist countries.[25]

Early in his career Bassols determined that Mexico's primary problem was how to intelligently distribute land to the peasants. In 1927 he conceived agrarian legislation containing a strong defense of the judicial rights of labor based on Mexico's historical conditions. He supported the antisocialist *ejido* (collective farm) as a controlled life, a core from which a sense of political, economic, and social belonging emanated, a place where displaced persons could affiliate and overcome their alienation.

Bassols claimed that without a healthy and productive rural proletariat Mexico could not industrialize,[26] and he advocated transferral of the means of production from the *hacendados* and foreign entrepreneurs to those who worked the land. Such thinking subsequently contributed to the progressive land reforms of the Cárdenas era.

Bassols believed that the indigenous folk were the backbone of the agrarian sector, the basic cultural component of Mexican society. He felt that by preserving the Indians' spiritual structure, while initiating scientific technology, Mexico could foster a social revolution.[27] He contended that Indian integration would hasten the abandonment of the traditional forms of production in favor of more equitable ones. Thus, he championed cultural relativity as a means of introducing new and progressive ideas.[28]

Bassols felt that Mexico had failed to educate its Indian population, especially the rural *campesinos*. He believed that the schools had created group or class differences and antagonisms that militated against the incorporation of the indigenous people into Mexican life.[29] He suggested beginning in the primary schools to imbue children with unselfish socialist ideas, to develop their interest in the state as a collectivist whole, to create Mexicanism that would enable people to relate to one another as equals.[30] Simultaneously, he asserted that rural education had to maintain traditional folklore, music, popular arts, poetry, and dance and blend the indigenous aesthetic values into Mexican life. He did not want to replace native culture with totally Western values.

As minister of education under Cárdenas, Bassols initiated, under Article 3 of the constitution, a program of socialized education to emancipate young Mexicans from the influence of the

Church and teach "scientific truth" in the schools.[31] His educational program sustained the doctrine of the distribution of wealth, took education out of the hands of the clergy, and had a profound and lasting affect upon Mexico from the primary schools through the national university.[32]

Bassols endeavored to educate his fellow Mexicans by clarifying nineteenth-century liberalism. He portrayed Benito Juárez and Miguel Hidalgo as representatives of a vaguely revolutionary movement, as leaders who began Mexico's social struggle, guided by romanticism and individualism, and who failed to recognize the true enemy.[33] To him, the inherent weakness of liberalism led to the takeover of Mexico by positivism, which prevented genuine revolution.

Bassols functioned as a critic of the Mexican Revolution, one who wanted to strengthen it by changing its orientation. For most of his life, he remained a loyal supporter of the movement, ever hopeful that it could be transformed from reformist capitalism to revolutionary socialism. He conceived of himself as a revolutionary devoted to restructuring Mexico's economy and body politic. He claimed that the capitalist world hindered the growth of Mexico and that only a new order could free his country from hunger.[34]

He maintained that the Mexican Revolution had a relationship to the Russian revolution—that both were part of the international struggle against general exploitation and class division. He did not subscribe to the idea that the Mexican Revolution was *sui generis* or without worldwide connections.[35]

During the 1930s Bassols collaborated with Vicente Lombardo Toledano in directing the socialist magazine *Futuro* and in founding the publishing house Editorial Revolucionario. He also was instrumental in getting refugees from the Spanish Civil War into Mexico where many of them became bulwarks of the nation's leftist and liberal intelligentsia.

He recognized the 1938 nationalization of oil as a major step in the natural progression of placing ownership of the land in the hands of the people and in destroying the political power of those who owned the land and its resources.[36] He lamented the fact that by 1940 the Mexican revolution had wound down. To help regenerate it, he thrust himself into the publication of the periodical *Combate,* which defended the vital interests of the people against foreign forces and those who would subsequently use World War II to enrich themselves,[37] and he worked through the Political Action League to counter the conservative-revisionist trend he saw taking over the Revolution. He spoke out against fascism in Italy, Germany, and Spain and pointed out that World War II encompassed two major components—the Axis conflict with the Allies and a class struggle, both derived from the contradictions of capitalism.

After World War II, Bassols contended that the United States viewed Latin America as a source of raw materials and envisioned using the human resources of the area for canon fodder in its Cold War drive to control the world. He also complained that the United States extracted three times what it invested in Mexico and thereby helped retard its growth.[38] He believed that the United States dominated the United Nations, but he hoped that the international organization would develop a close relationship between the emerging nations of Latin America, Asia, and Africa that could, in the future, work together to combat Yankee influence. Subsequently, he advocated Mexico's withdrawal from the United States-controlled United Nations.[39]

By 1949 Bassols considered the Mexican Revolution, led by the Revolutionary party, at a standstill, and two years later he helped found the socialist *Partido Popular,* which he hoped could restimulate the Revolution he saw falling into the hands of Mexico's powerful neighbor to the north and perhaps offset the 1947 Rio Treaty of Reciprocal Assistance adopted by the Organization of American States, which he claimed placed Latin America under a United States-led anticommunist alliance.[40]

By the time of his death in 1959, Bassols, independent, "plain" Marxist-humanist, had become more of a propagandist for socialism than a theoretician. He died disillusioned, believing that the Mexican Revolution, which had not even achieved the elementary goal of effective suffrage, had disappeared.[41]

Jesús Silva Herzog (1892–)

Early in his life Jesús Silva Herzog read the articles of the Flores Magón brothers and gained insight into anarchism. Subsequently, he befriended Aníbal Ponce of Argentina, whom he spoke of as the model socialist teacher working realistically toward a utopian goal and whose book *Educación y lucha de clases* (1936) (Education and Class Struggle) he referred to as the major work of its type in Spanish.[42] The study of Marx led Silva Herzog to affiliate briefly with the Mexican Communist party. At the same time he supported and criticized the Mexican Revolution—a role he has played as a diplomat, intellectual adviser, and active economist-administrator.

The victim of failing eyesight for over a quarter of a century, Silva Herzog nevertheless has maintained an exceptionally high rate of scholarly output. Close scrutiny of his writings, as well as his efforts on behalf of the respected magazine of social and political opinion *Cuadernos Americanos,* which he founded, reveals that he has used scientific Marxism primarily as a heuristic device, more a frame-work for critically analyzing problems than as an ideology that he embraced totally.

Silva Herzog's *El pensamiento socialista* (1937) (Socialist Thinking) demonstrated a fine understanding of the evolution of socialist thought from the Peloponnesian wars to the Mexican Revolution and traced the role of social and economic relations of production, *latifundismo,* and slavery from primitive tribal days through the feudal, capitalist, and imperialist stages of development.[43]

In addition to writing about socialist thought, Silva Herzog has delved into Latin American and world affairs. In so doing, he has adhered to the philosophy that each nation has to develop in conformity with its historical antecedents and geographical conditions;[44] yet he has always considered the problems of individual nations in the context of international relationships. For example, he viewed post-World War II industrialization in Latin America as a direct consequence of the Good Neighbor Policy, which he called the "white glove" replacing the "big stick," a change of form rather than content. He viewed the United States' expansionist policies as impediments to progress for the majority of nations, a situation that he predicted would prevail until capitalism was transformed "into a new society capable of superseding the bloody civilization of the merchant."[45]

He pointed out that the United States endeavored to control business, as well as ideology, in Latin America. He condemned the United States and its Organization of American States compatriots for severing ties to Castro's socialist Cuba for not being democratic while ignoring most of Latin America's right-wing dictators.[46] He criticized the hegemony of the United States and the Kennedy administration for trying to overthrow Cuba during the

1961 Bay of Pigs invasion and wondered how the Organization of American States could simultaneously condemn the Dominican Republic's aggression against Venezuela and overlook the United States' action against Cuba.[47]

Silva Herzog's life has paralleled the Mexican Revolution. His essays on the Revolution demonstrated that it did not follow Marxist principles but depicted its antibourgeois character. To him, the Revolution regulated, rather than destroyed, private property. He maintained that in 1910 the political leaders who opposed Díaz and sought power were not overly concerned about economic and social problems, nor were they receptive to the idea of class struggle, whereas the people were more interested in improving living conditions than in perfecting the governmental system and democracy. According to Silva Herzog, the revolutionary upsurge soon surpassed the aims of the original leaders, and the poor began to oppose the rich—peasants turned against landlords during the bloody preconstitution years.[48]

Silva Herzog analyzed Mexico's social classes and labor movement and concluded that the framers of the 1917 constitution were peasants, workers, military men, and professionals not influenced by Marx but by nineteenth-century liberalism. They produced an antibourgeois document that was popular, proagrarian, and nationalist. He pointed out that the constitution, even Articles 123 and 27, which dealt with the rights of labor and subsoil resources, accepted the concept of private property, that subsoil rights belonged to the nation, but most land belonged to individuals.[49]

Silva Herzog also developed the theme that Mexican thought was not unique or Marxist, but a product of numerous external ideologies as well as the social liberation of the 1857 constitution.[50]

Like Narciso Bassols, Silva Herzog saw in the Mexican Revolution the economic and social contradictions necessary to move toward socialism. He too believed that the Cárdenas era brought the greatest progress in terms of independence.[51] After Cárdenas nationalized oil, from May 1939 to August 1940, Silva Herzog put his advocacy of state-controlled industry into operation as general manager of Mexico's Office of Petroleum Distribution. To him, the oil expropriation signified a major step in resolving the problem of inequality between people. He hoped that it would lead to an equitable redistribution of Mexico's national wealth to enable the nation's people at least to be adequately fed.[52]

Silva Herzog claimed that by 1938 the Revolution had been taken over by a new bourgeoisie; nevertheless, Mexico had passed from feudalism to a precapitalist economy, which he equated with a new synthesis.[53] When the Party of the Mexican Revolution changed its name to the Party of the Institutional Revolution in 1946, he asserted that an institutionalized movement was not revolutionary, its structure and superstructure had not been transformed, and one social class had replaced another in power. What occurred in Mexico could not be simultaneously a revolution and institutionalized, as the former connoted continuous restructuring and the latter implied, at least, reforming the existing structure. Silva Herzog considered the Revolution over.[54]

Revolutionary fervor, he argued, waned due to a lack of sustaining ideology, and by the 1970s he assessed the movement as an abortive antibourgeois revolution. He noted that Mexico's leftists were often not communists and that they confused the principles of the Revolution with socialist ideas. Some believed that socialism consisted merely of paying good salaries to the workers, others felt that it meant following the essential doctrines of Christ, and a third element contended that it was the socialization of production. Silva Herzog realized that even to most educated Mexicans the whole of Marx was not understood—socialism, as well as the Revolution, meant various things to different people.[55] Like his friend Narciso Bassols he lamented the fact that what he wanted the Revolution to be had not come to pass.

Despite the failure of Mexico's disparate Left to turn the Revolution toward socialism, Silva Herzog maintained that intellectuals should continue to find new routes to solutions to social problems. He has always contended that Mexico's *pensadores* have an obligation to function as the architects of society. He has never lost his passion for eliminating pain, suffering, and injustice by blending the many Mexicos into an authentic nation enroute to constructing a socialist state. He has indicated that Mexico has a long way to go to attain its own socialist values, has noted that the humanism of the Classical ages and Jesus's teachings are inherent in the Mexican ethos, but they are not socialist in nature. He also has seen the influence of Plato in Mexico's concept of the state and social justice wherein the interest of the individual is subordinate to that of the state, but he has warned that this should not be misconstrued as an aspect of socialism in that in the Mexican state there exist distinct social classes. Silva Herzog depicted a class struggle in Athens and Sparta between the artisans or manual workers, the warriors and the philosopher class that governed[56] and drew an analogy between it and the situation that exists in contemporary Mexico. He also noted that both the Mexican state and Plato's Republic condoned private property[57] although the Greeks made provisions for private property based on equality.

Combining classical Marxist humanism with rationalism has led Silva Herzog to believe that Mexico has the ability to create its own social existence. He has continuously claimed that human progress consists essentially of thought leading to domination over natural and social forces and of putting these forces at the service of humanity. In Mexico, he believes capitalism, which extols individual gain, has turned man into a merchant not necessarily interested in human progress. But he insists that nothing in the world is static, that all is in a state of transformation, that history exists because people and their actions constantly change. Just as capitalism developed and represents a single historical stage, he envisions its contradictions eventually leading it to give way to socialism. History, he has explained, is on the side of humanity, and eventually exploitative capitalism will fall.[58]

While constructing his world view, Silva Herzog traced the elements of communism from an awareness of inequality in Aristotle's *On Politics* to Christ, to Thomas More's *Utopia*, to the present.[59] He explored the pre-Marxian origins of historical materialism and economic determinism, realized that Plato and Aristotle understood the importance of economics, but maintained that Marx deserves credit for inventing the economic interpretation of history because he put it all together.[60]

Silva Herzog concluded that Marxism affirms the dominant position of the economic factor in history, but it does not reject other influences such as politics and law.[61] He has criticized rigid communism and anticommunism and has pleaded for intelligent distinctions between socialism and its various forms. He has maintained that all theories of socialism share two elements: they are a force for the future and have peace as a goal. By way of illustrating the diversity within Marxism that Silva Herzog refers to so frequently, we note that he has disagreed with Lenin's dictum that imperialism is the last stage of capitalism. To him, Mexico has served as a prime example that for colonies or semicolonial countries imperialism is often the first stage.[62] With undiminished idealism, Silva Herzog has endeavored to convince his countrymen of Mexico's need to attain greater social, political, and economic autonomy within the capitalist system in order to begin the transformation to socialism. It is a tribute to his sagacity that the Cuban revolutionary leader and thinker Che Guevara looked to him for inspiration when drafting Cuba's nationalization legislation.

Vicente Lombardo Toledano (1894–1968)

Stimulated as a teenager by the ideas of Classical Greek democracy and Mexico's Generation of 1910, Vicente Lombardo Toledano studied with Antonio Caso, from whom he gained knowledge of the intuitionism of Henri Bergson's humanism, anti-Marxism, and liberalism. After visiting the United States in 1925, where he purchased his first copies of Marxist works, he returned home and obtained a government job involving the distribution of land to peasants, a position that enabled him to see that many of the social goals of the Mexican Revolution had been forgotten by the corrupt politicians and property owners who controlled it. This experience nurtured his interest in the working class and led him to become an evolutionary socialist and follower of the Second International.[63]

Lombardo read the works of Argentine socialist Juan Justo, whom he regarded as a major interpreter of Marx in South America and from whom he got the idea that internationalism and love of *la patria* were compatible in a socialist sense because the workers are the country. From Justo he learned that every nation contained two *patrias,* the *patria* of the exploited and the *patria* of the exploiters; but the workers belong to the true *patria*—the one of the impoverished majority rather than the well-off minority.[64]

A man of thought and action, Lombardo wrote many books, articles, and pamphlets, founded journals, and directed political groups—all focused primarily on the class struggle. His fertile mind also had a philosophical bent. For example, in well-publicized debates with Antonio Caso over idealism and materialism, Lombardo demonstrated scientifically how the idealists took refuge in religion and metaphysics.[65] His works emphasized that through dialectical materialism man could use nature to his benefit and by understanding the historical process open the possibility of transforming society into an advanced stage.[66]

Lombardo subsequently rejected his early belief that man could not bridge the gap between the organic and inorganic worlds and came to think of the unity of space, time, and matter as part of the mysteries of humanity that science could unravel.[67] He decided that a reciprocal relationship existed between man's material and spiritual needs and that meeting one would in turn benefit the other.

He maintained that existentialism, which, thanks to Miguel Unamuno and José Ortega y Gasset, had gained popularity in Mexico, was an easy way out for intellectuals who feared socialism. He also rejected pragmatism as a variation of irrationalism, which hypothesized that reason cannot handle all problems and action is the most important aspect of human development. He had no faith in the maxim "if you cannot think it out, try to work it out."[68] He thought that bourgeois philosophy relied increasingly on idealism and irrationalism in its struggle with proletarian thought or dialectical materialism and contended that the rejection by bourgeois thinkers of reason as a means to knowledge and progress aided capitalism and imperialism. Specifically, he blamed Arthur Schopenhauer for popularizing bourgeois idealism, categorized Friedrich Nietzsche and Sören Kierkegaard as major reactionary thinkers, for, respectively, denying evolutionary progress and stressing Christian salvation.[69]

Politically, Lombardo advocated "popular democracy," government based on the representation of diverse groups, but under working-class leadership, which would eventually lead to the means of production becoming public property and large landholdings being divided among the peasants.[70] He tried to explain some of his ideas to the Mexican people in ¿*Moscú o Pekín?* (1963) (Moscow or Peking?) where he expressed a philosophy encompassing the spectrum of life from natural law to the principles of development. He analyzed Mexico's class alignment by depicting the contradictions in the classes' different relationships to the means of production. He clarified the laws of Mexico's social development and presented his world view by showing the relationship of matter to political concerns.[71]

Lombardo viewed the Mexican Revolution as a continuation of

the nineteenth-century independence movement and *La Reforma*. To him the 1910 upheaval struck a blow at slavery, feudalism, and exploitation of national wealth by foreigners.[72] During the early 1920s, he interpreted the Mexican Revolution as socialist-oriented but gradually came to understand it as a capitalist movement pervaded by socialist rhetoric. He thought that Mexican Revolutionary nationalism was sincere but misunderstood as the nation was controlled by a few foreigners and natives whose primary objective was profit and who branded as traitors the socialists who fought for the well-being of the masses.

He praised the Revolution's accentuation of Mexico's cultural heritage and *indianismo* but also recognized Mexico's legacy from Spain. He emphasized that national pride counterbalanced Yankee imperialism, which he felt could destroy Mexico economically, politically, and culturally.[73]

He noted that Mexico's controlling bourgeoisie sometimes acted democratically and on behalf of the majority and at other times yielded to foreign pressures. He recognized that the Revolution broke up some *haciendas,* distributed land, initiated irrigation projects, and nationalized some industries and utilities; but under the rubric of state capitalism wherein foreigners blocked national capital formation, dependency deepened and corrupt *caudillismo* abounded.[74] He eventually opted to support the positive aspects of the revolutionary government and to criticize the negative ones.[75]

Lombardo saw labor as the only genuinely revolutionary class in Mexico and believed that unions should be the focal points of revolution. Borrowing from what he perceived as the Chinese experience, in later years he urged the proletariat, *campesinos,* petty bourgeoisie, and all who did not control the means of production to unite under his Popular party banner. He sustained the idea that the working class was an integral part of the "great Mexican family"[76] and that it had to ally with the democratic bourgeoisie to effect democracy. He doubted that the proletariat, on its own, would develop the consciousness to bring about great change.[77] By strict Marxist standards, he held a bourgeois view of what constituted the working class. He rationalized the inclusion of comparatively well-paid doctors, teachers, and lawyers into the working class by claiming that their ideology was determined by their loyalties not by their income.

Lombardo always followed Lenin's thinking on capitalism and

imperialism, viewing the contradiction between collective production and private appropriation as the major cause of the class
struggle. He thought that the final stage of capitalism was imperialism, which caused class conflict within developed countries, led
to clashes between competing imperialists, and caused colonies to
rebel against dominant powers.[78]

Before World War II he believed in Lenin's theory of the inevitability of war caused by imperialism, but during the postwar era
he contended that times and conditions changed and most of the
world's people, capitalists included, wanted peace, and thus they
strove to prevent World War III.[79]

During the Cold War, Lombardo accepted the Russian idea that
conflict between capitalist and socialist states was not inevitable.
He subscribed to the coexistence argument based on the idea that
nations cannot afford global war, which would lead them to destroy each other.[80]

In *La doctrina Monroe y el movimiento obrero* (1927) (The
Monroe Doctrine and the Worker's Movement) he first discussed
imperialism in print. He noted that the Monroe Doctrine had
changed from a nineteenth-century protective device to one sanc-
tioning intervention during the twentieth century. He designated
the Spanish-American War as the beginning of the domination by
U.S. capital in Latin America[81] and indicated that by the post-
World War II period the United States exercised greater political
and economic dominion there.

He accepted the standard Soviet interpretation of imperialism as
economic domination by foreign capital, not as territorial control.
Following this definition, he categorized the United States as the
major imperialist in the world, one which designed its policies to
prevent Latin American autonomy.[82] This thinking led him to
postulate a dependency theory akin to André Gunder Frank's "development of underdevelopment" concept long before it was articulated by the latter.

To Lombardo, Indian and land tenure questions ranked with
foreign economic incursions as Mexico's foremost problem, and
he found causal connections between them. In *El problema del
indio* (1973) (The Indian Problem) he indicated that the original
communal land and subsoil resources belonged to the people but
that a current need existed to incorporate the Indian into the *ejidal*
system, that new techniques were needed to make the Indians'

private production more beneficial and less exploitative. He also demonstrated the need to irrigate and reforest Indian communities, to diversify agriculture, to build cooperatives for production and sales, and to prohibit forced labor.[83]

His program for the Indians rejected Social Darwinism on the grounds that a class struggle emanating from colonial dependency, not racial problems, existed in Mexico.[84] He maintained that making the Spanish language dominant throughout Mexico would damage indigenous cultures, that the Indians' way of life did not have to be destroyed for them to understand how they were being exploited, that they should be taught elementary Spanish along with their own dialects to preclude being taken advantage of by others,[85] that it was possible for them to understand how capitalism affected them by eliminating their ignorance, not their culture. Like the Peruvians Mariátegui and Castro Pozo, Lombardo explained that one could interpret native reality from the perspective of historical materialism.[86]

Lombardo adopted the Soviet stance on diverse nationalities. He wanted to transform regions into proletarian-run centers for production without tampering with national cultures, which he felt could be reconciled to socialism by education. He believed that the 1910 Revolution had great virtue in reviving Mexican nationalism, whose strength was in diversity and which acted as a force against foreign influence. He advocated the adjustment of territorial political divisions to homogeneous ethnic groups, political autonomy for these groups, and the elimination of the internal colonialism that Pablo González Casanova popularized thirty years later.[87] Lombardo proposed a nationwide campaign against *latifundismo,* which included building respect for the social and cultural integrity of the indigenous people and a national understanding that retention of Indian culture enriches and strengthens the country.

On the matter of land tenure, Lombardo felt that the Mexican Revolution was antifeudal, popular, antiimperialist, reformist, but not collectivist-socialist. To him the *ejido* system represented a modern version of the *hacienda* of the *Porfiriato,* not an element of socialism.[88]

Extensive changes in the political, economic, and social structure of Mexican society could only come about, in Lombardo's estimation, through socialist reeducation of the literate minority and new educational values for the illiterate majority. He conceded that education during the colonial era, under the guidance of the Church, might have professed humanism and social justice, but as Christianity became institutionalized, it became a pillar of support for the ruling classes. Thus, Christian teachings in Mexico were used to justify the status quo in class relations. To Lombardo, an atheist, social justice had an economic base whereas the Church assigned it a moral one. He viewed Mexico's struggle as one of Church versus state, not the Revolution against religion.[89] He also considered religion an integral part of Mexican life and urged socialists not to attack it directly, going on the assumption that as socialism grew, the influence of religion would wane.

He believed that colonial Church-dominated education had been replaced by the positivist education of the reform, a philosophy carried over into the *Porfiriato*. The Revolution, which overthrew the *Porfiriato,* he thought, faced the task of secularizing education and forging it into a method for scientific explanation. Such an educational system, he believed, could not be brought about from the top down since university education in Mexico was reserved for the privileged. He asserted that socialist education had to emanate from teachers' unions propagating programs that defended their interests and those of the people.[90]

Lombardo stressed the obligation of intellectuals to bring socialism to fruition and criticized people of letters for seeking instant solutions for which they were not willing to sacrifice their possessions or their lives. Conversely, some of his socialist contemporaries accused him of being too bourgeois and personally ungiving. For instance, political scientist Joseph Starobin, after attending a peace conference with Lombardo in Mexico in December 1949, concluded that the Mexican was ambitious, lived off his connections to the Mexican government, but was also more realistic in terms of how the Left could make gains than were Mexico's Communists.[91]

Lombardo frequently disagreed with the thinking of Mexico's Communist party, which called him a chauvinist nationalist, a charge he denied. His battle with the Communist party reached its apogee in 1935 when the Communists criticized changes in the Mexican constitution to provide for "socialist education," which the party felt was impossible in a bourgeois society. Lombardo agreed in principle but believed that education could be socialist-oriented to help construct proletarian class consciousness. He contended that the intransigence of the party typified the factionalism on the Left, which hindered the acceptance of socialist ideas in Mexico.[92] Lombardo attacked the Communist party for its lack of ideological preparation and for failing to come to grips with the problems unique to Mexico's working class.[93] At the same time he criticized the Trotskyists as divisive sectarians, causing Trotsky to label him a bourgeois political dilettante.

In *Lombardo Toledano y el marxismo-leninismo* (1966) (Lombardo Toledano and Marxism-Leninism) Gerardo Unzueta searched for keys to Lombardo's doctrines.[94] The book demonstrated how Lombardo's thought deviated from orthodox Marxism. For example, Lombardo expected that, in some unexplained way, Mexico's transformation to socialism would emerge from the nation's social reality. At times he gave the impression that philosophy could bring social and political change. He sometimes showed little interest in the revolutionary activities of the masses as essential steps toward effecting change.[95] Unzueta depicted Lombardo as guilty of subjectivism in applying Marx to Mexico, called his *Partido Popular Socialista* a practitioner of "legal Marxism," as opposed to the illegal Marxism of the Communist party, and noted that Lombardo's and the *Partido Popular Socialista's* willingness to work with and through the Mexican government benefited the bourgeoisie, not the working classes.

Víctor Alba called Lombardo's Marxism unoriginal and devoid of political analysis[96] and referred to him as the "master of the Marxist bureaucratic school in Mexico."[97] On the other hand, his *Partido Popular* was the first to articulate the theory that the state bureaucracy had lost some of its political autonomy to the bourgeoisie, but without damaging Mexico's ruling party—a thesis its successor, the *Partido Popular Socialista*, abandoned.[98]

Despite criticism of his brand of Marxism from fellow *pensadores* and doctrinal differences with the Communists and Trotskyists, Lombardo continued to believe that he could unite Mexico's Left and at various times tried to lead the proletariat to power under the umbrella of the Popular party or the Popular Socialist party. By the end of his life the socialist world had undergone considerable change. A life-long supporter of the Russian revolution, he began to view the Chinese revolution, especially its agrarian program, as more suitable to Latin America, which lacked industrialization. He became an admirer of the human dignity attained in China and in Castro's Cuba but felt that Mexico had to follow its own path to socialism.

The name Vicente Lombardo Toledano still evokes controversy in socialist circles in Mexico. Scholars find it difficult to categorize his brand of Marxism but agree that it was unorthodox and flexible. However, he was a successful organizer of Mexican labor and the Confederation of Latin American Workers (CTAL), a humanitarian, a peace activist, and a champion of national political and economic self-determination and political democracy who believed that social justice could be attained in Latin America by the unification of intellectual and manual workers and their indestructable alliance with international labor.[99]

Alonso Aguilar Monteverde

New Left economist-political activist Alonso Aguilar Monteverde has blended the thinking of Marx, Lenin, Mao, Trotsky, and Mariátegui with a solid sense of history, as is evident by his *Teoría y política de desarrollo latino americano* (1967) (Theory and Politics of Latin American Development).[100] He concurs with his countryman Jesús Silva Herzog's belief that Mexico's Revolution has come to be directed by a bourgeois ruling class, which has tried, but failed, to avoid the violence inherent in capitalism. Although at times he has tended to polemicize, Aguilar has, nevertheless, established a fine reputation as director of the publishing house Nuestro Tiempo and the journal *Estrategia*, which have represented the point of view that about 1920, after the insurrectionary period of the Revolution, bourgeois political power began to be consolidated in Mexico.[101]

Aguilar's extensive studies of the Mexican economy, which emphasize foreign investment there, have led him to conclude that the nation suffers from the capitalism of underdevelopment wherein the process of accumulation differs from that in strong capitalist states. He found that the native bourgeoisie, which has run the economy, is weak and thus has depended on the outside world for direction.[102] He realizes that the recent public rhetoric of Mexico's governing class opposes dependency but that it is subordinate to capitalism and imperialism. He contends that there exists in Mexico a dominant class that allies itself with international capital, seeks its technology, and adheres to its industrial development.

Aguilar maintains that Mexico has a capitalist-mixed economy,[103] and he excels at proposing economic remedies. He goes on the supposition that his economic measures, once enacted successfully, would alleviate a good number of the country's political and social problems.[104] He believes that Mexico must deemphasize foreign capital and economic thinking and must concentrate on building native industry and forget the ideas of economic integration and planning set down by Raúl Prebisch, which serve as devices to force Mexico to obtain foreign financing.[105] He pleads for loosening ties to the United States whose policies toward Mexico have been predicated upon aggressive designs since 1889, when Secretary of State James G. Blaine inaugurated the Pan-American Union to facilitate inter-American trade, until the present. He illustrated this theory in *Pan-Americanism from Monroe to the Present: A View from the Other Side* (1968) and corroborated it in *Latin America and the Alliance for Progress* (1963), which depicted the alliance as a clever way to thwart the trend to the left and to build Latin American dependence upon the United States economically and ideologically.[106] Aguilar indicted Pan-Americanism under the United States-dominated Organization of American States and advocated a Latin American orientation away from its neighbor to the north and toward Africa and Asia, which, he contended, were interested in genuine development.[107]

In the area of internal politics, Aguilar has conceded that Mexico's ruling party, the *Partido Revolucionario Institucional* (PRI), has at times moderated injustice, mitigated exploitation, smoothed over conflicts, and established political order—acts directed toward the preservation of power and the existing social and economic system.[108] To him, the Revolution has been an antifeudal step toward capitalism. It reformed and updated agriculture, made possible the development of some resources, consolidated more capital in the state, brought about institutional and constitutional reforms, modernized the economy, advanced education and governmental administration, made some concessions to the masses, but primarily enhanced the lot of the petty bourgeoisie.[109]

In *La burguesía, la oligarquía, y el estado* (1973) (The Bourgeoisie, the Oligarchy, and the State),[110] written with Jorge Carrión, Aguilar noted that during the 1910–1917 period a sector of the bourgeoisie, kept out of power during the *Porfirato* (1876–1910) when Mexico's economy forged strong links to foreign in-

terests, took over. This new group of nationalist and antiimperialist rulers, for a time (1920–1940), moved toward aspects of state
capitalism where the public sector served the private, briefly modified relations with imperialist powers, but soon established connections with international capital and moved away from any
socialist orientations.[111] Moreover, the new governors successfully
combatted the class struggle by utilizing the rhetoric of "national
unity" under the Revolution.[112]

Aguilar believes that the PRI, or the Mexican state, thinks that
to maintain order it must mitigate the class struggle. It does this
by denying its existence and blaming national problems on in-
equitable distribution, which it claims can be rectified. Aguilar
claims that in truth the class struggle conditions the development
process; and until the former is resolved, distribution problems
will continue.[113] He maintains that in Mexico sovereignty theoretically resides in the people but that the Revolution has given it to a
government controlled by a bureaucratic middle class that de-
pends on the state for status and funds and functions in a basically
authoritarian fashion. Aguilar envisions great danger, possibly
even fascism, emanating from the concentration of power in the
hands of a Mexican bourgeoisie that does not advocate fundamental change.[114]

Whatever changes the Mexican Revolution has wrought, Aguilar believes, have been, for the most part, lost. He advocates a
proletarian alternative to the Revolution. He sees that the spirit of
the Revolution is not dead, "just old" and not revolutionary or
dynamic. He notes that the bourgeoisie has abolished the old oligarchy and the reformers and the reactionaries, that it controls the
means of production and maintains close connections between the
government and private industry. Thus, Mexico functions as a
top-to-bottom capitalist state. But he does not view the bourgeoisie as a monolithic class and consequently holds hope for future
change.[115]

An exponent of New Left thinking that has strong anarchist
overtones, Aguilar envisions the overthrow of capitalist-imperialist
power in Mexico by genuine revolution—the elimination of state
capitalism by encouraging the cultural revolutionary aspects of
Marxism-Leninism, by maintaining a permanent revolution aimed
at building a government based on direct democracy with minimal
bureaucratic control, by worker management of industry and stu-

dent control of universities, and by the pursuit of a flexible course toward socialism.

Pablo González Casanova (1922–)

One of the most widely recognized thinkers in contemporary Mexico is Pablo González Casanova. While training as a historian and sociologist, he read the works of Marx, Lenin, Mao, and Uruguayan Rodney Arismendi and subsequently wrote a Ph.D. dissertation under the direction of the famous French scholar Fernand Braudel, a member of the Annales School of history, which deemphasizes political narrative and stresses the analysis of long-term structure and trends. González Casanova gained enormous respect as an outspoken teacher of political sociology at the University of Mexico where he directed the Institute of Social Research, served as dean of its School of Political and Social Sciences, and because of his empathy with radical students was made rector of the university during the tumultuous days of the late 1960s.

Over the years González Casanova has been criticized by diverse Marxists, who have disagreed with his unorthodox thinking. Basically, he is a neo-Marxist. Like others who have followed the Frankfurt School, he has tended to Hegelianize Marxism, to stress its romantic and utopian aspects, to give it more existential than economic emphasis, and to focus on alienation rather than productivity. He has at times viewed Mexico as a dual society in which a pluralistic ruling class makes decisions independent of external influence. Thus, he has often employed diffusionist, rather than dependency, thinking in his analyses of Mexican development. He could be called a "nationalist Marxist" whose works demonstrate the contradictions inherent in all systems.

He has pleaded for creative syntheses by social scientists, integrating new methods with old, and adapting to new situations. For instance, he has maintained that in the social and juridical sciences there has been a tendency to study Mexican society in terms of ideas based upon European political experience, which he calls intellectual colonialism. He has worked for wider intellectual cooperation between Marxists and empiricists but has not been too hopeful that it will develop. He has been criticized by empirical sociologists, who have tended to isolate the capitalist system from time and space, and he has urged Marxist thinkers to go beyond placing the current socialist epoch in the context of its capitalist past. He holds that both positions are too extreme and that representatives of both ideologies must get together and stop talking past one another.[116] He opposes the false rigor of empiricism used by many social scientists and the dogmatism of some Marxists.

González Casanova believes that too often Marxist thinkers have failed to understand that capitalism and the forces of production have changed. He advocates providing a quantitative model leading to a modern and empirical Marxism and does this in his sociological studies of exploitation, which eliminate the old conception of exploitation as the ratio of surplus value to labor value and illustrate that, depending on circumstances, the ratio changes and the study of those circumstances is needed to understand the sociology of exploitation.[117] He also criticizes Mexican Marxists whom he feels have often applied the concept of class and social strata to the internal study of society without relating it to conflicts between nations whereas they have applied the idea of colonialism only to relations between nations.[118] In *La democracia en México* (1965) (*Democracy in Mexico,* 1970) he shows how the two are related.

To González Casanova, Marx's most original contribution was his method of analyzing human relationships in order to comprehend exploitation.[119] But he points out that in Marx's day all exploited people lived at minimum survival levels whereas today many exploited folks live above the base minimum. He contends that today's Marxists must adapt to different types of exploitation, which can even transcend class lines.[120] He demonstrates that exploitation refers to both a division of economic production and to human relations among those involved in the productive processes.

González Casanova shows that the democratic programs of dominant classes in Latin America have taken different forms. One program established a democratic regime without concessions to labor or in the areas of production or capital accumulation. This derived from the neo-Keynesian concept of greater state intervention in the economy, which meant no more participation in the economy by the people, but more by national enterprises. He explains this as part of a conservative program that demonstrates that democracy can exist without social justice or national liberation.[121]

He notes that the battle for democracy in Latin America has been detached from, and tied to, the struggle for independence, social justice, and power for the state. To him, Cuba represents the first Latin American example of a struggle for a different political system, for another type of society, for genuine structural change: socialism and redistribution. By 1979 he no longer viewed the Mexican experience as revolutionary, a fight for democracy perhaps, but not a struggle for a new society. In pondering the future of revolution in the area, he recognizes that there exist two large sectors engaged in the battle for socialism. One considers it vital to fight for democracy in order to move toward the struggle for socialism while the other holds that it is necessary to struggle for socialism directly.[122]

On the topic of the Mexican Revolution, González Casanova's unorthodox socialist views are most vivid. For example, he places the economy of the Revolution in the original "take-off" stage of capitalist accumulation but, paradoxically, contends that Mexico's rulers have the political knowledge of contemporary capitalism. To him, Mexico uses current capitalist ideology and structures to try to develop its class-divided society. He maintains that the proletariat must find solutions to today's problems by examining the existing backward structure, not by adhering to pure ideology.[123] His goal for Mexico is a peaceful transition to democratic socialism through a stage of welfare capitalism where the state guides the process and tries to reduce foreign-dominated internal exploitation. He believes that "as long as Mexico does not fully develop under capitalism, and internal colonialism is not removed, it will remain a single-party system, without the conditions for a proletarian mass party or a class struggle in its pure form."[124]

To González Casanova the single-party political system approximates the pre-Revolution rule by generals. In Mexico liberal constitutionality is theory not fact as power is not divided but resides in the leaders of the Revolution.[125] Nevertheless, he thinks that the Revolution has maintained peace, built a mixed economy with government help, and has increased Mexico's power of negotiation with the United States and foreign corporations. On these points he agreed with his wife's uncle, Vicente Lombardo Toledano, who believed that such government actions could hasten development and independence.

According to González Casanova, through the Cárdenas era to 1940, labor and the bourgeoisie allied against the landed aristocracy and foreign businesses to end the semifeudal relations of production and to initiate a national policy of capitalist development. But after 1940 the national bourgeoisie joined with foreign capitalists, emphasized manufacturing, and co-opted the urban and rural workers. He concurred with Marx that "the more the dominant class is capable of absorbing the best men of the oppressed classes, the more solid and dangerous is its domination,"[126] and he understands the enormous capacity of the Mexican government to co-opt potential revolutionaries.

Basically an independent Marxist, González Casanova has agreed with the Old Left, which has categorized the Mexican Revolution as an incomplete bourgeois social and political movement, in which the working class strives for a democratic national revolution, not socialism, and where the former process must be completed before the latter can begin. To prove that the bourgeois democratic-national revolution is incomplete, he cites constitutional violations by the government, the dictatorial nature of the ruling party, presidential despotism, and the undemocratic way labor unions and peasant leagues are run.[127] To him, "democracy exists to the extent that the people share the income, culture, and power; anything else is democratic folklore or rhetoric."[128]

González Casanova warns outside observers not to be misguided by what often appears as a leftward thrust among educated Mexicans. He notes that even the educated bourgeoisie in Mexico receive some exposure to Marxist thought, that many university students pass through a period of radical activism, and that Marxist rhetoric usually comes from the middle, not the lower, class.[129]

He views Mexico's leadership as primarily petty bourgeois. To him, the proletariat has not been adequately developed to be organized as a class, a condition that will prevail as long as internal colonialism persists. The proletariat is reformist and devoid of class consciousness despite its radical rhetoric. He agrees with Che Guevara that in countries like Mexico, where the government has come to power through some type of popular dialogue, fraudulent or not, and where a constitutional façade is maintained, a Cuban-style insurrection is impossible because the potential for civil struggle has not been exhausted.[130]

Although González Casanova's optimism of the 1960s has

waned, he still favors a popular alliance of peasants, urban workers, and the public sectors to complete the bourgeois political and social revolution necessary to build socialism. Opponents of this argument stress that the public bourgeoisie generally reduces to a political-military bureaucracy, which does not want to complete a bourgeois-democratic revolution. They point out that his theory of the unfinished character of political revolution hinges on the claim that it was a bourgeois revolution, but he makes the point that the logical form of bourgeois rule is democracy, and he disproves its existence in Mexico.[131]

The views of González Casanova coincide on some major issues with the ideas of other contemporary Mexican socialists whose thinking lack of space precludes us from analyzing in detail. For example, González Casanova concurred with the well-known writer-political activist José Revueltas (1914–1976) on a number of scores. They searched for a method to show how humanity could achieve a higher degree of consciousness and how to instill more creative, freer, and less dogmatic attitudes in Mexico's socialist revolutionaries. They saw glaring weaknesses in the Mexican Revolution, which they believed extended, to some degree, the positivist ideology of the *Porfiriato* that enabled imperialism to flourish. To them, the Revolution lacked the precise, ordered, ideological consciousness necessary to restructure society.[132] They agreed that no proletarian leadership emerged from the Revolution.[133] They challenged the high value Octavio Paz placed in *The Labyrinth of Solitude* on *mexicanidad* (Mexicanness), which they claimed legitimized undemocratic elections and the single-party state and projected a false image of political heterodoxy in Mexico.[134] To them, the bourgeois Revolution stifled class struggle and preserved class unity.

Rodolfo Stavenhagen (1932–)

The primary concerns of all of the Mexican radical *pensadores* we have discussed are touched upon in the almost legendary and dialectically oriented "Seven Fallacies About Latin America" written by González Casanova's younger colleague Rodolfo Stavenhagen. Benefiting from the works of Bassols, Silva Herzog, Lombardo Toledano, Aguilar and González Casanova, Stavenhagen's seven fallacies are as follows.

    1. He rejected the theory that Latin American nations are "dual

societies" (feudal and capitalist). He claimed that they are not integrated and, like González Casanova, explains their development in terms of internal colonialism.

2. He dismissed the diffusionist theory that progress in Latin America will come about by the spread of industrial products into the backward regions. He contended that progress in urban areas comes about at the expense of the hinterlands where unemployment grows and local craft industries are destroyed by bringing in goods manufactured by modern methods. Also, modernization creates a new class of middlemen, who draw capital out of the underdeveloped areas, thereby causing an unfavorable balance of trade between them and the developed regions.

3. Stavenhagen denied the premise that the existence of archaic traditional rural areas blocks the formation of an internal market and the development of progressive national capitalism. He asserted that the capitalist class has not tried to diversify agriculture for internal markets, to transform raw materials for use there, to increase industrialization, to reinvest in agriculture, or to strictly control foreign investment or limit imports or the manufacture of nonessential goods.

4. He discredited the idea that the national bourgeoisie has an interest in breaking the power of the landed oligarchy by noting that both groups often share the same agricultural, industrial, and financial interests.

5. Stavenhagen countered the belief that development in Latin America is the creation of a nationalist-progressive, dynamic middle class, which the area's governments should strive to stimulate. To him, the "middle sectors" buttress the ruling-power elites, which they are eager to join. He insisted that the growth of the middle sectors does not help solve the important problems of Latin America but often postpones solutions or sharpens the conflicts.

6. He condemned the notion that national integration in Latin America has been the product of miscegenation on the grounds that movement toward a more racially homogeneous society does not change the class structure, that genuine national integration requires the same values and opportunities for everybody, a situation that most members of the ruling class do not want. Also, he claimed that promiscegenationists are often racists, who endeavor to "whiten" or bring about the gradual disappearance of the Indians.

7. Finally, Stavenhagen found fallacious the belief that progress

in Latin America will only take place by means of an alliance between the workers and peasants as a result of their identity of interests. Here he deviated from the thinking of González Casanova and the orthodox Left. Historically, he noted, this alliance has not existed in Latin America. For instance, in Mexico where agrarian reform is capitalist in nature, peasants have become proprietors. Also, he showed that peasant and worker interests often differ. For example, agrarian reform frequently means less food for the cities and few funds for urban development. Benefits for urban workers, like pay raises, often come at the expense of the peasantry. He claimed that the peasants' revolutionary consciousness increases in inverse proportion to the possiblity of upward mobility; if more opportunities exist to go to the cities, peasants are less likely to be political.[135]

The topics contained in Stavenhagen's "Seven Fallacies" all relate to the Mexican Revolution and concern our socialist thinkers. Most of them, after struggling unsuccessfully to separate or reconcile the concerns of Mexican nationalism from or with the Revolution, would like to believe in the latter, but only on a few substantive issues does some consensus exist. Our *pensadores* agree that the large landowners, the rural-commercial bourgeoisie, and the upper-national bourgeoisie have combined to form a new national power elite in Mexico and have created a system of political domination and economic exploitation under which *ejido* holders (small estate owners) and farm laborers have suffered. To our Marxist thinkers, the existing system of neocolonial domination is subordinate to the Mexican economy as a whole and to foreign monopolies. Mexican Marxists, representing most sectarian points of view, think that dependence on foreign interests strengthens their country's bourgeoisie. They would also like to believe that it makes the ruling sector increasingly vulnerable to growing pressure by the peasant masses.

Adolfo Gilly

The Mexican Marxist *pensadores* whom we analyzed have displayed a greal deal of independent thought, ideological unorthodoxy, and willingness to innovate. Perhaps it is fitting to conclude this chapter by mentioning the work of the New Left journalist, historian, and political activist Adolfo Gilly, an Argentine who has adopted Mexico and whose analyses of the nation's history in many ways illustrate the same flexibility and creativity found in the work of his Mexican *compañeros,* most of whom share his dedication to theory and praxis.

Gilly's book *La Revolución interrumpida: México, 1910–1920: Una guerra campesina por la tierra y el poder* (The Interrupted Revolution: Mexico, 1910–1920: A Peasant War for Land and Power), written between 1966 and 1970 when he and some of his Trotskyist cohorts were in prison for violating Mexico's Law of Social Dissolution, searches for Marxist explanations of Mexican history.[136]

Gilly posits three interpretations of the Mexican Revolution. (1) Under his "bourgeois conception" it was a reformist movement from 1910 on, a continuous process with stages of slow and accelerated growth and interruptions under successive governments. In the eyes of its bourgeois leaders, this Revolution continues, but Gilly views it negatively as a permanently interrupted revolution. (2) He also stated that the Revolution can be categorized as a petty bourgeois movement with socialist trappings. If so, then the 1910 upheaval was the bourgeois democratic phase, which has only partially achieved its objective of destroying the power of the landed oligarchy and eliminating imperialism. Consequently, there must be another revolution. This interpretation contains the theory of national socialism refuted by Marx, Engels, and Lenin but revived by Stalin. It is predicated on the idea of adapting a socialist model to Mexico's conditions, much like what occurred in Russia, China, or Cuba. If we accept this interpretation, then we must conclude that the Mexican Revolution has fallen prey to national currents and to the nation's power elites, thus detracting from its original objectives. (3) Gilly also suggested that the Mexican Revolution could be explained as a proletarian and Marxist movement that has been interrupted. This, his preferred interpretation, holds that initially the *campesinos* and petty bourgeoisie developed an agrarian and anticapitalist antiimperialist threat. But the Revolution became dominated by bourgeois and petty bourgeois elements. It was interrupted in 1919–1920, again in 1940, and afterwards. Here Gilly applied Trotsky's theory of Permanent Revolution and saw the Mexican Revolution as dead. Economic development continued but social development did not.[137] In this interpretation, he viewed the new regime as unstable and noted that repeated attempts to replace it with total despotism have failed. Thus, the established rulers, whom he called "bonapartist and transitional," will someday be toppled by the proletarian revolution.[138] At the same time, Gilly concurred with the majority of Mexican Marxist thinkers who have contended that Mexico's ruling bureaucracy has incorporated part of the peasant revolution in order to keep it in line.[139] In this interpretation of the Mexican Revolution, a contradiction exists between Gilly's optimism and the fact that the nation's bureaucracy, led by a powerful president as well as the capitalist and imperialist sectors, continues to gain strength while little or no evidence exists that the Mexican workers are gaining power.

Gilly's diverse approaches to the Mexican Revolution together with the conglomeration of interpretations of that movement presented by his comrades and the contradictions in their various theories that remain unresolved exemplify the multifarious nature of socialist thought in Mexico best expressed by the phrase "each to his own Revolution."

10. Cuba

The first thing that the intellectual in the revolution discovers is his own ignorance. He has been so accustomed to pose foreign problems to himself and to talk only to hear himself talk that he does not understand that he is not prepared to accept the intellectual challenge of the revolution. Reality has exploded before his eyes and its power of transforming his life is incalculable. He then begins to grope between his old skepticism and the new enthusiasm.

Ambrosio Fornet

The Cuban revolution has opened a new arena for class struggle in Latin America, and its ideology has played a significant role in mobilizing mass commitment to social, political, and economic change in the region.

Prior to the Cuban revolution some Latin American nations had sought social change during the twentieth century through populist and generally nonviolent reform movements such as those initiated by Víctor Paz Estensorro in Bolivia, Juan José Arévalo and Jacobo Arbenz Guzmán in Guatemala, and Rómulo Betancourt in Venezuela. All of those efforts were devoid of ideology and conscious self-regulation by the working class. Although they all moved toward some state regulation of industry and commerce and endeavored to lessen dependence on foreign powers, they did not socialize the means of production or eliminate private property, and ultimately they fell victim to the forces of reaction or failed to live up to their reformist potential.

On the other hand, Fidel Castro's movement, carried out by guerrilla insurrection, a method Marx and Engels viewed as part of the larger concept of revolution, attained many of the objectives of the above-mentioned reform efforts. How Cuba's revolution defeated a government supported by the United States and established a socialist state so close to the world's most powerful capitalist nation is extremely important to Marxist thinkers throughout the world who view Cuba as a model for other underdeveloped nations and admit that Cuban socialism, although different from that envisioned by Marx, perhaps has greater applicability today than the ideas of the German scholar.

Although Marx and Engels approved of guerrilla warfare as a form of popular struggle, they, unlike the Cubans, did not link it to proletarian tactics for gaining power. Lenin believed that a proletarian party, or vanguard, was essential for revolution, and he pointed to the failure of the Paris Commune of 1871 as an example of a premature, ill-prepared, partyless revolution. Engels noted that the ruling classes, by perfecting their weapons and training their armies in new methods of warfare, determined the level of armed violence that the revolutionary parties had to overcome if they desired victory. Castro and his comrades proved Marx, Engels, and Lenin wrong.

The Cuban revolution did not arise from an ideological vacuum. It had many precursors. As early as 1868 when Cuban Creoles rebelled against Spain, an anarchist group first appeared on the island under the leadership of Saturnino Martínez, who had successfully organized a tobacco workers union. Cuba's anarcho-syndicalist movement gained members as disenchantment with the country's positivist elites grew among urban labor. The movement functioned until 1925 when President Gerardo Machado destroyed it by imprisoning or murdering its leaders.

While Cuba's anarchists struggled for existence, embryonic socialists like Enrique Roig began to write, during the 1880s, on Marxist theory in the newspapers *El Obrero* in Cienfuegos and *El Productor* in Havana.[1] Poet-writer Diego Vicente Tejera (1848–1903), who learned about socialism from utopians, anarcho-syndicalists, and the followers of the Second International whom he met in France, pressed publicly for Cuban independence from Spain and argued that once the break with the mother country took place, Cuba would find itself with two traditional political parties, liberals and conservatives. He felt that both would exploit the proletariat if it did not organize itself.

Cuban workers demonstrated their willingness to band together at the nation's first Worker's Congress in 1892 where they resolved: "The working class will not be emancipated until it embraces the ideas of revolutionary socialism."[2] Tejera took advantage of this worker solidarity and founded the Socialist party in 1899, which advocated pursuing a nonviolent democratic road to socialism once the Spanish were ousted from Cuba. In *Un sistema social práctico: Sus grandes líneas* (1897) (A Practical Social System: Its Major Lines) he outlined his conception of Cuban socialism. He envisioned a Cuban Workers party directing the country, allocating a greater share of income from production to the laboring class, raising wages, and improving working conditions. He strove for a transformation to socialism but opposed class struggle, believing that it would cause violence. He maintained that Cuban problems differed from those of Europe and required a different approach. He claimed that a spiritual revolution was necessary to attain the political, economic, and social redemption of Cuba's masses.[3] Although his thinking had little direct impact on Cuba during his lifetime, it affected subsequent generations of Cuban socialists as well as his friend José Martí (1835–1895), who had considerable influence on the course of Cuba's history.

Cuba's tradition of combining intellectual with active political struggle gained major impetus from Martí's efforts on behalf of Cuban independence. The Cuban poet-journalist was a romantic idealist, an antiimperialist who opposed U.S. hegemony in Cuba. He had some familiarity with the writings of Marx, and he knew the value of the proletariat as a backbone of revolutionary change. However, his social and political programs for Cuba lacked an economic base and scientific rigor. Martí believed in the unity of all fighters, the formation of a political party to lead the revolutionary movement, and the possibility of the movement engaging in armed struggle. He did not accept the concepts of class struggle or historical materialism. He advocated equality and representative democracy where all social strata cooperated, believed in private property and a form of capitalism that would not exploit the poor, and opposed government domination by one class or party.

Martí felt that Marx deserved to be honored because he favored the weak and supported rebellion and struggle. He erroneously depicted Marx as a critic without a program for change, as one who pointed out the injury but had no remedy for it.[4] Writing in *La América* of New York in 1884 Martí referred to socialism as a slavery of man serving the state.[5]

Carlos Rafael Rodríguez, the Communist party leader, assessing the role of Martí in the Cuban revolution, said:

One must not . . . attribute to Martí ideological bases that are alien to him and that distort his real significance. It is plausible, but it is artificial to probe the great man to extract from him a pretended socialist streak . . . in perspective we can see that no one was more the child of his times, more expressive of his class, more tied to the customs of his day, than José Martí. . . . The republic of Martí, therefore is democratic in its political aspect, and bourgeois in its social content.[6]

Roberto Fernández Retamar, director of Cuba's Center for José Martí Studies, asserts that Cuba does not try to make Martí a Marxist, which he was not, but tries to illuminate the ties between Martí's radical ideas and the ideology of the modern socialist revolution.[7]

Fidel Castro acknowledges the debt of the 26th of July Movement to the political and social philosophy of José Martí but claims that the nineteenth-century freedom fighter did not understand the necessity of eliminating the nation's odious form of capitalism in order to achieve genuine social and political change.

Carlos B. Baliño (1848–1926)

Carlos Baliño never achieved the fame of his friend José Martí as a newspaperman, freedom fighter, or thinker, but in many ways he was more of a precursor of Cuba's socialist revolution. Brought up in a revolutionary tradition by his father Carlos J. Baliño, an ardent opponent of Spanish colonialism, young Carlos worked with Cuba's laboring classes, particularly the tobacco workers, and was introduced to socialism during his early twenties. He eventually traveled to the United States where he met Martí and observed imperialism first hand.[8]

Baliño sought a liberating philosophy, one that would enable him to devise a plan for Cuban independence. He was initially attracted to anarcho-syndicalist ideas but later replaced them with the thoughts of Marx and Engels, which he read while working in a factory in the United States during the 1875 to 1881 period. In the United States he affiliated with Samuel Gompers and the workers movement, lectured extensively, and wrote for and published various newspapers championing Cuban liberation and the abolition of imperialism.[9]

He collaborated with José Martí to found the Cuban Revolutionary party in 1892 although his brand of militance included the scientific socialism of Marx and Engels and Martí's did not. At the beginning of the twentieth century Baliño returned to Cuba where he tried to popularize the idea that the breaking of ties to Spain did not bring genuine independence to Cuba since the United States dominated the island and Cuba's basic economic and social structures had not changed. He pointed out that there existed the need for economic liberty without which the idea of political liberty is diminished. He stressed the need for economic diversification and production for the internal market as essential to Cuban economic independence.[10]

In 1903 Baliño founded the *Club de Propaganda Socialista*, which served as the first nucleus in the nation to propagate Marxist ideas.[11] Two years later he organized the Socialist Workers Party of Cuba.[12] At the same time he produced his most famous written work, a pamphlet *Verdades Socialistas* (1905) (Socialist Truths), which stated that art and literature should be for all, not just the privileged classes; claimed that moral decay emanated from the system and could not be eliminated by reform crusades; condemned the concept of social evolution as contributing to people's willingness to accept their fate or to have faith; depicted socialism as a way of social planning and action and as an aspiration for justice; talked about practical matters such as nationalized railroads and socialized medicine; contended that equality of conditions and opportunity were not designed to strip people of their individuality or to regulate their actions;[13] and expressed a belief in the effectiveness of strikes in bringing justice to exploited workers.[14] The pamphlet represented the most articulate plea by a Cuban Marxist to that time, one effectively relating the plight of Cuba's workers to that of their international brethren.

By 1918 Baliño had become enamored of the Russian revolution and even wrote a poem identifying with that movement. The Soviet experience reenforced his confidence in the mission of the proletariat, whose cause he continued to promote vocally and in print. He excoriated the Platt Amendment which, at the end of the Spanish-American War, Washington insisted be inserted in Cuba's constitution and under whose provisions the United States had the right to intervene in Cuban affairs. He identified the plight of Cuba with U.S. imperialism as portrayed in Scott Nearing's *The American Empire*. In 1921 he translated that book into Spanish and added a prologue, which pointed out that U.S. capitalism had moved from a democratic spirit to one predicated on hegemony.[15]

Baliño remained active in the socialist movement until 1925 when he, along with Julio Antonio Mella, founded Cuba's Communist party. He and Mella worked to raise the consciousness of the Cuban people and pressured the government to abrogate the Platt Amendment, which it subsequently did in 1934.[16]

In addition to indicting U.S. imperialism, Baliño blamed many of Cuba's problems on its native bourgeoisie, which he called "hypocritical" and accused of not caring about the nation's hungry, miserable, and ignorant citizens. He advocated the end to what he loosely referred to as "Cuban slavery" wherein the means of production were controlled by foreigners and their native accomplices, and he agitated for socialism, which would place the means of production in the hands of the *campesinos*,[17] thereby elevating the ordinary Cuban person. He vociferously opposed discrimination against blacks, who, he realized, suffered the most under what he called Cuba's slavery system.

Until his death, Baliño struggled for socialism. Although he was not a profound or innovative Marxist *pensador,* he was an inspirational figure, the first of his breed—the original Cuban Marxist in the minds of his countrymen.

Julio Antonio Mella (1903–1929)

Cuban scholars often think of Julio Antonio Mella as the successor to Carlos Baliño despite the fact that they were colleagues and died within a few years of each other. Mella reenforced the thinking of Baliño, and he too served as an important precursor of the Cuban revolution.

During the 1920s Mella studied at the University of Havana where he became acquainted with the works of Peruvian Marxist José Carlos Mariátegui and Argentine thinker Aníbal Ponce and was influenced by the Mexican Revolution and the University Reform Movement. He saw university reform leading to national independence—a step in the direction of radical, systematic change for Cuba.[18] He developed a firm belief in cooperation between intellectual and manual laborers and, like Mariátegui, advocated university students' advancing the cause of the working classes. To attain that end, in 1922 he organized Cuba's first revolutionary student movement, the Federation of University Students. That movement served as a forerunner to other university movements in Cuba, including the one which spawned Fidel Castro three decades later.

Mella criticized the University of Havana, calling it a school of commerce where students went to learn how to make financial gains in life rather than a place dedicated to improving society.[19] This dissatisfaction caused him to help form the José Martí Popular University, which integrated over five hundred workers with students and professors striving to foster understanding. To Mella, Martí University existed to encourage new ideas rather than to inculcate those of the prevailing system, as did the University of Havana. He used Martí University as a vehicle to denounce the inhuman working conditions in Cuba, particularly on the sugar plantations. Because of its politics and antiimperialist stances, especially against the United States, the school was declared illegal by dictator Machado in 1927, and it ceased to function.[20]

While at the University of Havana, and later through Martí University, Mella located and tried to work out the antagonisms between intellectual and manual laborers. He realized that physical workers had difficulty seeing the "value" produced by the fruits of intellectual labor and thus tended to identify intellectuals with the bourgeoisie and the prevailing social system. He implored manual laborers to identify with the mental workers—to realize that both theory and practice were necessary to the struggle for socialism.[21] He wrote that the intellectual is a worker who endeavors to bring about justice from tyranny, an idea he borrowed from Uruguay's José Enrique Rodó. Mella thought that intellectuals should replace the functions of the priests, who had failed, and noted that those who worked for freedom were intellectuals but those who merely talked about it were hypocrites.[22] Although he was not antireligious, he was anticlerical, found the clergy to be reactionary, in opposition to scientific thinking, and overly influential in Cuba's schools. To combat this retrograde situation, he founded the Anti-Clerical League.[23]

Mella was enthusiastic about the Russian revolution, studied Soviet educational methods, and was impressed by the effective use of cultural committees in Russian factories, which brought theater, art, music, and history to the workers. He believed that workers had to be encouraged by intellectuals to further their education and to express themselves in the creative arts in order to make their lives more worthwhile, ideas he tried to popularize in Cuba. He undertook such projects, he said, not as a utopian but as a realist who thought that he could contribute to some progress in his lifetime.[24]

Mella used his talent for writing provocative, but not highly theoretical, essays and polemics to arouse consciousness and get across the socialist message in a precise and inspirational manner. He excelled at explaining, in Marxist terms, the contradictions inherent in post-World War I international, social, and economic conditions.[25] He understood the value of effective communication to the struggle for socialism and wrote pieces on how to write articles, stressing that they had to have a central theme, be expository, reach a broad audience, express a sense of the masses, and serve as an organizer for collective action.[26]

Mella also used his organizational and writing skills to promote the idea that the Cuban people would be emancipated only when they possessed a sense of themselves—when they understood their own culture.[27] He believed that art forms like Charlie Chaplin films and John Reed's book *Ten Days That Shook the World* were extremely useful tools to make Cubans aware of how they were exploited and what they could do to foster change.[28]

On the other hand, Mella viewed some types of popular culture as poor substitutes for work. For instance, to him sports like baseball, which became popular in Cuba during the Babe Ruth era, were promoted to make money, to hypnotize people or take the minds of the unemployed off of their troubles, and to direct their energies away from working on social problems. The Olympic Games, he said, primarily shifted the energies of middle-class youth away from work,[29] a point of view partially rejected by Castro, who feels that sports can promote a sense of team or collective spirit as well as physical well-being and provide heroes like boxer Teofilo Stevenson and sprinter Alberto Juantorena, Olympic Gold Medalists who serve society as unifying forces.

Mella did not consider Cuba's social, political, and economic problems isolated but part of an international situation created by capitalist imperialism. He advocated Latin American unification against the common enemy and thought radical change was especially feasible in Argentina, Brazil, Chile, and Peru where he believed it possible to impede the influence of the United States. He contended that in the Caribbean, where the United States already had troops maintaining the status quo, change would be difficult to bring about.[30]

To him Wall Street represented the primary oppressor of the Americas, operating under the guise of the Monroe Doctrine and in collusion with various Latin American native bourgeoisies.[31] He claimed: "The Bolivarian ideal ought to be our aspiration, that of Monroe is our death."[32] Mella feared a second world war provoked by capitalist greed and as an extension of class antagonisms. He used the term *fascism* to describe that condition before the word became fashionable.

He said that internationalism—solidarity and union with the oppressed of the rest of the nations—signified national liberation from the yoke of external imperialism.[33] Like Carlos Baliño, his ideas on imperialism were, in part, derived from Scott Nearing, with whom they agreed that revolution had to be directed against the dollar, not the United States per se.[34]

Mella and Baliño started the Cuban section of the Anti-Imperialist League of the Americas as a step toward building internationalism and unity in the hemisphere. League members, which included liberals and socialists, campaigned against Latin American dictators such as Juan Vicente Gómez in Venezuela and Peru's Augusto B. Leguía, whom them viewed as subservient to international capitalism.[35] Within the league Mella also established himself as Cuba's foremost expert on the Leninist concept of imperialism.

Mella and Baliño organized the Constitutional Congress of the Communist Party of Cuba held in August 1925 in Havana. Cuban dictator Machado responded to the formation of the Communist party by imprisoning Mella the following month. Mella immediately went on a hunger strike, whereupon he was exiled, first to Honduras then Guatemala. Finally, he settled in Mexico in 1926 where he began to work with the Mexican Communist party.

In 1926 he wrote *Glosas al pensamiento de José Martí* (Commentaries on the Thinking of José Martí), which exhorted Cubans to follow Martí's antifeudal, antiimperialist, prointernational, and proequal (black) rights postures. He showed how Martí's love for Cuba fit into the scheme of international solidarity for workers. In other words, Mella reconciled Cuban nationalism with internationalism.[36]

The following year Mella organized the National Association of Cuban Revolutionary Immigrants, a group, with chapters in Paris, New York, Madrid, Bogota and Mexico City, dedicated to intensifying the struggle against the Machado dictatorship. In *Cuba Libre*, the organization's journal, he wrote "¿Hacia dónde va

Cuba?" (1928) (Where Is Cuba Going?), explaining that the country's colonial position was analogous to that of Puerto Rico vis-
à-vis the United States and that Cuba needed a liberal-national,
democratic revolution to rectify the situation.[37]

At the same time that he prescribed for the ills of Cuba, he
inveighed against Peru's *Aprista* movement, which he believed negated the importance of the proletarian struggle in Latin America.
He contended that the working classes had to unite the other
classes and declared that *Aprismo* combatted socialism by neutral-
izing the actions of the true revolutionaries.[38] He criticized the
Apristas as reformist-opportunists who approved of private property and opposed imperialism, but not on the grounds of class or
as the final stage of capitalism.[39] Although the *Apristas* alluded to
"intellectual laborers," Mella asserted that they used the expression not to pertain to workers but rather to petty bourgeois
lawyers.[40] Moreover, he claimed that *Aprismo* was unscientific, a
vehicle for rhetoric, and that no genuine *Aprista* method existed.[41]

Mella's beliefs about the *Apristas* were buttressed by political
exiles from all over Latin America who belonged to the Anti-
Imperialist League, as did famous Mexicans like artists Diego Rivera and Davíd Alfaro Siqueiros and respected historian Isidro Fabela, who joined Mella in denouncing Cuba's Machado regime in
El Machete, the organ of Mexico's Communist party, and in *El
Libertador,* the Anti-Imperialist League periodical.[42]

Agents of the tyrant Machado assassinated Mella in Mexico on
January 10, 1929. Like his countryman José Martí, he became a
martyr to the cause of Cuban liberation. His standard interpretations of Marx and Lenin, couched in simple language, were instrumental in mobilizing thought in his nation and in forming its
revolutionary consciousness. In the tradition of Martí, but with a
Marxist twist, Mella made an indelible imprint on Cuba. His
thoughts have been translated into the reality of the Cuban revolution and its constitution, particularly aspects pertaining to mar-
riage, divorce, limitations on property rights, agrarian reform, antiimperialism, the eradication of illiteracy, and equal rights for
citizens of all colors and both sexes.

Juan Marinello (1898–1977)

A contemporary of Carlos Baliño and Julio Mella, Juan Marinello first gained national prominence in 1923 when he joined the

protesta de las trece (protest of the thirteen) against the corrupt government of Alfredo Zayas (1921–1925).

Marinello claimed that he and numerous colleagues were inspired by the writings of Argentine socialist Aníbal Ponce, who initially alerted them to the adverse affects of imperialism upon Cuba.[43] They also regarded Peru's José Mariátegui as an advanced thinker who intelligently defended Latin America against an international economic system that would retard the region's overall development.

A prolific pamphleteer, Marinello wrote on various topics, including politics and international economics, but specialized in literary criticism and the role of the writer in the revolution. His work included *Literatura hispanoamericana: Hombres, meditaciones* (Hispanic American Literature: Men and Meditations), which dealt with figures in Cuban literary life.[44]

Marinello was especially interested in José Martí, whose works he reinterpreted[45] and whom he considered a great artist and Cuba's premier writer. He demonstrated how Martí's liberalism served as a precursor of Cuban socialism. To him, Martí took the first necessary giant step toward throwing off Cuba's chains of oppression by advocating the solidarity of the peoples of Latin America. But Marinello pointed out that Martí did not think in materialist terms.[46] In *José Martí, escritor americano: Martí y el modernismo* (1958) (José Martí, American Writer: Martí and Modernism), Marinello demonstrated how the Cuban freedom fighter rejected modernists as artists.[47] He showed that to Martí modernism, which enjoyed considerable popularity in Cuba during the last years of the nineteenth century, attempted to preserve the aesthetic realm against intellectual, social, and historical forces threatening it. In another work, *Once ensayos martianos* (1964) (Eleven Essays on Martí), Marinello showed the indebtedness of the liberal Cuban to Spanish classicists, his universality, and his antiimperialist, anti-United States attitudes.[48] In the final analysis, Marinello felt that Martí defied categorization. He called him "the poet [who] expressing reality in an unaccustomed manner, transforms it within himself, makes it a part of his internal tumult, of his spiritual state of his dominating emotion."[49]

Marinello claimed that some of the major bourgeois Cuban intellectuals contributed to the barbarity of the pre-Castro era in Cuba.[50] He also maintained that a number of the nation's non-

Marxist literary giants, in addition to Martí, opposed imperialism, advocated liberty of action for communists, and served as "men of transition" to socialism. However, he illustrated that such thinkers as José Varona and Martí held different views of imperialism than did Lenin—to them it was a biological and social phenomenon, not one with an economic base.[51]

During the 1930s Juan Marinello attained national recognition as director of the magazine *Masas,* which he used to try to awaken the Cuban people to their plight as pawns in an international game over which they had little or no control. He portrayed Cuba as a dependent nation perpetually suffering from the reverberations of the conflicts within international capitalism.

He understood the causes of the tensions that resulted in excessive nationalist belligerency in Europe and predicted that a second world war would erupt as a consequence of competition for international markets. He feared that capitalist democracy would not be able to stem the tide of rising fascism and called the inability of France and England to defend democracy in the Spanish Civil War a sad portent.[52] He denounced wars predicated on imperialism but maintained that just wars included those that opposed colonialism, imperialism, and class oppression. He considered it essential to battle for national and international liberty and to defeat such horrors as fascism.[53]

Marinello stressed in 1940 that World War II would benefit the entrepreneurial class seeking new markets but not the masses. At that time he particularly identified with the laboring masses in the United States, who he felt did not want a war in which they stood to sustain the greatest casualties. After hostilities erupted in Europe, but before the Japanese attacked Pearl Harbor, he spoke of two types of democracy—the U.S. bourgeois type, which favored imperialism, and the Cuban communist antiimperialist form. He noted that World War II showed the contradiction between the two kinds of democracy and expressed the hope that the global conflict would open the way for the type of democracy he preferred—a people's democracy.

Marinello's thinking approached that of the New Left, which years later advocated "unitary democracy," which is distinguished from the "adversary democracy" of liberalism by distrust of representative institutions and prefers participation by all citizens in political deliberations and by decision rulings that require a consensus. "Unitary democracy" is inspired to some extent by Aristotle's concept of the polis as an association for the expression of civic friendship rather than the modern idea of the state as an instrument to serve private ends.

Marinello saw Cuba entering World War II on the side of the Allies both to foster democracy and counter imperialism. Following the thinking of Lenin, he believed it necessary for Cuba to attain bourgeois democracy, as existed in England and the United States, as a prelude to socialism. He hoped that the defeat of fascism would create a wave of popular revulsion in Cuba against its own governmental excesses, which would lead to a movement for democracy that would proceed against the imperialist aspects of bourgeois democracy and set in motion the next stage of the struggle for socialism.[54]

Marinello viewed the termination of World War II as the beginning of a new era in U.S. imperialism. He realized that wartime exigencies had shifted a great deal of Latin America's economic dependence from Europe to the United States, a situation that the hemisphere's most powerful nation would strive to maintain and exploit.[55]

During the post-World War II period he worked diligently to maintain the visibility and legality of Cuba's Communist party. He remained prominent in politics, and by 1956, when Fidel Castro began his battle against the government of Fulgencio Batista from the Sierra Maestre Mountains, Marinello served as head of Cuba's Communist party. After Castro's victory on January 1, 1959, Marinello played a role in reconciling the party with Castro's revolutionary forces, no simple task given the distrust of the latter for the former, which had for some years openly collaborated with the Batista administration while simultaneously contending that only a broad united front and mass action could create the conditions for the overthrow of Batista. Once Castro proved that other tactics, detailed on subsequent pages, could be successful, and the Batista regime was ousted and a modicum of accord was established between the Communist party and Castro's 26th of July Movement, Marinello served as rector of the University of Havana. He then turned a great deal of his attention toward the writing of polemics, especially ones exhorting his Cuban comrades in the various arts to focus their energies on projects illuminating socialist realism.[56]

Like Carlos Baliño and Juan Antonio Mella, Marinello helped popularize standard Marxist-Leninist ideas in Cuba, but in a somewhat innovative fashion. More significantly, he served as a major link between liberals of the Martí ilk, the country's communist old guard, and the insurrectionaries like Fidel Castro and Che Guevara, who engineered the revolution. Despite his collaboration with the Cuban revolution and contributions to Castro's unique and successful brand of socialism, Marinello never expressed radical changes in his orthodox Marxist thinking. He molded his ideas to fit new situations but continued in "sophisticated" Marxist fashion to seek answers to many of Cuba's problems.

Blas Roca (1908–)

Juan Marinello's *compañero* Francisco Calderío, better known as Blas Roca, also made the transition from old-guard Communism to *Fidelismo*. More of a theoretician than Marinello, Roca became well known in Cuban political and literary circles after the publication of his book *Los fundamentos del socialismo en Cuba* (The Fundamentals of Socialism in Cuba) in 1943, a volume of sufficient significance that the Castro regime updated and reissued it in 1962.

Roca's historically oriented primer on Cuban problems explained how the Spanish had turned Cuba's indigenous society into a slave society. According to him, after abolition Cuba entered the feudal stage, which preceded the establishment of capitalism under which some elements of feudalism endured. Roca provided a complete, easily understood analysis of the class structure in neocolonial Cuba. According to him, the nation languished under the control of the *latifundistas,* including U.S. landowners, the sugar bourgeoisie directed by U.S. companies, and Cuban middle-class importers and merchants. Further down on the social ladder in Cuba he placed the non-sugar-industry-related industrial bourgeoisie, followed by the urban and rural proletariat.[57]

Roca also provided a brief history of the Marxist movement in Cuba, crediting Carlos Baliño with being the driving force behind the Socialist Propaganda Club founded in 1903, which embraced Marxist doctrine, declared its solidarity with the program of the International, and eventually adopted the name Socialist Workers party.

Roca regarded the Cuban state before the revolution as a semicolonial dependency and felt that the Platt Amendment had miti-gated the principle of national independence.[58] To him, Cuba fit what Lenin called "unequal capitalist development" wherein the imperialist capitalist nations determine how rapidly, or not, the underdeveloped states develop, especially in a quasi-feudal *latifun-dista* type of nation with an agrarian and monocultural (sugar) orientation. He believed that liberation from the domination of the United States was a prerequisite to Cuban development[59] and attributed Cuba's periodic severe economic crises to capitalism and to the fact that the island dependency suffered greatly when the dominant nation experienced hard times and even when it went through mild recessions. Under independent socialism, he predicted that Cuba would not be subject to the major or minor fallout from changes in economic conditions in the capitalist world.

Roca has always maintained an acute interest in the attempts of various Latin American nations to break the bonds of dependency and to engender social reform. The Mexican Revolution intrigued him, and at a time when Mexico's President Lázaro Cárdenas was referred to as a "socialist" in many quarters in the Americas, Roca analyzed *Cardenismo* and found it to be a form of state capitalism that advanced Mexico's national independence but did not move the nation closer to socialism.[60]

Roca also sought potential models for Cuban change. He looked to Europe—the Catholic nations in particular—for ideas that could benefit his people. He found that France's worker-priest movement contributed to organizing the masses for action and inadvertently united the Left for the struggle against exploita-tion. Although his observations elicited little initial reaction in Cuba, in subsequent years liberation theology, which became popular in Latin America, corroborated Roca's belief that the Church, as one of the region's cultural institutions, could play a role in fostering radical change. Although he believed that mate-rial is not a product of the spirit—rather that the spirit is a pro-duct of material—he stressed that Cuba's Marxists have always defended the freedom of religion and opposed persecution of the Church, premises to which Castro adhered in subsequent years.[61]

Roca also traced the history of discrimination against blacks in Cuba[62] to the need for a labor base for the colonial plantations. His ideas on the pervasiveness of antiblack feeling and the need to eliminate it had considerable impact upon Castro's revolutionary government, one of whose greatest successes has been providing equality of opportunity to blacks. At the same time his work has displayed compassion for the *campesinos,* another group benefiting under the classless society.

The Communist leader and politician and one-time Stalinist, Blas Roca, like his comrade Juan Marinello, has devoted a lifetime to building a socialist community in Cuba. They reluctantly cooperated with the Batista administration as a means of maintaining legality for their party and providing for the safety of its members. When the Batista regime appeared to be crumbling, they threw their support to Castro's liberal and radical insurgents. After Castro's victory, when the revolution turned sharply to the left, Roca, the general secretary of the Communist party, *Partido Socialista del Pueblo* (PSP) (People's Socialist Party), became president of the Cuban revolution's first National Assembly and a highly respected member of Cuba's Communist party, which was headed by Castro. The Cuban revolution altered Roca's orthodox communist beliefs about viable strategies for successful social change, but his standard "sophisticated" interpretations of Marxism-Leninism stand in contrast to the thinking of some of Cuba's other Marxist *pensadores,* who have, as subsequent pages reveal, adapted more innovative and varied types of socialist thought to conditions peculiar to Cuba.

Carlos Rafael Rodríguez (1913–)

Another leader of Cuba's People's Socialist or Communist party, Carlos Rafael Rodríguez was sent by the PSP into the Sierra Maestra in June 1958 to make contact with Castro's guerrillas, and he, like Blas Roca, ultimately gained the trust of the *Fidelistas.*

Rodríguez, too, began his active political life at the University of Havana where he participated in the 1933 rebellion against dictator Gerardo Machado, which for the first time deeply involved Cuba's workers in the anticapitalist, antiimperialist struggle and began to socialize the working class on a mass basis, thereby adding to the revolutionary tradition upon which Castro subsequently built. By 1939 he had become a member of the Communist party's Central Committee and Politbureau. His comrades regarded him as the intellectual with the greatest theoretical knowledge of Marxism. During the period of the Communist party-Batista Alliance he served in the dictator's cabinet (1940–1944). Unlike his Stalinist colleague Blas Roca, Rodríguez tried to avoid leftist sectarianism as much as possible while in public office[63] and worked actively and through his writing to develop harmony among socialist factions in Cuba.

His pioneering work, *El marxismo y la historia de Cuba* (Marxism and the History of Cuba), published in 1944, condemned most histories of Cuba for focusing on the bourgeoisie. To him, most Cuban historians have been idealists and positivists who have not understood Marxist methodology. He illustrated the differences in the way capitalist and Marxist historians operate and articulated the need for scientific, well-documented analyses of Cuban history. He emphasized that Marxism is not solely an economic interpretation, that historical materialism is much more, that it studies social relations. Unlike Ranke and Macauley, who explained history in terms of treaties, diplomatic struggles, and parliamentary debates; Carlyle, who dealt with history in terms of heroes of given epochs; Hegel, who saw history as the march of a universal spirit or ideal of liberty; or Comte (influenced by Darwin), who viewed the example of the struggle of individuals and groups in a process of rigorous selection—Rodríguez stated that Marxism does not preclude all of these factors. He found the above facets subject to the forces and relations of production that determine the ideas of each epoch.[64]

Basing his analysis of Cuban history on the thinking of Engels, he found the genesis of the nation's struggle for independence from Spain in the political and property relations between Spain the metropolis and Cuba the satellite. From the first third of the nineteenth century, he said, the colonial relations of Spain with the island did not contribute to the development of Cuban economic forces or even the development of Cuba's bourgeoisie who wanted to control their own destiny and nation. Rodríguez believed that during the middle of the nineteenth century the Cuban middle class assumed a revolutionary posture in opposition to Spanish control in order to defend Cuban riches. Thus, the struggle with Spain was part of the larger capitalist conflict.[65] His contention is borne out by Marxist historian Sergio Aguirre with whom he worked and who agreed that the 1868 rebellion began as a bourgeois movement for national liberation whereas the violent upheaval of 1895 was an attempt to protect the national liberation of the democratic bourgeoisie.[66]

In *Cuba en el tránsito al socialismo (1953–1963)* (1978) (Cuba's Transition to Socialism [1953–1963]), a sequel to *El marxismo,* Rodríguez's scholarship falters a bit as he occasionally uses unsubstantiated rhetoric. In this history of the transformation of Cuba to socialism he used the word *communism* to refer to the higher stage of society that comes after socialism, as well as to designate the period when the means of production are initially converted to common property,[67] leading us to speculate that he advocated building socialism and communism simultaneously in Cuba. He refers to Cuba as one of the first countries in the world for which the term *neocolonialism* was appropriate, explaining that while the nation formally gained independence in 1903, the 1901 Platt Amendment put Cuba under the guardianship of U.S. monopoly capital until 1934.[68]

Rodríguez acknowledged that Marx's written references to Latin America were not always theoretically or factually sound but that they emanated from a viable global conception of history from which today's thinkers can extrapolate.[69] Rodríguez preferred Lenin's approach to the study of social reality, particularly his belief in abandoning old schemes for new ones more compatible with contemporary life—a lesson Castro learned well.[70] Rodríguez applied Lenin's theories on colonialism to Latin America and noted that by examining the peculiarities of the social composition of the Orient, Lenin came close to comprehending the Latin American situation, especially the plight of the peasants. By following Lenin's method of analyzing social reality and devising a plan for action, Rodríguez claimed that Castro threw off the old—the soldiers and the priests—and replaced them with the new—worker and peasant power[71]—thereby bringing about Latin America's first socialist revolution.[72]

Rodríguez viewed Cuba in the post-World War II era as part of a global movement toward socialism, which grew concurrently with the demise of worldwide colonialism. More specifically, he initially thought of Castro's 1953 attack on the Moncada barracks as a *putsch,* not a revolution, but he depicted Cuba, from the time Castro toppled Batista in 1959 until 1963, as in transition, going through an atypical democratic bourgeois phase where private capital still formed, where limited agrarian reform took place,[73] and where the radical nationalization of foreign property was an antiimperialist move.

He believed that Castro changed the direction of the bourgeois-democratic antiimperialist movement of the type advocated by José Martí to socialist revolution because Fidel knew that historically reform processes ousted the dominant political powers only temporarily. Castro's knowledge of the history of the short-lived reform movements in Guatemala between 1944 and 1954, in Bolivia between 1952 and 1964, and Colombia in 1948, enabled him to see that Cuba needed definite and permanent societal restructuring.[74]

Rodríguez noted that by the final days of the struggle against the Batista government, Castro was almost obsessed with destroying the dominant political class in Cuba,[75] a feat the *Fidelistas* carried out rather quickly once in power. Rodríguez also claimed that representatives of Cuba's Communist party met with Castro within weeks after the *Granma* landed on December 2, 1956, and Castro launched the crusade against Batista's regime.[76] He noted that by 1958 Castro respected and understood the Communists and felt the need to ally with them but was not an ideological comrade as he still harbored prejudices built upon a lifetime of exposure to anticommunism.[77] At the same time, Fidel told Rodríguez that it would be tactically unsound to alert the enemy by defining his revolutionary goals too clearly.[78] By April 1961 Castro told a group of workers: "Long live our socialist revolution."[79] But according to Rodríguez, not until the fall of 1963, with the advent of the second agrarian reform, did Cuba leave the transition (or reform) phase, at least insofar as agriculture was concerned, and start on the road to socialist revolution.[80]

Once Cuba's revolution was secured, Rodríguez became increasingly important as a liaison between the liberal revolutionaries, the Communist party, and the more radical socialists, and, subsequently, he served as Cuba's foreign minister, as a democratically elected member of its National Assembly, as vice-president, and as an ideological mentor whose "plain" Marxist ideas guided Cuba toward collective action and communism.

Ernesto "Che" Guevara (1927–1967)

Argentine-born physician Ernesto "Che" Guevara, the Cuban revolution's most prolific writer, Renaissance man, and folk hero, began to study Marxism seriously under the tutelage of Hilda

Gadea (who later became his first wife) in Guatemala in 1954, the year that a CIA-sponsored coup overthrew that nation's social-reformist government.

Che understood the value of cultivating the mind as a vital instrument in the revolutionary struggle. A man of action who felt compelled to put his ideas on paper, he wrote rather well, despite a penchant for obtuse or vague abstractions. Close examination of his works shows the influence of Jesús Silva Herzog, Immanuel Kant, Karl Marx, V. I. Lenin, Leon Trotsky, Joseph Stalin, Vo Nguyen Giap, Franz Fanon, Milovan Djilas, Ernest Mandel, José Carlos Mariátegui, and Paul Baran. Legend has it that Che always carried with him a copy of Pablo Neruda's *Canto general*—in the midst of heroic struggle he found time for poetry.[81] He stressed Mariátegui's idea of ethics in Marxism and the building of a proletarian humanism, one formed from the class struggle. He probably had read the Peruvian thinker's *Defensa del marxismo* (Defense of Marxism), which was republished in Castro's Cuba.

Che delved more deeply into political and social theory after Castro's victory. Then, like Marx and Lenin, he concentrated on the idea that "the emancipation of the working people will be the task of the working people themselves,"[82] which he realized had to start with a mass education program. He personally taught literature courses to groups of Cubans and issued them copies of *Don Quixote*,[83] which enabled them to build confidence and think in terms of progress as they viewed their teacher as a modern knight-errant who defeated the previously unconquerable foe.

Together with the massive literacy campaign he engineered, Che emphasized the role of art in the revolution. He believed that intellectuals should provide ideology through political theory as well as through artistic works. To him, culture and art had traditionally been used to free people (temporarily) from alienation after long work days. In prerevolutionary Cuba people had sought relief from alienation by communing with their environment—an escape which combatted the idea of art as a weapon of protest and change. He felt that art too often combined aspects of the socialist present and the dead past. He attacked socialist realism, which arose on the foundations of nineteenth-century class-oriented art, as basically capitalist and not truly expressing freedom. He sought a society that breeds the true artistic freedom, which comes with communism, and contended that art forms must not represent nature as a basically "positive" social reality, as an ideal society almost without the conflict and contradictions that the revolution seeks to illuminate.[84] At the same time, he believed that art could shift people away from the crass materialism of capitalism and get them to create aesthetic satisfactions to replace material ones.

Although Che put considerable stress on the cultural aspects of the revolution, his world renown came primarily from his exploits as a guerrilla fighter, tactician, and theorist. His concept of the catalytic role of the guerrilla departed from conventional Marxist thought and revised the thinking of Lenin. Lenin taught that one could move only when the objective and subjective conditions for revolution matured, a situation that was virtually nonexistent in Latin America in the 1960s. But Che thought that by using a catalyst, one could prepare the Latin American nations for the revolution.[85]

Inspired by Bakunin's beliefs that a social revolution could begin before a political one because even the finest army could not overcome irregular troops supported by the masses and that deeds provide the greatest encouragement to revolution, Che advocated beginning insurrections independently in the countryside to serve as catalysts for spreading the revolution to the cities.[86] He knew that Latin Americans saw the objective conditions for revolution—poverty, hunger, oppression—and believed that the subjective conditions—cognizance of the possibility of victory—could emerge only by engaging in armed struggle.[87]

Guevara dismissed the possibility of peaceful transformation to socialism in Latin America. While Marx and Lenin saw the urban proletariat as the most effective revolutionary force and thought that the cities were the place to launch the battle, Che concluded that the peasant could be the vehicle of liberation. He maintained that in underdeveloped Latin America rural guerrilla action was preferable because the most repressive forces of the incumbent regimes operated in the cities. Like Giap and Mao, Che advocated allying the guerrillas with the peasantry, which could be mobilized by implementing agrarian reform. To him, the peasants would fight to obtain land, and this constituted the mainspring of Third World revolution.

Che contradicted the theory adhered to by Latin America's Communist parties that they had to win political victories at the ballot box before beginning a conflict with the power elites. He knew that the essence of Marxism does not always come from books but can be derived from the revolutionary process. He disagreed with Lenin's dictum that "without a revolutionary theory there can be no revolution"[88] but did not dismiss the importance of theory.[89] To him, "The revolutionary makes the revolution and the revolution makes the revolutionary."[90] He disregarded Lenin's admonition: "Never play with insurrection" and Mao's plea to "engage in no battle you are not sure of winning."[91]

Guevara rejected coexistence, preferring confrontation as the best method of conducting relations between the growing socialist alliance and the capitalist nations in the process of losing their empires.[92] For example, he held that the United States' invasion of the Dominican Republic in 1965 stirred up nationalism and stimulated socialist opposition to capitalist intervention. He hoped that guerrilla actions throughout Latin America would elicit strong U.S. interventions and force confrontations leading to a continental war that would end with U.S. capitalism losing to Latin American socialism.

Insofar as Cuba's revolution was concerned, Che can be credited with two innovations. First, he viewed guerrilla war as a means to complete victory whereas the outstanding Marxist guerrilla warfare theoreticians Mao and Giap felt that guerrilla warfare had some limitations. Second, Che disproved, at least in Cuba, Mao and Lin Piao's contention that one had to prepare the rural people to await the right conditions for armed revolution.[93] To him, Cuba found its own road to socialism, one which included considerable improvisation.

When given the task of organizing Cuba's economy, Guevara became an advocate of planning as a creative device for development. He also preferred the Chinese position that it is better to advance economically on one's own than to rely upon more developed nations. He thought that all socialist states had the duty to assist one another in the struggle,[94] and he disliked the idea of Cuba relying too heavily on the Soviet Union.

Fidel Castro became increasingly oriented to the Soviet Union and wanted to concentrate on building Cuban communism whereas Guevara moved toward Trotskyism and the belief that the construction of socialism and communism in Cuba could come about, and be maintained, only by opening new revolutionary fronts in the Third World. Che concurred with Trotsky's views on

Permanent Revolution in the colonial nations and believed in proletarian internationalism. He originally thought that the role of vanguard parties was to help create conditions needed to seize power, but he subsequently rejected the Trotskyist notion that a vanguard is necessary to participate in the daily struggle of the masses or to win them to socialism in favor of the idea that the masses are already mentally committed to socialism.[95]

Guevara agreed with Lenin that imperialism represented the highest stage of capitalism. He argued for a grand strategy to defeat imperialism, a Third World unity that would take advantage of the contradictions of capitalism that he felt were leading to a worldwide explosion. He concurred with Marx's prediction that capitalism would disappear and make way for a new, socialist order and Lenin's conclusion that the transition to socialism could be accelerated by human actions.

To initiate action, he supported the *foco* theory. By *foco* he meant a center or nucleus of guerrilla operations rather than a base. A *foco* constituted a unit fighting in a specific province, not stationed in one place. The *foco* could be viewed as a force rather than a center or as the motor of the revolution providing the leadership, subjective conditions, and revolutionary fervor that lead to the creation of a people's army.[96]

French intellectual Régis Debray, who observed Guevara in Cuba and Bolivia, called the *foco* theory more than a strategy. To Debray, it represented an ethical philosophy recognizing that a person's lifestyle gradually determines his or her activities and demanding that revolutionaries be activists who impress others by what they do, not by what they say.[97]

Foco theorists maintain that orthodox Communist organization only benefits urbanites and ignores the peasants. They also believe that the *foco* philosophy combines Marxism with existentialism by using existing circumstances to start the revolution. *Foco* advocates diverge from more traditional Marxists because they believe that the rural guerrilla movement need not be led by a party and that a party will emerge once the guerrilla force is established and after it has brought liberation. They contend that the next stage of the revolution will be guided by a Marxist-Leninist party that functions to develop production and heighten consciousness.[98] On the other hand, Communists, Trotskyists, and Maoists argue that guerrilla warfare needs years of careful political and ideological preparation, and they see *foco* theorists as unscientific adventurers who avoid historical analysis.

One should not misinterpret Che's advocacy of the *foco* theory as small-scale thinking. He was a man of considerable vision, who predicted widespread insurrection in the form of multinational, coordinated people's wars around *focos*. He thought that the *foco* theory could be best applied to dictatorships of the kind perpetuated by Cuba's Fulgencio Batista, the Dominican Republic's Rafael Trujillo, and Nicaragua's Anastasio Somoza. He also realized that where a government had come to power through any form of popular consultation, fraudulent or not, and maintained at least a façade of constitutionality, it is exceedingly difficult to precipitate a guerrilla war since the possibilities of civil struggle have not been exhausted. Nevertheless, Che believed that in nations under the economic and ideological domination of the United States, like Venezuela, when significant social change ceased to occur, it might be worthwhile to create revolutionary *focos*.

After Guevara was murdered while trying to ignite a revolution in Bolivia in 1967, the *foco* theory lost considerable support in Latin America. Newer revolutionary theories emerged, especially ones emphasizing urban guerrilla warfare. But Che's writings on guerrilla warfare continued to be studied and profoundly influenced revolutionaries throughout the world. Their close analyses of his works revealed that he knew that the struggle had eventually to be conducted in the cities and that he believed that urban activists would grow in proportion to the successes of rural ventures as occurred in Cuba.

Che Guevara taught that a person ignorant of ideology may become a guerrilla but cannot survive combat without acquiring it. He believed that the revolutionary's social conscience grows with his military skill but that the latter could not carry one through the hardships of warfare. To him, the best fighter was the most politically aware person, one fit to lead after the victory, for he or she was more realistic and revolutionary than anyone who had not fought.[99]

Once victory had been achieved in Cuba, Che tried to construct an ideology that would hasten the transformation to socialism. Marx and Lenin envisioned socialist revolution in societies where the capitalist material base would be somewhat developed and where the proletariat had a high degree of consciousness. After the

Russian revolution it became apparent that the material base they expected did not exist; thus the Soviet leaders could not emphasize moral incentives as Marx had believed possible. Rather, they had to pay more attention to the material base. Che felt that the Cuban revolutionary government inherited many potentially corrupting capitalist ways alien to the revolution, including material incentives. In utopian fashion he defined *value* according to moral and social or human worth, not supply and demand. To him, the value of work was more important in human terms than in terms of economic efficiency. He viewed economic man as a monster created by capitalism and felt that the economic system should serve society, that money was worth no part of human life.[100]

Che disagreed with classical Marxists who contended that one first establishes a socialist economy, and after it succeeds one has the foundation for building a revolutionary mentality. He agreed with Mao's belief that one immediately constructs a revolutionary conscience, or else one runs the risk of holding on to capitalist incentives, as he thought occurred in the Soviet Union.[101] Che believed that moral incentives made people community-oriented, willing to volunteer to cut cane for the good of society, rather than to be compelled to do so by social pressures. He sought to develop in Cubans an inner desire to contribute to society without seeking society's approval or receiving remuneration.

His moral incentives concept, which derived from "each according to his ability, to each according to his need," implied the elimination of the market wages system of labor allocation. He understood that a policy of moral instead of material incentives could hinder the production so desperately needed for Cuban development. On the other hand, he knew that, politically, opting for moral over material incentives could enhance mobilization and give the people a greater sense of participation in the decision-making process. Socially, moral over material incentives could help eliminate class stratification, further income equalization, reduce alienation, and strengthen solidarity.

According to social democrat Michael Harrington, Che did not deny the objective need for material incentives but was unwilling to use them as a fundamental driving force. Harrington stated that Che erroneously assumed that the "Marxian vision of what man can become under conditions of democratically planned and socialized abundance, can be operative in a society of scarcity." He thought Che was overly idealistic and that moral incentives could not work in Cuba, that for people to be able to love each other there has to be material sufficiency, and that Che miscalculated that people will sacrifice and accept insufficiencies while building a material base.[102]

By the 1970s Cuba moved toward a balance of moral and material incentives. In keeping with Marx's *Critique of the Gotha Program,* Cuba found itself in the initial stages of socialism adhering to the premise "from each according to his ability, to each according to his work." Cuba accepted a more traditional interpretation of postcapitalist development based on the material base, followed by abundance, and then the creation of the new socialist person. While loyal supporters of the moral incentive concept believed that the change in policy would create competition and hostility instead of promote production, others rationalized the change as "collective incentives." Cuba's leaders found that even moral incentives could be egotistically motivated, that people could compete for them on a material basis. This raised the question to what extent psychological or spiritual materialism is possible.

In addition to introducing the idea of moral incentives into Cuban society, Che sought two other major goals after the military successes of the revolution—the creation of a new, more utopian, socialist person for the twenty-first century and the development of technology appropriate for life in the new Cuba. He believed that socialism could be constructed only in an ex-colonial dependency of the monocultural variety by simultaneously building technology and a new value system. Taking his lead from Karl Marx and Argentine Marxist Aníbal Ponce's *Humanismo burgués y humanismo proletario* (Bourgeois Humanism and Proletarian Humanism), Che decided:

> Man still needs to undergo a complete spiritual rebirth in his attitude toward his work, freed from the direct pressure of his social environment though linked to it by his new habits. That will be communism.[103]

Che concluded that to achieve freedom for the individual and human fulfillment, people must produce without being forced to sell themselves as commodities. To him, the socialist person needed vast inner resources, a sense of solidarity and service to the masses, and had to strive for total awareness.[104] Like Plato, Che believed that the realization of man lay within his community. He emphasized that the socialist revolution need not extinguish the individual in favor of the state and stressed the close dialectical unity between the individual and the mass in which both are interrelated; and the mass, as a whole composed of individuals, is thereby interrelated with the leader.[105] Che's thinking, thus preserves man's role in the state. He maintained that the new socialist-humanist Cuban person, by adhering to the theory of moral incentives, could combat bureaucracy.

Che's views on the new socialist person, adapted from the Russian and Chinese revolutions, have had considerable impact outside of Cuba. During the late 1960s and early 1970s they were accepted by radical groups in the United States, North Vietnam, and Latin America. They influenced, in varying degrees, numerous younger communists as well as the Colombian revolutionary priest Camilo Torres and his followers.[106] Che, not Fidel Castro, became the major inspiration and guide to the MIR, the far-left segment of the coalition that supported Salvador Allende's government in Chile. The MIR and the other factions in the Allende administration approved of Guevara's stress upon the spiritual element in Marxism—the fact that he was drawn to the humanism of the young Marx. Paradoxically, the most conservative groups in the coalition felt that Che supported communist totalitarianism—a non-Marxian concept.

Regardless of Guevara's theoretical strengths and weaknesses, he will be remembered as an opponent of Marxist sectarianism and as the existential socialist hero who gave his life for the revolution. Che realized that the Cuban revolution often diverged from Marxist theory.[107] He knew that economic, political, and social circumstances differed from place to place in Latin America and implored revolutionaries to deal with theory and creative practice in accord with the special conditions of their respective countries while refraining from mechanical thinking. He considered all of Latin America his native country and viewed the Cuban revolution as the first part of a larger struggle to eventually embrace and emancipate the entire region.

In *El socialismo y el hombre* (1966) (Socialism and Man) he visualized the future in the hands of youth and predicted that some day the party, as the vanguard for the masses, could give way to the latter when they were sufficiently educated for communism.[108] His ideas, but above all his romantic guerrilla fighter image, appealed to young people all over the world. Unfortunately, he may have hurt scientific revolution by giving young idealists the impression that all they have to do is take rifles to the hills and start the process of societal change.

Fidel Castro (1927–)

Scholars will debate for generations at what point in his life Fidel Castro, the son of an upper-middle-class family, became a socialist. For our purposes it is a moot point. Most observers agree that from his youth Castro displayed leadership ability, radical tendencies, and perhaps even humanist-socialist proclivities. While a student leader at the University of Havana during the late 1940s Fidel read some Marx but also came under the influence of Eduardo Chibas, an ardent nationalist who convinced him that there existed revolutionary potential in Cuba's bourgeoisie and its student movements, whose support Fidel subsequently used to achieve victory.

Castro's speeches and writings have always displayed a sense of history, and the strong influence of José Martí, whose works he first read while in high school. Fidel called Martí an antiimperialist reformer, not a Marxist, but noted that conditions were not ripe for Marxist revolution in Cuba during Martí's lifetime. Until Castro took control of Cuba in 1959 he publicly stood for a humanist revolution. Lionel Martin, a political scientist-journalist who knows Fidel quite well, indicated that behind the Cuban leader's reformist façade has always existed a revolutionary, who, from his religious background, has derived a social stance akin to primitive Christianity—the idea of justice and identification with the poor and humble. By the age of twenty, Fidel had become familiar with the thinking of his countryman Julio Antonio Mella and admitted to being somewhat of a utopian socialist.[109]

Upon his return from Colombia in 1948 where he witnessed the *Bogatazo,* in which Colombia's liberal presidential aspirant Jorge Gaítan was assassinated and his movement thwarted, Castro attended a Marxist study group where he read Lenin's *The State and Revolution* and *Imperialism: The Highest Stage of Capitalism* and developed a deeper appreciation of Marxist theory.[110]

After helping lead the abortive raid on the Moncada army barracks in 1953 that he hoped would spark a popular uprising to topple the Batista regime, Castro, while in prison, wrote the famous "History Will Absolve Me" speech. It was inspired to some extent by Antonio Guiteras's 1934 pamphlet *Joven Cuba* (Young Cuba) that supported antiimperialism and the idea that property is not an absolute right but a social function best guided by a state which controls the economy. Maurice Halperin, who taught at the University of Havana and initially supported the Cuban revolution, felt that the thinking of Guiteras deeply influenced Castro and led to his ideas on nationalization of subsoil rights, public services, agrarian reform, expropriation of large estates, and the creation of agricultural cooperatives.[111]

Castro based his early revolutionary activities on the belief in the legitimacy of revolution, a concept taken from the seventeenth- and eighteenth-century philosophers who challenged the "Divine Right of Kings" and advocated bourgeois revolution. In a legal brief filed against the 1953 Batista takeover he argued for "a new conception of the state, of society, of the judicial order based on profound historical and philosophical principles."[112]

Even before the Moncada debacle, Castro believed in the masses and in the "irreducible force of great ideas," which add up to the "Marxian dictum that when ideas take possession of the masses, they become a material force."[113] He reenforced these convictions while in prison for almost two years (1953–1955) by rereading Marx and Lenin along with the works of Mariátegui, José Ingenieros, Weber, Balzac, and Gorky. In a letter written while in prison, he noted having read Victor Hugo's study of the 1848 revolution and its aftermath—*Napoléon le petit*—and Marx's *The Eighteenth Brumaire of Louis Bonaparte,* and he commented that after comparing the two works, "one could appreciate the enormous difference between a scientific and realistic conception of history and a purely romantic interpretation." For Hugo "history is chance, for Marx a process governed by laws."[114]

At this time Castro took cognizance of Cuba's historic political instability, assessed the need for radical domestic social and economic change in the country, and expressed the desire to eliminate all forms of subservience to the United States. Subsequently, he blended these ideas with Marxist ideology to form *Fidelismo* or Castroism. He saw no contradictions between Martí's dream of a just society free of foreign domination, racism, and the power of the propertied interests and the socioeconomic teachings of Marx.

Not until December 2, 1961, did Castro announce publicly: "I am a Marxist-Leninist, and I will be a Marxist-Leninist until the last days of my life." He would dismiss charges of hypocrisy by declaring that his previous political stances were irrelevant to present conditions in Cuba, that one is entitled to change his mind, and that intellectual growth can foster ideological and philosophical change in an individual.

Castro came to believe that Marxism-Leninism means more than mere theory and philosophy, that it serves as a guide to daily considerations to solving the practical problems that have faced humanity since classical times. He holds definite views on the role of intellectuals and artists in the search for solutions to society's problems, the elimination of alienation, and furthering the revolution. He conceives of intellectuals and those in the fine and applied arts as part of society, not outsiders, and condemns systems where the cultured find ways to make the workers labor for them. He rejects the role of the intellectual as the "critical conscience of society." Thus, Cuba under Fidel's leadership has resisted having an intellectual or artistic class and has at times discouraged writers and other artists from engaging in individual "anticollectivist" criticisms of the revolution.

On the question of intellectual property Fidel says that anything that emanates from the intelligence of individuals, a book for example, fiction or nonfiction, ought to be the patrimony of all people. He believes, for instance, that authors deserve compensation but opposes copyrights, contending that books should be printed freely in all parts of the world.[115]

Despite some concern for the rights and responsibilities of Cuba's intellectual laborers, Castro does not consider himself one of them. While his day-to-day duties have precluded him from devoting a great deal of time to theorizing, he has become somewhat of a pragmatic philosopher and interpreter of Cuba's revolution for his people.

He has noted that "Whoever stops to wait for ideas to triumph among the majority of the masses before initiating revolutionary action will never be a revolutionary,"[116] meaning that fighting may not be mandatory at a given moment in a specific country but that it will ultimately have to be resorted to wherever there is to be revolution.

Fidel concluded: "Many times practice comes first and then theory. And our people are also an example of this because many, the vast majority of those who today proclaim themselves Marxist-Leninists, arrived at Marxism-Leninsim by way of revolutionary struggle."[117] To Fidel, sound Marxist principles often grow out of immediate circumstances. For example, the Cuban revolution began with a fundamentally nationalist orientation, but the struggle led to the development of a class consciousness, in turn leading to socialism.

By the time he controlled Cuba, Fidel understood that in a socialist society each person works according to his or her ability and receives compensation according to his or her work whereas under communism all people work according to their needs. He concluded that to eliminate suffering and deprivation in his country during the socialist phase, communism must be built simultaneously.[118]

Unlike the Soviets who believe it necessary to build communism after the consolidation of socialism, Fidel realized that after a capitalist society falls, it is characterized by remnants of material incentives, commodity production, profit motives, and a system of socialist enterprises linked by market relations. Thus, he urged the building of communism free of the old order—a communist sector wherein there exists voluntary labor and a new attitude toward work before the availability of material abundance. In other words, he maintained that the elimination of poverty depended on sacrifice and communist attitudes.[119] In a way this corresponds to Trotsky's theory of Permanent Revolution and rejects the orthodox Marxist concept of consecutive stages of the revolutionary process.

At the same time that Fidel deviated from some aspects of Soviet revolutionary theory, he adhered to the Soviet idea of constructing a new technological base to increase production. Simultaneously, he strove to create the new socialist person advocated by Che Guevara. Like Che, Fidel initially rejected Lenin's idea of control of the revolution by a Marxist-Leninist party. At the outset of the Cuban revolution Castro advocated the need for a vanguard that did not have to be Marxist-Leninist but could be composed of those who desired a revolution even if they were independent of parties.

Between 1962 and 1967 Latin America's Communist parties rejected Castro's thinking because he assigned leadership of the revolution to guerrillas not Communist cadres, and he praised the peasants, rather than the industrial proletariat, as the popular revolutionary army while downgrading urban political movements in favor of rural ones.[120]

In Chile in 1971 Fidel told a student group: "A revolutionary process it not yet a revolution." By then he had a clearer theoretical framework and felt that his 1959 efforts were not a revolution, and he put them into the classical "stage" schema, building toward revolution. Fidel realized that revolution cannot be made overnight and agreed with Marx about the historical process.[121] He maintained that the idea of constantly consolidating and adding to the revolutionary nucleus was the secret to success. He opposed leftist sectarianism, contending that basically minor differences of opinion should not be used to exclude potential allies. He believed that those who joined the movement need not possess advanced Marxist awareness, that initially all they had to do was agree on the need to free themselves from imperialism.[122]

When Cuba's new Communist party formed in 1965, Fidel made it clear that the organization would follow Cuban ideas and methods. He supported Che's beliefs that in Latin America the peasantry constitutes a class, which, because of its uncultured state and isolation, needs the revolutionary and political leadership of the urban working class and revolutionary intellectuals.[123] But he also understood that Marx never anticipated a revolutionary transformation in an underdeveloped nation like Cuba, which lacked industries and a class-conscious proletariat. Thus, Cuba followed its own revolutionary strategy—that a small number of well-organized dedicated people could at a propitious moment seize the state and retain power by actions that draw the masses to the revolution, a theory critics of Castro have labeled *Blanquism*.

The Cuban revolution proved that noncommunists can overthrow a capitalist state. Whether one chooses to call what initially occurred in Cuba a socialist, Third World, or eclectic revolution is immaterial. What matters is that Cuba eliminated a neocolonial situation run by a corrupt and socially unresponsive government supported on all levels by the United States. The new regime stressed the anti-United States struggle and sought and found some socialist solutions to national problems.

Castro has often remarked how much easier it was to destroy the old order than to create a new society that will work for Cuba. Subsequently, he came to view Marxist analysis as one of a number of devices to help achieve the latter. He contends that "Marxism is a revolutionary and dialectical doctrine, not a philosophical doctrine. It is a guide for revolutionary action, not a dogma. To try to press Marxism into a type of catechism is anti-Marxist."[124] To him, communists are distinguished by how they behave in action and struggle and must interpret reality from a scientific viewpoint and conduct themselves "as a revolutionary force, not as a pseudo-revolutionary church."[125]

Castro has both borrowed from and criticized Maoism, Trotskyism, and Soviet Communism. At this juncture Castro's Marxism represents a conglomeration of native, European, and Latin American socialist and antiimperialist thought. By the early 1980s Fidel had conceptualized a valid socialist ethos for Cuba, one that could both impose critical restraints on the society and heighten its consciousness. At the same time he agreed fundamentally with Marx that there can be no genuine revolution until there is a world revolution. "We are not stupid enough to believe that we can build a brave little communist state in splendid isolation,"[126] stated the Cuban revolutionary, who, as much as any individual in the twentieth century, has actively tried to spread socialism in the Third World.

One cannot question the uniqueness of the Cuban experience where the old capitalist order was destroyed without an enunciated theory. Revolutionary Left critics have accused the Cubans of turning from theory as a guide to action to action as a means of building theory and have noted that living intellectuals did not play a major role in the early stages of the revolution. After Castro's revolution took control of Cuba, his government supported movements designed to replicate its achievements elsewhere in Latin America. Cuba's inability to ignite and sustain similar revolutions in other parts of the hemisphere perhaps helped convince Fidel of the value of theory as a guide, and as the Cuban revolution has progressed, *pensadores* have become an increasingly important part of it.[127]

11. Conclusions

> Marxism has penetrated so profoundly into history that, in
> some way or other, at times without realizing it, we are all
> Marxists. Our moral judgments and categories, our idea of
> the future, our opinions about the present or about justice,
> peace, and war, everything—including our negations of
> Marxism—is impregnated with Marxism. It is now part
> of our intellectual lifeblood and our moral sensibility.
> Octavio Paz

This chapter contains observations and conclusions not clarified in
the introductory chapters or those dealing with specific countries.
It also attempts to tie together themes and problems that Latin
America's radical thinkers address continuously, seek to understand and resolve, and even often agree upon. A number of the
following comments raise more questions than they answer. Nevertheless, they provide further insights into the intellectual processes and endeavors that engage Latin America's left-wing
thinkers. At times, what these people write—like the diverse
Marxisms they represent—defies categorization. The following
paragraphs are intended to add cohesion to this volume and to
illustrate some of the doctrinal differences dividing Latin America's Left. With the latter in mind, this chapter will undoubtedly
disconcert some readers whose objections the writer hopes will
subsequently contribute to the dialectical process.

Like Thomas Kuhn who argued that a scientific revolution occurs when one paradigm replaces another, Latin America's socialist thinkers agree that social and political revolution can occur
only when the Marxist perspective replaces that of capitalism. For
the most part the *pensadores* with whom I have dealt are optimistic advocates of the notion of progress through a classless society
who live in class-conscious nations where status symbols and values such as titles, honors, and degrees abound. Although they
have dedicated their political lives to the cause of collectivism,
they draw a remarkable amount of individual attention. They, in
effect, often represent an antielitist elite.

The backgrounds of many of them have been middle class, but

they, for the most part, have developed proletarian values and share the belief that politics is the articulation of social, especially class, conflict. Basically, most of them think about and interpret the nature of the human condition, society, and history in terms set forth by major nineteenth-century thinkers. Some have added dimensions of their own. The majority of them have not been simply Marxists of the heart who profess socialism because they feel capitalism is corrupt but have also been political activists—a factor that has often detracted from the time available to them to attain greater theoretical depth. Political activism has sometimes forced them to adhere to party discipline or to support oversimplified theory or dogma that offended their intellectual sensibilities and diminished their credibility as critical thinkers. Nevertheless, the best among them are scholarly skeptics who stress the production of knowledge and the use of it to forge a new society. Generally, they retain their radicialism while not suffering from false illusions about their accomplishments.

Almost all of the *pensadores* discussed in this book agree that the power of the oppressors exists only as long as the masses obey them. In somewhat utopian fashion, they possess a vision of freeing humanity from exploitation and poverty by eliminating private property and using agricultural and industrial production to provide abundance for all. They think that populist and nonviolent reform movements generally do not work or foster only temporary political and social change. They believe in the need for a socialist revolution, but, as this volume has illustrated, extensive disagreement exists on what theories, tactics, and strategies to follow to obtain their objective.

Marxism has become a way of life for most of its Latin American practioners who engage in what Antonio Gramsci called the war for position on the cultural front. They endeavor to reverse their people's inability to think about the existing order as a system and to start them working for socialism. To do this, it is necessary to eliminate what Gramsci called "bourgeois ideological hegemony"—popular acceptance of the fundamental precepts of capitalism. Latin America's Marxists strive to replace the establishment thinkers who the Italian theoretician called experts in legitimation who endeavor to inculcate the beliefs of those who control capital.

Latin American radicals believe that genuine education—the

process of critical evaluation and questioning, not merely the dissemination of information—is a marvelous instrument of progress that will eventually help negate the "truths" of the prevailing system. Except for those who pursue liberation theology, they often choose not to dwell publicly on religion, which they realize forms an integral part of life in the region. But in private they frequently express contempt for the Church, which they feel has historically buttressed the capitalist system. They condemn liberalism for the same reason and for its inability to solve Latin America's problems. On the other hand, they view conservatism as striving for the type of power that lacks compassion for humanity.

Theoretically, these Marxists follow a dialectical thought process that entails constantly revising their ideas according to circumstances and conditions. They agree that ideas are not generated internally but derive from the outside material world, mostly from the changing sensory perceptions caused by the evolving system of production. They regard capitalism as enormously unjust and believe that it requires a continuous maldistribution of wealth in order to maintain itself. They have faith in inevitability or almost a scientific course of events leading to a millennium. In many ways this attitude corresponds to the belief in progress found among Latin American *pensadores* since they first encountered Enlightenment thinking.

The area's Marxists agree that capitalism and its colonial, neocolonial, and imperialist manifestations basically harm society and will eventually be rejected by the masses and eliminated. They emphasize labor as the major component of production, do not disregard the significance of technology to production; but in the final analysis, unlike the multinational corporations, they contend that the class struggle rather than technology is the prime factor in changing the world.

The task of these theoretically oriented individuals has been made difficult by the fact that the area's leaders have not traditionally followed flexible political theory. The colonial epoch left a legacy of aboslute authority. The postindependence era produced a tendency toward military leadership, which rejected political theory as a guide to action, and the intellectual heritage of the nineteenth century generally denied participant political values and engendered pessimism for them in the future.

Not until positivism gained acceptance during the last third of the nineteenth century did the belief develop in Latin America that political and social theory should be directed toward solving political and social problems. Positivism established some precedent for using political theory but also provided an elitist authoritarian philosophy to which Marxists could react.

As twentieth-century positivism abandoned its historicism, Marxism's insistence upon a concept of historical process moving forward toward rational ends stood out more clearly. By the beginning of the twentieth century Marxism had penetrated the liberal and reform thought of the area more deeply than indicated by the weak position of the socialist political and labor movements there.[1]

Latin America's socialist *pensadores* have continued to pursue an understanding of the historical and inextricable connections between politics and other areas of human culture. They believe that underdevelopment of political ideas results from economic underdevelopment under capitalism. They seek to start to rectify this situation by trying to define a political community that will enable the people of the region to govern themselves. In order to do this, they find it necessary to reject the beliefs that Latin America is locked into a traditional model of politics and that European or Asian Marxist theories of revolution can be adopted and implemented successfully without being modified to conform to local conditions.

Preceding chapters have shown that adapting certain Marxist values to Latin America proves exceedingly difficult. A few areas of socialist endeavor, like the development of a feminist perspective and the attainment of equal rights for women, have been virtually excluded from mention on previous pages as they have been in the region. Latin America's basically capitalist system has traditionally relied upon sexual inequality for greater generation of surplus value by such means as underpaying female workers, extracting free labor from housewives, and placing women in jobs not likely to lend themselves to unionization—a situation exacerbated by the area's exceedingly *macho* orientation, which places females in positions of extraordinary subordination.

All of the older generation of Latin America's major Marxist thinkers have been men, much to my disappointment. I sought in vain to locate women whose contributions merited inclusion in this book. It is also sad to report that in my opinion, until recently, the majority of Latin America's Marxist thinkers, reflecting the sexual discrimination that has kept women from their ranks, have pursued traditional male chauvinist arrangements in their domestic lives. Paradoxically, these men understand that Marx viewed the female-male relationship as the most natural human tie and believed that the study of it could determine a great deal about human development. The work of these men also paved the way for a younger generation of female Marxist *pensadores* such as Chile's Marta Harnecker and Vania Bambirra of Brazil, who early in their careers demonstrated enormous intellectual potential.

While Marxist thinkers in Europe and the United States have turned out a plethora of works on the elimination of alienation through sexual relations, the materialism of sex, and the exploitation of women as sex objects or as a labor force, Latin America's socialist writers have paid scant attention to the subject. This has occurred in a geographic area where sexual repression has caused a great deal of physical and psychological harm to members of all classes. Most of the socialist thinkers we have dealt with have not written about the social relations that contribute frequently to sexual abstinence, unfulfillment, and frustration. They sometimes justify their neglect of topics dealing with sexuality on the grounds that people do not die from lack of sex, but they cannot dismiss the fact that its absence often diminishes lives.

The writers discussed here believe that Marxism, despite its shortcomings, asks more questions, probes for more relationships, and investigates in greater depth than do other modes of analysis. They know that Marx considered absurd the idea of a Marxism per se, that he did not think in terms of a system of dogmas formulated for posterity, but rather he devised a set of principles reflecting the nature and development of society. They endeavor to use these principles to examine the changing reality in order to discover the sources of change and to help society meet its requirements.[2]

Most Latin American socialists understand that Marx expected people to attain communism in different ways, to develop diverse and creative analytical methods and forms. If they eventually prove more successful in effecting change than their bourgeois counterparts, it will probably be because their prescriptions for society are based on Latin-style revolutionary ideas, which began with a thorough country-by-country analysis designed to yield solutions to the problems of the entire region, which they believe have international origins and repercussions.

The innovative Marxists question Latin America's traditional nation-state model, which they contend retards ideological, political, and social emancipation. To them, war, crime, poverty, and alienation are not permanent fixtures of society but only of the nation-state, which they view as a transitory or historical phase. They reject the postulates born of positivism and rationalism that nations have a potential for development that stands in opposition to the potential of other nations and that each country has its own conception of societal development that it must protect and even impose upon countries with dissimilar philosophies.

Most scholars agree that creative Marxists, of one variety or another, have contributed to Latin America's political, social, and economic life. They concur that Marxism has stimulated a special interest in social democracy in the region, but except for brief periods, like the early twentieth century under the direction of groups like Argentina's Socialist party, social democracy never took hold in Latin America. However, the challenge of Marxism and the prospect of social-democratic change spurred others, such as the *Aprista*-type parties and the Christian Democrats, toward more intensive social and political programs and action. Over the years liberal reform-minded parties have at times understood and accepted economic determinism and the inevitability of history and also have incorporated some of Marxism's ideas and a great deal of its rhetoric into their nationalist programs, which in some instances have diminished the uniqueness and effectiveness of their Marxist rivals. For example, Marxist rhetoric often pervaded the Mexican Revolution, Uruguayan *Batllismo*, Peruvian *Aprismo*, and Bolivia's, Guatemala's, and Venezuela's capitalist-oriented "national revolutions" of the twentieth century.

Latin America's Marxist thinkers have often dealt realistically, sometimes brilliantly, with the area's problems. As "armed intellectuals" they have exhibited a deeper understanding of revolutionary situations than have non-Marxist analysts.[3] The creed of Marx, Engels, Lenin, Trotsky, and their followers has added considerably to the creative intellect of Latin America. It has raised the historical consciousness necessary to understand the economic, political, and social origins of the problems confronting the various nations, thereby improving the social sciences, which seek ways to improve the quality of life. In this vein no finer examples of Marxism's originality exist than, as our study has shown, its suggestions for solving the problems of the regions's Indians.

Even if Marxism has not been pursued to its logical conclusion, the area has benefited from its vision. As societies' problems have multiplied during the twentieth century, Marxist hope has provided solace for human maturity and has helped engender greater sensitivity and the spirit essential to the survival of humanity.

Throughout this book we have noted where Marxist-oriented intellectuals have influenced government in a positive fashion without holding office. Socialist pressures have brought changes in capitalist society—better wages, land reform, fewer working hours, improved housing, finer education, and social security. Marxists have also provided penetrating analyses of capitalism, which have enabled capitalists to strengthen their system. To some degree, Marxists share responsibility—perhaps inadvertently—for making capitalism more progressive. A good example is the Economic Commission for Latin America (ECLA) organized in 1948 as a part of the United Nations. Led by the thinking of Argentine economist Raúl Prebisch, ECLA'a attempts to deal with Latin American development also owed a debt to Marxism. ECLA posited a theory of asymmetry in relations between the center, the industrialized nations, and the periphery or underdeveloped countries—more specifically the United States and Latin America. To improve Latin America's economic and social situation, ECLA stressed the need for the state to assume a greater role in central planning, for economic integration among countries, and for structural reforms to alter the existing class situation. In essence, ECLA, supported by urban middle classes and liberal intellectuals, translated some fundamental Marxist ideas into a type of reformist state capitalism.[4]

The failures of liberalism and programs such as that espoused by ECLA to foster the development Latin America needed caused more of the region's intellectuals to abandon capitalism and seek solutions to societal deterioration in scientific socialism. They realized that since World War II the urban working classes (those fully employed) had grown and experienced a rise in living standards and were in a better position to become active politically. Marxist *pensadores* found, in the thinking of Antonio Gramsci, some answers to how to take advantage of the increased number of workers. The written works of the Italian Marxist gained considerable popularity in Latin America during the post-World War II period, especially his idea that to attain hegemony the working class must develop its ability to surpass capitalism in the area of managing the forces of production. Gramsci contended that socialist-oriented changes cannot await the collapse of the capitalist economy, but that socialists must intervene in capitalism and assert a leadership role in restructuring institutions. He thought that it is feasible to foster working-class leadership within the capitalist system, before it is transformed, by winning popular support to build more than a minimum parliamentary majority.

Until Fidel Castro's victory in Cuba and that country's progress under socialism, intellectuals in Latin America, tired of the unfulfilled promises of the Left, often referred to Marxism as outdated, a philosophy whose founders had little knowledge of Latin America. The Cuban revolution forced many of them to reexamine the applicability of scientific socialism to their region, to dig deeper into the vast store of Marxist literature and theory for ideas, such as those of Gramsci, which could be applied creatively to twentieth-century conditions.

By the 1960s the idea of Gustave LeBon in his classic *The Psychology of Socialism* (1899)—that the Latin people lacked solidarity and had a tradition of individualism that negated working in concert—[5] was condemned to oblivion, as was the antieconomic determinist and antidialectical influence of the Spanish philosopher Ortega, which had been popular for so long in the region. Such notions became regarded as antileftist propaganda even by Latin America's non-Marxist young humanists and social scientists who felt that no doubt existed about the immanent metaphysical character of Marxist ideology, which offers ultimate justification in a doctrine encompassing the reality of nature, people, and society. These young scholars, often disillusioned by the failure of capitalist "democratic processes," no longer viewed socialism as an ideology produced by the cultural evolution of their existence but not coinciding with their social and economic evolution, or a philosophy lacking in rigor and smacking of the illogicality of Bergson's stream-of-consciousness thinking.

To illustrate the greater receptivity to left-wing thinking among Latin American *pensadores,* we note that recently a small number of them have given credence to a "non-capitalist-path-to-socialism" theory. They maintain that in Third World states, by introducing democratic, antiimperialist, antifeudal reforms, a transition can be made from national liberation to socialist revolution. Their theory is based on the revolutionary potential of the petty bourgeois leaders in alliance with the peasants, the proletariat, semiproletarians, and other progressive elements. Such coalitions, theoretically, form national democracies where they hold power in a kind of stage of transition to socialism. Exponents of this theory do not believe that nations must first develop capitalism in order to generate a working class capable of building socialism or that capitalism is an international system that has reached its apogee. They feel that working-class direction is necessary to socialism but that after gaining political independence working-class political control is not essential. They contend that premature attempts to assert working-class leadership could split the progressive forces, weaken the working class, and open the possibility of counterrevolutionary developments and that a broad alliance of progressive forces offers the best revolutionary prospect.[6] The idea is supported, to a limited extent, by the thinking of both Marx and Lenin, who, at one point or another, admitted that backward countries could go through certain stages of development to communism without passing through the capitalist stage.

Although most Latin American Marxists reject the "noncapitalist path" on numerous grounds—the most prominient being its lack of classlessness, its foggy perceptions about the social relations of production during the noncapitalist phase, and the difficulty of tying bourgeois nationalist movements to socialism—the theory presents an interesting option to traditional Marxist thought. Significantly, the theory emphasizes that Third World nations cannot move directly to the transition to socialism. It corroborates the fact that in all socialist nations after the seizure of power a stage has always existed when the forces for socialism had to be put together.

The post-Castro generation of Latin American *pensadores,* both proponents and opponents of the "non-capitalist-path" theory, demonstrate a higher degree of sophistication than many of their predecessors. For instance, they understand that Latin America is unique in that its nations have achieved theoretical political sovereignty, do not require liberation in the usual colonial sense, but remain economically dependent and are not prime candidates for a European-type of socialist revolution.[7]

Many Latin American Marxists are familiar with dependency, a concept initially expressed, but not defined, during the eighteenth and nineteenth centuries, then forgotten for generations and later noted in Lenin's theory of imperialism, and which became popular in Latin America during the late 1960s and 1970s. They realize that economic dependence dimishes political and social autonomy, and they clarify the distinctions between independent and dependent nations. They generally accept the usefulness of dependency theories as heuristic and consciousness-raising devices but contend that they, unlike Marxism, contain no programs for action against imperialism or for altering relations of production and often fail to consider class conflict.

Today's Marxist *pensadores* realize that while Marx dealt with dependency in regard to Ireland, he never addressed Latin American-style problems of dependency, did not relate his ideas to millions of people, and never had any political power. But they know that if they are to ascend to power, they will have to deal with Latin American types of dependency, as well as represent and govern millions of people. Can they build Marxist parties to accomplish such goals and come to power in an area unaccustomed to tight party discipline? Although they have managed, from time to time, to establish the respectability of Marxism in university circles and even teach some students its rudiments, they have generally not developed organic ties to organized labor whose growth has been retarded by a slow modernization process and governmental suppression. Can they overcome the lack of tradition of party discipline and their failure to build strong ties to the working classes, which often derive from their inability to reconcile the role of nationalism with that of internationalism?

Does hope exist for a viable road to socialism in a region where the Left is frequently disorganized and disunited, especially by "ultraleftism"—wherein many dissident groups have broken away from majority Marxist parties and quarrel among themselves? Paradoxically, in Marxian terms such fissures are inevitable, but prevent solidarity.

While the Left splits doctrinal hairs, the national bourgeoisies' fear of socialism precludes them from fighting for national liberation. Thus, it often becomes possible for nationalist militaries to provide guarantees against socialism and even support capitalist reforms, such as occurred in Peru between 1968 and 1980 and in Panama after the takeover by the National Guard in 1968.

With all of the above obstacles in mind, we find considerable evidence to support the fact that it is unlikely that socialism can be built from above in Latin America. For socialism to be institutionalized in the area, there must exist, as it did in Cuba, a Marxist-Leninist organization within the national revolutionary or reformist movement to eventually take charge of the transformation. Consensus exists among Marxist thinkers that Cuba proved that noncommunists can overthrow capitalist states but that it takes a party, theory, and discipline to maintain a revolution. These factors were missing in the *Unidad Popular* government of Salvador Allende; thus the transition to socialism never got underway in Chile.[8]

While socialist thinkers can base conclusions—such as the one above stating the need for a Marxist-Leninist organization—upon historical analysis, they cannot expect history to conform totally to specific theories. They realize that to ask who speaks truly for Marxism is like asking who speaks most accurately for Christianity. They note that we must see the ambiguities in the socialist traditions altered by each generation and by each intellectual. They concur with Gramsci that Marxism "does not maintain the simple people at the level of their own primitive philosophy of common sense, but on the contrary leads them to a higher conception of life."[9] Thus, for example, Latin America's socialist thinkers must face the reality that the urban working class may not be the essential element in the Latin American revolution, that it might have to be recruited to the revolution on an individual basis because to some extent it exists as part of a quasi-privileged class. Also, they realize the potential political importance of the rural workers who are beginning to lose their sense of alienation from society and develop their own identity as the peasant class changes from a class by itself to a class for itself.

Latin American intellectual and manual workers are drawn to socialism with its belief that the objective conditons for social revolution exist and its promise that history is on their side and that better days, under unified left-wing leadership are ahead. Yet their dream of a perfect future is negated by their history of an imperfect past. They search for more facts and evidence, for precise and orderly paths to tred, to remove themselves from the medieval logicians whose rationalizations and spiritual intuitions have too frequently misguided the region's leaders.

For over four and a half centuries Latin America's religious leaders frequently fit into the "medieval logician" category. Recently this situation has changed as a result of Cuba's socialist development from the bottom up, which gave hope to many Latin Americans during the 1960s. After Fidel Castro took power, sympathy for leftist movements grew in the region, and in many countries generals began to seize political control for "national security reasons." As the military became highly visible, even in formerly politically democratic states like Argentina, Bolivia, Brazil, and Peru, some Catholic clergy, such as Colombia's Camilo Torres, assumed a new role expressing the discontent of the workers, peasants, students, and intellectuals.

By 1968, at the Medellin Latin American Bishops Conference, a new liberation theology emerged, one committing the Church to help the poor, to protect human rights, and to struggle for freedom from economic dependency. This unique Latin American contribution to Catholicism, later articulated in Gustavo Gutiérrez's *A Theology of Liberation* (1973),[10] is not a homogeneous school of thought, but contains diverse thrusts. It is generally based upon the belief that the people constitute the Church and that they must come to power if society is to be free and egalitarian. Liberation theology combines the Christian idea that man is alienated from God and his fellow beings with the Marxist notion that the system in which man works contributes to his alienation. Liberation theologians do not refer to a thorough long-term restructuring of society but to the elimination of alienation by taking the means of production away from individuals and giving them to higher institutions chiefly concerned with the common good.

Liberation theology per se should not be thought of as a Christian ideology of revolution. It is a process of reflection based on understanding the faith and the Christian commitment to liberation from an historical standpoint.

Liberation praxis, viewed historically, has been the exercise of charity. In Latin America it has been a reaction to institutionalized violence, as well as to the oppression of dependent capitalism. Its adherents constantly keep in mind that all facets of life contain a political dimension and seek God by fighting for the oppressed.[11]

While Marxism recognizes the dialectical relationship of the exploiters to the exploited, liberation theologians often feel that it forgets or disregards the dialectical tension revealed by history and confirmed by faith. Thus, they stress solidarity with exploited classes, view injustice as based upon the sin that breaks friendship with God and fellow humans, evangelize for radical liberation, and emphasize that their mission starts from faith but uses scientific reasoning.[12]

Liberation theology served as a transitional stage, or link, to the Christians for Socialism movement in Latin America. Within four years afer the Medellin conference thousands of "base communities" appeared in various parts of Latin America, advocating Christian thought and social action. These communities were frequently led by Christians for Socialism, who rejected the role of the Church as defender of the faith in the traditional sense of Catholics and capitalism opposing atheistic socialism. To a great degree the Christians for Socialism movement was inspired by Camilo Torres, who showed Christians how to reconcile their beliefs with Marxist thought.

Marx felt that religion would speak to people only as long as it helped them to achieve secular freedom.[13] In his own way, Pope Paul VI concurred in that belief as he, in May 1967, issued the encyclical *Popularum Progressio* criticizing imperialism, neocolonialism, and the dehumanizing waste of capitalism in light of poverty. Going on the premise that imperialism tries to keep people disunited and sets Christians against Marxists in order to thwart the revolutionary process, Dom Helder Camara, archbishop of Recife, Brazil, and fifteen other Third World bishops in 1967 asked the Church to condemn capitalism and to work with socialists towards social revolution. But not until the election of Salvador Allende in Chile in 1970 did the Christians for Socialism movement begin to grow rapidly.

By 1971, eighty priests in Chile alone openly supported Christians for Socialism. To them, more evangelical values existed in socialism than in capitalism. They referred to religion not as the opiate of the people but as a stimulus to liberation. They saw that the commitment of both God and Marx was fundamentally to humanity. They felt that no classes existed in the eyes of God, a point that caused a great deal of consternation within their own hierarchical and authoritarian Church.

By 1972 Christians for Socialism held its first formal Latin American convention in Santiago, Chile. Those attending agreed that Christian theology was conditioned by sociocultural forces with their inevitable sociopolitical implications. They concluded that Latin America's problems of unemployment, infant mortality, malnutrition, alcoholism, illiteracy, prostitution, increasing inequality between rich and poor, and racial discrimination were not the products of natural inadequacies or of some implacable God. On the contrary, they attributed these problems to a process determined by the will of humans, the will of a privileged minority that created and maintains an unjust society based on profit and competition.[14] They also deplored false models of economic growth, in particular Mexican and Brazilian developmentalism, which was supposedly implemented to help the workers and peasants but which hurt them and detracted from the goals of revolution.[15]

Those attending the 1972 convention, unlike most nonreligious Marxists, saw no incongruities between their Christianity and Marxism. They criticized the prevailing system for concealing the major effect of economic factors on class relationships and on political, cultural, and religious life.[16] Most of them concurred with these thoughts of Sergio Méndez Arceo, bishop of Cuernavaca, Mexico:

> Only socialism can give Latin America the authentic development it needs. . . . I believe that a socialist system is more in conformity with the Christian principles of brotherhood, justice, and peace. . . . I do not know what form this socialism should take, but that it is the general line that I should follow. In my overviews, it should be a democratic form of socialism.[17]

Sergio Méndez Arceo and the Christians for Socialism favor a return to the early principles of Christianity. They identify the suffering servant of Second Isaiah with the exploited workers.[18] They believe that the world view of Marxism and Christianity is historical. Theoretically, both are oriented to aid the struggle for justice and human emancipation, and both advocate a mixture of theory and praxis.

Christians for Socialism think that bourgeois society has used the Christian faith, turning it into a religion that legitimizes domination. They feel that somehow the Catholic Church has imparted a sacred character to capitalist democracy and liberty and conceives of "charity" as incompatible with revolution. They believe that the Church has perverted the concepts of social Christianity to the extent that human rights have become synonymous with the rights of the ruling class and, as such, are defended as essential elements of Christianity. Christians for Socialism assert that social Christianity endeavored to liberate humanity from the evils of capitalism, but historical analysis reveals that capitalism ended up using social Christianity for its own purposes. Thus, they contend, it became necessary for those who believed in the basic tenets of social Christianity to look elsewhere—to historical materialism— for insight into humanity's dilemmas. To cite a recent example, Christians for Socialism maintain that the publication of the International Telephone and Telegraph (ITT) papers that divulged U.S. and multinational company complicity in the overthrow of the democratically elected Allende government in Chile in 1973 came as a revelation to most Christians but did not surprise Marxists oriented to the lessons of history.[19]

Christians for Socialism contend that Marxism paves the way for a new economic system that can generate autonomous development at an accelerated pace and create a classless society that closely approximates a true brotherhood of man. They believe that religion will continue to be important as long as alienation remains a part of secular society and that the need for religion will disappear when humanity is truly free.

We do not have sufficient historical perspective to measure the full impact of liberation theology and the Christians for Socialism movement. We do know that they have helped debunk the myth that developmental capitalism, even at its reformist best, is beneficial to the majority of Latin Americans. They have mobilized workers, peasants, and some members of the lower middle class for the struggle against those who maintain social and political control in Latin America and for whom capitalism has been beneficial. Above all, they successfully challenged the idea that class struggle was incompatible with the message of the gospel because it was predicated on hatred, which caused violence.[20] Perhaps the fact that conservative Pope John Paul II traveled to Puebla, Mexico, in 1979 for the Latin American Bishops Conference, where he spoke against the progressive measures enacted at the 1968 Medellin conference and then in May 1980 ordered Roman Catholic clergy to disengage from secular politics, an order reiterated in

1981 to the clergymen serving in the highest echelons of Nicaragua's revolutionary government, attests to the effectiveness of Christians for Socialism.

This study has ascertained that Latin America's Marxists and their ideas have influenced social and political life in the region and even affected religion creatively. Our analysis leads us to agree with nonsocialist philosopher Robert Nisbet who writes:

> The revolutionary community, in the strict sense of the term, is the most recent, the most distinctively modern of all forms of community in Western thought. Few would deny that it has become one of the most honored in the ranks of intellectuals.[21]

Latin America's radical intellectuals have shown, in critical fashion, society's character, its limitations, its injustices, and its conflicts. They have subscribed to Marx's belief that "we develop new principles for the world out of its own existing principles," [22] that history represents man's work—people learning to master their world and control their destiny.[23] They endeavor to bring the capitalist world to understand itself, its needs, and its potential to create a new conceptual pattern necessary for political and social change.[24]

Unfortunately, classical Marxism's level of abstraction is often too high to deal effectively with mundane daily situations. It is frequently better suited to the study of broad historical contours than to that of the dynamics of individual institutions or groups whose relationships and conflicts contribute to the most common problems in Latin America. The works of many of the writers we have examined present overviews enabling us to comprehend the area's illnesses, but they frequently offer complex prescriptions for their cure, which are very difficult to administer.

In addition to their often impractically abstract or esoteric views, Latin America's Marxists at times display intolerance for one another's ideas and, moreover, become impatient with those who reject socialism. Intellectual arrogance has frequently split the Left internally as well as alienating potential converts or allies. Marx, who believed that some who disagreed with him did not make immoral judgments but often made valid decisions based upon the relations in which they stand and their class and individual values, would be horrified by the rigidity that at times exists on the Left in Latin America. If we retain Marx's open-mindedness, it is not important that we agree or disagree with the writers whose works we have scrutinized; it is sufficient to understand that they have advanced our knowledge about their societies and the possibility for revolutionary transformation in them.

Marxism has outlived all other forms of radicalism in Latin America because the strength of Marx's thought —and that of his prominent interpreters—outweighs that of other revolutionaries. Also, Marxism generally accepts the existence of, and even the need for, the region's capitalist system as a desirable step toward building socialism. Marxism eschews nihilism and presents a constructive program for the future. Besides, Marx's logic makes revolution for Latin America seem inevitable—a step in the human progression based upon a plausible philosophy of history.[25]

"Theory, my friend, is gray, but green is the eternal tree of life." This line from Goethe's *Faust* was often cited by Lenin when criticizing narrow-minded Marxists who failed to see life's new and unexpected developments.[26] Latin America's socialists continuously confront the question of which social or political theories to adhere to, how precisely they must or can be followed, or how to extrapolate from or develop them. For example, the region's orthodox Communists have traditionally categorized Latin America as a semifeudal state where unproductive agriculture thwarts industrialization and the building of the proletariat. Thus, Communist parties have urged the bourgeoisie to ally with workers and peasants to strip power from the landlords, who collude with foreign interests. This theory contains two elements that a number of Marxists cannot accept. It is not fully internationalist in that it advocates carrying out the dialectical process within the nation, and it often supports reformist middle-class political parties in the struggle against reactionaries.

Some of the thinkers whose works we have examined have rejected the orthodox view that Latin America is semifeudal and have contended that it has been part of the capitalist system since colonial days. To these people the area's monocultures under the control of landlords are part of capitalism, not an obstacle to its development. They see the agricultural sector allied with the urban merchants who promote the importation of manufactured goods, not industrializaton. They maintain that the bourgeoisie is tied to the existing power structure and imperialism and cannot be relied upon to help overthrow it.[27] Also, many contemporary Marxists have given up the old idea of bringing the petty bourgeoisie, especially the intelligentsia, into the socialist camp on the grounds that these elements have traditionally been nationalists and that nationalism will continuously be affected by imperialist domination.

Debates on such topics as whether Latin America is semifeudal or not or on the usefulness of the petty bourgeoisie to the revolution will continue among the region's Marxist groups. The popularity of the specific beliefs of the various sects will fluctuate periodically, and Marxist theory in general will go through cycles of greater and lesser development. To illustrate these points, we note that the triumph of the Russian revolution gave impetus to wider acceptance of socialist thought in Latin America between the world wars. Paradoxically, at that time, the dominance of Stalinist thought among the region's Marxists often hindered the development of socialist political and social ideas there.

In recent decades Marxist thought in Latin America has followed definite trends. After Castro's takeover in Cuba in 1959 until the early 1970s, neo-Marxist ideas, voluntarism, and dependency thinking frequently replaced more rigid "dead," "vulgar," and European-oriented Marxist thought in the region. Following the 1973 overthrow of the Allende regime in Chile, when hemispherewide suppression of revolutionary and popular movements and more overt U.S. support for anti-left-wing militarism made it difficult for Marxists to build ties to the popular classes and made conditions for revolution less propitious, many of the area's Marxist *pensadores* began to reject more eclectic neo-Marxist, voluntarist, and dependency thinking in favor of more theoretical Marxist stances, including classical and structuralist perspectives.

In contrast to dependency paradigms, which emphasized that precapitalist modes of production ended in Latin America when the area became part of the international capitalist system in the sixteenth century, scholars such as Mexico's Roger Bartra and Ecuador's Agustín Cuevas have of late stressed the structuralist view. They have maintained that precapitalist structures still exist in Latin America, that its countries are relatively autonomous and divided by class relations, and that these conditions emanate from internal contradictions.

Currently, the structuralist position represents a source of considerable critical debate among Latin American Marxists. Many accept the structuralist concept of the capitalist state. To them, better than any other theory, it explains the relationship of the area's numerous repressive military dictatorships to its class structures by showing how nondemocratic forms of control are established in capitalist societies when a leadership crisis occurs and no civilian segment of the power bloc can assert hegemony over the dominant classes or the bloc.[28]

Previous chapters have illustrated that while orthodox Communists have stood by their beliefs, other theories—such as the ones just posited above or the previously mentioned "non-capitalist-path" concept—tend to become part of new orthodoxies, which, in dialectical fashion, both inhibit and contribute to more innovative Marxist thought in Latin America.

Historically, in Latin America, as in most other places in the world, no authoritative Marxist interpretation or set of theories exists. We find only individual and collective judgments and evaluations. Nevertheless, Latin America has produced strong exponents of diverse Marxist thinking who have tried to construct workable philosophies for the region. Although their efforts often appear to have substantiated Chairman Mao's advice "let a hundred flowers bloom," they have helped develop regional unity as their analyses transcend national boundaries. Their quest for understanding in order to transform the world into a more rational place has, however, not always succeeded on the international level but has often had the non-Marxist result of giving a better sense of direction to individual nations. Paradoxically, these countries have, at times, become more aware of the deleterious effects of the imperialism of world powers and the need for international solidarity to combat it.

Although Marxists have not gained political control of Latin America, except for Cuba, and perhaps briefly in Chile and partially in Nicaragua, they have constantly challenged the ruling class and thereby placed some limits on its actions. They have forced some economic and social reforms, fostered hope for eventual reconciliation between practical politics and human emancipation, and presented a humanist way of delineating people and stimulating socioeconomic development and of redistributing material and spiritual goods.[29]

Marxist thought and action in Latin America have also inspired change in some of the English-speaking nations of the Caribbean and South America. Socialist governments gained control in Grenada under Maurice Bishop in 1979, in Jamaica under Michael Manley in 1976, and in British Guiana under Cheddi Jagan in 1957. Proof of the significant impact of Marxism upon the Caribbean and South America are the great lengths to which its opponents go to attempt to eliminate it.

As technology and modernity increase, the chances of successful socialist revolutions in the more industrially advanced Latin American nations, where most foreign capital is invested and more efficient elites rule, are reduced. Greater promise for revolutionary success exits in less developed countries as evidenced by the 1979 victory of Nicaragua's Sandinist Front of National Liberation, which destroyed dictator Anastasio Somoza's repressive state and began to replace it with a new social order responsive to the interests of the peasants and workers. The Sandinistas used the thinking of Lenin, Mao, Ho Chi Minh, Che Guevara, and Fidel Castro and the ideology of insurrection of their early twentieth-century populist and guerrilla hero Augusto Sandino to forge a flexible nonsectarian Third World Marxism based on Nicaragua's ethos.[30]

The nature of the Nicaraguan and Cuban revolutions and what occurs at this time of writing in El Salvador lead Latin America's Marxist intellectuals to conclude that they can interpret the world but that only the people have the power of numbers to change it. In light of pressures by the capitalist world to maintain ideological supremacy in Latin America, most of the region's nations rarely tolerate political opposition. Even in countries with electoral processes and constitutionalism like Colombia, the Dominican Republic, Mexico, and Venezuela, those in control permit no substantial active Marxist resistance.

Latin America's Marxist *pensadores,* whether they prefer a program of socialism advocated by Recabarren, Palacios, Mariátegui, Lombardo Toledano, Caio Prado Júnior, Camilo Torres, Che Guevara, or combinations or variations of the many themes mentioned in this volume, continue to fight an up-hill battle against their governments and their fellow citizens who have become one-dimensional, are unable to think dialectically, and are conditioned to accept less than the best possible state of being.

Glossary

Aprismo — Program of the Popular American Revolutionary Alliance

compañero — comrade or friend

campesino — a rural worker or peasant

caudillo(-ismo) — boss, chief (bossism)

cholo — Indian or person of mixed blood

criollo — a person born in America to European parents

descamisados — shirtless ones or Argentine workers

ejido — a collective or communal farm

encomienda — colonial system that granted Indians, and in effect land to Spanish soldiers.

estancia — a landed estate or ranch

foco — an insurrectional center

gamonalismo — rural bossism

golpe — a blow, strike, or coup d'état

hacendado, hacendista — owner of a landed estate

indigenismo, indianismo — a movement to assimilate Indians into civilization while preserving their culture

latifundios — large landed estates

pardo — a person of mixed black and white blood

peninsular — a resident of America born in Spain

pensador — a thinker

Porfiriato — the era (1876-1911) when Porfirio Díaz ruled Mexico

porteño — a resident of the port city of Buenos Aires, Argentina

Abbreviations

AD   *Acción Democrática* (Democratic Action party, Venezuela)

APRA   *Alianza Popular Revolucionaria Americana* (Popular American Revolutionary Alliance)

COB   *Central Obrera Boliviana* (Bolivian Labor Central)

COMIBOL   *Corporación Minera de Bolivia* (Bolivian Mining Corporation)

COPEI   *Comité de Organización Política Electoral Independiente* (Christian Democratic party, Venezuela)

ECLA   Economic Commission for Latin America

FIB   *Frente de la Izquierda Boliviana* (Bolivian Leftist Front)

FRAP   *Frente de Acción Popular* (Popular Action Front, Chile)

MAS   *Movimiento al Socialismo* (Movement to Socialism party, Venezuela)

MIR   *Movimiento Izquierda Revolucionaria* (Movement of the Revolutionary Left, Chile. Similarly named parties existed in Argentina and Venezuela.)

MLN   *Movimiento de Liberación Nacional* (National Liberation Movement, Uruguay's Tupamaros)

MNR   *Movimiento Nacionalista Revolucionario* (National Revolutionary Movement, Bolivia)

PIR   *Partido de la Izquierda Revolucionaria* (Party of the Revolutionary Left, Bolivia)

POR   *Partido Obrero Revolucionario* (Revolutionary Workers' party, Bolivia)

PRI   *Partido Revolucionario Institucional* (Party of the Institutional Revolution, Mexico)

PSOB   *Partido Socialista Obrero Boliviano* (Bolivian Socialist Workers' party)

PSP   *Partido Socialista del Pueblo* (People's Socialist party, Cuba)

RADEPA   *Razón de Patria* (Reason of the Fatherland, Bolivia)

Notes

Chapter 1. Introduction

1 Raymond Aron, "The Impact of Marxism in the Twentieth Century" in *Marxism in the Modern World,* ed. Milorad M. Drachkovitch, (Stanford: Hoover Institution Press, 1965), p. 1.

2 Charles H. Anderson, *The Political Economy of Social Class* (Englewood Cliffs, N.J.: Prentice-Hall, 1974), p. 3; and C. Wright Mills, *The Marxists* (New York: Delta, 1962), p. 96.

3 Harold Eugene Davis, *Latin American Thought: A Historical Introduction* (New York: Free Press, 1974), p. 232.

4 Edward B. Richards, "Marxism and Marxist Movements in Latin America in Recent Soviet Historical Writing," *Hispanic American Historical Review* 45(4) (Nov. 1965): 585.

5 John Lewis, *The Marxism of Marx* (London: Lawrence & Wishert, 1972), p. 192.

6 See Mills, *Marxists.*

7 Michael Harrington, *The Twilight of Capitalism* (New York: Simon & Schuster, 1976), p. 343.

8 Lewis, *Marxism of Marx,* p. 21.

9 E. J. Hobsbawm, "Karl Marx's Contribution to Historiography," in *Ideology in Social Science,* ed. Robin Blackburn (New York: Vintage, 1973), p. 274.

10 Ibid., pp. 273-74.

11 B.M. Boguslavsky et al., *ABC of Dialectical and Historical Materialism* (Moscow: Progress Pubs., 1976), pp. 246-47.

12 Donald C. Hodges, *Socialist Humanism: The Outcome of Classical European Morality* (St. Louis: Warren H. Green, 1974), p. 339. Hodges and Georg Lukács differ somewhat on the origins of socialist humanism.

13 Richard Wohl, "Intellectual History: An Historian's View," *Historian* 16 (Autumn 1953): 64-65.

14 John M. Cammett, *Antonio Gramsci and the Origins of Italian Communism* (Stanford: Stanford University Press, 1967), p. 201.

15 James Joll, *Antonio Gramsci* (New York: Penguin Books, 1977), pp. 122-24.

16 Throughout this book *Communist* written with a capital *C* refers to those people or parties with ties to the Soviet Union or the Communist International (Comintern). *Socialist* written with a capital *S* refers to specific Socialist (not Communist) parties or their members. *Communist* with a small *c* and *socialist* with a small *s* are generic terms.

Chapter 2. Marx and Marxism

1 Bertell Ollman, *Alienation: Marx's Conception of Man in Capitalist Society* (London: Cambridge University Press, 1971), pp. xii-xiv.

2 Albert William Levi, *Humanism and Politics* (Bloomington: Indiana University Press, 1969), p. 403.

3 F. V. Konstantinov et al., *The Fundamentals of Marxist-Leninist Philosophy* (Moscow: Progress Pubs., 1974), p. 330.

4 M. M. Bober, *Karl Marx's Interpretation of History* (New York: W. W. Norton, 1965), p. 128.

5 Julio Alvarez del Vayo, *The March of Socialism* (New York: Hill & Wang, 1974), p.5.

6 John Lewis, *The Marxism of Marx* (London: Lawrence & Wishert, 1972), p. 11.

7 Charles H. Anderson, *The Political Economy of Social Class* (Englewood Cliffs, N.J.: Prentice-Hall, 1974), pp. 7-8.

8 Ibid.

9 Lewis, *Marxism of Marx,* p. 216.

10 Eduardo Galeano, *Open Veins of Latin America* (New York: Monthly Review Press, 1973), p. 77.

11 Bober, *Karl Marx's Interpretation,* pp. 206-07.

12 Lewis, *Marxism of Marx,* p. 9.

13 Ernst Nolte, " The Relationship Between 'Bourgeois' and 'Marxist' Historiography," *History and Theory* 14 (1975): 66.

14 Ollman, *Alienation,* p. 124.

15 William Z. Foster, *Outline Political History of the Americas* (New York: International Pubs., 1951), p. 298.

16 Karl Marx and Friedrich Engels, *Materiales para la historia de América Latina* (Mexico City: Siglo XXI, 1975), pp. 28-33.

17 Ibid., 23-25.

18 Ibid., pp. 39-42.

19 Friedrich Engels, *Werke* (Berlin: Dietz Verlag, 1963), 29:280.

20 Karl Marx, "Bolívar y Ponte," *New American Encyclopedia* 3 (1858): 10.

21 Hal Draper, "Karl Marx and Simón Bolívar: A Note on Authoritarian Leadership in a National Liberation Movement," *New Politics* 7 (Winter 1968): 77.

22 Marx and Engels, *Materiales*, pp. 101-02.

23 Ibid., pp. 195-97.

24 Galeano, *Open Veins*, pp. 38-39, as quoted in Karl Marx, *Das Kapital*, 1: Ch. 3.

25 Marx and Engels, *Materiales*, pp. 175-76, 179.

26 Ibid., 327-39.

27 Ibid., pp. 317-20.

28 V. I. Lenin, *Imperialism: The Highest Stage of Capitalism* (New York: International Pubs., 1939), pp. 7, 15.

29 V. I. Lenin, *Lenin on the United States* (New York: International Pubs., 1970), pp. 608-09.

30 Lenin, *Imperialism*, p. 85; Jean François Revel, *The Totalitarian Temptation* (Garden City, N.Y.: Doubleday, 1977), p. 2.

31 Donald C. Hodges, *The Latin American Revolution: Politics and Strategy from Apro-Marxism to Guevarism* (New York: William Morrow, 1974), p. 68.

32 Ibid., pp. 81-82.

33 León Trotsky, *Por los estados unidos socialistas de América Latina* (Buenos Aires: Ediciones Coyoacán, 1961), pp. 13, 48-49.

34 Donald E. Davis, "Marxism and People's Wars," *Orbis* 15(4) (Winter 1972):1203.

35 Mostofa Rejai, ed., *Mao Tse-tung on Revolution and War* (Garden City, N.Y.: Doubleday, 1969), p. xv.

36 James Joll, *Antonio Gramsci* (New York: Penguin Books, 1977), pp. 15-16.

37 Antonio Gramsci, *Letters from Prison* (New York: Harper & Row, 1975), p. 43.

38 Ibid., p.40.

39 Joll, *Gramsci*, pp. 77-78.

40 Ibid., p. 92

41 Harold Eugene Davis, *Latin American Thought: A Historical Introduction* (New York: Free Press, 1974), p. 97.

42 Volodia Teitelboim, "Problems Facing Latin American Intellectuals," *World Marxist Review* 2 (12) (Dec. 1968): 69.

43 Victorio Codovilla, "The Ideas of Marxism-Leninism in Latin America," *World Marxist Review* 7(8) (Aug. 1964): 41.

44 Hobart A. Spalding, Jr., *Organized Labor in Latin America: Historical Case Studies of Urban Workers in Dependent Societies* (New York: Harper & Row, 1977), p. 27.

45 Codovilla, "Ideas of Marxism-Leninism," p. 42.

Chapter 3. Argentina

1 Julio Cortázar, *Herald Tribune* (International), April 5, 1979.

2 Harold Eugene Davis, ed., *Latin American Social Thought* (Washington, D.C.: University Press of Washington, D.C., 1961), p. 102.

3 Leopoldo Zea, *The Latin American Mind* (Norman: University of Oklahoma Press, 1963), p. 21.

4 Carlos M. Lombardi, *Las ideas sociales en la Argentina* (Buenos Aires: Editoriales Platina/Stilcograf, 1965), pp. 58-60.

5 G. D. H. Cole, *A History of Socialist Thought*, vol. 3, pt. 2: *The Second International, 1889-1914* (London: Macmillan, 1956), p. 826.

6 Lombardi, *Las ideas sociales*, p. 125.

7 Hobart A. Spalding, Jr., *Organized Labor in Latin America: Historical Case Studies of Urban Workers in Dependent Societies* (New York: Harper & Row, 1977), p. 6.

8 Cole, *History of Socialist Thought*, pp. 822-23.

9 José Luis Romero, *A History of Argentine Political Thought* (Stanford: Stanford University Press, 1963), p. 223.

10 See Vicente D. Sierra, *Historia de las ideas políticas en Argentina* (Buenos Aires: Ediciones Nuestra Causa, 1950).

11 Lombardi, *Las ideas sociales*, p. 159.

12 See Luis Pan, *Justo y Marx: El socialismo en la Argentina* (Buenos Aires: Ediciones Monserrat, 1964).

13 Alberto J. Pla, *Ideología y método en la historiografía Argentina* (Buenos Aires: Ediciones Nueva Visión, 1972), pp. 113-14.

14 See Pla, *Ideología*.

15 Lombardi, *Las ideas sociales*, p. 160.

16 Ibid., p.8

17 Américo Ghioldi, *Juan B. Justo. Sus ideas históricas, socialistas, filosóficas* (Buenos Aires: Ediciones Monserrat, 1964), p. 109.

18 Juan B. Justo, *Socialismo* (Buenos Aires: Tipografía "La Vanguardia," 1920).

19 Ibid., pp. 47–48.

20 Ghioldi, *Justo,* pp. 44–45.

21 Zea, *Latin American Mind*, pp. 233–35.

22 Jorge Abelardo Ramos, *Revolución y contrarevolución en la Argentina*, vol. 3: *La bella época, 1904–1922* (Buenos Aires: Editorial Plus Ultra, 1973), pp. 195–96. Ironically, Ugarte was expelled in 1913 from the Socialist party for his "internationalist position." Ugarte's written works were primarily one dimensional (antiimperialist) and not of sufficient theoretical depth to warrant inclusion among those of the authors mentioned in this chapter.

23 Richard J. Walter, *The Socialist Party of Argentina, 1890–1930* (Austin: University of Texas Press, 1977), pp. 117–18.

24 Ibid., p. 59.

25 Michael Harrington, *Socialism* (New York: Bantam Books, 1973), p. 125.

26 Cole, *History of Socialist Thought*, p. 830.

27 Ghioldi, *Justo*, p. 101.

28 Justo, *Socialismo*, p. 140.

29 Adolfo Dickmann, *Nacionalismo y socialismo* (Buenos Aires: Porter Hnos., 1933).

30 Enrique Dickmann, *Población e inmigración* (Buenos Aires: Editorial Losada, 1946).

31 Enrique Dickmann, *Ideas e ideales* (Buenos Aires: Agencia General de Librería y Publicaciones, 1920).

32 Jacinto Oddone, *Historia del socialismo argentino,* 2 vols. (Buenos Aires: Talleres Gráficos "La Vanguardia," 1934).

33 Jacinto Oddone, *Gremialismo proletario argentino* (Buenos Aires: Editorial La Vanguardia, 1949).

34 Romero, *History of Argentine Political Thought*, p. 204.

35 Walter, *Socialist Party*, pp. 75–76.

36 See Alfredo L. Palacios, *La justicia social* (Buenos Aires: Editorial Claridad, 1954).

37 Ibid., p. 74.

38 Pan, *Justo y Marx*, p. 135.

39 Alfredo L. Palacios *Masas y élites en Iberoamérica* (Buenos Aires: Editorial Columbia, 1960), pp. 45–46.

40 Ibid., pp. 67–68.

41 Alfredo L. Palacios, *Soberanía y socialización de industrias: Monopolios, latifundios, y privilegios de capital extranjero* (Buenos Aires: Editorial La Vanguardia, 1946), pp. 341–43.

42 Emilio Frugoni, *Génesis, esencia, y fundamentos del socialismo* (Buenos Aires: Editorial Américalee, 1947), p. 291.

43 Alfredo L. Palacios, *Nuestra América y el imperialismo* (Buenos Aires: Editorial Palestra, 1961).

44 Ibid., pp. 46–47.

45 See Alfredo L. Palacios, *Una revolución: La reforma agraria en Cuba* (Buenos Aires: Editorial Palestra, 1961).

46 Lombardi, *Las ideas sociales,* p. 170.

47 Ibid., pp. 142–49.

48 "Four South American Socialists," *Latin American Thought* 1(4) (July 1946):1.

49 Juan Antonio Salceda, *Aníbal Ponce y el pensamiento de Mayo* (Buenos Aires: Editorial Lautaro, 1957), pp. 187–88.

50 "Four South American Socialists," p. 1.

51 Aníbal Ponce, *Humanismo burgués y humanismo proletario* (Havana: Imprenta Nacional, 1962), p. 336.

52 Ibid., pp. 143–58.

53 Ibid., pp. 105–07.

54 Juan Marinello, *Contemporáneos* (Havana: Universidad Central de las Villas, 1964), pp. 164–66.

55 Ponce, *Humanismo*, pp. 18–21.

56 Salceda, *Ponce*, pp. 210–13.

57 Aníbal Ponce, *Educación y lucha de clases* (Havana: Imprenta Nacional de Cuba, 1961), pp. 12–14.

58 Ibid., pp. 147–49.

59 See ibid.

60 Rodolfo Ghioldi, *Escritos* (Buenos Aires: Editorial Anteo, 1975), pp. 7–8.

61 Ibid., pp. 124–38.

62 Lombardi, *Las ideas sociales*, p. 126.

63 Ibid., pp. 169–71.

64 R. Ghioldi, *Escritos*, pp. 79–89.

65 Ibid., pp. 81–87.

66 Ibid., p. 79.

67 Ibid., pp. 120–22.

68 Lombardi, *Las ideas sociales*, p. 170.

69 Rodolfo Ghioldi, *La política en el mundo* (Buenos Aires: Editorial Futuro, 1946), p. 47.

70 Ghioldi, *Escritos*, pp. 159–84.

71 See Rodolfo Ghioldi, *No puede haber revolución en la revolución* (Buenos Aires: Editorial Anteo, 1967).

72 Ghioldi, *Escritos*, pp. 97–101.

73 Américo Ghioldi, *Marxismo, socialismo, izquierdismo, comunismo, y la realidad argentina de hoy* (Buenos Aires: Ediciones Populares Argentinas, 1950), p. 17.

74 Ibid.

75 See Américo Ghioldi, *Juan B. Justo: Sus ideas históricas, socialistas, filosóficas* (Buenos Aires: Ediciones Monserrat, 1964).

76 Américo Ghioldi, *El socialismo en la evolución nacional* (Buenos Aires: Editorial La Vanguardia, 1946), p. 83.

77 A. Ghioldi, *Marxismo*, p. 157.

78 Américo Ghioldi, *El socialismo y la actual crisis argentina* (Buenos Aires: Partido Socialista, 1948), pp. 6–7.

79 Ibid., p. 31.

80 See Américo Ghioldi, *El arte de la conducción y las dictaduras modernas* (Montevideo: Ediciones La Vanguardia en el exilio, 1955).

81 See Codovilla's collected speeches and writings in his *Nuestro camino desemboca en la victoria* (Buenos Aires: Editorial Fundamentos, 1954).

82 From a July 1976 series of personal interviews with political scientist Joseph R. Starobin who, while foreign editor of the *Daily Worker,* conversed with Codovilla during the 1946–1947 period.

83 Victorio Codovilla, *¿Resisterá la Argentina al imperialismo yanqui?* (Buenos Aires: Editorial Anteo, 1948), p. 142.

84 Ibid., pp. 175–76.

85 Ibid., p. 282.

86 Ibid., pp. 144–45.

87 Ibid., p. 141.

88 Codovilla, *Nuestro camino,* pp. 578–79.

89 Ibid., p. 257.

90 Victorio Codovilla, "Unir a la mujeres en la lucha por sus derechos," in *Problemas y luchas de las mujeres,* ed. Partido Comunista (Buenos Aires: Partido Comunista, 1947), pp. 90–91.

91 Lombardi, *Las ideas sociales,* p. 163.

92 Codovilla, *Nuestro camino,* p 308.

92 Lombardi, *Las ideas sociales,* p. 163.

94 Jorge Abelardo Ramos, *El partido comunista en la política Argentina: Su histórica y su crítica* (Buenos Aires: Coyoacán, 1962), pp. 181–83.

95 Ibid.

96 Codovilla, *Nuestro camino,* p. 268.

97 Lombardi, *Las ideas sociales,* p. 167.

98 Victorio Codovilla, *Trabajos escogidos* (Buenos Aires: Editorial Anteo, 1972), 1:188–91.

99 Ibid., p. 207.

100 Lombardi, *Las ideas sociales,* pp. 165–67.

101 Silvio Frondizi, *El materialismo dialéctico* (La Plata: Centro Estudiantes Derecho, 1966).

102 Silvio Frondizi, *El estado moderno: Ensayo de crítica constructiva* (Buenos Aires: Roque Depalma, 1954), p. 51.

103 Ibid., pp. 138–49.

104 Ibid., pp. 95–124.

105 Ibid., p. 120.

106 Ibid., pp. 185–86.

107 Silvio Frondizi, *Teorías políticas contemporáneas* (Buenos Aires: Ediciones Macchi, 1965), pp. 203–06.

108 Ibid., pp. 17–20.

109 Ibid., pp. 131–41.

110 Ibid., pp. 74–75.

111 Silvio Frondizi, *La realidad argentina,* 2 vols. (Buenos Aires: Praxis, 1956).

112 He articulated these ideas a decade before André Gunder Frank spoke about the "development of underdevelopment" and Theotonio dos Santos wrote about dependency.

113 See Silvio Frondizi, *La revolución cubana: Su significación histórica* (Montevideo: Editorial Ciencias Políticas, 1961).

114 H. S. Ferns, *Argentina* (New York: Praeger, 1969), p. 262.

115 Liborio Justo, *Prontuario: Una autobiografía* (Buenos Aires: Ediciones Gure, 1956), p. 195.

116 Liborio Justo, *León Trotsky y el fracaso mundial del trotskyismo* (Lima: Fondo de Cultura Popular, 1975), pp. 5, 7.

117 Ibid., p. 15.

118 Ibid., pp. 162–65.

119 Ibid., pp. 128–37.

120 Justo, *Prontuario,* pp. 204–09.

121 Liborio Justo, *Pampas y lanzas: Fundamentos histórico-económico-sociales de la nacionalidad y de la conciencia nacional argentina* (Buenos Aires: Editorial Palestra, 1962), pp. 112–33.

122 Ibid., pp. 68–69.

123 Liborio Justo, *Bolivia: La revolución derrotada* (Buenos Aires: Juárez Editor, S.A., 1971), pp. 25–26.

124 Ibid., p. 72.

125 Ibid., p. 132.

126 Ibid., pp. 207–19.

127 Ibid., p. 202.

128 Ibid., pp. 237–38.

129 Ibid., pp. 266–71.

130 Ibid., pp. 283–84.

131 Jorge Abelardo Ramos, *Bolivarismo y marxismo* (Buenos Aires: A. Peña Lillo, 1969), p. 15.

132 See Jorge Abelardo Ramos, *Historia del stalinismo en la Argentina* (Buenos Aires: Editorial Rancagua, 1974).

133 See Ramos, *El partido communista.*

134 Jorge Abelardo Ramos, *El marxismo en los países coloniales* (Cochabamba, Bolivia: Editorial Universitaria, 1970), pp. 6–8.

135 Ibid., p. 12.

136 Ibid., p. 14.

137 Ibid., p. 25.

138 Jorge Abelardo Ramos, *Revolución y contrarevolución en la Argentina,* vol. 5: *La era del bonapartismo, 1943–1973* (Buenos Aires: Editorial Plus Ultra, 1977), p. 318.

139 See Jorge Abelardo Ramos, *América Latina: Un país* (Buenos Aires: Editorial Octubre, 1949).

140 Ramos, *Bolivarismo*, pp. 110–11.

141 Ibid., pp. 131–33.

142 Ramos, *El partido communista.*

143 Ibid., pp. 224–25.

144 Jorge Abelardo Ramos, *Revolución y contrarevolución en la Argentina*, vol 1: *Las masas y las lanzas, 1810–1862* (Buenos Aires: Editorial Plus Ultra, 1974), pp. 9–10.

145 Jorge Abelardo Ramos, *Revolución y contrarevolución en la Argentina.* vol. 2: *Del patriciado a la oligarquía, 1862–1904* (Buenos Aires: Editorial Plus Ultra, 1976), pp. 305–07.

146 Ramos, *Revolución y contrarevolucón*, 5:315–17.

147 Ramos, *Historia del stalinismo*, p. 178.

148 Ramos, *Revolución y contrarevolución*, 1:13.

149 Ramos, *Historia del stalinismo*, p. 183.

Chapter 4. Chile

1 Harold Eugene Davis, ed., *Latin American Social Thought* (Washington, D.C.: University Press of Washington, D.C., 1961), p. 161.

2 Helio Jaguaribe, "Marxism and Latin American Development," in *Marx and the Western World*, ed. Nicholas Lobkowicz (Notre Dame, Ind.: University of Notre Dame Press, 1967), p. 232.

3 Harry W. Laidler, *History of Socialism* (New York: Thomas Y. Crowell, 1968), p. 611.

4 Paul W. Drake, *Socialism and Populism in Chile, 1932–1952* (Urbana: University of Illinois Press, 1978), p. 143.

5 Ernst Halperin, *Nationalism and Communism in Chile* (Cambridge, Mass.: MIT Press, 1965), pp. 142–44.

6 See James Petras, *Politics and Social Forces in Chilean Development* (Berkeley and Los Angeles: University of California Press, 1970).

7 Halperin, *Nationalism*, p. 122.

8 Pablo Neruda, *Memoirs* (New York: Penguin Books, 1978), p. 266.

9 Ibid., p. 319.

10 See Luis Emilio Recabarren, *El pensamiento de Luis Emilio Recabarren*, (Santiago: Austral, 1971), vol. 1.

11 Fernando Alegría, *Recabarren* (Santiago: Editorial "Antares," 1938), p. 71.

12 Luis Emilio Recabarren, *Obras Escogidas* (Santiago: Editorial Recabarren, 1965), 1:10, and Harold Eugene Davis, *Revolutionaries,*

Traditionalists, and Dictators in Latin America (New York: Cooper Square, 1973), pp. 61–66.

13 Volodia Teitelboim, "Literature and Socialism," *World Marxist Review* 3(3) (March 1960):45.

14 Alegría, *Recabarren,* p. 156.

15 Recabarren, *Obras,* 1:102.

16 Ibid., p. 133.

17 Ibid., p. 107.

18 Alegría, *Recabarren,* pp. 128, 148.

19 Recabarren, *El pensamiento,* 1:143–55.

20 Ibid., p. 135.

21 Recabarren, *Obras,* 1:93–94.

22 Recabarren, *El pensamiento,* 1:84.

23 Julio César Jobet, *Recabarren: Los orígenes del movimiento obrero y del socialismo chilenos* (Santiago: Prensa Latino-Americana, 1955), p. 38.

24 Recabarren, *El pensamiento,* 2:31–33.

25 Recabarren, *Obras,* 1:17.

26 Recabarren, *El pensamiento,* 2:406.

27 Alegría, *Recabarren,* p. 136.

28 Recabarren, *El pensamiento,* 2:352.

29 Julio César Jobet, *Ensayo crítico del desarrollo económico-social de Chile* (Santiago: Editorial Universitaria, 1955), p. 140.

30 Alegría, *Recabarren,* p. 118.

31 See Recabarren, *El pensamiento,* vol. 1.

32 Jobet, *Ensayo crítico,* pp. xiii–xiv.

33 Jobet, *Recabarren.*

34 Jobet, *Ensayo crítico.*

35 Ibid., pp. xvii–xviii.

36 Ibid., p. xviii.

37 Ibid., p. 8.

38 Ibid., p. xix.

39 Ibid., p. 1.

40 Julio César Jobet, *Los fundamentos del marxismo* (Santiago: Prensa Latino-Americana, n.d.), p. 12.

41 Ibid., pp. 141–48.

42 Ibid., pp. 166–68.

43 Ibid., pp. 168–70.

44 Drake, *Socialism,* p. 309.

45 Rodney Arismendi, *Lenin, la revolución, y América Latina* (Montevideo: Ediciones Pueblos Unidos, 1970), pp. 379–425.

46 Halperin, *Nationalism,* pp. 245–46.

47 Ibid., p. 246.

48 Oscar Waiss, *Nacionalismo y socialismo en América Latina* (Buenos Aires: Ediciones Iguazú, 1961), pp. 173–82.

49 Ibid., pp. 37–38.

50 Ibid., p. 119.

51 Oscar Waiss, *Los problemas del socialismo contemporáneo* (Buenos Aires: Ediciones Iguazú, 1961), pp. 64–65.

52 Ibid., pp. 68–69.

53 Ibid., pp. 124–25.

54 Ibid., pp. 133–40.

55 Ibid., pp. 127–32.

56 Waiss, *Nacionalismo,* pp. 167–72.

57 Ibid., pp. 160–61.

58 Ibid., pp. 167–7ʻ

59 Ibid.

60 See Luis Vitale, *Interpretación marxista de la historia de Chile,* vol. 1: *Las culturas primativas: La conquista española* (Santiago: Ediciones de Prensa Latino-Americana, 1967).

61 Luis Vitale, "Latin America: Feudal or Capitalist?" in *Latin America: Reform or Revolution?* ed. James Petras and Maurice Zeitlin (Greenwich, Conn.: Fawcett, 1968), pp. 33–40.

62 Ibid.

63 Luis Vitale and Kalki Glausser R., *Acerca del modo de producción colonial en América Latina* (Medellin, Colombia: Ediciones Crítico, 1974), pp. 161, 183.

64 Ibid., p. 172.

65 Ibid., pp. 164–65.

66 Vitale, *Interpretación marxista,* 1:16–17.

67 Ibid., p. 17.

68 Vitale, "Latin America," pp. 41–42.

69 Ibid., p. 43.

70 Luis Vitale, *Los discursos de Clotario Blest y la revolución chilena* (Santiago: Editorial Por, 1961), pp. 61–62.

71 Ibid., pp. 56–57.

72 See ibid.

73 Ibid., pp. 67–71.

74 Ibid., pp. 75–77.

75 Ibid., pp. 93–95.

76 Vitale, *Interpretación marxista,* 1:7–8.

77 See Vitale, *Los discursos.*

78 Luis Vitale, "Fidelismo and Marxism," *International Socialist Review* 24 (Winter 1963):23.

79 Luis Vitale, "Predictions of the Founders of Marxism on the Development of World Revolution," in *Fifty Years of World Revolution*, ed. Ernest Mandel (New York: Merit Pubs., 1968), p. 38.

80 Ibid., pp. 40–41.

81 Ibid., p. 43.

82 Ibid., pp. 44–45.

83 Ibid., p. 46.

84 Ibid., p. 49.

85 Ibid., p. 35.

86 See Luis Vitale, *¿Y después de 4, qué? Perspectivas de Chile después de las elecciones presidenciales* (Santiago: Editorial Prensa Latino-Americana, 1970).

87 Volodia Teitelboim, "Literature and Socialism," *World Marxist Review* 3(3) (March 1960):45.

88 Volodia Teitelboim, *El oficio ciudadano* (Santiago: Nacimiento, 1973), pp. 82–84.

89 Volodia Teitelboim, "Problems Facing Latin American Intellectuals," *World Marxist Review* 2(2) (Dec. 1968):74.

90 Ibid.

91 Ibid., p. 68.

92 Teitelboim, *El oficio*, pp. 129–33.

93 William E. Ratliff, *Castroism and Communism in Latin America, 1959–1976: The Varieties of Marxist-Leninist Experience* (Washington, D.C.: American Enterprise Institute, 1976), p. 180.

94 Teitelboim, *El oficio*, p. 168.

95 Volodia Teitelboim, "The Failure in Chile and the Future of a Strategy," in *Marxism and Latin America*, ed. Luis E. Aguilar (Philadelphia: Temple University Press, 1978), p. 333.

96 Luis Corvalán, *Nuestra vía revolucionaria* (Santiago: Impresora Horizonte, 1964), p. 40.

97 Sergio Guilisasti Tagle, *Partidos políticos chilenos* (Santiago: Editorial Nacimiento, 1964), pp. 330–40.

98 See Corvalán, *Nuestra vía*.

99 Jorge Palacios, *Chile: An Attempt at "Historic Compromise": The Real Story of the Allende Years* (Chicago: Banner Press, 1979), p. 50.

100 Corvalán, *Nuestra vía*, p. 19.

101 Halperin, *Nationalism*, pp. 148–50.

102 Ibid., pp. 68–71.

103 Palacios, *Chile*, p. 42.

104 Ibid., p. 339.

105 Drake, *Socialism*, pp. 282, 290.

106 Raúl Ampuero Díaz, "Reflexiones sobre la revolución y el socialismo," in *Pensamiento teórico y político del partido socialista de Chile*,

ed. Julio César Jobet and Alejandro Chelén (Santiago: Empresa Editora Nacional Quimantu, 1972), pp. 151–64.

107 Guilisasti, *Partidos políticos*, pp. 298–306.

108 Halperin, *Nationalism*, pp. 151–53.

109 Raúl Ampuero Díaz, *La izquierda en punto muerto* (Santiago: Editorial Orbe, 1969), pp. 46–47.

110 Ibid., p. 59.

111 Ibid., p. 175–76.

112 Raúl Ampuero Díaz, *El socialismo ante el mundo de hoy* (Santiago: Prensa Latino-Americana, 1964), pp. 27–28.

113 Ampuero, *La izquierda*, pp. 151–53.

114 Ibid., pp. 156–69.

115 Guilisasti, *Partidos*, p. 301.

116 Ibid., pp. 300–04.

117 Halperin, *Nationalism*, p. 154.

118 Ampuero, *El socialismo*, pp. 27–28.

119 Ibid.

120 Ampuero, "Reflexiones," p. 157.

121 Halperin, *Nationalism*, p. 158.

122 Clodomiro Almeyda Medina, *Visión sociológica de Chile* (Santiago: Academia de las Escuelas de Ciencias Políticas y Administrativas, 1957), pp. 20–21.

123 Clodomiro Almeyda Medina, *Hacia un teoría marxista del estado* (Santiago: Universidad de Chile, Colección Cultura Política, 1948).

124 Almeyda, *Visión*, pp. 20–21.

125 Almeyda, *Hacia un teoría*, pp. 89–93.

126 Ibid., pp. 202–03.

127 Ibid., pp. 133–34.

128 Clodomiro Almeyda Medina, "Concepción marxista del hombre," in *Pensamiento Teórico*, ed. Jobet and Chelen, pp. 343–79.

129 Almeyda, *Hacia un teoría*, p. 154.

130 Clodomiro Almeyda Medina, *Reflexiones políticas* (Santiago: Prensa Latino-Americana, 1958), pp. 84–85.

131 Ibid., p. 34.

132 Halperin, *Nationalism*, p. 161.

133 Almeyda, *Reflexiones*, pp. 58–59.

134 Halperin, *Nationalism*, pp. 167–68.

135 Clodomiro Almeyda Medina, "The Foreign Policy of the Unidad Popular Government," in *Chile at the Turning Point: Lessons of the Socialist Years, 1970–1973*, ed. Federico G. Gil, Ricardo Lagos E., and Henry Landsberger (Philadelphia: Institute for Study of Human Issues, 1979), pp. 79–87.

136 Salvador Allende, *La contradicción de Chile* (Santiago: Talleres Gráficos, 1943), pp. 37–38.

137 Drake, *Socialism*, pp. 3–5.

138 Salvador Allende, *Chile's Road to Socialism* (Baltimore: Penguin Books, 1973), p. 61.

139 Salvador Allende, *El pensamiento de Salvador Allende*, ed. Hugo Latorre (Mexico City: Fondo de Cultura Económica, 1974), p. 272.

140 Guilisasti, *Partidos*, pp. 271–93.

141 Allende, *El pensamiento*, p. 272.

142 Régis Debray, *The Chilean Revolution: Conversations with Allende* (New York: Random House, 1971), p. 64.

143 Guilisasti, *Partidos*, p. 276.

144 Allende, *Chile's Road*, p. 57.

145 Frederico G. Gil, *The Political System of Chile* (Boston: Houghton Mifflin, 1966), p. 285.

146 Allende, *Chile's Road*, pp. 171–72.

147 Ibid., p. 12.

148 Salvador Allende, *Citas de compañero presidente* (Santiago: Ediciones Nueva República, 1973).

149 Guilisasti, *Partidos*, pp. 283–84.

150 Ibid., p. 288.

151 Ibid., p. 293.

152 Drake, *Socialism*, p. 321.

153 Donald C. Hodges, ed., *The Legacy of Che Guevara: A Documentary Study* (London: Thames & Hudson, 1977), p. 140.

154 See Julio Solar and Jacques Choncol, *Desarrollo sin capitalismo: Hacia un mundo comunitario* (Caracas: Nuevo Orden, 1964).

Chapter 5. Brazil

1 Vamireh Chacon, *História das idéias socialistas no Brasil* (Rio de Janeiro: Editôra Civilização Brasileira S.A., 1965), p. 413.

2 G. D. H. Cole, *A History of Socialist Thought*, vol. 3, pt. 2: *The Second International, 1889–1914* (London: Macmillan, 1956), p. 825.

3 Helio Jaquaribe, "Marxism and Latin American Development," in *Marx and the Western World*, ed. Nicholas Lobkowicz (Notre Dame, Ind.: University of Notre Dame Press, 1967), p. 237.

4 Ibid.

5 Chacon, *História*, pp. 265–72.

6 John W. F. Dulles, *Anarchists and Communists in Brazil, 1900–1935* (Austin: University of Texas Press, 1973), p. 5.

7 Ronald H. Chilcote, *The Brazilian Communist Party: Conflict*

and Integration, 1922–1972 (New York: Oxford University Press, 1974), p. 20.

8 See Dulles, *Anarchists,* for an excellent account.

9 Ibid., pp. 269–72.

10 Pedro Motta Lima, "Marxism-Leninism and Its Influence on Cultural Life in Brazil," *World Marxist Review* 5(10) (Oct. 1962):22.

11 Jacob Gorender, "Brazil in the Grip of Contradictions," *World Marxist Review* 6(2) (Feb. 1963):27–32.

12 Chilcote, *Brazilian Communist Party,* p. 130.

13 See Nelson Werneck Sodré, *A coluna Prestes* (Rio de Janeiro: Editôra Civilização Brasileira, 1978).

14 John Nasht, "The Prestes Saga," *Inter-American Monthly* 3 (Dec. 1945):43.

15 Sodré, *A coluna Prestes,* pp. 95–96.

16 Dulles, *Anarchists,* p. 420.

17 Abguar Bastos, *Prestes e a revolução social* (Rio de Janeiro: Editorial Calvino, 1946), pp. 250–317.

18 Chilcote, *Brazilian Communist Party,* p. 36.

19 Sodré, *A coluna Prestes,* p. 96.

20 "Four South American Socialists," *Latin American Thought* 1(4) (July 1946):24.

21 Bastos, *Prestes,* pp. 304–16.

22 Luiz Carlos Prestes, *Os comunistas na luta pela democracia* (Rio de Janeiro: Edições Horizonte, 1945), pp. 9–12.

23 Pablo Neruda, *Memoirs* (New York: Penguin Books, 1978), p. 312.

24 From statements by Joseph R. Starobin, political scientist, personal interviews, Hancock, Mass., July 1976.

25 Chilcote, *Brazilian Communist Party,* pp. 87–88.

26 Luiz Carlos Prestes, "Policy of the Military Dictatorship in Brazil," *World Marxist Review* 8(4) (April 1965):36.

27 Luiz Carlos Prestes, *Tribuna Popular,* Jan. 12, 13, 1973.

28 Luiz Carlos Prestes, "Lenin's Heritage and Fight Against Opportunism in the Brazilian Communist Party," *World Marxist Review* 13(11) (Nov. 1970):10–12.

29 See Bastos, *Prestes.*

30 Chilcote, *Brazilian Communist Party,* p. 130.

31 Ibid., p. 120.

32 Ibid., p. 96.

33 Starobin, interviews.

34 Ibid.

35 Ibid.

36 "Four South American Socialists," p. 203.

37 See Jorge Amado, *Vida de Luiz Carlos Prestes: Cavaleiro da esperança* (São Paulo: Martins, 1945).

38 See Leôncio Basbaum, *Uma vida em seis tempos (memórias)* (São Paulo: Editôra Alfa-Omega, 1976).

39 Leôncio Basbaum, *O processo evólutiva da história* (São Paulo: Editôra Edaglit, 1963), p. 147.

40 Ibid., p. 112.

41 Leôncio Basbaum, *História sincera da república*, 4 vols. (São Paulo: [various publishers], 1962–1968).

42 Basbaum, *O processo*, pp. 287–95.

43 Harold Eugene Davis, *Latin American Thought: A Historical Introduction* (New York: Free Press, 1974), p. 196.

44 See Leôncio Basbaum, *Alienação e humanismo* (São Paulo: Editôra Fulgor, 1967).

45 Basbaum, *Uma vida.*

46 Ibid., pp. 34–52.

47 Leôncio Basbaum, *História sincera da república de 1889 a 1930*, vol. 2 (São Paulo: Edicões LB, 1962), p. 427.

48 Ibid., p. 346.

49 Ibid., pp. 420–21.

50 Ibid., p. 435.

51 Ibid., p. 425.

52 Ibid., p. 438.

53 Leôncio Basbaum, *Sociología de materialismo* (Buenos Aires: Editorial Américalee, 1964), p. 349.

54 Ibid., pp. 350–54.

55 Ibid., p. 348.

56 For background, see Leôncio Basbaum, *História sincera da república de 1930 a 1960* (São Paulo: Editôra Edaglit, 1962), vol. 3.

57 Ibid., p. 270.

58 Leôncio Basbaum, *Caminhos brasileiros do desenvolvimento* (São Paulo: Editôra Fulgor, 1960), p. 20.

59 See André Gunder Frank, *Latin America: Underdevelopment or Revolution* (New York: Monthly Review Press, 1969); and Frank's *Capitalism and Underdevelopment in Latin America: Historical Studies of Chile and Brazil* (New York: Monthly Review Press, 1969).

60 Basbaum, *Caminhos*, pp. 184–91.

61 Basbaum, *Sociología*, p. 196.

62 Basbaum, *O processo*, pp. 106–07.

63 See ibid.

64 Ibid., p. 251.

65 Basbaum, *Sociología*, pp. 383–85.

66 Ibid., 378–79.

67 Basbaum, *História sincera*, 2:418.

68 Leôncio Basbaum, *História sincera da republica*, vol. 1 (São Paulo: Edicões LB, 1962), p. 17.

69 Ibid., pp. 11–16.

70 Basbaum, *Sociología*, pp. 380–81.

71 See Basbaum, *O processo*.

72 Chilcote, *Brazilian Communist Party*, p. 56.

73 See Caio Prado Júnior, *A revolução brasileira* (São Paulo: Editôra Brasiliense, 1966).

74 Caio Prado Júnior, *The Colonial Background of Modern Brazil* (Berkeley and Los Angeles: University of California Press, 1969), p. 21.

75 Caio Prado Júnior, "A Guide for the Historiography of the Second Empire," in *Perspectives on Brazilian History*, ed. E. Bradford Burns (New York: Columbia University Press, 1967), pp. 91–100.

76 Prado, *A revolução*, p. 158.

77 Ibid., pp. 33–114.

78 Caio Prado Júnior, *La revolución brasileño* (Buenos Aires: A. Peña, 1968), p. 13.

79 Caio Prado Júnior, *O mundo do socialismo* (São Paulo: Editôra Brasiliense, 1962), p. 107.

80 Ibid., p. 180.

81 Ibid., pp. 106–07.

82 Ibid., pp. 182–83.

83 Carlos Marighela, *For the Liberation of Brazil* (Baltimore: Penguin Books, 1971), p. 8.

84 Joaquin Camara Ferreira, "Marighela: Creative Life and Action," *Tricontinental Bulletin* 21–27 (Nov. 8, 1970–Feb. 1971):120–21.

85 Marighela, *For the Liberation*, p. 12.

86 Prestes, "Lenin's Heritage and Fight," pp. 12–17.

87 Marighela, *For the Liberation*, p. 138.

88 Ibid., pp. 145–46.

89 Ibid., p. 147.

90 Ibid., p. 150.

91 Ibid., p. 172.

92 Ibid., pp. 46–48.

93 Ibid., pp. 170–71.

94 "Four South American Socialists," p. 230.

95 Marighela, *For the Liberation*, pp. 19–23.

96 Ibid., p. 14.

97 Chacon, *História*, p. 333.

98 Nelson Werneck Sodré, *Formação histórica do Brasil* (São Paulo: Editôra Brasiliense, 1962).

99 Nelson Werneck Sodré, *História da burguesia brasileira* (Rio de Janeiro: Editôra Civilização Brasileira, 1967), p. 14.

100 Ibid., pp. 145–55.

101 Ibid., p. 176.

102 Ibid., pp. 372–89.

103 Sodré, *A coluna Prestes*, p. 12.

104 Ibid., pp. 64–75.

105 Nelson Werneck Sodré, *Evolución social y económica del Brasil* (Buenos Aires: Editorial Universitaria de Buenos Aires, 1964), pp. 83–88.

106 Nelson Werneck Sodré, *Ofício de escritor: Dialética da literatura* (Rio de Janeiro: Editôra Civilização Brasileira, 1965).

107 Ibid., p. 57.

108 Ibid., p. 148.

109 Ibid., pp. 58–61.

110 Nelson Werneck Sodré, *História da literatura brasileira* (Rio de Janeiro: Editôra Civilização Brasileira, 1976).

111 See Sodré, *Ofício de escritor*.

112 Ibid., p. 50.

113 Ibid., pp. 104–06.

Chapter 6. Peru

1 Helio Jaguaribe, "Marxism and Latin American Development," in *Marx and the Western World*, ed. Nicholas Lobkowicz (Notre Dame, Ind.: University of Notre Dame Press, 1967).

2 John M. Baines, *Revolution in Peru: Mariátegui and the Myth* (University: University of Alabama Press, 1972), p. 14.

3 See ibid.

4 Jesús Chavarría, *José Carlos Mariátegui and the Rise of Modern Peru, 1890–1930* (Albuquerque: University of New Mexico Press, 1979), p. 74.

5 Jorge del Prado, *Mariátegui y su obra* (Lima: Ediciones Nuevo Horizonte, 1946), p. 19.

6 José Carlos Mariátegui, *Seven Interpretive Essays on Peruvian Reality* (Austin: University of Texas Press, 1971), p. xi.

7 Harry E. Vanden, "Mariátegui: Marxismo, Communismo, and Other Bibliographic Notes," *Latin American Research Review* 14(3) (1979):75.

8 Augusto Salazar Bondy, *Historia de las ideas en el Perú contemporáneo*, 2 vols. (Lima: Francisco Moncloa, 1967), p. 314.

9 Quoted in Chavarría, *Mariátegui*, p. 170.

10 Ibid., pp. 85–86.

11 Martin S. Stabb, *In Quest of Identity: Patterns in the Spanish*

American Essay of Ideas, 1890–1960 (Chapel Hill: University of North Carolina Press, 1967), p. 116.

12 Jean Franco, *The Modern Culture of Latin America: Society and the Artist* (Harmondsworth, Eng.: Pelican Books, 1970), p. 115.

13 Robert E. McNicoll, "Intellectual Origins of Aprismo," *Hispanic American Historical Review* 23(3) (Aug. 1943):434.

14 The fullest and most sensitive account of Mariátegui's life and work is Chavarría's.

15 Mariátegui, *Seven Interpretive Essays*, p. xxxvi.

16 Ibid., p. xii.

17 José Carlos Mariátegui, *Historia de la crisis mundial: Conferencias, 1923, 1924* (Lima: Biblioteca Amauta, 1959), p. 15.

18 Daniel R. Reedy. "The Cohesive Influence of José Carlos Mariátegui on Peruvian Art and Politics," in *Artists and Writers in the Evolution of Latin America,* ed. Edward D. Terry (University: University of Alabama Press, 1969), p. 150.

19 Baines, *Revolution,* pp. 30–32.

20 Chavarría, *Mariátegui,* p. 149.

21 Ibid., p. 140.

22 See José Carlos Mariátegui, *Defensa del marxismo* (Lima: Biblioteca Amauta, 1959); Eugenio Chang-Rodríguez, *La literatura política de González Prada, Mariátegui, y Haya de la Torre* (Mexico City: Ediciones de Andrea, 1957), pp. 172–74.

23 Chavarría, *Mariátegui,* p. 134.

24 Ibid., p. 138.

25 José Aricó, ed., *Mariátegui y los orígenes del marxismo latino-americano* (Mexico City: Siglo XXI, 1978), pp. xviii–xix.

26 Vanden, "Mariátegui," p. 78.

27 Ibid., p. 77.

28 Chavarría, *Mariátegui,* p. 206, n. 13.

29 Harold Eugene Davis, ed. and trans., *Latin American Social Thought* (Washington, D.C.: University Press of Washington, D.C., 1961), p. 435.

30 Reedy, "Cohesive Influences," p. 152.

31 Aricó, ed., *Mariátegui,* p. 176.

32 Chang-Rodríguez, *La literatura,* p. 192.

33 Chavarría, *Mariátegui,* p. 153.

34 Salazar Bondy, *Historia,* pp. 319–21.

35 Mariátegui, *Historia de la crisis,* pp. 118–19.

36 See Chavarría, *Mariátegui,* for more detailed explanations.

37 Ibid., p. 172.

38 Chang-Rodríguez, *La literatura,* p. 182.

39 Prado, *Mariátegui,* p. 55.

40 Chang-Rodríguez, *La literatura*, pp. 187–88.
41 Mariátegui, *Seven Interpretive Essays*, p. 30.
42 Ibid., p. 76.
43 "Four South American Socialists," p. 1.
44 McNicoll, "Intellectual Origins," p. 437.
45 Prado, *Mariátegui*, p. 110.
46 Mario Benedetti, *El escritor latinoamericano y la revolución posible* (Buenos Aires: Editorial Alfa Argentina, 1974), p. 64.
47 Harold Eugene Davis, *Latin American Thought: A Historical Introduction* (New York: Free Press, 1974), p. 189.
48 Mariátegui, *Historia de la crisis*, pp. 166–67, 193–97.
49 Stabb, *In Quest of Identity*, p. 107.
50 Miguel Jorrín and John Martz, *Latin American Political Thought and Ideology* (Chapel Hill: University of North Carolina Press, 1970), pp. 331–32; and Salazar Bondy, *Historia*, p. 363.
51 Hildebrando Castro Pozo, *Del allyu al cooperativismo socialista* (Lima: Biblioteca de la Revista de Economía y Finanzas, 1936).
52 Ibid.
53 Ricardo Martínez de la Torre, *Apuntes para una interpretación marxista de historia social del Perú* (Lima: Vol. 1: Ediciones "Frente," 1935; vol. 2: Empresa Editora Peruana, 1948; vol. 3: Empresa Editora Peruana, 1949; vol. 4: Compañía Impresora Peruana, 1949).
54 See ibid., vol. 1.
55 Ricardo Martínez de la Torre, *De la reforma universitaria al partido socialista: Apuntes para una interpretación marxista de historia soical del Perú* (Lima: Ediciones Frente, 1945), pp. 30–56.
56 Donald C. Hodges, *The Latin American Revolution: Politics and Strategy from Apro-Marxism to Guevarism* (New York: William Morrow, 1974), p. 28.
57 Harold Eugene Davis, *Revolutionaries, Traditionalists, and Dictators in Latin America* (New York: Cooper Square, 1973), pp. 80–85.
58 Hugo Blanco, *Land or Death: The Peasant Struggle in Peru* (New York: Pathfinder Press, 1972), p. 62.
59 Ibid., p. 9
60 Robert J. Alexander, *Trotskyism in Latin America* (Stanford: Hoover Institution Press, 1973), p. 158.
61 Blanco, *Land or Death*, p. 64.
62 Ibid., p. 31.
63 David Chaplin, ed., *Peruvian Nationalism: A Corporatist Revolution* (New Brunswick, N.J.: Transaction Books, 1976), p. 283.
64 Héctor Béjar, *Peru 1965: Notes on a Guerrilla Experience* (New York: Monthly Review Press, 1969), p. 55.
65 Chaplin, *Peruvian Nationalism*, p. 286.

66 Richard Gott, *Guerrilla Movements in Latin America* (Garden City, N.Y.: Doubleday, 1972), p. 318.

67 Aníbal Quijano, "Tendencies in the Class Struggle in Peru," *Contemporary Marxism,* no. 1, Spring 1980, p. 55.

68 Aníbal Quijano, *Crisis imperialista y clase obrera en América Latina* (Lima: Quijano, 1974).

69 Ibid., p. 113.

70 Ibid., pp. 57–58.

71 Ibid., pp. 16–23.

72 Aníbal Quijano, "Tendencies in Peruvian Development and in the Class Structure," in *Latin America: Reform or Revolution,* ed. James Petras and Maurice Zeitlin (Greenwich, Conn.: Fawcett, 1968), pp. 289–90.

73 Ibid., p. 289.

74 Ibid., pp. 291–93.

75 Quijano, *Crisis imperialista,* pp. 70–71.

76 Ibid. p. 89.

77 Quijano, "Tendencies in Peruvian Development," p. 89.

78 Quijano, *Crisis imperialista,* pp. 38–46.

79 Aníbal Quijano, *Nationalism and Capitalism in Peru: A Study in Neo-Imperialism* (New York: Monthly Review Press, 1971), p. 5.

80 Ibid., p. 48.

81 Quijano, *Crisis imperialista,* pp. 76–79.

82 Ibid., pp. 79–85.

83 Ibid., pp. 14–15.

84 Aníbal Quijano, "Contemporary Peasant Movements," in *Elites in Latin America,* ed. Seymour Martin Lipset and Aldo Solari (New York: Oxford University Press, 1967), pp. 303–04.

85 Ibid., pp. 327–29.

86 Quijano, "Tendencies in the Class Struggle," p. 50.

87 Quijano, "Contemporary Peasant Movements," pp. 306–15.

88 Ibid., pp. 329–30.

Chapter 7. The Bolivarian Nations

1 Diego Montaña Cuéllar, *Colombia: País formal y país real* (Buenos Aires: Editorial Platina, 1963), p. 131.

2 Ibid., p. 134.

3 José Consuegra Higgins, *Lenin y la América Latina* (Barranquilla, Colombia: Ediciones Cruz del Sur, 1972), pp. 15–19.

4 Jorge Elíecer Gaitán, *Las ideas socialistas en Colombia* (Bogota: Casa del Pueblo, 1963).

5 Ibid., p. 31.

6 Ibid., p. 95.

7 Ibid., p. 109.

8 Ibid., p. 30.

9 Statements by Joseph R. Starobin, former foreign editor of the *Daily Worker,* personal interviews, Hancock, Mass., July 1976.

10 Montaña Cuéllar, *Colombia,* p. 281.

11 Diego Montaña Cuéllar, *Los partidos políticos y la realidad nacional* (Medellin, Colombia: Santander, 1944?).

12 Diego Montaña Cuéllar, *Sociología americana* (Bogota: Universidad Nacional de Colombia, 1950).

13 Ibid., p. 18.

14 Ibid., pp. 13–17.

15 Ibid., pp. 28–41.

16 Richard Gott, *Guerrilla Movements in Latin America* (Garden City, N.Y.: Doubleday, 1972), p. 255.

17 Montaña Cuéllar, *Colombia,* p. 283.

18 See José Consuegra Higgins, *El control de la natalidad como arma del imperialismo* (Buenos Aires: Editorial Galerna, 1969).

19 Ibid., pp. 20–21.

20 Ibid., pp. 23–27.

21 Ibid., p. 100.

22 Ibid.

23 Consuegra, *Lenin,* p. 73.

24 Ibid., p. 38.

25 Ibid., p. 48.

26 Harold Eugene Davis, *Revolutionaries, Traditionalists, and Dictators in Latin America* (New York: Cooper Square, 1973), p. 75.

27 Ibid.

28 Germán Guzmán, *Camilo Torres* (New York: Sheed and Ward, 1969), p. 64.

29 John Gerassi, ed., *Revolutionary Priest: The Complete Writings and Messages of Camilo Torres* (New York: Random House, 1971), p. 29.

30 Ibid., p. 354.

31 Ibid., p. 29.

32 Ibid., pp. 21–23.

33 Walter J. Broderick, *Camilo Torres: A Biography of the Priest-Guerrillero* (New York: Doubleday, 1975), p. 155.

34 Gerassi, ed., *Revolutionary Priest,* pp. 318, 357.

35 Camilo Torres Restrepo, *Camilo Torres: Por el Padre Camilo Torres Restrepo (1956–1966)* (Cuernavaca: Centro Intercultural de Documentación, 1966), p. 70.

36 Gerassi, ed., *Revolutionary Priest,* pp. 296–97.

37 Guzmán, *Torres,* p. 174.

38 Ibid., p. 78.

39 Ibid., p. 297.

40 See *NACLA Reports,* Sept.–Oct. 1978, pp. 43–44.

41 In this chapter I often speak of Camilo Torres as Camilo or Padre Camilo as he was referred to in print and in conversation in Colombia. In Chapter X and elsewhere in the book Fidel Castro and Ernesto Guevara are often cited, respectively, as Fidel and Che as they are known in Cuba.

42 Sheldon B. Liss, *Diplomacy and Dependency: Venezuela, the United States, and the Americas* (Salisbury, N.C.: Documentary Publications, 1978), p. 92.

43 Germán Carrera Damas, *Historiografía marxista venezolana y otros temas* (Caracas: Universidad Central de Venezuela, 1967), pp. 114–15.

44 Domingo Alberto Rangel, *Los andinos en el poder* (Caracas: Talleres Gráficos Universitarios, 1964).

45 Ibid., p. 21.

46 Ibid., p. 151.

47 Ibid., p. 232.

48 Domingo Alberto Rangel, *La revolución de las fantasías* (Caracas: Ediciones OFIDI, 1958).

49 Domingo Alberto Rangel, *Los mercaderes del voto: Estudio de un sistema* (Valencia, Venezuela: Vadell Hermanos, 1973), pp. 27–28.

50 Ibid., p. 13.

51 Ibid., p. 132.

52 Ibid., pp. 138–39.

53 Rangel, *Los andinos,* pp. 215–32.

54 Liss, *Diplomacy,* p. 192.

55 See Domingo Alberto Rangel, *La oligarquía del dinero,* vol. 3 of *Capital y desarrollo* (Caracas: Editorial Fuentes, 1971).

56 See Domingo Alberto Rangel, *El proceso del capitalismo contemporáneo en Venezuela* (Caracas: Universidad Central de Venezuela, 1968).

57 Germán Carrera Damas, "Estudio preliminar," in vol. 1 of *Materiales para el estudio de la ideología realista de la independencia* (Caracas: Universidad Central de Venezuela, Facultad de Humanidades y Educación, Instituto de Antropología e Historia, 1971), p. lxviii.

58 Ibid., p. lxvix.

59 Ibid., p. lxxv.

60 Ibid., p. lxxxv.

61 Ibid., p. lxxx.

62 Ibid., p. lxxix.

63 Ibid., p. lxxvi.

64 Germán Carrera Damas, "The Cult of the Liberator," in *The Liberator, Simon Bolivar: Man and Image,* ed. David Bushnell (New York: Knopf, 1970), p. 109.

65 Ibid.

66 See Carrera Damas, "Estudio preliminar."

67 Germán Carrera Damas, *La dimensión histórica en el presente de América Latina y Venezuela: Tres conferencias* (Caracas: Universidad Central de Venezuela, Facultad de Humanidades y Educación, 1972).

68 Ibid., pp. 82–83.

69 Ibid., p. 59.

70 Ibid., pp. 50–52.

71 Ibid., p. 62.

72 Ibid., pp. 62–76.

73 Ibid., pp. 99–103.

74 Teodoro Petkoff, *¿Socialismo para Venezuela?* (Caracas: Editorial Domingo Fuentes, 1970), p. 25.

75 See ibid.

76 Ibid., pp. 79–80.

77 Teodoro Petkoff, *Razón y pasión del socialismo: El Tema socialista en Venezuela* (Caracas: Ediciones Centauro, 1973).

78 Ibid., pp. 353–61.

79 Petkoff, *¿Socialismo para Venezuela?* pp. 42–43.

80 Petkoff, *Razón y pasión,* pp. 362–66.

81 Petkoff, *¿Socialismo para Venezuela?* pp. 129–30.

82 Petkoff, *Razón y pasión,* p. 115.

83 Teodoro Petkoff, "The Left on Trial," in *Marxism in Latin America,* ed. Luis E. Aguilar (Philadelphia: Temple University Press, 1978), pp. 397–98.

84 Ibid., p. 401.

85 Petkoff, *Razón y pasión,* p. 165.

86 Héctor Malavé Mata, *Formación histórica del antidesarrollo de Venezuela* (Havana: Casa de las Américas, 1974).

87 José A. Silva Michelena, *The Illusion of Democracy in Dependent Nations,* vol. 3 of *The Politics of Change in Venezuela* (Cambridge, Mass.: MIT Press, 1971).

88 Guillermo Francovich, *El pensamiento boliviano en el siglo XX* (Mexico City: Fondo de Cultura Económica, 1956), p. 103.

89 Enrique Anderson-Imbert, *Spanish American Literature: A History,* 2 vols. (Detroit: Wayne State University Press, 1969), 2:571.

90 Francovich, *El pensamiento,* pp. 103–04.

91 Guillermo Lora, *Historia del movimiento obrero boliviano, 1923–1933,* Vol. 3 (La Paz: Editorial Los Amigos, 1970), pp. 58–72.

92 Francovich, *El pensamiento,* p. 103.

93 Ibid., p. 105.

94 Ibid.

95 James M. Malloy and Richard Thorn, eds., *Beyond the Revolution: Bolivia Since 1952* (Pittsburgh: University of Pittsburgh Press, 1971), p. 66.

96 Ibid., p. 54.

97 Régis Debray, *Prison Writings* (London: Allen Lane, 1973), pp. 6–7.

98 Donald C. Hodges, *The Latin American Revolution: Politics and Strategy from Apro-Marxism to Guevarism* (New York: William Morrow, 1974), p. 102.

99 Herbert S. Klein, *Parties and Political Change in Bolivia, 1880-1952* (Cambridge: Cambridge University Press, 1969), p. 99.

100 Francovich, *El pensamiento*, p. 108.

101 "Four South American Socialists," *Latin American Thought* 1 (4) (July 1946): 2.

102 Francovich, *El pensamiento*, pp. 108-09.

103 Klein, *Parties*, p. 99.

104 See "Four South American Socialists."

105 Francovich, *El pensamiento*, p. 112.

106 James M. Malloy, *Bolivia: The Uncompleted Revolution* (Pittsburgh: University of Pittsburgh Press, 1970), p. 205.

107 See Francovich, *El pensamiento*.

108 Ibid., p. 110.

109 Lora, *Historia*, 3:299-304.

110 Malloy, *Bolivia*, pp. 95-96.

111 Tristán Marof, *La tragedia del altiplano* (Buenos Aires: Editorial Claridad, 1934), pp. 104-11.

112 Tristán Marof, *Ensayos y crítica: Revoluciones bolivianas, guerras internacionales, y escritores* (La Paz: Librería y Editorial "Juventud," 1961), pp. 67-68.

113 Anderson-Imbert, *Spanish-American Literature*, 2:533-34.

114 Tristán Marof, *El jefe: Comedia política* (La Paz: n. p., 1965).

115 See Tristán Marof, *La verdad socialista en Bolivia* (La Paz: La Editorial "Trabajo," 1938).

116 Marof, *Ensayos*, p. 138.

117 Tristán Marof, *La justicia del Inca* (Brussels: Librería Falk Fils, 1926), p. 25.

118 Lora, *Historia*, 3:299–304.

119 Ibid., p. 307.

120 Marof, *Ensayos*, p. 15.

121 Ibid., pp. 9–11.

122 See Marof, *La justicia*.

123 Marof, *La tragedia.*
124 Ibid.
125 Ibid., p. 10.
126 Ibid., pp. 27–29.
127 See Marof, *La justicia.*
128 Marof, *La tragedia,* pp. 67–69.
129 See Marof, *Ensayos.*
130 Marof, *La verdad socialista,* p. 1.

131 Guillermo Lora, *Historia del movimiento obrero boliviano,* La Paz: Editorial "Los Amigos del Libro": vol. 1: *1848–1900* (1967); vol. 2: *1900–1923* (1969); vol. 3: *1923–1933* (1970). An abridged one-volume work in English is *A History of the Bolivian Labour Movement* (Cambridge: Cambridge University Press, 1977).

132 Lora, *Historia,* 1:182.
133 Ibid., p. 233.
134 Ibid., vol 1.
135 Ibid., 2:204.
136 Ibid., 1:285–89.
137 Ibid., 2:197.
138 Ibid., p. 21.
139 Ibid., vol. 2.
140 Hodges, *Latin American Revolution,* pp. 85–107.

141 Guillermo Lora, *La revolución boliviana* (La Paz: Talleres Gráficos Bolivianos para "Difusión S.R.L., " 1963), pp. 397–407.

142 Hobart A. Spalding, Jr., *Organized Labor in Latin America: Historical Case Studies of Urban Workers in Dependent Societies* (New York: Harper & Row, 1977), pp. 215–17.

143 Ibid.

144 See Guillermo Lora, *Balance de la huelga minera* (La Paz: Ediciones "Masas," 1963).

145 Lora, *La revolución boliviana,* pp. 86–87.
146 Ibid., p. 109.

147 Guillermo Lora, *Las guerrillas: La concepción marxista contra el golpismo adventurero* (La Paz: Ediciones "Masas, " 1963).

148 Ibid., pp. 23–24.
149 Ibid., pp. 16–17.
150 Ibid., pp. 13–15.
151 Ibid., pp. 20–23.

Chapter 8. Uruguay

1 Martin Weinstein, *Uruguay: The Politics of Failure* (Westport, Conn.: Greenwood Press, 1975), pp. 22–23.

2 Arturo Ardao, *La filosofía en el Uruguay en el siglo XX* (Mexico City: Fondo de Cultura Económica, 1965 6), p. 134.

3 Emilio Frugoni, *La revolución del machete: Panorama político del Uruguay* (Buenos Aires: Colección Claridad, 1935), pp. 216–18.

4 Ibid., pp. 170–211.

5 See ibid.

6 Ardao, *La filosofía*, pp. 134–35.

7 Emilio Frugoni, *Ensayos sobre marxismo* (Montevideo: Claudio García y Cia, 1936), pp. 37–55.

8 Ibid.

9 José Consuegra Higgins, *Apuntes de economía política* (Bogota: Ediciones Tercer Mundo, 1964), p. 135.

10 Ibid., pp. 137–38.

11 Emilio Frugoni, *Génesis, esencia, y fundamentos del socialismo* (Buenos Aires: Editorial Americalee, 1947).

12 Ibid., pp. 45–49.

13 Ibid., pp. 255–74.

14 Ibid., pp. 371–83.

15 Rodney Arismendi, *Problemas de una revolución continental* (Montevideo: Ediciones Pueblos Unidos, 1962), pp. 508–11.

16 Ibid., p. 515.

17 Ibid., pp. 519–56; and Rodney Arismendi, *La filosofía del marxismo y el Señor Haya de la Torre* (Montevideo: Editorial América, 1946), pp. 20–21.

18 Arismendi, *Problemas,* p. 368; and Rodney Arismendi, "On the Role of the National Bourgeoisie in the Anti-Imperialist Struggle," *World Marxist Review* 2 (6) (June 1959): 36–38.

19 Rodney Arismendi, "On the Role of the National Bougeoisie in the Anti-Imperialist Struggle," *World Marxist Review* 2 (5) (May 1959):38.

20 Arismendi, *Problemas,* pp. 195–97.

21 Rodney Arismendi, *Lenin: La Revolución, y América Latina* (Montevideo: Ediciones Pueblos Unidos, 1970).

22 Arismendi, "On the Role," *World Marxist Review,* May 1959, p. 35.

23 See Arismendi, *Lenin.*

24 Rodney Arismendi, "On the Dialectics of Peaceful Coexistence and Revolutionary Change," *World Marxist Review,* 19 (1) (Jan. 1976):8–10.

25 Arismendi, *Problemas,* p. 52.

26 Arismendi, "On the Role," *World Marxist Review,* May 1959, p. 35.

27 Francisco R. Pintos, *Historia del Uruguay (1851–1938): Ensayo de interpretación materialista* (Montevideo: Ediciones Pueblos Unidos, 1946), pp. 28–29.

28 Ibid., pp. 93–109. See Francisco R. Pintos, *Batlle y el proceso histórico* (Montevideo: C. García, 1960).

29 Francisco R. Pintos, *Ubicación de Artigas* (Montevideo: Ediciones Pueblos Unidos, 1965).

30 Francisco R. Pintos, *Historia del movimiento obrero del Uruguay* (Montevideo: Corporación Gráfica, 1960).

31 Donald C. Hodges, ed. and trans., *Philosophy of the Urban Guerrilla: The Revolutionary Writings of Abraham Guillén* (New York: William Morrow, 1973), pp. 3–4.

32 Ibid., pp. 22, 150–51; and Abraham Guillén, *La rebelión del tercer mundo* (Montevideo: Ed. Andes, 1969), pp. 201–03.

33 Abraham Guillén, *Dialéctica de la política* (Montevideo: Editorial Cooperativa Obrera Gráfica, 1967), pp. 45–46.

34 Hodges, ed., *Philosophy*, pp. 29–30.

35 See Abraham Guillén, *Desafío al pentágono* (Montevideo: Editorial Andes, 1969).

36 Hodges, ed., *Philosophy*, pp. 23–24.

37 Ibid., pp. 28–29.

38 Ibid., pp. 34–35.

39 Abraham Guillén, *Estrategia de la guerrilla urbana* (Montevideo: Editorial Manuales del Pueblo, 1966), pp. 42–52.

40 Donald C. Hodges, ed., *The Legacy of Che Guevara: A Documentary Study* (London: Thames & Hudson, 1977), p. 58.

41 Hodges, ed., *Philosophy*, pp. 6–7.

42 Ibid., p. 35.

43 Ibid., p. 41.

44 James Kohl and John Litt, *Urban Guerrilla Warfare in Latin America* (Cambridge, Mass: MIT Press, 1974), pp. 227–36.

45 Hartmut Ramm, *The Marxism of Régis Debray: Between Lenin and Guevara* (Lawrence, Kansas: Regents Press of Kansas, 1978), pp. 165–66.

46 Hodges, ed., *Legacy*, p. 36.

47 Hodges, ed., *Philosophy*, pp. 256–71.

48 Abraham Guillén, quoted in Introduction to *Marxism in Latin America*, ed. Luis E. Aguilar (Philadelphia: Temple University Press, 1978), p. 71, n. 20.

49 Kohl and Litt, *Urban Guerrilla Warfare*, p. 191.

Chapter 9. Mexico

1 Gastón García Cantú, *El socialismo en México: Siglo XIX* (Mexico City: Ediciones Era, 1969), pp. 189–98.

2 Ibid., p. 46.

3 Víctor Alba, *Las ideas sociales contemporáneas en México* (Mexico City: Fondo de Cultura Económica, 1960), pp. 102–03.

4 García Cantú, *El socialismo*, pp. 134–35.

5 Carlos M. Rama, *Mouvements ouvrières et socialistes: L'Amérique Latine (1492–1936)* (Paris: Les Editions Ouvrières, 1959), pp. 19–20.

6 García Cantú, *El socialismo*, p. 108.

7 Ibid., pp. 340–45.

8 Jesús Silva Herzog, *El pensamiento económico, social, y político de México, 1810–1964* (Mexico City: Instituto Mexicano de Investigaciones Económicas, 1967), pp. 551–62.

9 Victor Alba, *The Mexicans: The Making of a Nation* (New York: Praeger, 1967), pp. 108, 244.

10 Silva Herzog, *El pensamiento*, p. 517.

11 Jesús Silva Herzog, *El pensamiento económico en México* (Mexico City: Fondo de Cultura Económica, 1947), pp. 164–71.

12 Silva Herzog, *El pensamiento económico, social*, p. 520.

13 Ibid., p. 518.

14 Ibid., p. 519.

15 Ibid., p. 525.

16 Octavio Paz, *The Labyrinth of Solitude: Life and Thought in Mexico* (New York: Grove Press 1961), pp. 155–57.

17 Donald C. Hodges, *The Latin American Revolution: Politics and Strategy from Apro-Marxism to Guevarism* (New York: William Morrow, 1974), pp. 44–46.

18 José Consuegra Higgins, *Lenin y la América Latina* (Barranquilla, Colombia: Ediciones Cruz del Sur, 1972), pp. 109–11.

19 Luis G. Monzón, *Detalles de la educación socialista implantables en México* (Mexico City: Secretaría de Educación Pública, Comisión Editora Popular, Talleres Gráficos de la Nación, 1936), p. 19.

20 León Trotsky, *Por los estados unidos socialistas de América Latina* (Buenos Aires: Ediciones Coyoácan, 1961), p. 20.

21 Alba, *Las ideas sociales*, p. 207.

22 See Narcisco Bassols, *Obras* (Mexico City: Fondo de Cultura Económica, 1964).

23 Ibid., pp. 25–27.

24 Jesús Silva Herzog, *Una vida en la vida de México* (Mexico City: Siglo XXI, 1972), pp. 139–40.

25 Bassols, *Obras*, pp. 409–19.

26 Silva Herzog, *El pensamiento económico, social*, p. 566.

27 Alba, *Las ideas sociales*, p. 351.

28 Vicente Lombardo Toledano, *El problema del indio* (Mexico City: SepSetentas, 1973), pp. 28–29.

29 Silva Herzog, *El pensamiento económico, social*, p. 571.

30 Bassols, *Obras*, p. 140.

31 Joe C. Ashby, *Organized Labor and the Mexican Revolution*

Under Lázaro Cárdenas (Chapel Hill: University of North Carolina Press, 1967), p. 23.

32 Bassols, *Obras*, p. 128.

33 Ibid., pp. 23–25.

34 Ibid., pp. 4–6.

35 Rodney Arismendi, *Problemas de una revolución continental* (Montevideo: Ediciones Pueblos Unidos, 1962), p. 367.

36 Bassols, *Obras*, p. 382.

37 Ibid., pp. 457–59.

38 Silva Herzog, *El pensamiento económico, social*, p. 575.

39 Bassols, *Obras*, p. 512.

40 Ibid., pp. 674–75.

41 Ibid., p. 855.

42 Silva Herzog, *Una vida*, p. 178.

43 See Jesús Silva Herzog, *El pensamiento socialista* (Mexico City: La Universidad Obrera de México, 1937).

44 Jesús Silva Herzog, *Inquietud sin tregua: Ensayos y artículos escogidos, 1937–1965* (Mexico City: Cuadernos Americanos, 1965), p. 276.

45 Alonso Aguilar, *Pan-Americanism from Monroe to the Present: A View from the Other Side* (New York: Monthly Review Press, 1968), p. 70.

46 Silva Herzog, *Una vida*, p. 33.

47 See Silva Herzog, *Inquietud sin tregua*.

48 Julio Alvarez del Vayo, *The March of Socialism* (New York: Hill & Wang, 1974), pp. 296–97.

49 Silva Herzog, *Una vida*, p. 151.

50 See Jesús Silva Herzog, ed., *Trajectoria ideológica de la Revolución mexicana, 1919–1917: Del manifesto del partido liberal de 1906 a la consitución de 1917* (Mexico City: Cuadernos Americanos, 1963).

51 Alba, *La ideas sociales*, p. 219.

52 Ibid., p. 232.

53 Ibid., p. 233.

54 Silva Herzog, *Una vida*, pp. 301–08.

55 Arnaldo Córdova, *La ideología de la revolución mexicana* (Mexico City: Ediciones Era, 1973), p. 340.

56 Silva Herzog, *Inquietud sin tregua*, pp. 191–201.

57 Silva Herzor, *El pensamiento socialista*, pp. 30–38.

58 Silva Herzorg, *Inquietud sin tregua*, pp. 191–201.

59 Ibid., pp. 248–80.

60 Ibid., pp. 295–305.

61 Silva Herzog, *El pensamiento socialista*, p. 112.

62 Ibid., p. 16.

63 Robert P. Millon, *Mexican Marxist: Vicente Lombardo Toledano* (Chapel Hill: University of North Carolina Press, 1966), p. 182.

64 Vicente Lombardo Toledano, "The Mexican Flag and the Proletariat," in *Nationalism in Latin America*, ed, Samuel Baily (New York: Knopf, 1971), pp. 142–44.

65 See Vicente Lombardo Toledano and Antonio Caso, *Idealismo vs. materialismo dialéctico* (Mexico City: Universidad Obrera de México, 1963).

66 Vicente Lombardo Toledano, *La batalla de las ideas en nuestro tiempo* (Mexico City: Universidad Nacional Autónoma de México, 1959), p. 20.

67 Vicente Lombardo Toledano, *Escritos filosóficos* (Mexico City: Editorial México Nuevo, 1937), pp. 207–10.

68 Lombardo, *La batalla*, pp. 15–18.

69 Ibid., pp. 9–18.

70 Miguel Jorrín and John Martz, *Latin American Political Thought and Ideology* (Chapel Hill: University of North Carolina Press, 1970), pp. 224–25.

71 Gerardo Unzueta, *Lombardo Toledano y el marxismo-leninismo* (Mexico City: Fondo de Cultura Popular, 1966), p. 15; and see Vicente Lombardo Toledano, *¿Moscú o Pekín? La vía mexicana hacia el socialismo* (Mexico City: Partido Popular Socialista, 1963).

72 Unzueta, *Lombardo*, p. 159.

73 Millon, *Mexican Marxist*, pp. 35–6; and Vicente Lombardo Toledano, *La perspectiva de México: Una democracia del pueblo* (Mexico City: Ediciones de Partido Popular, 1956), pp. 101–03.

74 See Millon, *Mexican Marxist*.

.75 Ibid., pp. 59–60.

76 Severo Iglesias, *Sindicalismo y socialismo en México* (Mexico City: Editorial Grijalbos, S.A., 1970), p. 131.

77 Unzueta, *Lombardo*, p. 155.

78 Millon, *Mexican Marxist*, p. 29.

79 Ibid., p. 116.

80 Ibid., p. 29.

81 Ibid., p. 22.

82 Ibid., p. 42.

83 See Lombardo, *El problema del indio*.

84 Ibid., pp. 7–8.

85 Ibid; see his introduction.

86 Ibid., pp. 31–35.

87 Ibid., p. 37.

88 Alba, *Las ideas sociales*, p. 307.

89 Millon, *Mexican Marxist*, p. 78.

90 Lombardo, *El problema del indio*, p. 74.

91 Statement by Joseph R. Starobin, former foreign editor of the *Daily Worker*, personal interviews, Hancock, Mass. July 1976.

92 Millon, *Mexican Marxist,* p. 37.

93 Ibid., p.36.

94 Sheldon B. Liss, "Relaciones internacionales de México: ¿Donde están los yanquis?" in *Investigaciones contemporáneas sobre historia de México* (Mexico City: Universidad Nacional Autónoma de México, El Colegio de México, University of Texas, 1971), p. 560.

95 Unzueta, *Lombardo,* pp. 120–21.

96 Víctor Alba, *Historia del comunismo en América Latina* (Mexico City: Ediciones Occidentales, 1954), pp. 56–57.

97 Alba, *Las ideas sociales,* pp. 242–43.

98 Donald C. Hodges and Ross Gandy, *Mexico, 1910–1976: Reform or Revolution?* (London: Zed Press, 1979), pp. 109–10.

99 Millon, *Mexican Marxist,* p. 130.

100 Alonso Aguilar Monteverde, *Teoría y política de desarrollo latino americano* (Mexico City: Universidad Nacional Autónoma de México, 1967).

101 Hodges and Gandy, *Mexico,* p. 102.

102 Alonso Aguilar Monteverde, *Hacia un cambio radical: Ensayos* (Mexico City: Editorial Nuestro Tiempo, 1975), pp. 31, 119.

103 Aguilar, *Hacia un cambio radical.*

104 Ibid., pp. 190–91.

105 See Aguilar, *Teoría y política.*

106 Alonso Aguilar Monteverde, *Latin America and the Alliance for Progress* (New York: Monthly Review Press, 1963), pamphlet.

107 Liss, "Relaciones," p. 554.

108 Aguilar, *Hacia un cambio radical,* p. 56.

109 Ibid., p. 201.

110 Alonso Aguilar Monteverde and Jorge Carrión, *La burguesía, la oligarquía, y el estado* (Mexico City: Editorial Nuestro Tiempo, 1973).

111 Hodges and Gandy, *Mexico,* p. 105.

112 Aguilar, *Hacia un cambio radical,* p. 226.

113 Ibid., p. 214.

114 Ibid., pp. 233–35.

115 Ibid., pp. 64, 128.

116 Joseph A. Kahl, *Modernization, Exploitation, and Dependency in Latin America* (New Brunswick, N.J.: Transaction Books, 1976), pp. 109–10; and Pablo González Casanova, *La categoría del desarrollo económico y la investigación en ciencias sociales* (Mexico City: Universidad Nacional Autónoma de México, Instituto de Investigaciones Sociales, 1967), p.69.

117 Kahl, *Modernization,* p. 100.

118 Pablo González Casanova, "Internal Colonialism and Natural Development," in *Latin American Radicalism,* ed. Irving L. Horowitz, Josué de Castro, and John Gerassi (New York: Vintage, 1969), p. 118.

119 Kahl, *Moderization,* p. 106.

120 Ibid., p. 112.

121 Pablo González Casanova, "The Crisis of the State and the Struggle for Democracy in Latin America," *Contemporary Marxism,* no. 1, Spring 1980, pp. 67–68.

122 Ibid., pp. 65–66.

123 Pablo González Casanova, "Proletarian Conscience and Marxist Rhetoric," in *Marxism in Latin America,* ed. Luis E. Aguilar (Philadelphia: Temple University Press, 1978), p. 310.

124 Pablo González Casanova, *Democracy in Mexico* (New York: Oxford University Press, 1970), p. 195.

125 Kahl, *Modernization,* p. 81.

126 Ibid., pp. 89–90.

127 Hodges and Gandy, *Mexico,* p. 90.

128 González Casanova, *Democracy in Mexico,* p. 194.

129 González Casanova, "Proletarian Conscience," p. 309.

130 González Casanova, *Democracy in Mexico,* pp. 108–09.

131 Hodges and Gandy, *Mexico,* pp. 91–92.

132 José Revueltas, "En torno a las opiniones de Cosío Villegas: Crisis y destino de México," in *Is the Mexican Revolution Dead?* ed. and trans, Stanley R. Ross (New York: Knopf, 1966).

133 See José Revueltas, *Un proletariado sin cabeza* (Mexico City: Ediciones de la Liga Leninista Espartaco, 1962).

134 Roberto Simón Crespi, "José Revueltas (1914–1976): A Political Biography," *Latin American Perspectives* 6 (3) (Summer 1979): 101–02.

135 Rodlofo Stavenhagen, "Seven Fallacies About Latin America," in *Latin America: Reform or Revolution?* ed. James Petras and Maurice Zeitlin (Greenwich, Conn.: Fawcett, 1968), pp. 13–31.

136 Adolfo Gilly, *La Revolución interrumpida: México, 1910–1920: Una guerra campesina por la tierra y el poder* (Mexico City: Ediciones "El Caballito," 1971), p. 5.

137 Ibid., p. 387.

138 Hodges and Gandy, *Mexico,* p. 83.

139 Ibid., pp. 85–87.

Chapter 10. Cuba

1 See Blas Roca, *Los fundamentos del socialismo en Cuba* (Havana: Ediciones Populares, 1962).

2 Maurice Halperin, *The Rise and Decline of Fidel Castro* (Berkeley and Los Angeles: University of California Press, 1974), p. 4.

3 Harold Eugene Davis, *Revolutionaries, Traditionalists, and Dictators in Latin America* (New York: Cooper Square, 1973), pp. 55–59.

4 José Martí, "On the Death of Karl Marx," in *Marxism in Latin America,* ed. Luis E. Aguilar (Philadelphia: Temple University Press, 1978), pp. 102–03.

5 Herbert L. Matthews, *Revolution in Cuba* (New York: Charles Scribner's, 1975), p. 223.

6 Richard B. Gray, "José Martí and Social Revolution in Cuba," *Journal of Inter-American Studies,* 5 (2) (April 1963): 256.

7 *Times of the Americas,* March 29, 1978, p.2.

8 Gaspar Jorge García Galló et al., eds., *Carlos B. Baliño: Apuntes históricos sobre sus actividades revolucionarias* (Havana: Partido Comunista de Cuba, 1967), pp. 20–21.

9 Ibid., pp. 42–43.

10 Carlos B. Baliño, *Documentos de Carlos Baliño* (Havana: Departamento "Colección Cubana" de la Biblioteca Nacional José Martí, 1964), pp. 33, 36.

11 García Galló et. al., eds., *Baliño,* pp. 81–84.

12 Ibid., p. 85.

13 Baliño, *Documentos* pp. 43–53.

14 García Galló et al., eds., *Baliño,* pp. 55–59.

15 Baliño, *Documentos,* p. 64.

16 García Galló, et al., eds., *Baliño,* pp. 35–37.

17 Baliño, *Documentos,* p. 33.

18 See Julio Antonio Mella, *Escritos revolucionarios* (Mexico City: Siglo XXI, 1978).

19 Ibid., p. 17.

20 Ibid., pp. 22–23.

21 Julio Antonio Mella, *Julio Antonio Mella en el Machete: Antología parcial de un luchador y su momento histórico* (Mexico City: Fondo de Cultura Popular, 1968), pp. 244–46.

22 Mella, *Escritos,* pp. 44–45.

23 Ibid., p. 24.

24 Ibid., pp. 58–59.

25 See Mella, *Mella.*

26 Ibid., pp. 256–57.

27 Mella, *Escritos,* pp. 49–50.

28 Ibid., p. 243.

29 Ibid., pp. 157–58; and Mella, *Mella,* pp. 276, 291.

30 Mella, *Mella,* p. 22.

31 Ibid., p. 23.

32 Mella, *Escritos,* p. 19.

33 Roca, *Los fundamentos,* p. 95.

34 Mella, *Escritos,* p. 70.

35 Ibid., pp. 74–77.

36 Ibid., p. 26.

37 Ibid., pp. 28–29.

38 Ibid., p. 28.

39 Julio Antonio Mella, *La lucha revolucionaria contra el imperialismo: ¿Qué es el APRA?* (Mexico City, 1928), p. 5.

40 Ibid., pp. 12–17.

41 Ibid., pp. 16–19.

42 Mella, *Escritos*, p. 25.

43 Juan Marinello, *Contemporáneos* (Havana: Universidad Central de las Villas, 1964), p. 169; see also Juan Marinello, *Ocho notas sobre Aníbal Ponce* (Buenos Aires: Cuadernos de Cultura, 1958), pamphlet.

44 Juan Marinello, *Literatura hispanoamericana: Hombres, meditaciones* (Mexico City: Universidad Nacional, n.d.).

45 See Juan Marinello, *Once ensayos martianos* (Havana: Comisión Nacional Cubana de la UNESCO, 1964).

46 Ibid., p. 193.

47 See Juan Marinello, *José Martí, escritor Americano: Martí y el modernismo* (Mexico City: Editorial Grijalbo, 1958).

48 Marinello, *Once ensayos.*

49 Harold Eugene Davis, *Latin American Thought: A Historical Introduction* (New York: Free Press, 1974), p. 130.

50 Marinello, *Contemporáneos*, p. 229.

51 See ibid.

52 Juan Marinello, *Cuba contra la guerra imperialista* (Havana: Ediciones Sociales, 1940), pp. 8–9.

53 Ibid., pp. 22–23.

54 Ibid., pp. 24–27.

55 See Marinello, *Once ensayos.*

56 See Juan Marinello, *Conversación con nuestros pintores abstractos* (Santiago de Cuba: Universidad de Oriente Departamento de Extensión y Relaciones Culturales, 1960).

57 Carlos Rafael Rodríguez, *Cuba en el tránsito al socialismo (1953–1963): Lenin y la cuestión colonial* (Mexico City: Siglo XXI, 1978), pp. 30–45.

58 Roca, *Los fundamentos*, p. 60.

59 Ibid., pp. 16–22.

60 Ibid., p. 109.

61 Ibid., p. 98.

62 Ibid., pp. 50–56.

63 Matthews, *Revolution in Cuba*, p. 225.

64 Carlos Rafael Rodríguez, *El marxismo y la historia de Cuba* (Havana: Editorial Páginas, 1944), pp. 3–24.

65 Ibid.

66 Sergio Aguirre, *Seis actitudas de la burguesía cubana en el siglo XIX* (Havana: Editorial Páginas, 1944), pp. 25–47.

67 Rodríguez, *Cuba en el tránsito* p. 13.

68 Ibid., p. 16.

69 Ibid., p. 166.

70 Ibid., pp. 232–33.

71 José Consuegra Higgins, *Lenin y la América Latina* (Barranquilla, Colombia: Ediciones Cruz del Sur, 1972), pp. 111–24.

72 Ibid.

73 Rodríguez, *Cuba en el tránsito,* p. 137.

74 Ibid., pp. 104–05.

75 Ibid., p. 103.

76 Lionel Martin, *The Early Fidel: Roots of Castro's Communism* (Secaucus, N.J.: Lyle Stuart, 1978), p. 198.

77 Rodríguez, *Cuba en el tránsito,* p. 107.

78 Martin, *Early Fidel,* p. 220.

79 Rodríguez, *Cuba en el tránsito,* pp. 130–35.

80 Ibid., pp. 146–54.

81 Pablo Neruda, *Memoirs* (New York: Penguin Books, 1978), p. 323.

82 Michael Lowy, *The Marxism of Che Guevara* (New York: Monthly Review Press, 1973), p. 23.

83 Ibid., p. 33.

84 Ernesto Guevara, "On Art and Revolution," *Praxis,* Winter 1976, p. 396.

85 Donald C. Hodges, *The Latin American Revolution: Politics and Strategy from Apro-Marxism to Guevarism* (New York: William Morrow, 1974), p. 165.

86 Donald C. Hodges, ed., *The Legacy of Che Guevara: A Documentary Study* (London: Thames & Hudson, 1977), p. 58.

87 Ibid., pp. 20–21.

88 Ibid., p. 20.

89 Hartmut Ramm, *The Marxism of Régis Debray: Between Lenin and Guevara* (Lawrence, Kansas: Regents Press of Kansas, 1978), pp. 7–9.

90 Ernesto Guevara, "The Philosophy of Che Guevara," taped interview (Hollywood, Ca.: Center for Cassette Studies, 1965).

91 Jay Mallin, ed., *"Che" Guevara on Revolution* (Coral Gables: University of Miami Press, 1969), p. 13.

92 Ramm, *Marxism,* pp. vii–viii.

93 Mallin, ed., *"Che" Guevara,* pp. 11–12.

94 Guevara, "Philosophy of Che Guevara."

95 Joseph Hansen, *The Leninist Strategy of Party Building: The De-*

bate on Guerrilla Warfare in Latin America (New York: Pathfinder Press, 1979), pp. 296–97.

96 John Gerassi, ed., *The Coming of the New International* (New York: World Pub., 1971), p. 57.

97 John Gerassi, *Towards Revolution,* 2 vols. (London: Weidenfeld & Nicolson, 1971), 2:425.

98 Hodges, ed., *Legacy of Che Guevara,* pp. 26–27.

99 Andrew Sinclair, *Che Guevara* (New York: Viking Press, 1970), p. 30.

100 Ibid., pp. 67–68.

101 Ibid., p. 67.

102 Michael Harrington, *The Twilight of Capitalism* (New York: Simon & Schuster, 1976), pp. 177–78.

103 Ernesto Guevara, "Notes on Socialism and Man," *International Socialist Review* 27(Winter 1966): 21.

104 Lowy, *Marxism,* pp. 27–28.

105 Betram Silverman, ed., *Man and Socialism in Cuba* (New York: Atheneum, 1973), p. 340.

106 Hodges, ed., *Legacy of Che Guevara,* pp. 48–49.

107 See Guevara, "Notes on Socialism and Man."

108 Davis, *Latin American Thought,* p. 199; and Ernesto Guevara, *El socialismo y el hombre* (Montevideo: Nativa Libros, 1966), p. 13.

109 Martin, *Early Fidel,* pp. 23, 28–30.

110 Ibid., p. 64.

111 Halperin, *Rise and Decline,* pp. 10–12.

112 Martin, *Early Fidel,* p. 101.

113 Ibid., p. 107.

114 Ibid., p. 154.

115 Fidel Castro, "On Intellectual Property," in *Writing in Cuba Since the Revolution,* ed. Andrew Salkey (London: Bogle-L'Overture, 1977), pp. 150–51.

116 Martin Kenner and James Petras, eds., *Fidel Castro Speaks* (New York: Grove Press, 1969), p. 146.

117 Ramm, *Marxism* p. 58.

118 Hodges, ed., *Legacy of Che Guevara,* pp. 152–53.

119 Ibid., pp. 49–50.

120 David Childs, *Marx and the Marxists* (London: Ernest Benn, 1973), pp. 313–14.

121 Fidel Castro, *Fidel in Chile* (New York: International Pubs., 1972), p. 65.

122 Ibid., pp. 72–73.

123 Matthews, *Revolution in Cuba,* pp. 255–56.

124 Ibid., p. 237.

125 Fidel Castro, "Speech of March 13, 1967," in *Cuba in Revolution,* ed. Rolando E. Bonachea and Nelson P. Valdés (Garden City, N.Y.: Anchor-Doubleday, 1972), pp. 540–41.

126 K. S. Karol, *Guerrillas in Power* (New York: Hill & Wang, 1970), p. 384.

127 Havana served as Latin America's center of ferment for Marxist thought from the 1960s until roughly the middle of the 1970s when most of the political exiles from the region's anticommunist dictatorships chose to congregate in Mexico City.

Chapter 11. Conclusions

1 Harold Eugene Davis, ed., *Latin American Social Thought* (Washington, D.C.: University Press of Washington, D.C., 1961), p. 368.

2 Longino Becerra, "Latin America: Two epochs and Marxism-Leninism," *World Marxist Review* 2(7) (July 1968):92.

3 Leopold Labedz, ed., *Revisionism: Essays on the History of Marxist Ideas* (New York: Praeger, 1962), p. 16.

4 Helio Jaguaribe, "Marxism and Latin American Development," in *Marx and the Western World,* ed. Nicholas Lobkowicz (Notre Dame, Ind.: University of Notre Dame Press, 1967), pp. 245–47.

5 See Gustave LeBon, *The Psychology of Socialism* (Wells, Vt.: Fraser, 1965); initially published in 1899.

6 Clive Thomas, "The Non-Capitalist Path as Theory and Practice of Decolonization and Socialist Transformation," *Latin American Perspectives* 5(2) (Spring 1978):11–19.

7 Hartmut Ramm, *The Marxism of Régis Debray: Between Lenin and Guevara* (Lawrence, Kansas: Regents Press of Kansas, 1978), p. 178.

8 Ibid., p. 187.

9 Michael Harrington, *The Twilight of Capitalism* (New York: Siman & Schuster, 1976), p. 47.

10 Rosino Gibellini, ed., *Frontiers of Theology in Latin America* (Maryknoll, N.Y.: Orbis Books, 1979), p. ix.

11 Ibid., pp. 2, 10, 16, 17.

12 Ibid., pp. 54–55.

13 Thomas Dean, *Post-Theistic Thinking: The Marxist-Christian Dialogue in Radical Perspective* (Philadelphia: Temple University Press, 1975), p. 235; taken from Karl Marx, *Capital* (London, 1930), 1:53–54.

14 John Eagleson, ed., *Christians and Socialism* (Maryknoll, N.Y.: Orbis Books, 1975), pp. 163–64.

15 Ibid., p. 164.

16 Ibid., p. 171.

17 Ibid., pp. viii–ix

18 Donald C. Hodges, *Socialist Humanism: The Outcome of Classical European Morality* (St. Louis: Warren H. Green, 1974), pp. 246, 252.

19 Eagleson, ed., *Christians*, p. 111.

20 Ibid., p. 236.

21 Robert Nisbet, *The Social Philosophers: Community and Conflict in Western Thought* (New York: Thomas Y. Crowell, 1973), p. 317.

22 T.B. Bottomore, *Sociology as Social Criticism* (New York: Pantheon, 1974), pp. 210–11.

23 John Lewis, *The Marxism of Marx* (London: Lawrence & Wishert, 1972), p. 21.

24 Ibid., p. 22.

25 Nisbet, *Social Philosophers*, p. 282.

26 F.V. Konstantinov et al., *The Fundamentals of Marxist-Leninist Philosophy* (Moscow: Progress Pub., 1974), p. 275.

27 Margaret E. Rowntree, "Spanish American Marxian Politacal Theory," Ph.D. diss., University of California, Berkeley, 1968, pp. 224–25.

28 Richard L. Harris, "The Influence of Marxist Structuralism on the Intellectual Left in Latin America," *Insurgent Sociologist* 9(1) (Summer 1979):62–73.

29 Jaguaribe, "Marxism," pp. 244–45.

30 Harry E. Vanden, "The Ideology of Insurrection," in *Nicaragua in Revolution*, ed. Thomas W. Walker (New York: Praeger, 1982), pp. 41–62.

Bibliography

Original Works—Books and Pamphlets

Aguilar Monteverde, Alonso. *Latin America and the Alliance for Progress.* New York: Monthly Review Press, 1963.

—. *Teoría y política de desarrollo latino americano.* Mexico City: Universidad Nacional Autónoma de México, 1967.

—. *Pan-Americanism from Monroe to the Present: A View from the Other Side.* New York, Monthly Review Press, 1968.

—. *Hacia un cambio radical: Ensayos.* Mexico City: Editorial Nuestro Tiempo, 1975.

Aguilar Monteverde, Alonso, and Jorge Carrión. *La burguesía, la oligarquía, y el estado.* Mexico City: Editorial Nuestro Tiempo, 1972.

Aguirre, Manuel Agustín. *América Latina y el Ecuador.* Quito: Editorial Universitaria, 1959.

—. *El socialismo científico.* Quito: Editorial Universitaria, 1963.

—. *Imperialismo y militarismo en la América Latina.* Montevideo: Sandino, 1968(?).

Aguirre, Sergio. *Seis actitudas de la burguesía cubana en el siglo XIX.* Havana: Editorial Páginas, 1944.

Alatas, Syed Hussein. *Intellectuals in Developing Societies.* London: Frank Cass, 1977.

Alba, Víctor. *Historia del comunismo en América Latina.* Mexico City: Ediciones Occidentales, 1954.

—. *Las ideas sociales contemporáneas en México.* Mexico City: Fondo de Cultura Económica, 1960.

—. *The Mexicans: The Making of a Nation.* New York: Praeger, 1967.

Albert, Michael. *What Is to Be Undone: A Modern Revolutionary Discussion of Classical Left Ideologies.* Boston: Porter Sargent, 1974.

Alegría, Fernando. *Recabarren.* Santiago: Editorial "Antares," 1938.

Alexander, Robert J. *Communism in Latin America.* New Brunswick, N.J.: Rutgers University Press, 1957.

————. *The Bolivian National Revolution.* New Brunswick, N.J.: Rutgers University Press, 1958.

————. *The Communist Party of Venezuela.* Stanford: Hoover Institution Press, 1969.

————. *Trotskyism in Latin America.* Stanford: Hoover Institution Press, 1973.

Alisky, Marvin. *Uruguay: A Contemporary Survey.* New York: Praeger, 1969.

Allende, Salvador. *La contradicción de Chile.* Santiago: Talleres Gráficos, 1943.

————. *Chile's Road to Socialism.* Baltimore: Penguin Books, 1973.

————. *El pensamiento de Salvador Allende.* Mexico City: Fondo de Cultura Económica, 1974.

Almeyda Medina, Clodomiro. *Hacia un teoría marxista del estado.* Santiago: Universidad de Chile, Colección Cultura Política, 1948.

————. *Visión sociológica de Chile.* Santiago: Academia de las Escuelas de Ciencias Políticas y Administrativas, 1957.

————. *Reflexiones políticas.* Santiago: Prensa Latino-Americana, 1958.

Althusser, Louis. *Positions (1964-1975).* Paris: Editions Sociales, 1976.

Alvarez del Vayo, Julio. *The March of Socialism.* New York: Hill & Wang, 1974.

Amado, Jorge. *Vida de Luiz Carlos Prestes: Cavaleiro da esperança.* São Paulo: Martins, 1945.

Ampuero Díaz, Raúl. *El socialismo ante el mundo de hoy.* Santiago: Prensa Latino-Americana, 1964.

————. *La izquierda en punto muerto,* Santiago: Editorial Orbe, 1969.

Anderson, Charles H. *The Political Economy of Social Class.* Englewood Cliffs, N.J.: Prentice-Hall, 1974.

Anderson, Thomas P. *Matanza: El Salvador's Communist Revolt of 1932.* Lincoln: University of Nebraska Press, 1971.

Anderson-Imbert, Enrique. *Spanish American Literature: A History.* 2 vols. Detroit: Wayne State University Press, 1969.

Angell, Alan. *Politics and the Labour Movement in Chile.* London: Oxford University Press, 1972.

Ardao, Arturo. *La filosofía en el Uruguay en el siglo XX.* Mexico City: Fondo de Cultura Económica, 1956.

Arismendi, Rodney. *La filosofía del marxismo y el Señor Haya de la Torre.* Montevideo: Editorial América, 1946.

————. *Problemas de una revolución continental.* Montevideo: Ediciones Pueblos Unidos, 1962.

————. *Lenin: La revolución y América Latina.* Montevideo: Ediciones Pueblos Unidos, 1970.

Ashby, Joe C. *Organized Labor and the Mexican Revolution Under*

Lázaro Cárdenas. Chapel Hill: University of North Carolina Press, 1967.

Avineri, Shlomo. *The Social and Political Thought of Karl Marx.* Cambridge: Cambridge University Press, 1971.

Baines, John M. *Revolution in Peru: Mariátegui and the Myth.* University: University of Alabama Press, 1972.

Baliño, Carlos B. *Documentos de Carlos Baliño.* Havana: Departamento "Colección Cubana" de la Biblioteca Nacional José Martí, 1964.

———. *Apuntes históricos sobre sus actividades revolucionarias.* Havana: Partido Comunista de Cuba, 1967.

de Barros, Almiro Bica Buys. *Os movimentos sociais e o socialismo.* Rio de Janeiro: José Konfino, 1956.

Basbaum, Leôncio, *Caminhos brasileiros do desenvolvimento.* São Paulo: Editôra Fulgor, 1960.

———. *História sincera da república,* vol. 1: São Paulo: Edições LB, 1962; vol 2: *de 1889 a 1930,* São Paulo: Edições LB, 1962; vol. 3: *de 1930 a 1960,* São Paulo: Editôra Edaglit, 1962; vol. 4: *de 1961 a 1967,* São Paulo: Editôra Alfa Omega, 1968.

———. *O processo evólutivo da história.* São Paulo: Editôra Edaglit, 1963.

———. *Sociología de materialismo.* Buenos Aires: Editorial Américalee, 1964.

———. *Alienação e humanismo.* São Paulo: Editôra Fulgor, 1967.

———. *Uma vida em seis tempos (memórias).* Saõ Paulo: Editôra Alfa-Omega, 1976.

Bassols, Narciso. *Obras.* Mexico City: Fondo de Cultura Económica, 1964.

Bastos, Abguar. *Prestes e a revolução social.* Rio de Janeiro: Editorial Calvino, 1946.

———. *História da política revolucionária no Brasil.* Vol. 1: 1900-1932. Rio de Janeiro: Conquista, 1969.

Beals, Carleton. *Latin America: World in Revolution.* London: Abelard-Schuman, 1963.

Béjar, Héctor. *Peru 1965: Notes on a Guerrilla Experience.* New York: Monthly Review Press, 1969.

Benedetti, Mario. *El escritor latinoamericano y la revolución posible.* Buenos Aires: Editorial Alfa Argentina, 1974.

Bernardo, Robert M. *The Theory of Moral Incentives in Cuba.* University: University of Alabama Press, 1971.

Blanco, Hugo. *Land or Death: The Peasant Struggle in Peru.* New York: Pathfinder Press, 1972.

Bober, M. M. *Karl Marx's Interpretation of History.* New York: W. W. Norton, 1965.

Boguslavsky, B. M., et al. *ABC of Dialectical and Historical Materialism.* Moscow: Progress Publishers, 1976.

Boorstein, Edward. *The Economic Transformation of Cuba.* New York: Monthly Review Press, 1968.

Bottomore, T. B. *Sociology as Social Criticism.* New York: Pantheon, 1974.

Bremauntz, Alberto. *La batalla ideológica en México.* Mexico City: Ediciones Jurídico Sociales, 1962.

Broderick, Walter J. *Camilo Torres: A Biography of the Priest-Guerrillero.* New York: Doubleday, 1975.

Cammett, John M. *Antonio Gramsci and the Origins of Italian Communism.* Stanford: Stanford University Press, 1967.

Camus, Albert. *The Rebel: An Essay on Man in Revolt.* New York: Random House, 1956.

Careaga, Gabriel. *Los intelectuales y la política en México.* Mexico City: Editorial Extemporáneos, 1971.

Carnero Checa, Genaro. *El aguila rampante: El imperialismo yanqui sobre América Latina.* Mexico City: Ediciones Seminario Peruano, 1956.

Carrera Damas, Germán. *Tres temas de historia.* Caracas: Universidad Central de Venezuela, Facultad de Humanidades y Educación, 1961.

———. *Historiografía marxista Venezolana y otros temas.* Caracas: Universidad Central de Venezuela, 1967.

———. *La dimensión histórica en el presente de América Latina y Venezuela: Tres conferencias.* Caracas: Universidad Central de Venezuela, Facultad de Humanidades y Educación, 1972.

Castellanos, Jorge. *Raíces de la ideología burguesa en Cuba.* Havana: Editorial Páginas, 1944.

Castro, Fidel. *Fidel in Chile.* New York: International Publishers, 1972.

Castro Pozo, Hildebrando,. *Nuestra comunidad indígena.* Lima: El Lucero, 1924.

———. *Del ayllu al cooperativismo socialista.* Lima: Biblioteca de la Revista de Economía y Finanzas, 1936.

Chacon, Vamireh. *História das idéias socialistas no Brasil.* Rio de Janeiro: Editôra Civilização Brasileira, S.A., 1965.

Chang-Rodríguez, Eugenio. *La literatura política de González Prada, Mariátegui, y Haya de la Torre.* Mexico City: Ediciones de Andrea, 1957.

Chavarría, Jesús. *José Carlos Mariátegui and the Rise of Modern Peru, 1890-1930.* Albuquerque: University of New Mexico Press, 1979.

Chilcote, Ronald H. *The Brazilian Communist Party: Conflict and Inte-*

gration, 1922-1972. New York: Oxford University Press, 1974.

Childs, David. *Marx and the Marxists.* London: Ernest Benn, 1973.

Clark, Martin. *Antonio Gramsci and the Revolution That Failed.* New Haven: Yale University Press, 1977.

Cockcroft, James D. *Intellectual Precursors of the Mexican Revolution, 1900-1913.* Austin: University of Texas Press, 1968.

Codovilla, Victorio. *¿Resisterá la Argentina al imperialismo yanqui?* Buenos Aires: Editorial Anteo, 1948.

———. *Nuestro camino desemboca en la victoria.* Buenos Aires: Editorial Fundamentos, 1954.

———. *Trabajos escogidos.* Vol. 1. Buenos Aires: Editorial Anteo, 1972.

Cole, G. D. H. *A History of Socialist Thought.* London: Macmillan: Vol. 3, pt. 2: *The Second International, 1889-1914,* 1956; vol. 4, pt. 2: *Communism and Social Democracy, 1914-1931,* 1958; vol. 5: *Socialism and Fascism, 1931–1939,* 1960.

Consuegra Higgins, José. *Apuntes de economía política.* Bogota: Ediciones Tercer Mundo, 1964.

———. *El control de la natalidad como arma del imperialismo.* Buenos Aires: Editorial Galerna, 1969.

———. *Lenin y la América Latina.* Barranquilla, Colombia: Ediciones Cruz del Sur, 1972.

Córdova, Arnaldo. *La ideología de la Revolución mexicana.* Mexico City: Ediciones Era, 1973.

Corvalán, Luis. *Chile y el nuevo panorama mundial.* Santiago: Partido Comunista de Chile, 1959.

———. *Cosas nuevas en el campo.* Santiago: Imprenta Lautaro, 1960.

———. *Nuestra vía revolucionaria.* Santiago: Impresora Horizonta, 1964.

Crawford, W. Rex. *A Century of Latin American Thought.* Cambridge, Mass.: Harvard University Press, 1961.

Cruz Costa, João. *A History of Ideas in Brazil.* Berkeley and Los Angeles: University of California Press, 1964.

Davis, Harold Eugene. *Social Science Trends in Latin America.* Washington, D.C.: The American University Press, 1950.

———. *Revolutionaries, Traditionalists, and Dictators in Latin America.* New York: Cooper Square, 1973.

———. *Latin American Thought: A Historical Introduction.* New York: Free Press, 1974.

Dean, Thomas. *Post-Theistic Thinking: The Marxist-Christian Dialogue in Radical Perspective.* Philadelphia: Temple University Press, 1975.

Debray, Régis. *The Chilean Revolution: Conversations with Allende.* New York: Random House, 1971.

————. *Prison Writings.* London: Allen Lane, 1973.

————. *Che's Guerrilla War.* Baltimore: Penguin Books, 1975.

Dickmann, Adolfo. *Nacionalismo y socialismo.* Buenos Aires: Porter Hermanos, 1933.

Dickmann, Enrique. *Democracia y socialismo.* Buenos Aires: Serafín Ponziniblio, 1917.

————. *Ideas e ideales.* Buenos Aires: Agencia General de Librería y Publicaciones, 1920.

————. *Páginas socialistas.* Buenos Aires: n.p., 1928.

————. *Población e inmigración.* Buenos Aires: Editorial Losada, 1946.

————. *Recuerdos de un militante socialista.* Buenos Aires: Editorial Vanguardia, 1949.

Diggins, John P. *The American Left in the Twentieth Century.* New York: Harcourt Brace Jovanovich, 1973.

Dix, Robert H. *Colombia: The Political Dimensions of Change.* New Haven: Yale University Press, 1967.

Drake, Paul W. *Socialism and Populism in Chile, 1932–1952.* Urbana: University of Illinois Press, 1978.

Dulles, John W. F. *Anarchists and Communists in Brazil, 1900–1935.* Austin: University of Texas Press, 1973.

Engels, Friedrich. *Werke.* Berlin: Dietz Verlag: Vol. 4, 1959; vols. 28, 29, 1963.

Feinberg, Richard E. *The Triumph of Allende: Chile's Legal Revolution.* New York: Mentor, 1972.

Ferns, H. S. *Argentina.* New York: Praeger, 1969.

Foster, William Z. *Outline Political History of the Americas.* New York: International Publishers, 1951.

Franco, Jean. *The Modern Culture of Latin America: Society and the Artist.* Harmondsworth, Eng.: Pelican Books, 1970.

Francovich, Guillermo. *El pensamiento boliviano en el siglo XX.* Mexico City: Fondo de Cultura Económica, 1956.

Frank, André Gunder. *Capitalism and Underdevelopment in Latin America: Historical Studies of Chile and Brazil.* New York: Monthly Review Press, 1969.

Freyre, Gilberto. *Order and Progress.* New York: Knopf, 1970.

Frondizi, Silvio. *El estado moderno: Ensayo de crítica constructiva.* Buenos Aires: Roque Depalma, 1954.

————. *La realidad argentina.* 2 vols. Buenos Aires: Praxis, 1956.

————. *La revolución cubana: Su significación histórica.* Montevideo: Editorial Ciencias Políticas, 1961.

————. *Teorías políticas contemporáneas.* Buenos Aires: Ediciones Macchi, 1965.

——. *El materialismo dialéctico.* La Plata: Centro Estudiantes Derecho, 1966.

Frugoni, Emilio. *La revolución de machete: Panorama político del Uruguay.* Buenos Aires: Colección Claridad, 1935.

——. *Ensayos sobre marxismo.* Montevideo: Claudio García y Cía, 1936.

——. *Génesis, esencia, y fundamentos del socialismo.* 2 vols. Buenos Aires: Editorial Américalee, 1947.

Gaitán, Jorge Elíecer. *Las ideas socialistas en Colombia.* Bogota: Casa del Pueblo, 1963.

Galeano, Eduardo. *Guatemala: Occupied Country.* New York: Monthly Review Press, 1969.

——. *Open Veins of Latin America.* New York: Monthly Review Press, 1973.

de Gandía, Enrique. *Historia de las ideas políticas en la Argentina.* 4 vols. Buenos Aires: Ediciones Depalma, 1960–1967.

García Cantú, Gastón. *El socialismo en México: Siglo XIX.* Mexico City: Ediciones Era, 1969.

García Montes, Jorge, and Antonio Alonso Avila. *Historia del partido comunista de Cuba.* Miami: Ediciones Universal, 1970.

Gerassi, John. *Towards Revolution.* 2 vols. London: Weidenfeld & Nicolson, 1971.

Ghioldi, Américo. *El socialismo en la evolución nacional.* Buenos Aires: Editorial La Vanguardia, 1946.

——. *El socialismo y la actual crisis argentina.* Buenos Aires: Partido Socialista, 1948.

——. *Marxismo, socialismo, izquierdismo, comunismo, y la realidad argentina de hoy.* Buenos Aires: Ediciones Populares Argentinas, 1950.

——. *Juan B. Justo: Sus ideas históricas, socialistas, filosóficas.* Buenos Aires: Ediciones Monserrat, 1964.

Ghioldi, Rodolfo. *La política en el mundo.* Buenos Aires: Editorial Futuro, 1946.

——. *Acerca de la cuestión agraria argentina.* Buenos Aires: Editorial Fundamentos, 1953.

——. *Escritos.* Buenos Aires: Editorial Anteo: Vol. 1, 1975; vol. 2, 1976.

Gil, Federico G. *The Political System of Chile.* Boston: Houghton Mifflin, 1966.

Gilio, Maria Esther. *The Tupamaro Guerrillas: The Structure and Strategy of the Urban Guerrilla Movement.* New York: Saturday Review Press, 1972.

Gilly, Adolfo. *Inside the Cuban Revolution*. New York: Monthly Review Press, 1964.

———. *La Revolución interrumpida: México, 1910–1920: Una guerra campesina por la tierra y el poder*. Mexico City: Ediciones "El Caballito," 1971.

Gómez, Eugenio. *Historia del partido comunista del Uruguay*. Montevideo: Editorial Elite, 1961.

Gómez-Quiñones, Juan. *Sembradores: Ricardo Flores Magón y el partido liberal mexicano: A Eulogy and Critique*. Los Angeles: UCLA Chicano Studies Center Publications, Monograph No. 5, 1977.

González Casanova, Pablo. *La ideología norteamericana sobre inversiones extranjeras*. Mexico City: Dirección General de Publicaciones, Universidad Nacional Autónoma de México, 1955.

———. *Las categorías del desarrollo económico y la investigación en ciencias sociales*. Mexico City: Universidad Nacional Autónoma de México, Instituto de Investigaciones Sociales, 1967.

———. *Sociología de la explotación*. Mexico City: Siglo XXI, 1969.

———. *Democracy in Mexico*. New York: Oxford University Press, 1970.

González Prada, Manuel. *Horas de lucha*. Lima: El Progreso Literario, 1908.

———. *Anarquía*. Santiago: Ediciones Ercilla, 1936.

———. *Propaganda y ataque*. Buenos Aires: Ediciones Iman, 1939.

Gott, Richard. *Guerilla Movements in Latin America*. Garden City, N.Y.: Doubleday, 1972.

Gramsci, Antonio. *Letters from Prison*. New York: Harper & Row, 1975.

Gray, Richard B. *José Martí, Cuban Patriot*. Gainesville: University of Florida Press, 1962.

Green, Gil. *Revolution Cuban Style*. New York: International Publishers, 1970.

Grompone, Antonio M. *La ideología de Batlle*. Montevideo: Editorial Arca, 1967.

Guardia Mayorga, César A. *Reconstruyendo el aprismo*. Arequipa, Peru, 1945.

Guevara, Ernesto. *Reminiscences of the Cuban Revolutionary War*. New York: Grove Press, 1968.

———. *Socialism and Man in Cuba and Other Works*. London: Stage I, 1968.

Guilisasti Tagle, Sergio. *Partidos políticos chilenos*. Santiago: Editorial Nacimiento, 1964.

Guillén, Abraham. *Teoría de la violencia.* Buenos Aires: Editorial Jamcana, 1965.

——. *Estrategia de la guerrilla urbana.* Montevideo: Editorial Manuales del Pueblo, 1966.

——. *Dialéctica de la política.* Montevideo: Editorial Cooperativa Obrera Gráfica, 1967.

——. *Desafío al pentágono.* Montevideo: Editorial Andes, 1969.

——. *La rebelión del tercer mundo.* Montevideo: Editorial Andes, 1969.

Guzmán, Germán. *Camilo Torres.* New York: Sheed and Ward, 1969.

Guzmán Böckler, Carlos, and Jean-Loup Herbert. *Guatemala: Una interpretación histórico-social.* Mexico City: Siglo XXI, 1972.

Halperin, Ernst. *Nationalism and Communism in Chile.* Cambridge, Mass.: MIT Press, 1965.

Halperin, Maurice. *The Rise and Decline of Fidel Castro.* Berkeley and Los Angeles: University of California Press, 1974.

Hansen, Joseph. *The Leninist Strategy of Party Building: The Debate on Guerrilla Warfare in Latin America.* New York: Pathfinder Press, 1979.

Harrington, Michael. *Socialism.* New York: Bantam Books, 1973.

——. *The Twilight of Capitalism.* New York: Simon & Schuster, 1976.

Hart, John M. *Anarchism and the Mexican Working Class, 1860–1931.* Austin: University of Texas Press, 1978.

Haya de la Torre, Víctor Raúl. *Y después de la guerra, ¿que?* Lima: Editorial Talleres PTCM, 1946.

Hearder, Harry. *Ideological Commitment and Historical Interpretation.* Cardiff: University of Wales Press, 1969.

Heilbroner, Robert L. *Marxism: For and Against.* New York: W. W. Norton, 1980.

Heliodoro Valle, Rafael. *Historia de las ideas contemporáneas en Centro-América.* Mexico City: Fondo de Cultura Económica, 1960.

Herman, Donald, L. *The Comintern in Mexico.* Washington, D.C.: Public Affairs Press, 1974.

Hodges, Donald C. *The Latin American Revolution: Politics and Strategy from Apro-Marxism to Guevarism.* New York: William Morrow, 1974.

——. *Socialist Humanism: The Outcome of Classical European Morality.* St. Louis: Warren H. Green, 1974.

——. *Argentina, 1943–1976: The National Revolution and Resistance.* Albuquerque: University of New Mexico Press, 1976.

Hodges, Donald C., and Ross Gandy. *Mexico, 1910–1976: Reform or Revolution?* London: Zed Press, 1979.

Hoffman, John. *Marxism and the Theory of Praxis.* New York: International Publishers, 1975.

Horowitz, Irving Louis. *Revolution in Brazil.* New York: E. P. Dutton, 1964.

———. *Cuban Communism.* New Brunswick, N.J.: Transaction Books, 1977.

Huberman, Leo, and Paul M. Sweezy. *Socialism in Cuba.* New York: Monthly Review Press, 1969.

Huneeus, Pablo, et al. *Chile: El costo social de la dependencia ideológica.* Santiago: Editorial del Pacifico, 1973.

Hyams, Edward. *The Millennium Postponed: Socialism from Sir Thomas More to Mao Tse-Tung.* New York: Taplinger, 1974.

Iglesias, Severo. *Sindicalismo y socialismo en México.* Mexico City: Editorial Grijalbos, S.A., 1970.

Jacobini, H. B. *A Study of the Philosophy of International Law as Seen in the Work of Latin American Writers.* The Hague: Martinus Nijhoff, 1954.

Jobet, Julio César. *Ensayo crítico del desarrollo económico-social de Chile.* Santiago: Editorial Universitaria, 1955.

———. *Los fundamentos del marxismo.* Santiago: Prensa Latino-Americana, nd.

———. *Recabarren: Los orígenes del movimiento obrero y del socialismo chilenos.* Santiago: Prensa Latino-Americana, 1955.

Joss, James. *Antonio Gramsci.* New York: Penguin Books, 1977.

Jorrín, Miguel, and John Martz. *Latin American Political Thought and Ideology.* Chapel Hill: University of North Carolina Press, 1970.

Justo, Juan B. *Socialismo.* Buenos Aires: Tipografía "La Vanguardia," 1920.

———. *Internacionalismo y patria.* Buenos Aires: La Vanguardia, 1933.

Justo, Liborio (Quebracho). *Prontuario: Una autobiografía.* Buenos Aires: Ediciones Gure, 1956.

———. *Pampas y lanzas: Fundamentos histórico-económico-sociales de la nacionalidad y de la conciencia nacional argentina.* Buenos Aires: Editorial Palestra, 1962.

———. *Bolivia: La revolución derrotada.* Buenos Aires: Juárez Editor, S.A., 1971.

———. *León Trotsky y el fracaso mundial del trotskysmo.* Lima: Fondo de Cultura Popular, 1975.

Kahl, Joseph A. *Modernization, Exploitation, and Dependency in Latin America.* New Brunswick, N.J.: Transaction Books, 1976.

Karol, K. S. *Guerrillas in Power.* New York: Hill & Wang, 1970.

Kiernan, V. G. *Marxism and Imperialism*. New York: St. Martin's Press, 1974.

Kilroy-Silk, Robert. *Socialism Since Marx*. New York: Taplinger, 1972.

Klein, Herbert S. *Parties and Political Change in Bolivia, 1880–1952*. Cambridge: Cambridge University Press, 1969.

Kohl, James, and John Litt. *Urban Guerrilla Warfare in Latin America*. Cambridge, Mass.: MIT Press, 1974.

Konstantinov, F. V., et al. *The Fundamentals of Marxist-Leninist Philosophy*. Moscow: Progress Publishers, 1974.

Lafertte G., Elías. *Hacia la transformación económica y política de Chile por la vía de la unión nacional*. Santiago: Ediciones Nueva América, 1945.

———. *Vida de un comunista*. Santiago: Talleres Gráficos Horizonte, 1961.

Laidler, Harry W. *History of Socialism*. New York: Thomas Y. Crowell, 1968.

Lavretski, J. *Salvador Allende*. Moscow: Editorial Progreso, 1978.

LeBon, Gustave. *The Psychology of Socialism*. Wells, Vt.: Fraser, 1965.

Lenin, V. I. *Imperialism: The Highest Stage of Capitalism*. New York: International Publishers, 1939.

———. *Lenin on the United States*. New York: International Publishers, 1970.

Levi, Albert William. *Humanism and Politics*. Bloomington: Indiana University Press, 1969.

Levine, Robert M. *The Vargas Regime: The Critical Years, 1934–1938*. New York: Columbia University Press, 1970.

Lewis, John. *The Marxism of Marx*. London: Lawrence & Wishert, 1972.

Lichtheim, George. *Marxism: An Historical and Critical Study*. London: Routledge & Kegan Paul, 1961.

———. *A Short History of Socialism*. New York: Praeger, 1970.

Lipschütz, Alejandro. *Marx y Lenin en la América Latina y los problemas indigenistas*. Havana: Casa de las Américas, 1974.

Liss, Sheldon B. *Diplomacy and Dependency: Venezuela, the United States, and the Americas*. Salisbury, N.C.: Documentary Publications, 1978.

Lombardi, Carlos M. *Las ideas sociales en la Argentina*. Buenos Aires: Editoriales Platina/Stilcograf, 1965.

Lombardo Toledano, Vicente. *La doctrina Monroe y el movimiento obrero*. Mexico City: Talleres Linotipográficos "La Lucha," 1927.

———. *Escritos filosóficos*. Mexico City: Editorial México Nuevo, 1937.

———. *Nuestra lucha por la libertad.* Mexico City: Universidad Obrera de México, 1941.

———. *Las luchas proletarias de Veracruz.* Jalapa: Editorial Barricada, 1942.

———. *La rebelión del mundo colonial contra el imperialismo.* Mexico City: n.p., 1950.

———. *La evolución de México durante la primera mitad del siglo XX.* Mexico City: n.p., 1956.

———. *La perspectiva de México: Una democracia del pueblo.* Mexico City: Ediciones de Partido Popular, 1956.

———. *La batalla de las ideas en nuestro tiempo.* Mexico City: Universidad Nacional Autónoma de México, 1959.

———. *¿Moscú o Pekin? La vía mexicana hacia el socialismo.* Mexico City: Partido Popular Socialista, 1963.

———. *El problema del indio.* Mexico City: SepSetentas, 1973.

Lombardo Toledano, Vicente, and Antonio Caso, *Idealismo vs. materialismo dialéctico.* Mexico City: Universidad Obrera de México, 1963.

Lombardo Toledano, Vicente, Xavier Icaza, et al. *Marxismo y anti-marxismo.* Mexico City: Editorial Futuro, 1934.

Lora, Guillermo. *Balance de la huelga minera.* La Paz: Ediciones "Masas," 1963.

———. *Las guerrillas: La concepción marxista contra el golpismo adventurero.* La Paz: Ediciones "Masas," 1963.

———. *La revolución boliviana.* La Paz: Talleres Gráficos Bolivianos para "Difusión S.R.L.," 1963.

———. *Perspectivas de la revolución boliviana.* La Paz: Editorial "Masas," 1964.

———. *Historia del movimiento obrero boliviano.* La Paz: Editorial "Los Amigos del Libro": Vol 1: *1848–1900,* 1967, vol. 2: *1900–1923,* 1969, vol. 3: *1923–1933,* 1970.

———. *A History of the Bolivian Labour Movement.* Cambridge: Cambridge University Press, 1977.

Lowy, Michael. *The Marxism of Che Guevara.* New York: Monthly Review Press, 1973.

Macaulay, Neill. *The Prestes Column: Revolution in Brazil.* New York: New Viewpoints, 1974.

Madariaga, José Luis. *¿Que es la izquierda nacional? Manual del socialismo revolucionario.* Buenos Aires: Ediciones IA, 1969.

Malavé Mata, Héctor. *Formación histórica del antidesarrollo de Venezuela.* Havana: Casa del las Américas, 1974.

Malloy, James M. *Bolivia: The Uncompleted Revolution.* Pittsburgh: University of Pittsburgh Press, 1970.

Mañach, Jorge. *Martí: Apostle of Freedom.* New York: Devin-Adair, 1950.

Mariátegui, José Carlos. *Defensa del marxismo.* Lima: Biblioteca Amauta, 1959.

———. *Historia de la crisis mundial: Conferencias, 1923, 1924.* Lima: Biblioteca Amauta, 1959.

———. *Seven Interpretive Essays on Peruvian Reality.* Austin: University of Texas Press, 1971.

Marighela, Carlos. *For the Liberation of Brazil.* Baltimore: Penguin Books, 1971.

Marinello, Juan. *Cuba contra la guerra imperialista.* Havana: Ediciones Sociales, 1940.

———. *Contemporáneos.* Havana: Universidad Central de las Villas, 1964.

———. *Once ensayos martianos.* Havana: Comisión Nacional Cubana de la UNESCO, 1964.

Marof, Tristán (Gustavo Adolfo Navarro). *La justicia del Inca.* Brussels: Librería Falk Fils, 1926.

———. *La tragedia del altiplano.* Buenos Aires: Editorial Claridad, 1934.

———. *La verdad socialista en Bolivia.* La Paz: La Editorial "Trabajo," 1938.

———. *Ensayos y crítica: Revoluciones bolivianos, guerras internacionales, y escritores.* La Paz: Librería y Editorial "Juventud," 1961.

———. *El jefe: Comedia política.* La Paz: n.p., 1965.

Márquez Fuentes, Manuel, and Octavio Rodríguez Araujo. *El partido comunista mexicano.* Mexico City: Ediciones El Caballito, 1973.

Martin, Lionel. *The Early Fidel: Roots of Castro's Communism.* Secaucus, N.J.: Lyle Stuart, 1978.

Martínez Bello, Antonio. *Ideas sociales y económicas de José Martí.* Havana: La Verónica, 1940.

Martínez de la Torre, Ricardo. *De la reforma universitaria al partido socialista: Apuntes para un interpretación marxista de historia social del Perú.* Lima: Ediciones "Frente," 1945.

———. *Apuntes para una interpretación marxista de historia social del Perú.* Lima: Vol. 1, Ediciones "Frente," 1935; vol. 2, Empresa Editora Peruana, 1948; vol. 3, Empresa Editora Peruana, 1949; vol. 4, Compañía Impresora Peruana, 1949.

Martz, John D. *Colombia: Contemporary Political Survey.* Chapel Hill: University of North Carolina Press, 1962.

Marx, Karl. *A Contribution to the Critique of Political Economy.* New York: International Publishers, 1970.

Marx, Karl, and Friedrich Engels. *Materiales para la historia de América Latina.* Mexico City: Siglo XXI, 1975.

Marx, Karl, Friedrich Engels, and V.I. Lenin. *Anarchism and Anarcho-Syndicalism.* New York: International Publishers, 1972.

Matthews, Herbert L. *Revolution in Cuba.* New York: Scribner's, 1975.

May, Henry E. *The Enlightenment in America.* New York: Oxford University Press, 1976.

McLellan, David. *Karl Marx: His Life and Thought.* New York: Harper & Row, 1973.

Mella, Julio Antonio. *La lucha revolucionaria contra el imperialismo: ¿Qué es el APRA?* Mexico City, 1928.

———. *Julio Antonio Mella en el Machete: Antología parcial de un luchador y su momento histórico.* Mexico City: Fondo de Cultura Popular, 1968.

———. *Escritos revolucionarios.* Mexico City: Siglo XXI, 1978.

Miliband, Ralph. *Marxism and Politics.* Oxford: Oxford University Press, 1977.

Millon, Robert P. *Mexican Marxist: Vicente Lombardo Toledano.* Chapel Hill: University of North Carolina Press, 1966.

———. *Zapata: The Ideology of a Peasant Revolutionary.* New York: International Publishers, 1969.

Mills, C. Wright. *Listen Yankee: The Revolution in Cuba.* New York: Ballantine Books, 1960.

———. *The Marxists.* New York: Delta, 1962.

———. *Power, Politics, and People: The Collected Essays of C. Wright Mills.* New York: Oxford University Press, 1963.

Miranda, José P. *Marx en México: Plusvalía y política.* Mexico City: Siglo XXI, 1972.

Montaña Cuéllar, Diego. *Sociología américana.* Bogota: Universidad Nacional de Colombia, 1950.

———. *Colombia: País formal y país real.* Buenos Aires: Editorial Platina, 1963.

Monzón, Luis G. *Detalles de la educación socialista implantables en México.* Mexico City: Secretaría de Educación Pública, Comisión Editora Popular, Talleres Gráficos de la Nación, 1936.

Neruda, Pablo. *Memoirs.* New York: Penguin Books, 1978.

Nisbet, Robert. *The Social Philosophers: Community and Conflict in Western Thought.* New York: Thomas Y. Crowell, 1973.

Nunn, Frederick M. *Chilean Politics, 1920–1931: The Honorable Mission of the Armed Forces.* Albuquerque: University of New Mexico Press, 1970.

O'Connor, James. *The Origins of Socialism in Cuba*. Ithaca: Cornell University Press, 1970.

Oddone, Jacinto. *Historia del socialismo argentino*. 2 vols. Buenos Aires: Talleres Gráficos "La Vanguardia," 1934.

———. *Gremialismo proletario argentino*. Buenos Aries: Editorial La Vanguardia, 1949.

Ollman, Bertell. *Alienation: Marx's Conception of Man in Capitalist Society*. London: Cambridge University Press, 1971.

Orrego, Antenor. *El pueblo continente: Ensayos para una interpretación de la América Latina*. Santiago: Ercilla, 1939.

Osorio Lizarazo, J. A. *Gaitán: Vida, muerte, y permanente presencia*. Buenos Aires: Ediciones López Negri, 1952.

Palacios, Alfredo L. *Soberanía y socialización de industrias: Monopolios, latifundios, y privilegios de capital extranjero*. Buenos Aires: Editorial La Vanguardia, 1946.

———. *La justicia social*. Buenos Aires: Editorial Claridad, 1954.

———. *Masas y élites en Iberoamérica*. Buenos Aires: Editorial Columbia, 1960.

———. *Nuestra América y el imperialismo*. Buenos Aires: Editorial Palestra, 1961.

Palacios, Jorge. *Chile: An Attempt at "Historic Compromise": The Real Story of the Allende Years*. Chicago: Banner Press, 1979.

Pan, Luis. *Justo y Marx: El socialismo en la Argentina*. Buenos Aires: Ediciones Monserrat, 1964.

Paz, Octavio. *The Labyrinth of Solitude: Life and Thought in Mexico*. New York: Grove Press, 1961.

———. *The Other Mexico: Critique of the Pyramid*. New York: Grove Press, 1972.

Peñaloza, Juan Ramón. *Trotsky ante la revolución nacional latinoamericana*. Buenos Aires: Editorial Indoamérica, 1953.

Petkoff, Teodoro. *¿Socialismo para Venezuela?* Caracas: Editorial Domingo Fuentes, 1970.

———. *Razón y pasión del socialismo: El tema socialista en Venezuela*. Caracas: Ediciones Centauro, 1973.

Petras, James. *Politics and Social Forces in Chilean Development*. Berkeley and Los Angeles: University of California Press, 1970.

———. *Critical Perspectives on Imperialism and Social Class in the Third World*. New York: Monthly Review Press, 1978.

Pintos, Francisco R. *Historia del Uruguay (1851–1938): Ensayo de interpretación materialista*. Montevideo: Ediciones Pueblos Unidos, 1946.

Pla, Alberto J. *Ideología y método en la historiografía Argentina*. Buenos Aires: Ediciones Nueva Visión, 1972.

Poblete Troncoso, Moisés, and Ben G. Burnet. *The Rise of the Latin American Labor Movement*. New Haven: College and University Press, 1960.

Ponce, Aníbal. *Educación y lucha de clases*. Havana: Imprenta Nacional de Cuba, 1961.

————. *Humanismo burgués y humanismo proletario*. Havana: Imprenta Nacional, 1962.

Poppino, Rollie. *International Communism in Latin America: A History of the Movement, 1917–1963*. Glencoe, N.Y.: Free Press, 1964.

Prado Júnior, Caio. *Historia económica del Brasil*. Buenos Aires: Editorial Futuro, 1959.

————. *Evolução política do Brasil e outros estudos*. São Paulo: Editôra Brasiliense, 1961.

————. *O mundo do socialismo*. São Paulo: Editôra Brasiliense, 1962.

————. *A revolução brasileira*. Sao Paulo: Editôra Brasiliense, 1966.

————. *La revolución brasileña*. Buenos Aires: A. Peña, 1968.

————. *The Colonial Background of Modern Brazil*. Berkeley and Los Angeles: University of California Press, 1969.

————. *Estruturalismo de Lévi-Strauss: Marxismo de Louis Althusser*. São Paulo: Editôra Brasiliense, 1971.

Prado, Jorge del. *Mariátegui y su obra*. Lima: Ediciones Nuevo Horizonte, 1946.

Prestes, Luiz Carlos. *Os comunistas na luta pela democracia*. Rio de Janeiro: Edições Horizonte, 1945.

Quartim, João. *Dictatorship and Armed Struggle in Brazil*. New York: Monthly Review Press, 1971.

Quijano, Aníbal. *Nationalism and Capitalism in Peru: A Study in Neo-Imperialism*. New York: Monthly Review Press, 1971.

————. *Crisis imperialista y clase obrera en América Latina*. Lima: Quijano, 1974.

Raguso, Stefano. *Los orígenes de la izquierda y de la derecha en la literatura política*. Caracas: Edime, 1969.

Rama, Carlos M. *Mouvements ouvrières et socialistes: L'Amérique Latine (1492–1936)*. Paris: Les Editions Ouvrières, 1959.

Ramm, Hartmut. *The Marxism of Régis Debray: Between Lenin and Guevara*. Lawrence, Kansas: Regents Press of Kansas, 1978.

Ramos, Jorge Abelardo. *América Latina: Una País*. Buenos Aires: Editorial Octubre, 1949.

————. *El partido comunista en la política argentina: Su historia y su crítica*. Buenos Aires: Coyoacán, 1962.

————. *Historia de la nación latinoamericana*. Buenos Aires: A. Peña Lillo, 1968.

———. *Bolivarismo y marxismo.* Buenos Aires: A. Peña Lillo, 1969.

———. *El marxismo en los países coloniales.* Cochabamba, Bolivia: Editorial Universitaria, 1970.

———. *Historia del stalinismo en la Argentina.* Buenos Aires: Editorial Rancagua, 1974.

———. *Revolución y contrarevolución en la Argentina.* Buenos Aires: Editorial Plus Ultra: Vol. 1: *Las masas y las lanzas, 1810–1862,* 1974; vol. 2: *Del patricidado a la oligarquía, 1862–1904,* 1976; vol. 3: *La bella epoca, 1904–1922,* 1973; vol. 5: *La era del bonapartismo, 1943–1973,* 1977.

Rangel, Domingo Alberto. *La revolución de las fantasías.* Caracas: Ediciones OFIDI, 1958.

———. *País ocupado.* Caracas: Pensamiento Vivo, 1960.

———. *Historia económica de Venezuela.* Caracas: Pensamiento Vivo, 1962.

———. *Los andinos en el poder.* Caracas: Talleres Gráficos Universitarios, 1964.

———. *El proceso del capitalismo contemporáneo en Venezuela.* Caracas: Universidad Central de Venezuela, 1968.

———. *Capital y desarrollo.* 2 vols. Caracas: Instituto de Investigaciones Económicas y Sociales, 1969–1970.

———. *La oligarquía del dinero.* Vol. 3 of *Capital y desarrollo.* Caracas: Editorial Fuentes, 1971.

———. *Los mercaderes de voto: Estudio de un sistema.* Valencia, Venezuela: Vadell Hermanos, 1973.

Ratliff, William E. *Castroism and Communism in Latin America, 1959–1976: The Varieties of Marxist-Leninist Experience.* Washington, D.C.: American Enterprise Institute for Public Policy Research, 1976.

Ravines, Eudocio. *El momento político.* Lima: Ediciones Peruanas, 1945.

———. *The Yenan Way.* New York: Scribner's, 1951.

———. *La gran estafa.* Santiago: Editorial del Pacífico, 1957.

Recabarren, Luis Emilio. *El socialismo.* Iquique, Chile: El Despertar, 1912.

———. *Obras escogidas.* Vol. 1. Santiago: Editorial Recabarren, 1965.

———. *El pensamiento de Luis Emilio Recabarren.* 2 vols. Santiago: Austral, 1971.

Revel, Jean François. *The Totalitarian Temptation.* Garden City, N.Y.: Doubleday, 1977.

Revueltas, José. *Un proletariado sin cabeza.* Mexico City: Ediciones de la Liga Leninista Espartaco, 1962.

Reynolds, Charles V. *Theory and Explanation in International Politics.* New York: Harper & Row, 1974.

Ribeiro, Darcy. *The Americas and Civilization*. New York: E. P. Dutton, 1971.

Roca, Blas. *Los fundamentos del socialismo en Cuba*. Havana: Ediciones Populares, 1962.

Rodríquez, Carlos Rafael. *El marxismo y la historia de Cuba*. Havana: Editorial Páginas, 1944.

———. *Cuba en el tránsito al socialismo (1953–1963): Lenin y la cuestión colonial*. Mexico City: Siglo XXI, 1978.

Rodríguez López, Juan. *Socialismo en el Uruguay*. Montevideo: Palacio de Libro, 1928.

Romanell, Patrick. *Making of the Mexican Mind: A Study in Recent Mexican Thought*. Notre Dame, Ind.: University of Notre Dame Press, 1967.

Romero, José Luis. *A History of Argentine Political Thought*. Stanford: Stanford University Press, 1963.

Rubel, Maximilien, and Margaret Manale. *Marx Without Myth: A Chronological Study of His Life and Work*. New York: Harper & Row, 1975.

Salazar Bondy, Augusto. *Historia de las ideas en el Perú contemporáneo*. 2 vols. Lima: Francisco Moncloa, 1967.

Salceda, Juan Antonio. *Aníbal Ponce y el pensamiento de Mayo*. Buenos Aires: Editorial Lautaro, 1957.

Sánchez, Luis Alberto. *Nueva historia de la literatura americana*. Buenos Aires: Editorial Americalee, 1943.

Sánchez Reulet, Aníbal. *Contemporary Latin American Philosophy*. Albuquerque: University of New Mexico Press, 1954.

Sartre, Jean-Paul. *Sartre on Cuba*. New York: Ballantine Books, 1961.

Schmitt, Karl, M. *Communism in Mexico*. Austin: University of Texas Press, 1965.

Schumpeter, Joseph A. *The Great Economists from Marx to Keynes*. New York: Oxford University Press, 1951.

Shragin, Victor. *Chile, Corvalán, Struggle*. Moscow: Progress Publishers, 1980.

Sierra, Vicente D. *Historia de las ideas políticas en Argentina*. Buenos Aires: Ediciones Nuestra Causa, 1950.

Silva Herzog, Jesús. *El pensamiento socialista*. Mexico City: La Universidad Obrera de México, 1937.

———. *El pensamiento económico en México*. Mexico City: Fondo de Cultura Económica, 1947.

———. *Inquietud sin tregua: Ensayos y artículos escogidos, 1937–1965*. Mexico City: Cuadernos Americanos, 1965.

———. *El pensamiento económico, social, y político de México, 1810–*

1964. Mexico City: Instituto Mexicano de Investigaciones Económicas, 1967.

———. *Una vida en la vida de México.* Mexico City: Siglo XXI, 1972.

Silva Michelena, José A. *The Illusion of Democracy in Dependent Nations.* Vol. 3 of his *The Politics of Change in Venezuela.* Cambridge, Mass.: MIT Press, 1971.

Silva Solar, Julio, and Jacques Choncol. *Desarrollo sin capitalismo: Hacia un mundo comunitario.* Caracas: Nuevo Orden, 1964.

Sinclair, Andrew. *Che Guevara.* New York: Viking Press, 1970.

Smith, Peter H. *Argentina and the Failure of Democracy: Conflict Among Political Elites, 1904–1955.* Madison: University of Wisconsin Press, 1974.

Snow, Peter G. *Argentine Radicalism.* Iowa City: University of Iowa Press, 1965.

Sodré, Nelson Werneck. *Introdução a revolução brasileira.* Rio de Janeiro: José Olympio, 1958.

———. *Formação histórica do Brasil.* São Paulo: Editôra Brasiliense, 1962.

———. *Evolución social y económica del Brasil.* Buenos Aires: Editorial Universitaria de Buenos Aires, 1964.

———. *História da burguesia brasileira.* Rio de Janeiro: Editôra Civilização Brasileira, 1967.

———. *Ofício de escritor: Dialética da literatura.* Rio de Janeiro: Editôra Civilização Brasileira, 1965.

———. *Fundamentos da estética marxista.* Rio de Janeiro: Editôra Civilização Brasileira, 1968.

———. *História da literatura brasileira.* Rio de Janeiro: Editôra Civilização Brasileira, 1976.

———. *A coluna Prestes.* Rio de Janeiro: Editôra Civilização Brasileira, 1978.

Soler, Ricaurte. *Formas ideológicas de la nación panameña.* Panama City: Ediciones De La Revista "Tareas," 1964.

Spalding, Hobart A., Jr. *Argentine Sociology from the End of the Nineteenth Century to World War One.* Buenos Aires: Instituto Torcuato di Tella Centro de Investigaciones Sociales, 1968.

———. *Organized Labor in Latin America: Historical Case Studies of Urban Workers in Dependent Societies.* New York: Harper & Row, 1977.

Stabb, Martin S. *In Quest of Identity: Patterns in the Spanish American Essay of Ideas, 1890–1960.* Chapel Hill: University of North Carolina Press, 1967.

Stavenhagen, Rudolfo. *Social Classes in Agrarian Societies.* Garden City, N.Y.: Doubleday, 1975.

Stevenson, John Reese. *The Chilean Popular Front*. Philadelphia: University of Pennsylvania Press, 1942.

Swomley, John M., Jr. *Liberation Ethics*. New York: Macmillan, 1972.

Teitelboim, Volodia. *El amanecer del capitalismo y la conquista de América*. Santiago: Editorial Nueva América, 1943.

————. *El oficio ciudadano*. Santiago: Nacimiento, 1973.

Thomas, Clive Y. *Dependence and Transformation: The Economics of the Transition to Socialism*. New York: Monthly Review Press, 1974.

Torres Restrepo, Camilo. *Camilo Torres: Por el Padre Camilo Torres Restrepo (1956–1966)*. Cuernavaca: Centro Intercultural de Documentación, 1966.

Torres Rivas, Edelberto. *Procesos y estructuras de una sociedad dependiente*. Santiago: Ediciones Prensa Latino-América, 1969.

————. *Interpretación del desarrollo social centroamericano*. San Jose, Costa Rica: Editorial Universitaria Centro-Americana, 1971.

Trotsky, León. *Por los estados unidos socialistas de América Latina*. Buenos Aires: Ediciones Coyoacán, 1961.

Tucker, Robert C. *The Marxian Revolutionary Idea*. New York: W. W. Norton, 1969.

Turner, Frederick C. *The Dynamic of Mexican Nationalism*. Chapel Hill: University of North Carolina Press, 1968.

Ugarte, Manuel. *The Destiny of a Continent*. New York: Knopf, 1925.

Unzueta, Gerardo. *Lombardo Toledano y el marxismo-leninismo*. Mexico City: Fondo de Cultura Popular, 1966.

Urriola Marcucci, Ornel E. *Dialéctica de la nación panameña: Período republicano*. Panama City: Ediciones Momento, 1972.

Urrutia, Miguel. *The Development of the Colombian Labor Movement*. New Haven: Yale University Press, 1969.

Vitale, Luis. *Los discursos de Clotario Blest y la revolución chilena*. Santiago: Editorial Por, 1961.

————. *Historia de movimiento obrero*. Santiago: Editorial Por, 1962.

————. *Interpretación marxista de la historia de Chile*. Santiago: Ediciones de Prensa Latino-Americana: Vol. 1: *Las culturas primitivas: La conquista española*, 1967; vol. 2: *La colonia y la revolución de 1810*, 1972; vol. 3: *La independencia política, la rebelión de las provincias, y los decenios de la burguesía comercial y terrateniente*, 1971.

Vitale, Louis, and Kalki Glausser R. *Acerca del modo de producción colonial en América Latina*. Medellin, Colombia: Ediciones Crítico, 1974.

Waiss, Oscar. *Nacionalismo y socialismo en América Latina*. Buenos Aires: Ediciones Iguazú, 1961.

———. *Los problemas del socialismo contemporáneo.* Buenos Aires: Ediciones Iguazú, 1961.

Walter, Richard J. *The Socialist Party of Argentina, 1890–1930.* Austin: University of Texas Press, 1977.

Weinstein, Martin. *Uruguay: The Politics of Failure.* Westport, Conn.: Greenwood Press, 1975.

Wesson, Robert G. *Why Marxism?* New York: Basic Books, 1976.

Williams, William A. *The Great Evasion: An Essay on the Contemporary Relevance of Karl Marx and on the Wisdom of Admitting the Heretic into the Dialogue About America's Future.* Chicago: Quadrangle, 1964.

Wolpin, Miles D. *Cuban Foreign Policy and Chilean Politics.* Lexington, Mass.: Lexington Books, 1972.

Zea, Leopoldo. *The Latin American Mind.* Norman: University of Oklahoma Press, 1963.

———. *El pensamiento latinoamericano.* 2 vols. Mexico City: Editorial Pormarca, 1965.

Zeitlin, Irving M. *Capitalism and Imperialism: An Introduction to Neo-Marxian Concepts.* Chicago: Markham, 1972.

Zum Felde, Alberto. *Proceso intelectual del Uruguay.* Montevideo: Editorial Claridad, 1941.

———. *Indice crítico de la literatura hispanoamericana: Los ensayistas.* Mexico City: Editorial Guarania, 1954.

Articles and Unpublished and Miscellaneous Materials

Aguirre, Manuel Agustín. "Report From Ecuador." In *Whither Latin America?* Carlos Fuentes et al. New York: Monthly Review Press, 1963.

Alexander, Robert J. "Aprismo, Is It Socialist?" *Modern Review* 1 (Nov. 1947):682–90.

Allende, Salvador. "Chile Begins Its March Towards Socialism." *New World Review* 39(1) (Winter 1971):26–37.

Almeyda Medina, Clodomiro. "Concepción marxista del hombre." In *Pensamiento teórico y político del partido socialista de Chile.* Edited by Julio César Jobet and Alejandro Chelén R. Santiago: Empresa Editora Nacional Quimantu, 1972.

———. "The Foreign Policy of the Unidad Popular Government." In *Chile at the Turning Point: Lessons of the Socialist Years, 1970–1973.* Edited by Federico G. Gil, Ricardo Lagos E., and Henry Landsberger. Philadelphia: Institute for Study of Human Issues, 1979.

Ampuero Díaz, Raúl. "Reflexiones sobre la revolución y el socialismo."

In *Pensamiento teórico y político del partido socialista de Chile.* Edited by Julio César Jobet and Alejandro Chelén R. Santiago: Empresa Editora Nacional Quimantu, 1972.

Arismendi, Rodney. "On the Role of the National Bourgeoisie in the Anti-Imperialist Struggle." *World Marxist Review* 2(5) (May 1959):29–39.

———. "On the Role of the National Bourgeoisie in the Anti-Imperialist Struggle." *World Marxist Review* 2(6) (June 1959):31–39.

———. "Lenin: Revolutionary Communist and Revolutionary Leader." *World Marxist Review* 13(5) (May 1970):92–102.

———. "How Victory Was Forged." *World Marxist Review* 18(5) (May 1975):15–22.

———. "On the Dialectics of Peaceful Coexistence and Revolutionary Change." *World Marxist Review* 19(1) (Jan. 1976):3–15.

Aron, Raymond. "The Impact of Marxism in the Twentieth Century." In *Marxism in the Modern World.* Edited by Milorad M. Drachkovitch. Stanford: Hoover Institution Press, 1965.

Becerra, Longino. "Latin America: Two Epochs and Marxism-Leninism." *World Marxist Review* 2(7) (July 1968):86–93.

Benedetti, Mario. "Relaciones entre el hombre de acción y el intelectual." *Casa de las Américas* 7 (March-April 1968):116–20.

Bernstein, Harry. "Marxismo en México, 1917–1925." *Historia Mexicana* 7 (April-June 1958):497–516.

Blanksten, George I. "Fidel Castro and Latin America." In *Latin American Politics.* Edited by Robert D. Tomasek. Garden City, N.Y.: Anchor Books, 1966.

Camara Ferreira, Joaquim. "Marighela: Creative Life and Action." *Tricontinental Bulletin* 21–27 (Nov. 8, 1970–Feb. 1971):119–23.

Carrera Damas, Germán. "The Cult of the Liberator." In *The Liberator, Simón Bolívar: Man and Image.* Edited by David Bushnell. New York: Knopf, 1970.

———. "Estudio preliminar." In *Materiales para el estudio de la ideología realista de la independencia.* Vol. 1. Caracas: Universidad Central de Venezuela, Facultad de Humanidades y Educación, Instituto de Antropología e Historia, 1971.

Central Committee of the Communist Party of Argentina. "A Revolution in the Revolution Is Impossible (1967)." In *Models of Political Change in Latin America.* Edited by Paul Sigmund. New York: Praeger, 1970.

Chavarría, Jesús. "The Intellectuals and the Crisis of Modern Peruvian Nationalism: 1870–1919." *Hispanic American Historical Review* 50(2) (May 1970):257–78.

Codovilla, Victorio. "Unir a las mujeres en la lucha por sus derechos." In *Problemas y luchas de las mujeres*. Edited by Partido Comunista. Buenos Aires: Partido Comunista, 1947.

———. "The Ideas of Marxism-Leninism in Latin America." *World Marxist Review* 7(8) (Aug. 1964):40–49.

Colombo, Eduardo. "Anarchism in Argentina and Uruguay." In *Anarchism Today*. Edited by David E. Aster and James Joll. New York: Doubleday, 1971.

Corvalán, Luis. "The Alliance of Revolutionary Anti-Imperialist Forces in Latin America (1967)." In *Models of Political Change in Latin America*. Edited by Paul Sigmund. New York: Praeger, 1970.

Cotler, Julio. "The Concentration of Income and Political Authoritarianism in Peru." In *The Politics of Antipolitics: The Military in Latin America*. Edited by Brian Loveman and Thomas M. Davies, Jr. Lincoln: University of Nebraska Press, 1978.

Crespi, Roberto Simón. "José Revueltas (1914–1976): A Political Biography." *Latin American Perspectives* 6(3) (Summer 1979):93–113.

Davis, Donald E. "Marxism and People's Wars." *Orbis* 15(4) (Winter 1972):1194–1205.

Davis, Harold Eugene. "Political Philosophies in the Caribbean." In *The Caribbean: Contemporary Trends*. Edited by A. Curtis Wilgus. Gainesville: University of Florida Press, 1953.

———. "The History of Ideas in Latin America. *Latin American Research Review* 3 (Fall 1968):23–44.

Dias, Giocondo. "Some Problems of the Class Struggle in Brazil." *World Marxist Review* 12 (Jan 1964):21–25.

Draper, Hal. "Karl Marx and Simón Bolívar: A Note on Authoritarian Leadership in a National Liberation Movement." *New Politics* 7 (Winter 1968):64–77.

Dudley, William S. "Waldo Frank North American Pensador." In *Columbia Essays in International Affairs: The Dean's Papers*. Vol. 3. Edited by A. W. Cordier. New York: Columbia University Press, 1968.

Echeverría, Evelio. "Bolshevism and the Spanish American Social Novel." *Latin American Literary Review* 41 (Spring-Summer 1976):89–95.

Erickson, Kenneth Paul, Patrick V. Peppe, and Hobart A. Spalding, Jr. "Research on the Urban Working Class and Organized Labor in Argentina, Brazil and Chile: What Is Left to Be Done?" *Latin American Research Review* 9(2) (Summer 1974):115–42.

Fortuny, José Manuel. "Has the Revolution Become More Difficult in

Latin America?" *World Marxist Review* 8(8) (August 1965):38–45.

"Four South American Socialists." *Latin American Thought* 1(4) (July 1946).

Galeano, Eduardo. "Latin America and the Theory of Imperialism." In *Lenin Today*. Edited by Paul M. Sweezy and Harry Magdoff. New York: Monthly Review Press, 1970.

Ghioldi, Rodolfo, "Socialist Democracy, an Inspiring Example." *World Marxist Review* 15(1) (Jan. 1975):61–68.

Gilbert, Felix. "Intellectual History: Its Aims and Methods." In *Historical Studies Today*. Edited by Felix Gilbert and Stephen R. Graubard. New York: W. W. Norton, 1972.

González Casanova, Pablo. "Internal Colonialism and National Development." In *Latin American Radicalism*. Edited by Irving Louis Horowitz, Josué de Castro, and John Gerassi. New York: Vintage, 1969.

———. "The Crisis of the State and the Struggle for Democracy in Latin America." *Contemporary Marxism.* no. 1, Spring 1980, pp. 64–69.

Gorender, Jacob. "Brazil in the Grip of Contradictions." *World Marxist Review* 6(2) (Feb. 1963):27–32.

Graham, Richard. "Brazil: The National Period." In *Latin American Scholarship Since World War II*. Edited by Roberto Esquenazi-Mayo and Michael C. Meyer. Lincoln: University of Nebraska Press, 1971.

Gray, Richard, B. "José Martí and Social Revolution in Cuba." *Journal of Inter-American Studies* 5(2) (April 1963):249–56.

Greene, John C. "Objectives and Methods in Intellectual History." *Mississippi Valley Historical Review* 44(1) (June 1957):58–74.

Guevara, Ernesto. "The Philosophy of Che Guevara." Taped interview. Hollywood, Ca.: Center for Cassette Studies, 1965.

———. "Notes on Socialism and Man." *International Socialist Review* 27 (Winter 1966):18–23.

———. "On Art and Revolution." *Praxis*. Winter 1976, p. 396.

Hansen, Joseph. "Ideology of the Cuban Revolution. *International Socialist Review,* Summer 1960, pp. 74–78.

Harding, Timothy F. "Revolution Tomorrow: The Failure of the Left." *Studies on the Left* 4(4) (Fall 1964):30–55.

———. "Dependency, Nationalism and the State in Latin America." *Latin American Perspectives* 3(4) (Fall 1976):3–11.

Harris, Richard L. "The Influence of Marxist Structuralism on the Intellectual Left in Latin America." *Insurgent Sociologist* 9(1) (Summer 1979):62–73.

Hart, John M. "Nineteenth-Century Urban Labor Precursors of the Mexican Revolution: the Development of an Ideology." *The Americas* 30(3) (Jan. 1974):297–318.

Heilbroner, Robert. "Inescapable Marx." *New York Review of Books,* June 29, 1978.

Higham, John. "Intellectual History and Its Neighbors." *Journal of the History of Ideas* 15(3) (June 1954):339–47.

Hobsbawm, Eric J. "From Social History to the History of Society." *Daedalus* 100(1) (Winter 1971):20–45.

———. "Karl Marx's Contribution to Historiography." In *Ideology in Social Science.* Edited by Robin Blackburn. New York: Vintage, 1973.

Jaguaribe, Helio. "Marxism and Latin American Development." In *Marx and the Western World.* Edited by Nicholas Lobkowicz. Notre Dame, Ind.: University of Notre Dame Press, 1967.

Liss, Sheldon B. "Relaciones internacionales de México: ¿Dónde están los yanquis?" In *Investigaciones contemporáneas sobre historia de México.* Mexico City: Universidad Nacional Autónoma de México, El Colegio de México, University of Texas Press, 1971.

Lombardo Toledano, Vicente. "The Mexican Flag and the Proletariat." In *Nationalism in Latin America.* Edited by Samuel Baily. New York: Knopf, 1971.

Mac-Laurin, Dámaso. "Los intelectuales en el comunismo de la Argentina." *Estudios Sobre El Comunismo* 6 (April-June 1958):71–78; and 8 (Jan.-March 1958):72–77.

Magdoff, Harry. "Is There a Noncapitalist Road?" *Monthly Review* 30(7) (Dec. 1978):1–10.

Martí, José. "Homage to Marx." In *The Quest for Change in Latin America.* Edited by W. Raymond Duncan and James N. Goodsell. New York: Oxford University Press, 1970.

Martz, John D. "Venezuela's Generation of '28: The Genesis of Political Democracy." *Journal of Inter-American Studies* 6(1) (Jan. 1964):17–32.

Marx, Karl. "Bolívar y Ponte." *New American Encyclopedia* 3 (1858).

Masur, Gerhard. "Foreign Political Ideologies in the Caribbean." In *The Caribbean: Its Political Problems.* Edited by A. Curtis Wilgus. Gainesville: University of Florida Press, 1962.

McNicoll, Robert E. "Intellectual Origins of Aprismo." *Hispanic American Historical Review* 23(3) (Aug. 1943):424–40.

——— "Hegel and Latin America Today." *Journal of Inter-American Studies* 6(1) (Jan. 1964):129–31.

Mesa-Lago, Carmelo. "Ideological, Political, and Economic Factors in the

Cuban Controversy on Material Versus Moral Incentives."
Journal of Inter-American Studies and World Affairs 14(1)
(Feb. 1972):49–111.

———. "Building Socialism in Cuba: Romantic Versus Realistic Approach." *Latin American Perspectives* 3(4) (Fall 1976):117–21.

Miliani, Domingo. "Utopian Socialism: Transitional Thread from Romanticism to Positivism in Latin America." *Journal of the History of Ideas.* no. 4, Oct.-Dec. 1963, pp. 523–58.

Miró Quesada, Francisco. "The Impact of Metaphysics on Latin American Ideology." *Journal of the History of Ideas,* no. 4, Oct.-Dec. 1963, pp. 539–52.

Motta Lima, Pedro. "Marxism-Leninism and Its Influence on Cultural Life in Brazil." *World Marxist Review* 5(10) (Oct. 1962):19–25.

Nasht, John. "The Prestes Saga." *Inter-American Monthly* 3 (Dec. 1945):14–15, 43–45.

Nolte, Ernst. "The Relationship Between 'Bourgeois' and 'Marxist' Historiography." *History and Theory* 14(1) (1975):57–73.

Nun, José. "Notes on Political Science and Latin America." In *Social Science in Latin America.* Edited by Manuel Diégues Júnior and B. Wood. New York: Columbia University Press, 1967.

O'Connor, James. "The Foundations of Cuban Socialism." *Studies on the Left* 4(4) (Fall 1964):97–117.

Ojeda, Fabricio. "Toward Revolutionary Power." In *Latin American Radicalism.* Edited by Irving Louis Horowitz, Josué de Castro, and John Gerassi. New York: Vintage, 1969.

de la Peña, Alcira. "Cuba and Marxism." *World Marxist Review* 6(6) (June 1963):75–78.

Prado Júnior, Caio. "A Guide for the Historiography of the Second Empire." In *Perspectives on Brazilian History.* Edited by E. Bradford Burns. New York: Columbia University Press, 1967.

Prestes, Luiz Carlos. "Grand Propects of Building Communism and Strengthening Peace." *World Marxist Review* 2(1) (June 1959):16–18.

———. "Policy of the Military Dictatorship in Brazil." *World Marxist Review* 8(4) (April 1965):34–39.

———. "Lenin's Heritage and Fight Against Opportunism in the Brazilian Communist Party." *World Marxist Review* 13(11) (Nov. 1970):10–17.

Quijano, Aníbal. "Contemporary Peasant Movements." In *Elites in Latin America.* Edited by Seymour Martin Lipset and Aldo Solari. New York: Oxford University Press, 1967.

————. "Tendencies in Peruvian Development and in the Class Structure." In *Latin America: Reform or Revolution?* Edited by James Petras and Maurice Zeitlin. Greenwich, Conn.: Fawcett, 1968.

————. "Tendencies in the Class Struggle in Peru." *Contemporary Marxism*, no. 1, Spring 1980, pp. 43–55.

Ratliff, William E. "Chinese Communist Cultural Diplomacy Toward Latin America, 1949–1960." *Hispanic American Historical Review* 49(1) (Feb. 1969):53–79.

Reedy, Daniel R. "The Cohesive Influence of José Carlos Mariátegui on Peruvian Art and Politics." In *Artists and Writers in the Evolution of Latin America*. Edited by Edward D. Terry. University: University of Alabama Press, 1969.

Revueltas, José. "En torno a las opiniones de Cosío Villegas: Crisis y destino de México." In *Is the Mexican Revolution Dead?* Edited and translated by Stanley R. Ross. New York: Knopf, 1966.

Richards, Edward B. "Marxism and Marxist Movements in Latin America in Recent Soviet Historical Writing." *Hispanic American Historical Review* 45(4) (Nov. 1965):577–90.

Romagnolo, David J. "The So-Called Law of Uneven and Combined Development." *Latin American Perspectives* 2(1) (Spring 1975):7–31.

Rowntree, Margaret E. "Spanish American Marxian Political Theory." Ph.D. dissertation (Political Science). University of California, Berkeley, 1968.

Simon, S. Fanny. "Anarchism and Anarcho-Syndicalism in South America." *Hispanic American Historical Review* 26(1) (Feb. 1964):38–59.

Skidmore, Thomas E. "The Historiography of Brazil, 1889–1964." *Hispanic American Historical Review* 56(1) (Feb. 1976):81–109.

Starobin, Joseph R. Personal Interviews with the former foreign editor of the *Daily Worker*. Conducted during July 1976 in Hancock, Massachusetts.

Stavenhagen, Rodolfo. "Seven Fallacies About Latin America." In *Latin America: Reform or Revolution?* Edited by James Petras and Maurice Zeitlin. Greenwich, Conn.: Fawcett, 1968.

————. "Classes, Colonialism, and Acculturation." In *Masses in Latin America*. Edited by Irving Louis Horowitz. New York: Oxford University Press, 1970.

————. "Aspectos sociales de la estructura agraria en México." In *Latin American Civilization*. Vol. 2. Edited by Benjamin Keen. Boston: Houghton Mifflin, 1974.

Teitelboim, Volodia. "Literature and Socialism." *World Marxist Review* 3(3) (March 1960):45–50.

———. "Problems Facing Latin American Intellectuals." *World Marxist Review* 2(12) (Dec. 1968):68–75.

———. "For the Complete Independence of Our America." *World Marxist Review* 18(9) (Sept. 1975):30–43.

Terán Gómez, Luis. "El ocaso del socialismo." *Journal of Inter-American Studies* 2(3) (July 1960):276–93.

Thomas, Clive. "The Non-Capitalist Path as Theory and Practice of Decolonization and Socialist Transformation." *Latin American Perspectives* 5(2) (Spring 1978):10–28.

Vanden, Harry E. "The Ideology of Insurrection." In *Nicaragua in Revolution.* Edited by Thomas W. Walker. New York: Praeger, 1982.

———. "Mariátegui: Marxismo, Comunismo, and Other Bibliographic Notes." *Latin American Research Review* 14(3) (1979):61–86.

Vitale, Luis. "Fidelismo and Marxism." *International Socialist Review* 24 (Winter 1963):23–24, 31.

———. "Which Road for Chile?" *International Socialist Review* 25(3) (Summer 1964).

———. "Latin America: Feudal or Capitalist?" In *Latin America: Reform or Revolution?* Edited by James Petras and Maurice Zeitlin. Greenwich, Conn.: Fawcett, 1968.

———. "Predictions of the Founders of Marxism on the Development of World Revolution." In *Fifty Years of World Revolution.* Edited by Ernest Mandel. New York: Merit Publishers, 1968.

Waiss, Oscar. "El carácter de la revolución latinoamericana." In *Pensamiento teórico y político del partido socialista de Chile.* Edited by Julio César Jobet and Alejandro Chelén R. Santiago: Empresa Editora Nacional Quimantu, 1972.

Wiener, Philip P. "Some Problems and Methods in the History of Ideas." *Journal of the History of Ideas* 22(4) (Oct.-Dec. 1961):531–48.

Welter, Rush. "The History of Ideas in America: An Essay in Redefinition." *Journal of American History* 51(4) (March 1965):599–614.

Wohl, R. Richard. "Intellectual History: An Historian's View." *Historian* 16 (Autumn 1953):62–77.

Zamora, Oscar. "The Differences Between Maoism and Guevaraism." In *Models of Political Change in Latin America.* Edited by Paul Sigmund. New York: Praeger, 1970.

Zea, Leopoldo. "Philosophy and Thought in Latin America." *Latin American Research Review* 3(2) (Spring 1968):3–16.

Edited Works

Adams, Richard N., et al. *Social Change in Latin America Today*. New York: Vintage, 1960.

Adler, John H., and Paul W. Kunets, eds. *Capital Movements and Economic Development*. New York: St. Martin's Press, 1967.

Aguilar, Luis E., ed. *Marxism in Latin America*. Philadelphia: Temple University Press, 1978.

Alexander, Robert J., ed. and trans. *Aprismo: The Ideas and Doctrines of Víctor Raúl Haya de la Torre*. Kent, Ohio: Kent State University Press, 1973.

Aptheker, Herbert, ed. *Marxism and Christianity*, New York: Humanities Press, 1968.

Aricó, José, ed. *Mariátegui y los orígenes del marxismo latinoamericano*. Mexico City: Siglo XXI, 1978.

Bartley, Russell H., ed. and trans. *Soviet Historians on Latin America: Recent Scholarly Contributions*. Madison: University of Wisconsin Press, 1978.

Bogotá, el Concejo de, eds. *Colección Jorge Eliécer Gaitán: Documentos para una biografía*. Bogota: Imprenta Municipal, 1949.

Bonachea, Rolando E., and Nelson P. Valdés, eds. *Cuba in Revolution*. Garden City, N.Y.: Anchor-Doubleday, 1972.

―――. *Revolutionary Struggle 1947–1958: The Selected Works of Fidel Castro*. Cambridge, Mass.: MIT Press, 1972.

Bushnell, David, ed. *The Liberator, Simón Bolívar: Man and Image*. New York: Knopf, 1970.

Cavalcanti, Pedro, and Paul Piccone, eds. *History, Philosophy, and Culture in the Young Gramsci*. St. Louis: Telos Press, 1975.

Chaplin, David, ed. *Peruvian Nationalism: A Corporatist Revolution*. New Brunswick, N.J.: Transaction Books, 1976.

Ch'en, Jerome, ed. *Mao*. Englewood Cliffs, N.J.: Prentice-Hall, 1969.

Chilcote, Ronald H., ed. *Revolution and Structural Change in Latin America: A Bibliography on Ideology, Development, and the Radical Left (1930–1965)*. 2 vols. Stanford: Hoover Institution Press, 1970.

Chilcote, Ronald H., and Joel C. Edelstein, eds. *Latin America: The Struggle with Dependency and Beyond*. New York: Schenkman Publishers, 1974.

Connor, James E., ed. *Lenin on Politics and Revolution*. New York: Pegasus, 1968.

Davis, Harold Eugene, ed. and trans. *Latin American Social Thought*. Washington, D.C.: University Press of Washington, D.C., 1961.

Drachkovitch, Milorad M., ed. *Marxism in the Modern World*. Stanford: Hoover Institution Press, 1965.

Eagleson, John, ed. *Christians and Socialism*. Maryknoll, N.Y.: Orbis Books, 1975.

Fernández Moreno, César, ed. *América Latina en su literatura*. Mexico City: Siglo XXI, 1972.

Freedman, Robert, ed. *Marxist Social Thought*. New York: Harcourt Brace, 1968.

Gerassi, John, ed. *Venceremos: The Speeches and Writings of Che Guevara*. New York: Simon & Schuster, 1968.

―――. *The Coming of the New International*. New York: World Publishing, 1971.

―――. *Revolutionary Priest: The Complete Writings and Messages of Camilo Torres*. New York: Random House, 1971.

Gibellini, Rosino, ed. *Frontiers of Theology in Latin America*. Maryknoll, N.Y.: Orbis Books, 1979.

Goodsell, James, N., ed. *Fidel Castro's Personal Revolution in Cuba: 1959–1973*. New York: Knopf, 1975.

Herman, Donald L., ed. *The Communist Tide in Latin America*. Austin: University of Texas Press, 1973.

Hoare, Quintin, and John Mathews, eds. *Antonio Gramsci: Selections from Political Writings (1910–1920)*. New York: International Publishers, 1977.

Hoare, Quintin, and Geoffrey Nowell Smith, eds. *Selections from the Prison Notebooks of Antonio Gramsci*. London: Lawrence & Wishart, 1971.

Hodges, Donald C., ed. *The Legacy of Che Guevara: A Documentary Study*. London: Thames & Hudson, 1977.

―――, ed. and trans. *Philosophy of the Urban Guerrilla: Revolutionary Writings of Abraham Guillén*. New York: William Morrow, 1973.

Hodges, Donald C., and Robert Elias Abu Shanab, eds. *National Liberation Fronts, 1960–1970*. New York: William Morrow, 1972.

Huberman, Leo, and Paul M. Sweezy, eds. *Régis Debray and the Latin American Revolution*. New York: Monthly Review Press, 1968.

Jobet, Julio César, and Alejandro Chelén R., eds. *Pensamiento teórico y político del partido socialista de Chile*. Santiago: Empresa Editora Nacional Quimantu, 1972.

Johnson, Dale L., ed. *The Chilean Road to Socialism*. Garden City, N.Y.: Doubleday, 1973.

Jordan, Z. A., ed. *Karl Marx: Economy, Class, and Social Revolution*. New York: Scribner's, 1971.

Kenner, Martin, and James Petras, eds. *Fidel Castro Speaks*. New York: Grove Press, 1969.

Labedz, Leopold, ed. *Revisionism: Essays on the History of Marxist Ideas.* New York: Praeger, 1962.

Mallin, Jay, ed. *"Che" Guevara on Revolution.* Coral Gables: University of Miami Press, 1969.

Malloy, James M., and Richard Thorn, eds. *Beyond the Revolution: Bolivia Since 1952.* Pittsburgh: University of Pittsburgh Press, 1971.

Nash, June, Juan Corradi, and Hobart Spalding, Jr., eds. *Ideology and Social Change in Latin America.* New York: Gordon and Breach Science Publishers, 1977.

Pomeroy, William J., ed. *Guerrilla Warfare and Marxism.* New York: International Publishers, 1968.

Radosh, Ronald, ed. *The New Cuba: Paradoxes and Potentials.* New York: William Morrow, 1976.

Rejai, Mostofa, ed. *Mao Tse-tung on Revolution and War.* Garden City, N.Y.: Doubleday, 1969.

Salkey, Andrew, ed. *Writing in Cuba Since the Revolution.* London: Bogle-L'Overture, 1977.

Schram, Stuart R., ed. *The Political Thought of Mao Tse-tung.* New York: Praeger, 1969.

Silverman, Bertram, ed. *Man and Socialism in Cuba.* New York: Atheneum, 1973.

Smelser, Neil, ed. *Karl Marx on Society and Social Change.* Chicago: University of Chicago Press, 1973.

Stavenhagen, Rodolfo, ed. *Agrarian Problems and Peasant Movements in Latin America.* Garden City, N.Y.: Doubleday, 1970.

Tibol, Raquel, ed. *Julio Antonio Mella en el Machete.* Mexico City: Fondo de Cultura Popular, 1968.

Waxman, Chaim I., ed. *The End of Ideology Debate.* New York: Funk & Wagnalls, 1968.

Wesson, Robert, ed. *Communism in Central America and the Caribbean.* Stanford: Hoover Institution Press, 1982.

Zammit, J. Ann, ed. *The Chilean Road to Socialism.* Sussex: University of Sussex, 1973.

Zea, Leopoldo, ed. *Antología pensamiento social y político de América Latina.* Washington, D.C.: Unión Panamericana, 1964.

INDEX

Aguilar Monteverde, Alonso, 226–229, 235
Aguirre, Sergio, 254
Aguirre Cerda, Pedro, 81, 99
Alba, Víctor, 207, 225
Alianza Popular Revolucionaria Americana (APRA), 140, 144, 147, 187, 194
Allende, Salvador, 74, 81, 86–91, 93–95, 98–102, 264, 281, 285, 288
Alliance for Progress, 53, 94, 154, 197, 227
Almeyda Medina, Clodomiro, 95–98, 100
Alves, Mario, 119
Amado, Jorge, 7, 106, 112
American Historical Association, 11
Ampuero Díaz, Raúl, 93–95
Anarcho-syndicalism, 33, 34, 40, 41, 103, 127, 149, 239, 241
Añaya, Ricardo, 179, 180, 189
Anderson-Imbert, Enrique, 174
Andesia, 64
Annales School, 229
Anti-Imperialist League of the Americas, 246, 247
Antiintellectual, 11
Anti-Kommunism, 165
Aprismo, 4, 139, 140, 151, 161, 175, 187, 194, 247, 276
Apristas, 83, 137, 139, 140, 144, 146, 175, 247, 276
Aquinas, Thomas, 87
Arbenz Guzmán, Jacobo, 238
Arce, José Antonio, 66, 175, 177–179, 189
Arcos, Santiago, 72, 80
Arévalo, Juan José, 165, 196, 238
Argentina, 22, 33, 34, 39–71, 78, 108, 149, 193, 198, 199, 245, 282; Association of May, 39, 41; Catholic Church, 61; Communist party, 41, 42, 51–53, 56–58, 60, 69; *descamisados*, 55; *emphyteusis*, 48; Generation of 1837, 39;

International Socialist party, 51, 56; *justicialismo*, 59; Movement of the Revolutionary Left (MIR), 60; National League of Teachers, 51; Popular Left Front, 67; Radical party, 57, 60; Revolutionary Socialist Workers party, 67, 68; Revolutionary Workers' League, 64; Sepoy Left, 67; Socialist party, 40, 41, 43, 44, 46, 49, 51–53, 56, 59, 60, 70, 276, 296 n.22; Socialist Party of the National Revolution, 68; *Unión Cívica de la juventud*, 43
Arguedas, Alcides, 182
Arismendi, Rodney, 82, 154, 195–198, 204, 229
Aristotle, 218, 250
Aron, Raymond, 1
Artigas, José, 193, 198
Assis, Machado de, 112
Atlantic Charter, 36
Augustine, Saint, 87
Axis, 99, 114, 214

Bakunin, Mikhail, 75, 128, 183, 201, 207, 258
Baliño, Carlos B., 241–243, 246, 247, 251
Baliño, Carlos J. 241
Balzac, Honoré de, 266
Bambirra, Vania, 11, 275
Bancroft, Herbert H., 20
Baran, Paul, 257
Baranquilla Plan, 161
Barbusse, Henri, 129, 181
Barreto, Lima, 34
Barreto, Tobías, 104
Bartra, Roger, 288
Basbaum, Leôncio (*pseud.* Augusto Machado), 103, 112–117, 126
Bassols, Narciso, 211–214, 216, 217, 235
Bastos, Abguar, 110
Batista, Fulgencio, 26, 37, 93, 250, 253–256, 261, 265, 266

Batlle y Ordóñez, José, 190–192, 195, 196, 198
Battle of Ayacucho, 20
Baudin, Louis, 178
Beard, Charles, 166
Belaúnde, Víctor Andrés, 137
Belaúnde-Terry, Fernando, 143
Bemis, Samuel Flagg, 53
Bergson, Henri, 219, 278
Bernstein, Eduard, 43
Betancourt, Rómulo, 161, 171, 196, 238
Bilbao, Francisco, 32, 72, 75
Bishop, Maurice, 290
Bismarck, Otto von, 40
Black Legend, 85
Blaine, James G., 227
Blanc, Louis, 206
Blanco Galdós, Hugo, 139–143, 147
Blanqui, Auguste, 201, 206
Blest, Clotario, 87
Bolívar, Simón, 4, 20, 21, 68, 69, 162, 167, 182
Bolivarismo, 167, 168
Bolivia, 34, 65, 66, 83, 145, 147, 159, 174–89, 256, 260, 261, 282; Bolivian Labor Central (COB), 177; Communist party, 66; *Corporación minera de Bolivia* (COMIBOL), 187; Front of the Left (FIB), 178; mines, 177, 181, 186; National Revolution, 128, 137, 176, 177, 185, 187, 188, 276; National Revolutionary Movement (MNR), 66, 177, 187; Party of the Revolutionary Left (PIR), 178–180; Reason of the Fatherland (RADEPA), 184; Regional Workers' Party, 67; Revolutionary Workers party (POR), 181, 185; Socialist Workers' party, 181, Thesis of Pulacayo, 186, 187; Tupac Amaru Revolutionary Group, 184; University Federation, 177; Women Workers' Federation, 175; Workers' Literary Centers, 175; Workers' Social Center, 175
Bolsheviks, 34, 104, 143
Brandão, Otávio, 105
Braudel, Fernand, 229
Brazil, 22, 34, 41, 51, 56, 57, 103–126,

145, 149, 159, 197–199, 245, 282; Action for National Liberation group, 122; Armed Revolutionary Vanguard, 119; Brazilian Writers Association, 106; Communist party, 105, 106, 108–111, 115, 117–120, 124; National Liberation Alliance or "Popular Front," 109; *Novo estado,* 124, 126; Revolutionary Communist party, 119; Socialist party, 104, 105; *tenentismo,* 107, 124
Bressaro, Hugo, 140
British Guiana, 290
Buchanan, James, 21
Bukharin, Nikolai, 131, 176
Bukovsky, Vladimir, 91

Cabet, Etienne, 75
Calderío, Francisco. *See* Roca, Blas
Calmon, Pedro, 116
Camara, Dom Helder, 283
Cárdenas, Lázaro, 64, 210, 212, 216, 232, 252
Carlyle, Thomas, 254
Carranza, Venustiano, 208
Carrera Damas, Germán, 166–169, 172, 173
Carrión, Jorge, 227
Caso, Antonio, ?11, 219
Castile, 31
Castro, Cipriano, 163
Castro, Fidel, 38, 48, 50, 51, 63, 88, 91, 93, 109, 116, 119, 136, 155, 158, 162, 171, 188, 197, 215, 226, 238, 239, 241, 245, 250, 251, 253, 255–257, 259, 264–270, 278, 282, 288, 290, 315 n.41
Castroism (*Fidelismo*), 74, 251, 265–270
Castro Pozo, Hildebrando, 131, 138–139, 141, 143, 223
Caudillismo, 18
Chaco Boreal, 176
Chaco War, 66, 176, 178, 184
Chaplin, Charlie, 112, 245
Charles V (King of Spain), 31
Chavarría, Jesús, 130
Chekhov, Anton, 181
Chibas, Eduardo, 265
Chilcote, Ronald, 111

Chile, 21, 32, 34, 41, 57, 72–102, 143, 145, 159, 184, 201, 245, 269, 281, 285, 288, 289; Catholic Church, 91; Communist party, 73–77, 81, 89–94; Communitarian socialism, 102; Democratic party, 73; Equality Society, 72; Generation of 1930, 79; Movement of the Revolutionary Left (MIR), 264; Popular Front, 73, 74, 81, 82, 86, 87, 99; Popular Unity Government (*Unidad Popular*), 81, 88, 90, 91, 95, 98, 102, 281; Radical party, 81, 82; Socialist Labor party, 73, 76; Socialist party, 73–75, 79, 81, 91, 93, 94, 99, 100; "Socialist Republic," 73, 86; Trotskyist Popular Socialist party, 81; *Unión Socialista Popular* (USP), 94; *vía pacífica*, 82, 93; Workers' Front Thesis, 99

China, 27, 37, 101, 197, 226, 236

Chinese Revolution, 25–27, 37, 74, 221, 225, 259, 264

Chinese socialism, 27, 83, 92, 98, 119

Christ, Jesus, 78, 157, 217

Christians for Socialism, 61, 159, 160, 282–286

CIA, 114, 122, 200, 203, 257

Clarté Circle, 181

Clausewitz, Karl von, 24, 55, 188

Codesio, Julia, 137

Codovilla, Victorio, 51, 56–59, 112, 299 n.82

Cold War, 37, 42, 56, 57, 66, 89, 93, 111, 214, 222

Colombia, 34, 35, 147, 149–160, 256, 265, 282, 290; Army of National Liberation, 157, 159; *Bogatazo*, 265; Catholic Church, 156, 157, 159, 252; Communist party, 153; Conservative party, 156, 158; *la violencia*, 151, 156, 158; Liberal party, 149, 151, 156, 158; National Front, 156; People's United Front, 159

Comintern, 23, 34, 35, 73, 133, 192

Comte, Auguste, 32, 40, 154, 190, 254

Comuneros, 31

Confederation of Latin American Workers (CTAL), 226

Constant, Benjamin, 103

Consuegra Higgins, José, 153–155

Corporativism, 96, 97

Cortázar, Julio, 7, 39

Corvalán, Luis, 91–93

Costa Rica, 35

Croce, Benedetto, 28, 132

Cuba, 21, 22, 26, 32, 34, 35, 48, 50, 51, 53, 57, 63, 84, 87, 88, 91, 93, 101, 109, 116, 153, 155, 158, 162, 168, 171, 188, 197, 200, 215, 216, 219, 226, 236, 238–270, 278, 281, 282, 288, 289; Anti-Clerical League, 244; Bay of Pigs, 216; *Club de Propaganda Socialista*, 242, 251; Communist party, 240, 242, 243, 246, 250, 253, 254, 256, 269; Cuban Revolutionary party, 241; Federation of University Students, 243; *Fidelistas*, 256; *Granma*, 256; guerrilla warfare and, 239, 253, 258–261; material incentives, 262; Moncada, 255, 265, 266; moral incentives, 262; National Association of Cuban Revolutionary Immigrants, 246; People's Socialist party, 253; Socialist party, 239; Socialist Workers party, 242, 251; 26th of July Movement, 241, 250

Cuban Revolution, 24, 48, 62, 63, 67, 69, 74, 81, 87, 91, 92, 94, 119, 141, 153, 162, 203, 238, 247, 251, 253, 262, 264–269, 278, 290

Cuevas, Augustín, 288

Cunha, Euclides da, 103, 105

Darío, Rubén, 35, 89, 182, 194

Darwin, Charles, 14, 154, 254

Davila, Carlos, 73

Davis, Harold Eugene, 2

Debray, Régis, 53, 119, 141, 260

Dialectics, 3, 9, 14–16, 31, 61, 133, 190, 220

Díaz, Porfirio, 206, 216

Dickmann, Adolfo, 46, 56

Dickmann, Enrique, 46, 56

Diffusionist theory, 53

Djilas, Milovan, 116, 117, 257

Dominican Republic, 35, 159, 216, 259, 290

Dos Santos, Theotonio, 11, 300 n.112

Dostoevski, Fyodor, 89, 181

Drake, Paul, 74

Dumas, Emile, 40

Duvalier, François, 37

Eastman, Max, 131

Echeverría, José Esteban, 32, 39, 40, 42, 47, 49, 153

Economic Commission for Latin America (ECLA), 277

Ecuador, 35

Eisenstein, Serge, 83

Elbrick, Charles Burke, 122

El Dorado, 20, 40

El Salvador, 35, 290

Encomienda system, 85

Engels, Friedrich, 9, 14, 15, 19–22, 62, 87, 90, 100, 121, 158, 236, 238, 239, 241, 254, 276

England, 30, 33, 56, 70, 144, 168, 176, 185, 198, 205, 249, 250; British (mentioned), 20, 21, 34, 113, 124, 133, 152, 184, 195

Erasmus, 50

Eurocommunism, 169

Fabela, Isidro, 48, 247

Fanon, Franz, 137, 162, 257

Fernández Retamar, Roberto, 241

Ferri, Enrico, 45

Fichte, Johann, 14

Fifth International, 64

Figueiredo, Antônio Pedro, 103

Figueres, José, 196

First International, 22

Flores Magón, Ricardo, 207, 214

Flores Magón brothers, 214

Foco theory, 69, 121, 141, 143, 158, 171, 188, 201–203, 260, 261

Fontes, Silverio, 103

Fornet, Ambrosio, 238

Fourier, Charles, 32, 75, 205

Fourth International, 64, 141

France, 33, 239, 249, 252; French (mentioned), 20, 21, 32

Francovich, Guillermo, 174, 176

Frank, André Gunder, 114, 173, 222, 300 n.112

Frank, Waldo, 63

Frankfurt School, 229

French Revolution, 98, 194

Freudian analysis, 132

Freyre, Gilberto, 116

Freyre, Ricardo Jaime, 186

Frondizi, Arturo, 60

Frondizi, Silvio, 59–63, 82

Frugoni, Emilio, 190–195, 198, 204

Furtado, Celso, 164

Gadea, Hilda, 256, 257

Gaitán, Jorge Elíecer, 150, 153, 158, 265

Galdames, Luis, 79, 80

Gamonalismo, 66, 136, 141

Garibaldi, Guiseppe, 206

García Márquez, Gabriel, 7

Garra, Lobodón. See Justo, Liborio

George, Henry, 208

Germany, 24, 30, 36, 52, 57, 176, 214; German (mentioned), 32

Ghioldi, Américo, 42, 43, 46, 51–56, 108, 112

Ghioldi, Rodolfo, 42, 49, 51–56, 108, 112

Gilly, Adolfo, 235–237

Gobetti, Piero, 132

Goethe, Johann Wolfgang von, 287

Gómez, Juan Vicente, 160, 161, 163, 246

Gompers, Samuel, 241

González, José María, 206

González Casanova, Pablo, 223, 229–235

González Prada, Manuel, 127, 128, 131, 136, 137, 143

Good Neighbor Policy, 26, 56, 57, 64, 215

Gordon, Lincoln, 114

Gorender, Jacob, 106

Gorky, Maxim, 125, 266

Goulart, João, 111, 114

Gramsci, Antonio, 7–9, 13, 28–30, 38,

78, 112, 125, 132, 134, 170, 199, 272, 277, 278, 281
Grenada, 289, 290
Grompone, Antonio, 190
Grove, Marmaduke, 73, 86
Guatemala, 83, 197, 256, 257
Guatemalan Revolution, 137, 276
Guevara, Ernesto, 38, 119, 141, 158, 177, 187, 201–203, 219, 232, 251, 256–265, 268, 290, 315 n.41
Guillén, Abraham, 121, 199–204; and urban guerrilla warfare, 199–204
Guillén, Nicolás, 49
Guiteras, Antonio, 266
Gutiérrez, Gustavo, 282

Haiti, 35
Halperin, Ernst, 74
Halperin, Maurice, 266
Harnecker, Marta, 11, 275
Harrington, Michael, 4, 262
Hart, A. B., 25
Haya de la Torre, Víctor Raúl, 7, 35, 64, 78, 95, 128, 129, 137, 139, 140, 145, 175, 195–197
Hegel, Georg Wilhelm Friedrich, 14, 16, 19, 20, 94, 254
Hegelian theory, 2, 8, 26, 44, 229
Helferding, Rudolf, 24
Heraclitus, 31
Hidalgo, Manuel, 155, 213
Hitler, Adolph, 36, 52, 55, 135
Hobson, John, 24
Ho Chi Minh, 290
Hodges, Donald, 25, 293 n.12
Hugo, Victor, 266
Humboldt, Alexander von, 153

Ibáñez, Carlos, 73, 86, 95, 98
Iglesia, Pablo, 75
Incas, 20, 66, 135, 136, 181
India, 19, 152, 165
Indianismo, 35, 135, 138, 140, 149, 179–181, 183, 207, 221–223
Industrial Revolution, 22, 120

Ingenieros, José, 34, 48, 49, 105, 131, 175, 186, 266
International Monetary Fund (IMF), 53
International Telephone and Telegraph Co. (ITT), 285
International Working Men's Association, 32
Irazabal, Carlos, 161
Ireland, 19
Italy, 30, 36, 176, 214

Jagan, Cheddi, 290
Jamaica, 22, 290
Japan, 176, 201, 249
Jaurès, Jean, 43, 46, 47, 53, 75, 104
Jobet, Julio César, 78–81
John XXIII (Pope), 156
John Paul II (Pope), 285
Juantorena, Alberto, 245
Juárez, Benito, 213
Justo, Agustín P., 63, 64
Justo, Juan B., 42–46, 51, 53–56, 65, 70, 75, 192, 219
Justo, Liborio [pseuds. Quebracho and Lobodón Garra], 25, 63–67

Kant, Immanuel, 14, 40, 52, 61, 104, 257
Kennedy, John F., 215
Keynesian, 230
Kierkegaard, Sören, 220
Korn, Alejandro, 52
Krausism, 190
Kropotkin, Peter, 104, 128, 207
Kuhn, Thomas, 10, 271

Lacerda, Carlos, 106
Lafertte, Elías, 89
Lahlman, Herman, 40
Laminnais, Félicité de, 72
Laski, Harold, 60, 96
Latifundismo 34, 48, 58, 65, 195, 215, 223
Latin American Union, 48
League of Nations, 135
LeBon, Gustave, 278
Lechín, Juan, 177

Lefevre, Henri, 53, 97
Leguía, Augusto, 129, 246
Lenin, Vladimir Ilyich, 1, 23–27, 30, 34, 38, 48, 49, 55, 66, 67, 76, 78, 83, 84, 87, 90–92, 100, 102, 104, 105, 108, 110, 113, 114, 132, 133, 143, 150–155, 160, 161, 164, 170, 175, 195–197, 203, 208–210, 221, 222, 226, 229, 236, 239, 247, 249, 250, 252, 255, 257–261, 265, 268, 276, 279, 280, 287, 290
Leninism, 28, 34, 51, 246
Leroux, Pierre, 39
Liberation theology, 282–286
Lin Piao, 259
Lombardi, Carlos, 42
Lombardo Toledano, Vicente, 7, 205, 210, 213, 219–226, 231, 235, 290
London, Jack, 182
Lora, Guillermo, 182, 185–189

Macaulay, T. B., 254
Machado, Gerardo, 239, 244, 246, 247, 253
Mahan, Alfred Thayer, 53
Malatesta, Enrico, 40
Malavé Mata, Héctor, 173
Malthus, Thomas Robert, 154
Man, Henri de, 132
Mandel, Ernest, 257
Manifest Destiny, 53, 82
Manley, Michael, 290
Mao Zedong, 26, 28, 38, 52, 93, 134, 141, 143, 187, 200, 226, 229, 258, 259, 262, 289, 290
Maoism, 74, 119, 143, 270
Maoists, 7, 28, 203, 260
Marcuse, Herbert, 113, 170
Mariátegui, José Carlos, 48, 66, 73, 75, 82, 84, 89, 127–143, 146, 149, 151, 154, 162, 175, 178, 182, 183, 187, 196, 223, 226, 248, 257, 266, 290
Marighela, Carlos, 110, 119–123, 202; advocates urban guerrilla warfare, 119–123
Marinello, Juan, 49, 247–251, 253
Maritain, Jacques, 155

Marof, Tristán [pseud. Gustavo Adolfo Navarro], 178, 181–185, 189
Martí, José, 4, 48, 49, 155, 191, 240, 241, 244, 246–249, 251, 265
Martin, Lionel, 265
Martínez, Saturnino, 239
Martínez de la Torre, Ricardo, 138–139
Marx, Karl, 1–5, 9–38, 40, 43–45, 47, 49, 52–55, 62, 67, 69, 73, 84, 86–88, 90, 100, 103, 104, 108, 112, 113, 117, 120, 130–133, 138, 140, 147, 150, 152–158, 162, 165, 173, 183, 186, 188, 193, 194, 197, 201, 205, 207–210, 215–219, 226, 229, 230, 232, 236, 238–241, 247, 255, 257, 258, 260, 261, 263–266, 269, 275, 276, 279, 280, 283, 286, 287; Asiatic mode of production, idea of, 66
Matos Romero, Manuel, 161
Maximalists, 34
Medellín Conference of Latin American Bishops, 160, 282, 283
Mella, Julio Antonio, 187, 242–247, 251, 265
Méndez Arceo, Sergio, 284
Mexican Revolution, 49, 105, 128, 137, 161, 166, 179, 194, 207–211, 213–217, 219–221, 223, 224, 226–228, 231–233, 235–237, 243, 252, 276
Mexico, 20, 32, 34, 35, 64, 83, 122, 142, 145, 159, 166, 205–237, 246, 252, 290; *Cardenismo*, 252; Catholic Church, 224; Communist party, 209, 215, 224, 225, 246, 247; *ejido*, 222, 223, 235; *Gran Círculo de Obreros*, 206; Indianism, 212; *La Reforma*, 221; *Partido Popular*, 214, 221, 225; *Partido Popular Socialista*, 225; Party of the Institutional Revolution (PRI), 217, 227, 228; Party of the Mexican Revolution (PRM), 217; Political Action League, 214; *Porfiriato*, 206, 223, 224, 227, 233
Michlet, Jules, 72
Mills, C. Wright, 2, 3, 60, 87
Mitrione, Dan, 203, 204
Molina Enríquez, Andrés, 182

Monroe Doctrine, 21, 26, 53, 94, 177, 222, 245
Montaña Cuéllar, Diego, 151–153, 157
Monzón, Luis, 209, 210
Mora, José María Luis, 205
More, Thomas, 183, 218
Morelos, José María, 155
Mournier, Emmanuel, 157
Mussolini, Benito, 36, 55, 86
Mutual Security Acts of 1951 and 1952, 66

National Liberation Alliance, 51
Navarro, Gustavo Adolfo. *See* Marof, Tristán
Nearing, Scott, 242, 246
Neruda, Pablo, 4, 7, 72, 74, 89, 109, 257
New Deal, 62
Newton, Isaac, 14
Nicaragua, 35, 48, 286, 290; Sandinist Front of National Liberation, 290
Nieto, Rafael, 208, 209
Nietzsche, Friedrich, 52, 131, 220
Nisbet, Robert, 286
Non-capitalist-path-to-socialism theory, 278–279
North Vietnam, 264

Oddone, Jacinto, 46
Oliveira, Nestor Peixoto, 104
Ollman, Bertell, 13
Olympic Games, 245
Organization of American States, 57, 98, 214–216, 227
Ortega y Gasset, José, 38, 52, 131, 151, 220, 278
Ostend Manifesto, 21
Owen, Robert, 75

Palacios, Alfredo L., 42, 43, 46–49, 56, 70, 75, 186, 290
Pan, Luis, 42, 52
Panama, 22, 35, 48, 150, 281; Canal, 139; Isthmus, 21
Pan Americanism, 48, 177, 197
Pan American Union, 63, 227
Paraguay, 35, 176; *Febreristas,* 83

Paris Commune, 22, 32, 40, 206, 207, 239; Communards, 33
Paul VI (Pope), 283
Paz, Octavio, 209, 233, 271
Paz Estensorro, Víctor, 176, 238
Pedro I (Emperor of Brazil), 103
Pedro II (Emperor of Brazil), 104
Pérez Jiménez, Marcos, 37, 163, 169
Permanent Revolution, Trotsky's theory of. *See under* Trotsky, Leon
Perón, Eva, 55
Perón, Juan, 55, 58, 59, 62, 69–71
Peronismo, 4, 55, 58, 59, 70, 71, 74
Peronista, 55, 58, 69
Peru, 20, 21, 35, 127–148, 245, 246, 281, 282; Artisans Union, 127; Catholic Church, 136, 137, 142; Communist party, 141; General Confederation of Workers, 129; Generation of 1919, 128; *indigenismo,* 127, 128, 143; Peruvianism, 142, 143; Socialist party, 129, 133, 138
Pesce, Hugo, 132
Petkoff, Teodoro, 169–173
Pink Legend, 85
Pinochet, Augusto, 95, 102
Pintos, Francisco R., 198–199, 204
Pla, Alberto, 42
Plato, 217, 218, 263
Platt Amendment, 48, 242, 243, 252, 255
Plekhanov, Georgy, 176
Ponce, Aníbal, 49–52, 56, 182, 214, 243, 248, 263
Popular Front, 36
Popularum Progressio, 283
Porteños, 52, 53, 65
Portugal, 31, 68, 103, 123
Positivism, 2, 6, 32, 49, 52, 103, 127, 190, 213, 273, 274, 276
Prado, Caio, Júnior, 116–119, 126, 290
Prebisch, Raúl, 53, 200, 227, 277
Prescott, William H., 20
Prestes, Luiz Carlos, 51, 56, 107, 113, 119, 123, 124, 126, 197
Prestes Column, 107, 113, 123, 124
Prestismo, 108, 110, 113, 123, 124, 126
Proudhon, Pierre-Joseph, 75, 128, 205, 206

Provincianos, 52, 53
Puebla Conference of Latin American Bishops, 285
Puerto Rico, 21, 48, 247
Puiggrós, Rodolfo, 11, 118

Quebracho. *See* Justo, Liborio
Quijano, Aníbal, 11, 143–148
Quinet, Edgar, 72
Quixote, Don, 112, 257

Ramírez, Gerardo F., 186
Ramos, Jorge Abelardo, 21, 67–71
Ramos, Samuel, 211
Rangel, Domingo Alberto, 162–166, 171, 173
Ranke, Leopold von, 254
Recabarren, Luis Emilio, 75–79, 82, 86, 91, 154, 186, 290
Reed, John, 245
Renaissance, 30, 50
Repetto, Nicolás, 43
Revueltas, José, 233
Rhodakanaty, Plotino, 205, 206
Ricardo, David, 17
Rio Treaty of 1947, 214
Risorgimento, 32
Rivera, Diego, 4, 247
Rivera, Silvia, 11
Roca, Blas [pseud. Francisco Calderío], 251–253
Rodó, José Enrique, 35, 182, 244
Rodríguez, Carlos Rafael, 154, 240, 253–256
Rodríguez, Simón, 182
Roig, Enrique, 239
Romania, 101
Romero, José Luis, 84
Roosevelt, Franklin D., 63, 64
Rosas, Juan Manuel de, 39, 65, 70
Rouma, Georges, 178
Rousseau, Jean-Jacques, 61, 182, 211
Roy, N. M., 209, 210
Royal Dutch Shell, 176
Russia. *See* Soviet Union
Russian Revolution, 23, 30, 34, 41, 73, 75, 104, 105, 110, 127, 133, 149, 155, 161, 195, 210, 213, 225, 242, 244, 262, 264, 288
Ruth, George Herman "Babe," 245

Saco, Carmen, 137
Saint Simon, Henri de, 32, 39, 40
Salazar Bondy, Augusto, 129
Sánchez, Luis Alberto, 128, 140
Sandino, Augusto, 48, 290
Sarmiento, Domingo F., 44, 54, 59, 65, 131
Sartre, Jean-Paul, 62, 112
Savitski, Silvestre, 149
Schopenhauer, Arthur, 220
Second International, 41, 191, 239
Sendic Antonaccio, Raúl, 203
Seoane, Manuel A., 175
Shakespeare, William, 50
Sierra, Santiago, 206
Sierra, Vicente, 41
Silva Bernardes, Artur da, 107
Silva Herzog, Jesús, 49, 208, 211, 214–219, 226, 235, 257
Silva Michelena, José, 173
Sino-Soviet split, 38, 95
Siqueiros, Davíd Alfaro, 247
Smith, Adam, 17, 18
Social Darwinism, 223
Social science, 9
Sodré, Nelson Werneck, 121, 123–126
Somoza, Anastasio, 261, 290
Sorel, Georges, 55, 68, 129, 132
Sori, Pietro, 40
Soviet Union, 21, 30, 37, 51, 52, 64, 76, 91–93, 96, 108, 109, 110, 112, 116, 117, 142, 168, 170, 181, 196, 201, 222, 223, 236, 259, 262
Soviet-United States Alliance, 36, 105
Spain, 20, 68, 84, 85, 89, 144, 155, 166–168, 199, 214, 239, 254
Spanish-American (Cuban) War, 222, 242
Spanish Civil War, 75, 199, 213, 249
Spencer, Herbert, 40, 43, 154
Spengler, Oswald, 131
Stalin, Joseph, 25, 26, 52, 64, 67, 109, 112, 153, 210, 236, 257
Stalinism, 57, 74, 95, 142, 187, 288

Standard Oil of New Jersey, 176, 184
Starobin, Joseph R. 111, 151, 224, 299
n.82
Stavenhagen, Rodolfo, 233–235
Stevenson, Teofilo, 245
Strachey, John, 211
Stroessner, Alfredo, 37
Structuralism, 288–289
Suárez, Francisco, 47
Surinam, 22

Tehuantepec, Isthmus of, 21
Teitelboim, Volodia, 89, 91–93
Tejada, Luis, 149
Tejera, Diego Vicente, 239
Third International, 41, 161, 181
Tiradentes, 105
Titoism, 74
Togliatti, Palmiro, 132
Tolstoy, Leo, 113, 181, 186
Torres Restrepo, Camilo, 149, 155–160,
171, 197, 264, 282, 283, 290, 315
n. 41
Trotsky, Leon, 25, 26, 52, 64–68, 76,
86–88, 116, 134, 140–142, 164, 176,
186, 210, 225, 226, 236, 257, 259,
268, 276; theory of Permanent Revolu-
tion, 25, 28, 142, 186, 236, 260, 268
Trotskyists, 7, 25, 26, 41, 66, 67, 84,
140, 143, 177, 183, 185, 187, 188,
203, 225, 236, 260, 270
Trujillo, Rafael, 37, 261
Truman, Harry S., 57
Truman Doctrine, 57
Turró, R. 193

Ugarte, Manuel, 44, 48, 67, 131, 296
n. 22
Unamuno, Miguel, 193, 220
United Nations, 36, 66, 214, 277
United States, 3, 11, 21, 22, 24–26, 28,
31, 33–38, 275, 277, 285, 288; Agency
for International Development (AID),
122, 203; and Argentina, 42, 48, 52,
53, 56, 62, 63, 66, 68–70; and Bolivia,
176, 177, 181, 182, 184, 185, 187,
189; and Brazil, 109, 110, 113, 114,

121, 122; and Chile, 79, 94, 97, 101;
and Colombia, 150, 152, 153, 156,
157; and Cuba, 238, 240–245, 247–
251, 255, 259, 264, 266, 269; Defense
Department, 200; and Mexico, 207,
208, 210, 214–216, 219, 221, 222,
227, 231; and Peru, 135, 144, 145; and
Uruguay, 194, 195, 198, 200, 201; and
Venezuela, 162, 165, 166, 168–174
Universal Interoceanic Canal Co., 22
University Reform Movement, 34, 41, 50,
52, 63, 70, 130, 139, 149, 177, 186,
243
Unzueta, Gerardo, 225
Urquidi Morales, Arturo, 175, 179, 180,
189
Uruguay, 34, 41, 78, 123, 190–204; *Batllismo*, 190, 192, 194, 195, 276;
Catholic Church, 196; Communist
party, 191, 195, 198; *Guillenismo*, 201;
Socialist party, 191, 192; Tupamaros,
192, 202–204

Valdelomar, Abraham, 129
Vargas, Getulio, 26, 105, 108, 109, 118,
124, 126
Varona, José, 249
Vasconcelos, José, 135

Vásquez Vela, Gonzalo, 210
Venezuela, 35, 69, 160–174, 216, 246,
261, 276, 290; Catholic Church, 172;
Christian Democratic party (COPEI),
165, 174; Committee of Democratic
Defense, 160; Communist party, 161,
164; Communist Youth Group, 169;
Democratic Action party (AD), 83, 161,
162, 164, 165, 171, 174; Generation of
'28, 160–163, 173; Movement of the
Revolutionary Left (MIR), 162; Move-
ment to Socialism (MAS), 164, 169,
170; petroleum, 164, 165, 174;
Workers Front, 160; Workers National
Front, 160
Viana, Oliveira, 116
Victoriano, José, 72
Vicuña Mackenna, Benjamin, 32

Vitale, Luis, 84–89
Vo Nguyen Giap, 187, 257–259

Waiss, Oscar, 81–84
Wall Street, 245
Wang Fu-chih, 27
War of the Pacific, 66, 128, 185
Warsaw Pact, 92
Weber, Max, 266
Wiesse, María, 137
Worker-Priest Movement, 252
World War I, 34, 41, 51, 73, 104, 135
World War II, 3, 36, 37, 42, 48, 51, 55, 57, 59, 62, 64, 66, 70, 99, 105, 106, 114, 135, 145, 157, 171, 176, 196, 214, 222, 249, 250, 277, 278

Yankeephobia, 35
Yupanqui, Dionisio Inca, 21
Yugoslavian socialism, 83, 95, 101; system of worker management, 94

Zavala, Silvio, 84
Zayas, Alfredo, 248
Zea, Leopoldo, 2, 195
Zionism, 84
Zola, Emile, 107
Zum Felde, Alberto, 190, 195